THE AWARD MOVIES

THE AWARD MOVIES

ROY PICKARD

A Complete Guide from A to Z

FREDERICK MULLER LIMITED
LONDON

First published in Great Britain, 1980 by
Frederick Muller Limited, London, NW2 6LE

British Library Cataloguing in Publication Data

Pickard, Roy
The award movies a complete guide from A-Z
1. Moving-pictures — Awards
I. Title
791.43 PN1993.5.A1

ISBN 0-584-10370-0

Typeset by Texet, Leighton Buzzard, Bedfordshire.
Printed in Great Britain by Redwood Burn Ltd., Trowbridge & Esher

For my father . . .

who first brought it all alive with tales of Rex Ingram and *Scaramouche,* the chariot race in *Ben-Hur* and Cagney in *The Public Enemy.*

Stills by courtesy of: Allied Artists; Artificial Eye; Avco Embassy; British Lion; Cinerama; Columbia; Compton; Curzon Films; Embassy Pictures; EMI; Filmsonor/Vera Film/Fono Roma; Gala; Greenwich Films; ITC; MGM; Paramount; Reggane Film/ONCIC; Svensk Filmindustri; 20th Century-Fox; United Artists; Universal; Vic/Appia Films; Warner Bros.

Preface

This book has been written as a companion to set alongside *The Oscar Movies.*

It presents, for the first time in one volume, every 'best picture' named in the last fifty years by the top award organizations in America, Britain and Europe.

Its basic task is to provide information in a simple, easy-to-read manner. It is not intended to be a definitive work on the greatest films ever made although many are to be found among its pages. But it is intended to reflect what voters and juries have *thought* were the best in the history of sound cinema.

'Best' is an emotive word. Critics and historians shy away from it and tend to dismiss the compiling of 'ten best lists' as being little more than parlour games. Yet, when polls are suggested by intellectual magazines, those same critics are only too eager to come forward and try their hands at the best movie game.

This book eliminates personal opinion by drawing on nine major organizations and festivals that have presented best film awards over a long period of time.

From America there are the selections of the Oscar Academy, the New York Critics and the National Board of Review; from Britain there are the British Academy Awards, first established in 1947; and from Europe there are the winners from the festivals at Venice, Cannes, Berlin, Karlovy Vary and Moscow.

Together, they represent a unique portrait of film history over the last fifty years and reveal how tastes have changed — and continue to change — with the passing of time.

How to use the book? Well, in much the same way as one uses *The Oscar Movies*. The films are listed in A to Z order so just check your title against the respective letter of the alphabet and you will find the movie — plus information about its best film awards, a synopsis and cast and credits.

If the picture isn't included it means that it hasn't earned a best picture award. It's as simple as that!

Part II performs a different function and includes not only the history of each award organization but also all the leading prize-winners — best actor, actress, director, etc. — in year order. This section is a valuable historical supplement and a useful source of cross-reference with the award movies in the first part of the book.

Although, on occasion, I have commented on the justice of certain awards, I have mostly left judgment in abeyance and left you, the reader, to scoff at what might appear to be a ludicrous award e.g. *The Shoes Of The Fisherman*, or blink, disbelievingly at an entry that states that Wellman's classic *The Ox-Bow Incident did* receive a best picture prize in 1943.

Here they are then, over 300 movies that have emerged as prize-winners from the glitter of Oscar night, the beaches of Cannes and the splendour of the Venice Lido. Westerns and musicals, dramas and comedies from all over the world, films that have passed into history or are still part of the current movie scene.

Films that, whether we like it or not, are known as 'the best!'

Roy Pickard,
August, 1980

Part One

THE MOVIES

The 318 films listed in alphabetical order in this section of the book constitute all the top 'best picture' winners of the last fifty years. The list has been compiled from the awards of the American and British Film Academies; the New York Critics Circle; the National Board of Review; and the prizes presented at the Cannes, Venice, Berlin, Moscow and Karlovy Vary Festivals.

For a check on the history of each award organization and festival see page 145.

THE ACCUSED (Czechoslovakia)

Awards (1)
Grand Prix Karlovy Vary, 1964

At first glance, a tense courtroom drama about an engineer arrested because of his misuse of public funds; beneath the surface a sharp probe into socialist bureaucracy and an exposé of corruption in certain areas of Czech society. A courageous film, shot in almost documentary fashion by Ján Kádár and Elmar Klos who have worked in harness for most of their long careers. In 1965 they filmed *The Shop On Main Street*, the first Czech film to win an Oscar.

A Czech State Film Production, directed by Ján Kádár and Elmar Klos. Screenplay by Vladimir Valenta, Ján Kádár and Elmar Klos, based on a story by Lenka Hašková. Photographed by Rudolf Milič. Music by Zdeněk Liška. 90 minutes.

Starring Vlado Muller, Jaroslav Blažek, Miroslav Macháček, Zora Jirakova.

Note: This picture is also known under the title *The Defendant*.

ADOPTION (Hungary)

Awards (1)
Golden Bear Berlin, 1975

Poignant account of the life of a forty-two-year-old widowed factory worker who eventually succeeds in finding an identity when she befriends a troubled teenager and adopts a small child. The only Hungarian success at the Berlin festival; realistically filmed by Márta Mészáros, a woman director in her forties, and played to near perfection by Kati Berek in the leading role.

Hunn Játékfilmstúdió, Hungarofilm. Directed by Márta Mészáros. Screenplay by Márta Mészáros, Gyula Hernádi and Ferenc Grünwalsky. Photographed by Lajos Koltai. Music by György Kovács. 89 minutes.

Starring Kati Berek, László Szabo, Gyöngyvér Vigh, Dr. Árpád Perlaky, Peter Fried, István Szöke, Florá Kádár, János Boross, Erzsi Varga.

AFFECTION (Bulgaria)

Awards (1)

Grand Prix	Moscow, 1973

One of the most recent attempts to convey contemporary Bulgarian life on screen; a problem romance that examines the unhappiness of a young woman sent to a mountain resort for therapy but who is still yearning for her lost love and unable to communicate with those around her. A prize-winner at Moscow where it shared the honours with *Oklahoma Crude* and *That Sweet Word Liberty*. Known also under the title of *Love*.

A Filmbulgaria Production, directed by Lyudmil Staikov. Screenplay by Alexander Karasimeonov. Photographed by Boris Janakiev. Music by Simeon Pironkov. 100 minutes.

Starring Violetta Doneva, Nevena Kokanova, Ivan Kondov, Nikolai Binev, Stefan Danailov.

ALICE DOESN'T LIVE HERE ANYMORE (USA)

Awards (1)

Best Film	British Academy Award, 1975

A newly-widowed woman (Ellen Burstyn) tries to cope with economic survival and create a new life for herself and her twelve-year-old son in modern day America. A fifties-type melodrama of the Douglas Sirk variety, given a new look by the imaginative approach of director Martin Scorsese. Ellen Burstyn won the Hollywood Oscar as best actress; the film won the best picture award of the British Film Academy which rated it ahead of the three other nominees; *Barry Lyndon*, *Dog Day Afternoon* and *Jaws*.

A Warner Bros. Picture, directed by Martin Scorsese. Screenplay by Robert Getchell. Photographed in Technicolor by Kent L. Wakeford. 112 minutes.

Starring Ellen Burstyn, Kris Kristofferson, Billy Green Bush, Diane Ladd, Lelia Goldoni, Lane Bradbury, Vic Tayback, Jodie Foster, Harvey Keitel.

Note: *Alice Doesn't Live Here Anymore* was first released in America in 1974.

ALL ABOUT EVE (USA)

Awards (3)

Best Film	American Academy Award, 1950
Best Film	New York Critics, 1950
Best Film, Any Source	British Academy Award, 1950

The meteoric rise of an unscrupulous young actress (Anne Baxter) who worms her way into the confidence of a fading Broadway star (Bette Davis) then cheats, blackmails and lies her way to the top of her profession. Still the wittiest of all backstage movies with an unrepeatable cast – Davis, Baxter, George Sanders, Celeste Holm, Thelma Ritter – firing off Mankiewicz epigrams every two minutes! A hit with all the major award organizations except the National Board of Review which placed it second behind *Sunset Boulevard*.

A Twentieth Century-Fox Picture, directed by Joseph L. Mankiewicz. Screenplay by Joseph L. Mankiewicz, based on the story 'The Wisdom Of Eve' by Mary Orr. Photographed by Milton Krasner. Music by Alfred Newman. 138 minutes.

Starring Bette Davis, Anne Baxter, George Sanders, Celeste Holm, Gary Merrill, Hugh Marlowe, Thelma Ritter, Marilyn Monroe, Gregory Ratoff.

ALL QUIET ON THE WESTERN FRONT (USA)

Awards (1)
Best Film — American Academy Award, 1929/30

An anguished cry against the futility of war, following the experiences of a group of young German soldiers who are first disillusioned by the death and destruction they find at the front then slowly killed, one by one, during the darkest days of the First World War. Now fifty years old but still as powerful as ever, *The Deer Hunter* and *Apocalypse Now* notwithstanding. The film was the first Universal picture to win an American Oscar; the second, *The Sting*, won forty-three years later!

A Universal Picture, directed by Lewis Milestone. Screenplay by Del Andrews, Maxwell Anderson and George Abbott, based on the novel by Erich Maria Remarque. Photographed by Arthur Edeson. 138 minutes.

Starring Lew Ayres, Louis Wolheim, John Wray, George 'Slim' Summerville, Raymond Griffith, Russell Gleason, William Bakewell, Scott Kolk.

Note: *All Quiet On The Western Front* was one of the films included in the National Board of Review's 'ten best' list of 1930.

ALL THAT JAZZ (USA)

Awards (1)
Golden Palm — Cannes, 1980

The American concern with death infiltrates the musical *genre* as Bob Fosse traces the final months in the life of ruthless Broadway choreographer Roy Scheider as he drives himself steadily towards a fatal heart attack. Reputedly autobiographical, frequently self-indulgent (with shades of latter day Fellini) but always visually exciting – especially in the musical sequences. A surprise co-winner (along with *Kagemusha*) of the 1980 Cannes festival and the first musical to earn the Golden Palm since *The Umbrellas Of Cherbourg*.

A Columbia/Twentieth Century Fox Picture, directed by Bob Fosse.

Screenplay by Robert Alan Aurthur and Bob Fosse. Photographed in Technicolor by Giuseppe Rotunno. Music arranged and conducted by Ralph Burns. Choreography by Bob Fosse. 123 minutes.

Starring Roy Scheider, Jessica Lange, Ann Reinking, Leland Palmer, Cliff Gorman, Ben Vereen, Erzsebet Foldi.

ALL THE KING'S MEN (USA)

Awards (2)

Best Film	American Academy Award, 1949
Best Film	New York Critics, 1949

Broderick Crawford in the best role of his career as the crusading Willie Stark, a roughneck backwater politician who rises swiftly to become governor of his midwestern state but is then corrupted by power and destroyed by the hand of an assassin. Based on the career of Louisiana's Huey 'Kingfish' Long and winner of two major American best picture awards. Not included, however, in the ten best list of the National Board of Review.

A Columbia Picture, directed by Robert Rossen. Screenplay by Robert Rossen, based on the novel by Robert Penn Warren. Photographed by Burnett Guffey. Music by Louis Gruenberg. 109 minutes.

Starring Broderick Crawford, John Ireland, John Derek, Joanne Dru, Mercedes McCambridge, Anne Seymour.

ALL THE PRESIDENT'S MEN (USA)

Awards (2)

Best Film	New York Critics, 1976
Best English Language Film	National Board of Review, 1976

The movie that proved that political films *can* make money at the box-office; a part-thriller, part-documentary account of the activities of Washington Post journalists Carl Bernstein and Bob Woodward whose post-Watergate investigations brought about the downfall of the Nixon administration. The film was a fancied contender at Oscar time following the awards of the New York Critics and National Board of Review. The boxing 'sleeper' *Rocky*, however, took the best picture Academy Award.

A Wildwood Enterprises/Warner Bros. Picture, directed by Alan J. Pakula. Screenplay by William Goldman, based on the book by Carl Bernstein and Bob Woodward. Photographed in Technicolor by Gordon Willis. Music by David Shire. 138 minutes.

Starring Dustin Hoffman, Robert Redford, Jack Warden, Martin Balsam, Hal Holbrook, Jason Robards, Jane Alexander, Meredith Baxter, Ned Beatty, Stephen Collins.

ALPHAVILLE (France/Italy)

Awards (1)

Golden Bear	Berlin, 1965

Jean-Luc Godard's comic strip about secret agent Lemmy Caution who is sent into another galaxy to track down a missing scientist in a computerised anti-human state. Taken a little too seriously by New Wave enthusiasts of the sixties, but enjoyable on a two-dimensional science-fiction level and making ingenious use of Paris — neon streets, shiny office blocks, etc. — as a township of the future. Top attractions: girl assassins in white swimsuits who dispose of their victims with knives if machine guns haven't already finished the job!

Chaumiane Production-Film Studio. Written and directed by Jean-Luc Godard. Photographed by Raoul Coutard. Music by Paul Misraki. 100 minutes.

Starring Eddie Constantine, Anna Karina, Akim Tamiroff, Howard Vernon, László Szabo, Michel Delahaye, Jean-André Fieschi.

AMARCORD (Italy/France)

Awards (3)

Best Foreign Language Film	American Academy Award, 1974
Best Film	New York Critics, 1974
Best Foreign Language Film	National Board of Review, 1974

Fellini travels back to the thirties and his youth in provincial Italy when Fascism under Mussolini was in firm control. The setting is a small North Italian town; the story no more than a series of isolated episodes about the whores, soldiers, priests, policemen and ordinary people who lived there during the period. A triple award winner in America, the film marked the fifth occasion that a Fellini picture had been named the year's best by the New York Critics. The title *Amarcord* is the Roman dialect for 'I Remember.'

F.C.Produzioni (Rome)/P.E.C.F. (Paris). Directed by Federico Fellini. Screenplay by Federico Fellini and Tonino Guerra. Photographed in Technicolor by Giuseppe Rotunno. Music by Nino Rota. 123 minutes.

Starring Puppela Maggio, Magali Noel, Armando Brancia, Ciccio Ingrassia, Nandino Orfei, Luigi Rossi, Bruno Zanin, Gianfilippo Carcano, Josiane Tanzili.

AN AMERICAN IN PARIS (USA)

Awards (1)

Best Film	American Academy Award, 1951

Director Vincente Minnelli and hoofer Gene Kelly together in post-war Paris and doing wonders with an already magnificent Gershwin score. The story — footloose American painter Kelly pursues Parisienne

Leslie Caron — is of no consequence. The music counts for everything. Highlights: 'Our Love is Here to Stay', a Kelly/Caron duet on the banks of the Seine; 'I Got Rhythm' danced by Kelly with some French street urchins; and a seventeen-minute ballet designed in different scenes in the styles of Dufy, Renoir, Utrillo, Van Gogh, etc.

A Metro-Goldwyn-Mayer Picture, directed by Vincente Minnelli. Screenplay by Alan Jay Lerner. Photographed in Technicolor by Alfred Gilks and John Alton (ballet). Music and lyrics by George and Ira Gershwin. Musical direction by Johnny Green and Saul Chaplin. 113 minutes.

Starring Gene Kelly, Leslie Caron, Oscar Levant, Georges Guetary, Nina Foch.

ANNA KARENINA (USA)

Awards (1)

Mussolini Cup	Venice, 1935

Garbo as Tolstoy's doomed Russian woman who flaunts convention by embarking on a passionate affair with a young army officer then commits suicide when she is abandoned both by her lover and humiliated husband. Tragedy with the elegant MGM touch and the only Garbo film to win a major prize in any form of competition. The film's Venice success was achieved in the face of strong opposition from *David Copperfield* and John Ford's *The Informer*. It did not figure in the ten best picture Oscar nominations of 1935.

A Metro-Goldwyn-Mayer Picture, directed by Clarence Brown. Screenplay by Clemence Dane and Salka Viertel, based on the novel by Leo Tolstoy. Photographed by William Daniels. Music by Herbert Stothart. 95 minutes.

Starring Greta Garbo, Fredric March, Basil Rathbone, Freddie Bartholomew, Maureen O'Sullivan, May Robson, Reginald Owen, Reginald Denny.

ANNIE HALL (USA)

Awards (3)

Best Film	American Academy Award, 1977
Best Film	New York Critics, 1977
Best Film	British Academy Award, 1977

The story and eventual break-up of the 'nervous romance' between Jewish comedian Alvy Singer (Woody Allen) and his neurotic, delightfully kooky girl friend, Annie Hall (Diane Keaton). An autobiographical movie that ranges from wisecracking comedy to melancholy and then back again and which became a 'sleeper' of the seventies when it took several major awards on both sides of the Atlantic. How good it really is remains to be seen. Perhaps Allen himself hit the truth on the head: 'Hardly my 8½ . . . more my 2½'.

A United Artists Picture, directed by Woody Allen. Screenplay by Woody Allen and Marshall Brickman. Photographed in De Luxe Color by Gordon Willis. 93 minutes.

Starring Woody Allen, Diane Keaton, Tony Roberts, Carol Kane, Paul Simon, Shelley Duvall, Janet Margolin, Colleen Dewhurst, Christopher Walken.

APARAJITO (India)

Awards (1)

Golden Lion	Venice, 1957

The continuing struggles of the penniless scholar of *Pather Panchali* who, in this second film in Ray's trilogy, leaves his village with the surviving members of his family — his wife and son — and starts a new life in the city of Benares. After the death of the father, the film concentrates on the relationship between the growing boy and his mother and on the latter's attempts to earn enough money to send her son to the University of Calcutta. See also *The World Of Apu*.

Produced and directed by Satyajit Ray. Screenplay by Satyajit Ray, based on the novel by Bidhutibhustan Bandapadhaya. Photographed by Subrata Mitra. Music by Ravi Shankar. 113 minutes.

Starring Pinaki Sen Gupta, Smaran Ghosal, Karuna Banerjee, Kanu Banerjee, Ramani Sen Gupta. Charu Ghosh.

THE APARTMENT (USA)

Awards (3)

Best Film	American Academy Award, 1960
Best Film	New York Critics, 1960
Best Film, Any Source	British Academy Award, 1960

Typically mordant Billy Wilder comedy about a frustrated young insurance clerk (Jack Lemmon) who discovers that the quickest way to gain promotion — and the key to the executive washroom — is by hiring out his apartment to his bosses for their extra-marital activities. For many, the perfect Wilder movie, skilfully treading the tightrope between comedy and tragedy, but for critics at the 1960 Venice festival where the film officially represented the United States, 'not really of festival calibre!'

A Mirisch Company Production (released by United Artists), directed by Billy Wilder. Screenplay by Billy Wilder and I. A. L. Diamond. Photographed in Panavision by Joseph LaShelle. Music by Adolph Deutsch. Art Direction by Alexander Trauner. 125 minutes.

Starring Jack Lemmon, Shirley MacLaine, Fred MacMurray, Ray Walston, David Lewis, Jack Kruschen, Joan Shawlee, Edie Adams.

Note: The Apartment shared the New York Critics Award with the British made *Sons And Lovers*.

APOCALYPSE NOW (USA)

Awards (1)

Golden Palm	Cannes, 1979

A journey into madness as Francis Ford Coppola transfers Conrad's *Heart Of Darkness* to Vietnam and follows Martin Sheen up-river on a trip to assassinate renegade colonel Marlon Brando. An American helicopter raid to the strains of 'The Ride Of The Valkyries' numbs the senses; Brando's eventual appearance brings the whole piece crashing down into static literary melodrama. But some brilliant passages and a prize-winner at Cannes in 1979 (see also *The Tin Drum*).

An Omni Zoetrope Production (distributed by United Artists), directed by Francis Ford Coppola. Screenplay by John Milius and Francis Ford Coppola, based on the novel *Heart Of Darkness* by Joseph Conrad. Photographed in Technovision and Technicolor by Vittorio Storaro. Music by Carmine Coppola and Francis Ford Coppola. 141 minutes in 70 mm. 153 minutes (with end title sequence) in 35 mm.

Starring Marlon Brando, Robert Duvall, Martin Sheen, Frederic Forrest, Albert Hall, Sam Bottoms, Larry Fishburne, Dennis Hopper, G. D. Spradlin, Harrison Ford, Jerry Ziesmer, Scott Glenn.

THE APPRENTICESHIP OF DUDDY KRAVITZ (Canada)

Awards (1)

Golden Bear	Berlin, 1974

The adventures of a pretentious young Jewish boy who graduates from high school in the late forties and determines to make good — no matter what the means. In many ways, the 'What Makes Sammy Run?' story transferred to post-war Montreal, sometimes dramatic, often humorous but always deftly played by Richard Dreyfuss as the teenage hustler, Jack Warden as his taxi driver father and Denholm Elliott as a drunken arty film director. The film remains the only Canadian production ever to receive a major best picture award.

An International Cinemedia Centre Production, in co-operation with the Canadian Film Development Corporation, Welco United Canada, Famous Players and Bellevue-Pathe. Directed by Ted Kotcheff. Screenplay by Mordecai Richler, based on his own novel. Photographed in Bellevue-Pathe Color and Panavision by Miklos Lente. Music supervised by Stanley Myers. 121 minutes.

Starring Richard Dreyfuss, Micheline Lanctot, Jack Warden, Randy Quaid, Joseph Wiseman, Denholm Elliott, Henry Ramer, Joe Silver, Zvee Scooler.

AROUND THE WORLD IN 80 DAYS (USA)

Awards (3)

Best Film	American Academy Award, 1956
Best Film	New York Critics, 1956
Best American Film	National Board of Review, 1956

David Niven as Jules Verne's Victorian adventurer Phileas Fogg who wagers £20,000 with members of the London Reform Club that he can circle the globe in eighty days. Fifty stars help and hinder him along the way, among them: Marlene Dietrich as the owner of a Barbary Coast saloon, Peter Lorre as a Japanese steward, Fernandel as a Paris coachman and Charles Boyer as a representative of Thomas Cook. A spectacular entertainment, much lauded in the USA but ignored by the British Film Academy who failed to list it in their *sixteen* nominations for the best picture of 1956.

A Michael Todd Production (released by United Artists), directed by Michael Anderson. Screenplay by S. J. Perelman, James Poe and John Farrow, based on the novel by Jules Verne. Photographed in Eastman Color and Todd-AO by Lionel Lindon. Music by Victor Young. 165 minutes.

Starring David Niven, Cantinflas, Robert Newton, Shirley MacLaine and fifty stars in cameo roles.

ARTISTES AT THE TOP OF THE BIG TOP: DISORIENTATED
(West Germany)

Awards (1)
Golden Lion Venice, 1968

Bizarre film about the daughter of a circus artiste who determines to create a 'reformed circus' that will meet the needs of modern society and also be worthy of her dead father. Many critics have found it to be an expression of other things besides, e.g. 'a corrosion of all idealism', 'an analysis of the progress of the German cinema' and 'a satire on modern economics.' Whatever its meaning, it was the last film to win the Golden Lion at Venice before the festival's sad decline into a non-event in the early seventies.

Kairos Film. Written and directed by Alexander Kluge. Photographed (partly in Eastman Color) by Günther Hörmann and Thomas Mauch. 103 minutes.

Starring Hannelore Hoger, Siegfried Graue, Alfred Edel, Bernd Höltz, Eva Oertel, Kurt Jürgens, Gilbert Houcke, Wanda Bronska-Pampuch.

THE ASCENT (USSR)

Awards (1)
Golden Bear Berlin, 1977

Religious parable about a Russian partisan officer who resists Nazi torture and becomes a Christ-like figure when he sacrifices his life for his comrades. Huge close-ups and stark camerawork helped the film become a prize-winner at Berlin although the jury spent fourteen hours in heated debate before naming it best of the festival over Bresson's *The Devil, Probably*. The picture was directed by Soviet woman director Larissa Shepitko who was killed in a car accident in the summer of 1979.

A Mosfilm Production, directed by Larissa Shepitko. Screenplay by Yuri Klepikov and Larissa Shepitko, based on the story *Sotnikov* by Vassil Bykov. Photographed by Vladimir Tchuchnov. Music by Alfred Schnittke. 105 minutes.

Starring Boris Plotnikov, Vladimir Gostjuchin, Sergei Yakoviev, Ludmila Polyakova, Viktoria Goldentul.

UNE AUSSI LONGUE ABSENCE (France/Italy)

Awards (1)

Golden Palm	Cannes, 1961

The film that shared the 1961 Cannes Prize with Bunuel's *Viridiana*; a Resnais-styled puzzle about a woman café proprietor (Alida Valli) living in a village on the outskirts of Paris, who believes that an amnesiac tramp (Georges Wilson) is the husband she lost in the war, 'missing believed killed.' In true Resnais fashion the audience is no wiser at the end of the film than it was at the beginning. Director Henri Colpi was a former cutter for Resnais and shot the film in six weeks.

Societé Cinematographique Lyre/Procinex/Galatea. Directed by Henri Colpi. Screenplay by Marguerite Duras and Gérard Jarlot, from a story by Duras. Photographed in Dyaliscope by Marcel Weiss. Music by Georges Delerue. 90 minutes.

Starring Alida Valli, Georges Wilson, Jacques Harden, Diana Lepvrier, Catherine Fontenay, Amédée, Charles Blavette, Paul Faivre.

AUTUMN SONATA (West Germany)

Awards (1)

Best Foreign Language Film	National Board of Review, 1978

Ninety-two minutes in the company of celebrated concert pianist Ingrid Bergman as she visits her lonely daughter Liv Ullmann for the first time in seven years. The result — as mother and daughter confront each other with raw emotion — is an acting *tour-de-force* and a powerful examination of artistic temperament and its responsibilities. The first and only time that Ingmar directed Ingrid!

A Personafilm for ITC, written and directed by Ingmar Bergman. Photographed in Eastman Color by Sven Nykvist. 92 minutes.

Starring Ingrid Bergman, Liv Ullmann, Lena Nyman, Halvar Björk, Arne Bang-Hansen, Gunnar Björnstrand, Erland Josephson, Georg Løkkeberg, Linn Ullmann, Knut Wigert, Eva von Hanno.

BALLAD OF A SOLDIER (USSR)

Awards (1)
Best Film, Any Source British Academy Award, 1961

Lyrical tale of a young Russian soldier who earns a six-day respite from the war and uses the time to make the long journey home to see his mother. His experiences along the way with men and woman all affected by the war — crippled veterans, faithless wives, a young country girl — make up a haunting, often quite beautiful picture which shared the best picture award of the British Film Academy in 1961. The other recipient of the year's British 'Oscar' was Robert Rossen's *The Hustler.*

A Mosfilm Studios Production, directed by Grigori Chukrai. Screenplay by Valentin Yoshov and Grigori Chukrai. Photographed by Vladimir Nikolayev and Eva Saveleva. Music by Mikhail Ziv. 92 minutes.

Starring Vladimir Ivashov, Sharma Prokhorenko, Antonina Maximova, Nikolai Kruchkov, Ievgeni Urbanski.

Note: Ballad Of A Soldier was first released in Russia in 1959.

BARRY LYNDON (Britain)

Awards (1)
Best English Language Film National Board of Review, 1975

Stanley Kubrick goes back instead of forward in time for an eighteenth century odyssey about an Irish opportunist who attains status through a rich marriage but finishes poverty-stricken and crippled after journeying through the battlefields and gambling houses of Europe. A meticulous adaptation of Thackeray's *The Memoirs Of Barry Lyndon, Esq*; for many a wearisome experience, for Kubrick devotees a masterpiece. Narrated by Michael Hordern.

A Hawk Films/Peregrine Production for Warner Bros. Written and directed by Stanley Kubrick, based on the novel by William Makepeace Thackeray. Photographed in Eastman Color by John Alcott. Music adaptation by Leonard Rosenman. 187 minutes.

Starring Ryan O'Neal, Marisa Berenson, Patrick Magee, Hardy Kruger, Steven Berkoff, Gay Hamilton, Marie Kean, Diana Koerner, Murray Melvin.

Note: Barry Lyndon shared the award of the National Board of Review with Robert Altman's *Nashville*.

THE BATTLE OF ALGIERS (Algeria/Italy)

Awards (1)
Golden Lion — Venice, 1966

Semi-documentary account of the long years of underground activity that led to the end of French rule in Algeria. Praised for its pictorial qualities — crowd scenes, imaginative use of close-ups, etc. — the film was a controversial winner at Venice where it was boycotted by the French because of its sympathies for the Algerian cause. Its Golden Lion award was met with boos at the prize-giving, many critics feeling that the honour should have gone to *Balthazar*, directed by the perennially unlucky Robert Bresson.

Igor Film/Casbah Films. Directed by Gillo Pontecorvo. Screenplay by Franco Solinas. Story by Gillo Pontecorvo. Photographed in CinemaScope by Marcello Gatti. Music by Ennio Morricone and Gillo Pontecorvo. 120 minutes.

Starring Jean Martin, Yacef Saadi, Brahim Haggiag, Tommaso Neri, Fawzia El-Kader, Samia Kerbash, Mohamed Ben Kassen, Ugo Paletti.

THE BATTLE OF STALINGRAD (USSR)

Awards (1)
Grand Prix — Karlovy Vary, 1949

Epic production about the Soviet's heroic defence of Stalingrad in 1942. Alexei Diki as a cool Stalin directing operations from the Kremlin and M. Astangov as a ranting Hitler offer real-life caricatures; the Russian and German newsreel cameras provide a sobering commentary on the enormous losses sustained by both sides.

A Mosfilm Production, directed by Vladimir Petrov. Screenplay by Nikolai Virta. Photographed by Yuri Yekelchik. Music by Aram Khachaturian. 149 minutes.

Starring Alexei Diki, Yuri Shumsky, Boris Livanov, Nikolai Simonov, Nikolai Plotnikov, M. Astangov.

BECKET (Britain)

Awards (1)
Best English Language Film — National Board of Review, 1964

The story of Thomas Becket, Archbishop of Canterbury, and his turbulent relationship with Norman king, Henry II during the struggles between church and state in twelfth century England. Impeccable sets and costumes, plus dialogue of a quality only rarely heard in period films were the key factors in the National Board of Review naming the picture best of the year. Oscar winner *My Fair Lady* was runner-up in the Board's ten best list.

A Paramount Picture, directed by Peter Glenville. Screenplay by Edward Anhalt, based on the play by Jean Anouilh. Photographed in

Technicolor and Panavision by Geoffrey Unsworth. Music by Laurence Rosenthal. Production Design by John Bryan. 148 minutes.

Starring Richard Burton, Peter O'Toole, John Gielgud, Donald Wolfit, Martita Hunt, Pamela Brown, Paolo Stoppa, Gino Cervi, David Weston, Felix Aylmer.

BELLE DE JOUR (France/Italy)

Awards (1)

Golden Lion	Venice, 1967

Luis Buñuel at his most mischievous; a version of Joseph Kessel's novel about a wealthy young surgeon's wife who indulges her masochistic fantasies by working as a part time prostitute in a Paris brothel. Erotic, wickedly funny and that rarest of cinema achievements – a work of art that entertains. The beautiful Catherine Deneuve is the tormented wife, Geneviève Page the lesbian madam of her brothel.

Paris Film (Paris)/Five Films (Rome). Directed by Luis Buñuel. Screenplay by Luis Buñuel and Jean-Claude Carrière, based on the novel by Joseph Kessel. Photographed in Eastman Color by Sacha Vierny. Art Direction by Robert Clavel. 104 minutes.

Starring Catherine Deneuve, Jean Sorel, Michel Piccoli, Geneviève Page, Francisco Rabal, Pierre Clementi, Georges Marchal.

BEN-HUR (USA)

Awards (3)

Best Film	American Academy Award, 1959
Best Film	New York Critics, 1959
Best Film, Any Source	British Academy Award, 1959

Christianity versus paganism in ancient Rome and, symbolically, white horses versus black horses when good guy Charlton Heston (Ben-Hur) takes on bad guy Stephen Boyd (Messala) in the famous eleven-minute chariot race. The most Oscared film of all time – eleven awards, one for each minute of the race – and honoured also by the New York Critics and the British Film Academy. The only dissenting vote came from The National Board of Review who placed the film second behind Fred Zinnemann's more delicate tale of religion, *The Nun's Story*.

A Metro-Goldwyn-Mayer Picture, directed by William Wyler. Screenplay by Karl Tunberg, based on the novel by General Lew Wallace. Photographed in Technicolor and Camera 65 by Robert L. Surtees. Music by Miklos Rozsa. Art Direction by William A. Horning and Edward Carfagno. 212 minutes.

Starring Charlton Heston, Jack Hawkins, Stephen Boyd, Hugh Griffith, Martha Scott, Cathy O'Donnell, Haya Hayareet, Sam Jaffe, Finlay Currie, Frank Thring.

THE BEST YEARS OF OUR LIVES (USA)

Awards (3)

Best Film	American Academy Award, 1946
Best Film	New York Critics, 1946
Best Film, Any Source	British Academy Award, 1947

Poignant drama of three American ex-servicemen and the problems they face when readjusting to civilian life after World War II. A model of its kind, despite the passing of thirty years, primarily because of its optimism and the sympathetically drawn characters of the three men — middle-aged army sergeant Fredric March, air corps officer Dana Andrews and sailor Harold Russell, in real life a handless veteran of the war. Only the National Board of Review failed to select the film as best of the year, placing it third behind *Henry V* and Rossellini's *Open City*.

A Samuel Goldwyn Production (released by RKO), directed by William Wyler. Screenplay by Robert E. Sherwood, based on the novel by MacKinlay Kantor. Photographed by Gregg Toland. Music by Hugo Friedhofer. 165 minutes.

Starring Fredric March, Myrna Loy, Dana Andrews, Teresa Wright, Virginia Mayo, Harold Russell, Cathy O'Donnell, Hoagy Carmichael, Gladys George, Ray Collins.

BICYCLE THIEVES (Italy)

Awards (4)

Best Foreign Language Film	American Academy Award, 1949
Best Foreign Language Film	New York Critics, 1949
Best Film	National Board of Review, 1949
Best Film, Any Source	British Academy Award, 1949

The desperate attempts of an Italian labourer and his son to search for the stolen bicycle that is so essential to the father in his newly obtained job as a billposter — a job on which the future livelihood of his family depends. One of the key films of the Italian neo-realistic movement, set in the poverty-stricken streets of post-war Rome and, for many years, considered to be one of the ten best pictures ever made.

A PDS (Enic) Umberto Scarpelli Production, directed by Vittorio De Sica. Screenplay by Cesare Zavattini, based on the story by Luigi Batolini. Photographed by Carlo Montuori. Music by Alessandro Cicognini. 90 minutes.

Starring Lamberto Maggiorani, Enzo Staiola, Lianella Carell, Gino Saltamerenda, Vittorio Antonucci.

Note: Bicycle Thieves was first shown in Italy in 1948. The film is known as *The Bicycle Thief* in the United States.

THE BIRDS,THE BEES AND THE ITALIANS (France/Italy)

Awards (1)
Golden Palm Cannes, 1966

Three amusing tales of provincial Italy, the first focussing on the adultery of a doctor's wife, the second on the bigamy of a bank clerk and the third on the mass seduction of a well-endowed but under-age farm girl. Virna Lisi, Gastone Moschin and Franco Fabrizi help interpret Pietro Germi's social observations of life in small town Italy. The film was Germi's successor to his earlier comedies, *Divorce-Italian Style* and *Seduced And Abandoned* and shared the Cannes prize with *A Man And A Woman.*

Dear Film/R.P.A./Les Films du Siecle. Directed by Pietro Germi. Screenplay by Age and Scarpelli, Luciano Vincenzoni and Pietro Germi. Photographed by Aiace Parolin. Music by Carlo Rustichelli. 115 minutes.

Starring Virna Lisi, Gastone Moschin, Nora Ricci, Alberto Lionello, Olga Villi, Franco Fabrizi, Beba Loncar, Gigi Ballista, Aldo Puglisi.

BLACK AND WHITE IN COLOUR (France/Switzerland/Ivory Coast)

Awards (1)
Best Foreign Language Film American Academy Award, 1976

Mocking tale about the evils of war, set in French West Africa in 1915 and focussing on a handful of easy-going Frenchmen who attack a nearby German community when they belatedly discover they are supposed to be enemies. The first feature of Jean-Jacques Annaud and the surprise Oscar winner of 1976.

Reggane Films/SFP (Paris)/Artco Film Productions (Zurich)/Société Ivoirienne de Production (Abidjan). Directed by Jean-Jacques Annaud. Screenplay by Georges Conchon and Jean-Jacques Annaud. Photographed in Eastman Color by Claude Agostini, Eduardo Serra and Nanamoudou Magassouda. Music by Pierre Bachelet and Mat Camison. 100 minutes.

Starring Jean Carmet, Jacques Dufilho, Catherine Rouvel, Jacques Spiesser, Dora Doll, Maurice Barrier, Claude Legros, Jacques Monnet.

BLACK ORPHEUS (France/Italy)

Awards (2)
Best Foreign Language Film American Academy Award, 1959
Golden Palm Cannes, 1959

Marcel Camus' spectacular updating of the Orpheus legend, set both in the dusty shanty towns of Rio and the city's colourful streets during the orgiastic days of the carnival. The film follows the tragic destinies of Orpheus, a young Brazilian tram driver, and his Eurydice, a black peasant girl fleeing from a menacing suitor whom she eventually recognises as death. Conceived as one long ballet with dialogue and played out by a cast of non-professionals.

Dispatfilm Paris/Gemma Cinematografica. Directed by Marcel Camus. Screenplay by Jacques Viot. Photographed in Eastman Color by Jean Bourgoin. Music by Antonio Carlos Jobim and Luis Bonfa. 98 minutes.

Starring Brenno Melio, Marpessa Dawn, Ademar Da Sylva, Lourdes De Oliveira, Lea Garcia.

BLOW-UP (Britain/Italy)

Awards (1)
Golden Palm — Cannes, 1967

Antonioni as ambiguous as ever in a film that combines an abstract, intellectual view of the swinging London of the sixties with an intriguing mystery story about a young fashion photographer (David Hemmings) who finds that he has accidentally photographed a murder being committed in a London park. The mystery is never solved; as usual with Antonioni the film's message is open to question. With this picture Antonioni became the only man to have directed best films at all three major European festivals — Cannes, Venice and Berlin.

A Bridge Film for Metro-Goldwyn-Mayer, directed by Michelangelo Antonioni. Screenplay by Michelangelo Antonioni and Tonino Guerra. Photographed in Metrocolor by Carlo Di Palma. Music by Herbie Hancock. 110 minutes.

Starring Vanessa Redgrave, Sarah Miles, David Hemmings, John Castle, Jane Birkin, Gillian Hills, Peter Bowles, Verushka.

Note: Blow-Up was first shown in New York in December, 1966.

BREAD AND CHOCOLATE (Italy)

Awards (1)
Best Foreign Language Film — New York Critics, 1978

Satire plus farce plus romance as an accident-prone waiter tries to make a go of it in prosperous Switzerland so that he can summon his wife and family from Italy. The sharp observations of the problems of immigrant workers helped earn the film the New York Critics Award four years after it had received a Silver Lion at Berlin.

Verona Cinematografica. Directed by Franco Brusati. Screenplay by Franco Brusati, Iaia Fiastri and Nino Manfredi. Story by Brusati. Photographed in Eastman Color by Luciano Tovoli. Music direction by Daniele Patrucchi. 112 minutes.

Starring Nino Manfredi, Anna Karina, Johnny Dorelli, Paolo Turco, Ugo D'Alessio, Federico Scrobogna, Gianfranco Barra, Giorgio Cerioni.

Note: Bread And Chocolate was first released in 1974.

THE BRIDGE (West Germany)

Awards (1)

Best Foreign Film	National Board of Review, 1961

Seven German schoolboys are ordered to defend the bridge of their town against the advancing Allies in the last days of World War II. By the film's close the bridge is a scene of senseless carnage and only one of the boys is alive. Powerful anti-war film of the early sixties, directed by Bernhard Wicki who subsequently directed the German sequences of Zanuck's *The Longest Day*.

Fono Film/Jochen Severin. Directed by Bernhard Wicki. Screenplay by Bernhard Wicki, Michael Mansfeld and Karl-Wilhelm Vivier, based on the book by Manfred Gregor. Photographed by Gerd von Bonin. Music by Hans-Martin Majewski. 102 minutes.

Starring Volker Bohnet, Fritz Wepper, Michael Hinz, Frank Glaubrecht, Karl Michael Balzer, Volker Lechtenbrink, Günther Hoffmann, Cordula Trantow, Wolfgang Stumpf, Günter Pfitzmann.

Note: The Bridge was first shown in West Germany in October, 1959.

THE BRIDGE ON THE RIVER KWAI (Britain)

Awards (4)

Best Film	American Academy Award, 1957
Best Film	New York Critics, 1957
Best American Film	National Board of Review, 1957
Best Film, Any Source	British Academy Award, 1957

Anti-war adventure about the construction by British prisoners-of-war of a Japanese railway bridge in the Burmese jungle and its eventual destruction by a British commando unit. The 'war is madness' theme is highlighted by the conflict of wills between the veteran Japanese commandant (Sessue Hayakawa) and the British colonel (Alec Guiness) in charge of the bridge-building. David Lean's first epic; based on the novel by Pierre Boulle which, in turn, was based on a true incident in World War II. A winner of all the major American and British best picture awards.

A Horizon Pictures-Columbia Production, directed by David Lean. Screenplay by Pierre Boulle (and, uncredited, Michael Wilson and Carl Foreman), based on his novel. Photographed in Technicolor and CinemaScope by Jack Hildyard. Music by Malcolm Arnold. 161 minutes.

Starring Alec Guinness, William Holden, Jack Hawkins, Sessue Hayakawa, James Donald, Geoffrey Horne, Andre Morell.

Note: The National Board of Review listed *Kwai* as an American film in their ten best list of 1957; on most occasions the film is referred to as a British production.

THE BROADWAY MELODY (USA)

Awards (1)
Best Film American Academy Award, 1928/29

Bessie Love and Anita Page as two country girls who try to carve out careers on the Broadway stage but find themselves romantically involved with vaudeville hoofer Charles King. The oldest plot in the world but brand new in 1929 when director Harry Beaumont put it all together and came up with the first musical to win a best picture Oscar. Top songs: 'The Wedding Of The Painted Doll', 'You Were Meant For Me' and 'Give My Regards To Broadway.'

A Metro-Goldwyn-Mayer Picture, directed by Harry Beaumont. Screenplay by Sarah Y. Mason. Dialogue by Norman Houston and James Gleason. Story by Edmund Goulding. Photographed (with 2-color Technicolor sequences) by John Arnold. Songs by Nacio Herb Brown, Arthur Freed, George M. Cohan and Willard Robison. 110 minutes.

Starring Anita Page, Bessie Love, Charles King, Jed Prouty, Kenneth Thomson, Edward Dillon, Mary Doran, Eddie Kane, J. Emmett Beck.

BUFFALO BILL AND THE INDIANS, OR SITTING BULL'S HISTORY LESSON (USA)

Awards (1)
Golden Bear Berlin, 1976

The private torment of an ageing Buffalo Bill Cody (Paul Newman) as he slowly comes to realise that he is nothing more than a hollow fake and has allowed the truth about himself to be buried beneath the popular myth. Set in 1885 within the confines of Cody's Wild West Show, the film marked Robert Altman's second European festival success and followed his prize-winning *M.A.S.H.* at Cannes six years earlier.

Dino De Laurentiis Corporation/Lion's Gate Films/Talent Associates-Norton Simon. Directed by Robert Altman. Screenplay by Alan Rudolph and Robert Altman, suggested by the play *Indians* by Arthur Kopit. Photographed in De Luxe-General Color and Panavision by Paul Lohmann. Music by Richard Baskin. 123 minutes.

Starring Paul Newman, Joel Grey, Burt Lancaster, Kevin McCarthy, Harvey Keitel, Allan Nicholls, Geraldine Chaplin, John Considine, Robert Doqui, Mike Kaplan, Bert Remsen.

BUSHIDO (Japan)

Awards (1)
Golden Bear Berlin, 1963

A brutal chronicle of how the Samurai spirit manifested itself, tracing the fortunes of a peasant family over four generations — from the turn of the seventeenth century to the break-up of the master-servant ethos in post World War II Japan. Kinnosuke Nakamura features as six members of the family. The film shared the 1963 Berlin prize with *Il Diavolo.*

A Toei Company Production, directed by Tadashi Imai. Screenplay by Naoyuki Suzuki from an original story by Norio Nanjo. Photographed in ToeiScope by Makoto Tsuboi. Music by Toshiro Mayuzumi. 123 minutes.

Starring Kinnosuke Nakamura, Masayuki Mori, Kyoko Kishida, Yoshiko Mita, Ineko Arima, Shinjiro Ebara.

BUTCH CASSIDY AND THE SUNDANCE KID (USA)

Awards (1)

Best Film	British Academy Award, 1970

Affectionate account of the final years of two of the West's most colourful outlaws who operated from their Wyoming hideout, 'Hole In The Wall', before perishing at the hands of the Bolivian cavalry. A highly regarded western that lost out at awards time in America but succeeded in Britain because of its later 1970 release date. The film remains only the fourth western – *Cimarron, The Ox-Bow Incident* and *High Noon* are the others – to have been named best picture in over fifty years of award history.

A Twentieth Century-Fox Picture, directed by George Roy Hill. Screenplay by William Goldman. Photographed in De Luxe Color and Panavision by Conrad Hall. Music by Burt Bacharach. 110 minutes.

Starring Paul Newman, Robert Redford, Katharine Ross, Strother Martin, Henry Jones, Jeff Corey, Cloris Leachman.

Note: Butch Cassidy And The Sundance Kid opened in the United States in September 1969 and qualified for the 1969 American Oscar Awards.

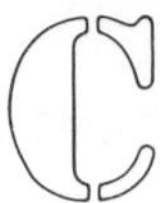

CABARET (USA)

Awards (2)

Best English Language Film	National Board of Review, 1972
Best Film	British Academy Award, 1972

The amorous adventures of cabaret singer Sally Bowles (Liza Minnelli) in Berlin just prior to the Nazis rise to power. As a piece of movie entertainment, spectacularly successful; as an adaptation of the musical play, less than satisfactory, losing several songs along the way and never quite evoking enough sleaziness to be totally convincing. Joel Grey (in a repeat of his Broadway role) co-stars as the lurid MC of the Kit Kat Klub, joining Minnelli in one of the new songs specially written for the film: 'Money, Money, Money!'

An ABC Pictures Corporation/Allied Artists Production, directed by Bob Fosse. Screenplay by Jay Presson Allen, based on the musical play by Joe Masteroff (book), John Kander (music) and Fred Ebb (lyrics). Photographed in Technicolor by Geoffrey Unsworth. 123 minutes.

Starring Liza Minnelli, Michael York, Helmut Griem, Joel Grey, Fritz Wepper, Marisa Berenson.

LA CAGE AUX FOLLES (France/Italy)

Awards (1)

Best Foreign Language Film	National Board of Review, 1979

A twenty-year homosexual relationship between a night club owner and a drag queen is rudely interrupted when the former's son brings home the girl he wants to marry — the daughter of a leading figure in the Union for Moral Order! French farce, set in St. Tropez, that follows a predictably chaotic course after an imaginative opening few reels.

Les Productions Artistes Associés (Paris)/Da.Ma.Produzione (Rome). Directed by Edouard Molinaro. Screenplay and adaptation by Francis Véber, Edouard Molinaro, Marcello Danon and Jean Poiret, based on the play by Poiret. Photographed in Eastman Color by Armando Nannuzzi. Music by Ennio Morricone. 91 minutes.

Starring Michel Serrault, Ugo Tognazzi, Michel Galabru, Claire Maurier, Remi Laurent, Benny Luke, Carmen Scarpitta, Luisa Maneri.

CAMERA BUFF (Poland)

Awards (1)
Grand Prix Moscow, 1979

Farcical (and satirical) comedy about a young factory worker who becomes a maniacal photography enthusiast when he purchases a camera to photograph his newly born daughter. After winning a prize in an amateur contest, he goes on to transcend his amateur status, destroy his marriage and photograph 'life as it really is.' A parody of both politics and culture (especially the film industry) and a comedy of some substance. One of three films to earn the 1979 Moscow Grand Prix. The others: *Seven Days In January* and *Christ Stopped At Eboli.*

A Film Polski Production, Film Unit Tor, Warsaw. Directed by Krzysztof Kieślowski. Screenplay by Kieślowski and Jerzy Stuhr. Photographed in Eastman Color by Jacek Petrycki. Music by Krzysztof Knittel. 112 minutes.

Starring Jerzy Stuhr, Malgorzata Zabkowska, Ewa Pokas, Stefan Czyzewski, Jerzy Nowak, Tadeusz Bladecki, Marek Litewka.

CANTATA OF CHILE (Cuba)

Awards (1)
Grand Prix Karlovy Vary, 1976

Political film that combines the music, poems and myths of Chile to illustrate the country's continued exploitation by European invaders — from the Spanish conquistadors to the less warlike but equally ruthless economic barons of recent times. At the heart of the film is a turn of the century strike at a British owned nitrate mine which led to the massacre of 3,600 workers by Chilean troops. Made by the director of the earlier, prize-winning *Lucia.*

ICAIC. Written and directed by Humberto Solas. Photographed in Eastman Color by Jorge Herrera. Music by Leo Brouwer. 119 minutes.

Starring Nelson Villagra, Shenda Román, Eric Heresmann, Alfredo Tornquist, Leonardo Perucci, Peggy Cordero, Flavia Ugalde, Luz Maria Laguerrigue.

THE CANTERBURY TALES (Italy/France)

Awards (1)
Golden Bear Berlin, 1972

A group of pilgrims journey to Canterbury and enjoy both their own adventures and the tales they tell each other along the way. An Italian's view of Merrie England, some way removed from Chaucer and rather closer to modern porn as Pasolini uses the stories to comment on human greed and indulge in elbow nudging naughtiness. Pasolini appears in the film as Chaucer, transcribing the stories for posterity.

P.E.A. Cinematografica (Rome)/Les Productions Artistes Associés

(Paris). Directed by Pier Paolo Pasolini. Screenplay by Pier Paolo Pasolini, based on the stories by Geoffrey Chaucer. Photographed in Technicolor by Tonino Delli Colli. 109 minutes.

Starring Pier Paolo Pasolini, Laura Betti, J.P. Van Dyne, Derek Deadman, George Bethell Datch, Hugh Griffith, Josephine Chaplin, Oscar Fochetti, Guiseppe Arrigo, Elizabetta Genovese.

CAPRICIOUS SUMMER (Czechoslovakia)

Awards (1)

Grand Prix	Karlovy Vary, 1968

Three ageing friends — a swimming master, a retired army officer and a parson — are suddenly bewitched by a beautiful young tightrope walker when she visits their town with her partner one memorable summer's day. All three make a play for the girl's attentions. All three fail. In the end the troupe moves on leaving the three men more regretful than ever of their lost youth. A wryly humorous film, set at the turn of the century and reminiscent of Renoir in its overall mood and the lazy beauty of its colour photography.

Barrandov Film Studio for Československý Film. Directed by Jiří Menzel. Screenplay by Jiří Menzel and Václav Nývlt, based on the novel by Vladislav Vančura. Photographed in Eastman Color by Jaromír Šofr. Music by Jiří Šust. 75 minutes.

Starring Rudolf Hrušínský, Vlastimil Brodský, František Řehák, Míla Myslíková, Jana Drchalová, Jiří Menzel.

UN CARNET DE BAL (France)

Awards (1)

Mussolini Cup	Venice, 1937

Bittersweet Duvivier film about a lonely young widow (Marie Bell) who decides to trace her former suitors when she comes across their names on an old dance programme. Sadness, disillusionment and a discovery of dreams unfulfilled lie at the end of her quest. Louis Jouvet is a night club owner, Pierre Blanchar a back street abortionist, Harry Baur a monk, Fernandel a barber and Raimu a small town mayor. Maurice Jaubert's haunting waltz became one of the most famous film themes of the thirties.

Sigma (P. Frogerais). Directed by Julien Duvivier. Screenplay by Julien Duvivier, Jean Sarment, Pierre Wolff, Yves Mirande and Bernard Zimmer. Photographed by Michel Kelber. Music by Maurice Jaubert. 109 minutes.

Starring Marie Bell, Françoise Rosay, Harry Baur, Pierre Blanchar, Raimu, Louis Jouvet, Fernandel, Pierre Richard-Willm, Milly Mathis, Robert Lynen.

CASABLANCA (USA)

Awards (1)
Best Film — American Academy Award, 1943

A rain-soaked Bogart waiting for Bergman at a Paris station; Paul Henreid leading the 'Marseillaise'; Claude Rains slyly leaving all options open and, of course, Dooley Wilson singing 'As Time Goes By' at Rick's place. In short, just about the perfect screen melodrama, blending intrigue and romance, menace and sophistication in a manner that only Hollywood at its most skilful could accomplish. The Oscar Academy alone recognised the film's quality and voted it best of 1943.

A Warner Bros. Picture, directed by Michael Curtiz. Screenplay by Julius J. Epstein, Philip G. Epstein and Howard Koch, based on *Everybody Comes To Rick's*, an unproduced play by Murray Burnett and Joan Alison. Photographed by Arthur Edeson. Music by Max Steiner. 102 minutes.

Starring Humphrey Bogart, Ingrid Bergman, Paul Henreid, Claude Rains, Conrad Veidt, Sydney Greenstreet, Peter Lorre, S. Z. Sakall, Dooley Wilson.

CAVALCADE (USA)

Awards (1)
Best Film — American Academy Award, 1932/33

Noel Coward's affectionate homage to his countrymen; a panorama of English history from 1889 to World War I and its aftermath, mirrored through the experiences and sacrifices of an upper class English family. Elegant performances and plenty of spectacular highlights – The Boer War, The Sinking of the Titanic, Zeppelin raids, etc. Also a best picture Oscar winner in a year when *42nd Street, I Am A Fugitive From A Chain Gang* and *Little Women* were among those up for the award.

A Fox Picture, directed by Frank Lloyd. Adaptation and dialogue by Reginald Berkeley, based on the play by Noel Coward. Photographed by Ernest Palmer. Art Direction by William Darling. 115 minutes.

Starring Diana Wynyard, Clive Brook, Ursula Jeans, Margaret Lindsay, Frank Lawton, Una O'Connor, Herbert Mundin, Irene Brown.

Note: Cavalcade was one of the films included in the National Board of Review's 'ten best list' of 1933.

CAVALIER OF THE GOLD STAR (USSR)

Awards (1)
Grand Prix — Karlovy Vary, 1951

Leisurely tale of a demobilized Russian soldier who persuades the inhabitants of his village to build a power station that will supply electricity to all farms in the area. Not exactly the most riveting of themes although the camerawork is fine and a comely dairy-maid offers compensations for the ponderous Stalinistic ideas amalgamated in the film.

A Mosfilm Production, directed by Yuri Raisman. Screenplay by B. Churskov, based on the novel by S. Babayevsky. Photographed in Magicolor by S. Urusevsky. Music by T. Khrennikov. 95 minutes.

Starring Sergei Bondarchuk, A. Chemodurov, A. Kanayeva, Boris Chirkov, N. Komissarov.

THE CHILDHOOD OF IVAN (USSR)

Awards (1)
Golden Lion — Venice, 1962

Impressions of war as seen through the eyes of a twelve-year-old boy who has seen his mother killed by the Germans and is cared for by a group of Soviet soldiers who try to protect him from the conflict. Not the most famous of Venice prize-winners (it shared the 1962 award with the Italian *Family Chronicle*) but one that has stood the test of time rather better than most. The poetic photography is inspired by the work of Russian master director Alexander Dovzhenko.

A Gorki Studio Production, released by Mosfilm. Directed by Andrei Tarkowski. Screenplay by Vladimir Bogomolov and Mikhail Papava. Photographed by Vladimir Iousov. 95 minutes.

Starring Kolia Bourliaiev, Z. Zoubov, E. Jarikov, S. Krilov, N. Griko.

CHRIST STOPPED AT EBOLI (Italy/France)

Awards (1)
Grand Prix — Moscow, 1979

The bleak day-to-day life of Lucanian peasants in Mussolini's Italy as seen through the eyes of a young Italian living in political exile because of his anti-fascist activities in the Ethiopian war. A lovingly photographed film, set in 1935, and comprising a series of vignettes of village life in Italy's poorest region, south of Naples. From the autobiographical book of the same name by writer-painter Carlo Levi and, along with the Polish comedy *Camera Buff* and Bardem's *Seven Days In January*, winner of the first prize at Moscow.

RAI-TV 2/Vides Cinematografica (Rome)/ Action Films (Paris). Directed by Francesco Rosi. Screenplay by Francesco Rosi, Tonino Guerra and Raffaele La Capria, based on the novel by Carlo Levi. Photographed in Technospes colour by Pasqualino De Santis. Music by Piero Piccioni. 151 minutes.

Starring Gian Maria Volonté, Paolo Bonacelli, Alain Cuny, Lea Massari, Irene Papas, François Simon.

CHRONICLE OF THE YEARS OF EMBERS (Algeria)

Awards (1)
Golden Palm — Cannes, 1975

Spectacle — Third World style — in a sweeping three-hour epic about the experiences of a poor peasant family living through five crucial periods in Algerian history. The film chronicles the development of Algerian revolutionary thought between the years 1939 and 1954 and is reputedly the most expensive ever made in Africa.

An O.N.C.I.C. Production, directed by Mohammed Lakhdar-Hamina. Screenplay by Mohammed Lakhdar-Hamina and Tewfik Fares. Photographed in Eastman Color and 70mm by Marcello Gatti. Music by Philippe Arthuys. 170 minutes.

Starring Jorge Voyagis, Mohammed Lakhdar-Hamina, Larbi Sekkal, Cheik Nourredine, Hassan Hassani, M. Kouiret, Leila Shenna, Francois Maistre.

CIMARRON (USA)

Awards (1)

Best Film — American Academy Award, 1930/31

Edna Ferber saga chronicling the rise of an Oklahoma frontier town from a rip-roaring lawless community to a rich, industrialized city of the twentieth century. The filming of the famous Cherokee Strip land stampede entailed the use of 1050 vehicles, 3500 horses, 5000 players and 35 cameras in pits, trucks and aeroplanes! The statistics have stood the film in good stead. It is still the only western to have won a best picture Oscar.

An RKO-Radio Picture, directed by Wesley Ruggles. Screenplay by Howard Estabrook, based on the novel by Edna Ferber. Photographed by Edward Cronjager. 130 minutes.

Starring Richard Dix, Irene Dunne, Edna May Oliver, Estelle Taylor, William Collier, Jr., George E. Stone, Roscoe Ates, Stanley Fields.

Note: Cimarron was one of the films included in the 1931 'ten best list' of the National Board of Review.

CINDERELLA (USA)

Awards (1)

First Prize — Berlin, 1951

The first of Walt Disney's attempts to translate an established fairy tale into a full-length animated cartoon. A fresh, lively little movie with several animal characters added to the established Cinderella story line: Gus and Jaq, a couple of domestic mice; Bruno, an affable dog, and an arrogant, pampered black cat named Lucifer. Top song: 'Bibbidi-Bobbidi-Boo.'

A Walt Disney Production, released by RKO Radio. Direction by Wilfred Jackson, Hamilton Luske and Clyde Geronimi. Production supervised by Ben Sharpsteen. Photographed in Technicolor. Music direction by Oliver Wallace and Paul Smith. Songs by Mack David, Jerry Livingston and Al Hoffman. 74 minutes.

Note: Cinderella was voted best of the Berlin festival by a public vote and was also rated as the best musical. It was first released in America in 1950.

THE CITADEL (Britain)

Awards (2)

Best Film	New York Critics, 1938
Best English Language Film	National Board of Review, 1938

Robert Donat as A. J. Cronin's Welsh mining doctor who almost loses his idealism during his rise to fame and fortune as a healer of the idle rich in Harley Street. A kind of 'Fame Is The Spur' of medicine and the closest director King Vidor ever came to directing an Oscar winning movie. Hollywood's choice in 1938, however, was Capra's *You Can't Take It With You*. The New York Critics and National Board of Review both offered compensations with best film awards.

A Metro-Goldwyn-Mayer Picture, directed by King Vidor. Screenplay by Ian Dalrymple, Frank Wead, Elizabeth Hill and Emlyn Williams, based on the novel by A. J. Cronin. Photographed by Harry Stradling. Music by Louis Levy. 110 minutes.

Starring Robert Donat, Rosalind Russell, Ralph Richardson, Rex Harrison, Emlyn Williams, Penelope Dudley Ward, Francis L. Sullivan, Mary Clare, Cecil Parker.

CITIZEN KANE (USA)

Awards (2)

Best Film	New York Critics, 1941
Best American Film	National Board of Review, 1941

The life and death of an American newspaper tycoon, pieced together by a newsreel reporter as he seeks the truth about the man behind the legend by interviewing those people most closely connected with him during his lifetime. Orson Welles' masterwork and a film yet to be toppled from many critics' lists as the best movie of all time. Hollywood's Oscar Academy recognised Welles' achievement by voting the film a solitary writing award. Welles, Joseph Cotten and Agnes Moorehead all made their screen debuts in the film.

An RKO-Radio Picture, directed by Orson Welles. Screenplay by Herman J. Mankiewicz and Orson Welles. Photographed by Gregg Toland. Music by Bernard Herrmann. 119 minutes.

Starring Orson Welles, Dorothy Comingore, Joseph Cotten, Everett Sloane, George Coulouris, Ray Collins, Ruth Warrick, Erskine Sanford, William Alland, Agnes Moorehead.

CLAIRE'S KNEE (France)

Awards (1)

Best Foreign Language Film	National Board of Review, 1971

Delicate, quietly erotic Eric Rohmer film made up of a series of summer interludes between a man on the brink of middle-age and a seventeen-year-old girl with whom he falls passionately in love. The girl's perfect right knee is the part of her anatomy which almost (although not quite) leads the man to succumb to her charms. Gossamer thin and talkative; number five in Rohmer's 'six moral fables', preceeded by *My Night At Maud's* and followed by *Love In The Afternoon.*

Les Films du Losange. Written and directed by Eric Rohmer. Photographed in Eastman Color by Nestor Almendros. 106 minutes.

Starring Jean-Claude Brialy, Aurora Cornu, Béatrice Romand, Laurence de Monaghan, Michèle Montel, Gérard Falconetti, Fabrice Luchini.

Note: Claire's Knee was first shown in France in 1970.

CLEAR SKIES (USSR)

Awards (1)

Grand Prix	Moscow, 1961

A young girl falls in love with a Russian test pilot, bears his child when he leaves for the war but finds that all is not sweetness and light when he returns home safely from a prison camp. Something of a watershed in the Soviet cinema of the post-Stalin era, raising questions about illegitimate children, alcoholic heroes, patriotism and Stalinistic dogma. Filmed in classical style by Grigori Chukrai, director of the award winning *Ballad Of A Soldier*, and joint winner (with Japan's *The Island*) of the 1961 Moscow Festival.

A Mosfilm Studios Production, directed by Grigori Chukrai. Screenplay by Daniil Khrabrovitsky. Photographed in Sovcolor by Sergei Poluyanov. Music by Mikhail Ziv. 90 minutes.

Starring Nina Drobysheva, Ievgeni Urbanski, N. Kuzmina, Vitaliy Konyayev, G. Kulikov.

A CLOCKWORK ORANGE (Britain)

Awards (1)

Best Film	New York Critics, 1971

Startling version of Anthony Burgess' novel about a nightmare society of the future where a loathsome young thug and his apelike gang of 'droogs' rape and pillage at will. The authorities seek to curb the youth's violence by experimental shock treatment. The treatment fails and the thug returns to his former self. The film's message? That free-will and individuality should be preserved at all costs. The only Stanley Kubrick picture to win a New York Critics best picture award.

A Warner Bros./Polaris Production, directed by Stanley Kubrick. Screenplay by Stanley Kubrick, based on the novel by Anthony Burgess. Photographed in colour by John Alcott. 136 minutes.

Starring Malcolm McDowell, Patrick Magee, Michael Bates, Warren Clarke, John Clive, Adrienne Corri, Carl Duering, Paul Farrell.

CLOSE FRIENDS (USSR)

Awards (1)
Grand Prix — Karlovy Vary, 1954

Three former boyhood friends – a famous architect, a well-known surgeon, and the head of a research institute – meet again in Moscow for a river holiday and discover how their characters and ideals have changed since childhood. Directed by Mikhail Kalatozov who, in 1958, was responsible for the award winning *The Cranes Are Flying* and later, the spectacular *The Red Tent*. Co-winner, along with *Salt Of The Earth*, of the 1954 Karlovy Vary Festival.

A Mosfilm Studios Production, directed by Mikhail Kalatozov. Screenplay by A. Galic and K. Isajev. Photographed in Sovcolor by M. Magidson. Music by T. Chrennikov. 100 minutes.

Starring Vasili Merkurjev, Boris Chirkov, A. Borisov, A. Gribov, L. Gricenkova, L. Sagalova.

CLOSELY OBSERVED TRAINS (Czechoslovakia)

Awards (1)
Best Foreign Language Film — American Academy Award, 1967

The sexual experiences of a shy young apprentice when he starts work as a platform guard in a quiet country railway station in wartime Czechoslovakia. Gently amusing for the most part; ultimately disturbing in its abrupt change of mood and tragic finale. The first film of noted director Jiří Menzel (see also *Capricious Summer*).

Barrandov Film Studio, for Československý Film, directed by Jiří Menzel. Screenplay by Jiří Menzel and Bohumil Hrabal, based on the novel by Hrabal. Photographed by Jaromír Šofr. Music by Jiří Šust. 89 minutes.

Starring Václav Neckář, Jitka Bendová, Vladimír Valenta, Libuše Havelková, Josef Somr, Alois Vachek.

Note: Closely Observed Trains was first released in Czechoslovakia in 1966.

CONFESSIONS OF A NAZI SPY (USA)

Awards (1)
Best English Language Film — National Board of Review, 1939

Anti-Nazi propaganda with Edward G. Robinson, who began the thirties in the gutter as *Little Caesar*, ending the decade in more sympathetic fashion as an FBI agent who smashes a Nazi spy ring operating in the United States. Based on the revelations of an ex-G-man and on spy trials held in the U.S. just before the war, the film remains one of the surprise best film winners of all time. The National Board of Review placed it first ahead of such heavyweight contenders as *Wuthering Heights, Stagecoach, Ninotchka, Young Mr. Lincoln, Goodbye Mr. Chips* and *Mr. Smith Goes To Washington.*

A Warner Bros. Picture, directed by Anatole Litvak. Screenplay by Milton Krims and John Wexley, based on articles by Leon G. Turrou. Photographed by Sol Polito. 102 minutes.

Starring Edward G. Robinson, Francis Lederer, George Sanders, Paul Lukas, Henry O'Neill, Dorothy Tree, Lya Lys, Grace Stafford.

CONFESSIONS OF A POLICE INSPECTOR (Italy)

Awards (1)

Grand Prix	Moscow, 1971

The Italian Mafia under the celluloid microscope as honest cop Martin Balsam tries to bring a crooked building contractor and a syndicate gangster to justice. A rough, tough flashy thriller revealing how Mafia corruption extends from village level, through the police force to the highest seats of power. The film shared the 1971 Moscow Prize with *White Bird With A Black Mark* and *Live Today, Die Tomorrow.*

Euro International Films/Explorer Film '58. Directed by Damiano Damiani. Screenplay by Damiano Damiani and Salvatore Laurani. Story by Damiani and Fulvio Gicca Palli. Photographed in Technicolor (prints by DeLuxe) and Techniscope by Claudio Ragora. Music by Riz Ortolani. 105 minutes.

Starring Martin Balsam, Franco Nero, Marilù Tolo, Claudio Gora, Arturo Dominici, Michele Gammino, Luciano Lorcas.

THE CONVERSATION (USA)

Awards (2)

Golden Palm	Cannes, 1974
Best English Language Film	National Board of Review, 1974

Echoes of *Blow-Up* in a darkly ambiguous thriller about a professional bugging expert who becomes uneasy when he suspects that one of his tapes will lead to murder. A technical *tour-de-force* and a disturbing warning about how easily the devices of modern technology can erode the values of our society. Francis Ford Coppola's first win at Cannes (see also *Apocalypse Now*).

A Coppola Company/Paramount Production, written and directed by Francis Ford Coppola. Photographed in Technicolor by Bill Butler. Music by David Shire. 113 minutes.

Starring Gene Hackman, John Cazale, Allen Garfield, Frederic Forrest, Cindy Williams, Michael Higgins, Elizabeth MacRae, Teri Garr, Harrison Ford, Mark Wheeler, Robert Duvall.

LES COUSINS (France)

Awards (1)

Golden Bear	Berlin, 1959

The unhappy experiences of an innocent young provincial student

(Gérard Blain) when he is flung headlong into the sophisticated undergraduate world dominated by his arrogant cousin (Jean-Claude Brialy). Chabrol's first (and only) festival success, skilfully capturing the atmosphere of an amoral young Parisian society and revealing, for the first time, the director's flair for the flamboyant and gift for exploring complex character relationships.

A AJYM Production, written and directed by Claude Chabrol. Dialogue by Paul Gégauff. Photographed by Henri Decaë. Music by Paul Misraki. 103 minutes.

Starring Gérard Blain, Jean-Claude Brialy, Juliette Mayniel, Claude Cerval, Guy Decomble, Corrado Guarducci, Geneviève Cluny, Michèle Meritz, Stéphane Audran.

THE CRANES ARE FLYING (USSR)

Awards (1)

Golden Palm	Cannes, 1958

Moving drama about the life of a young Russian girl from the time of her tragic love affair with a young student to her days in Siberia nursing wounded Soviet soldiers. Set in World War II and to date the only Russian winner of the Golden Palm at Cannes. Tatiana Samoilova won international recognition for her performance in the leading role.

A Mosfilm Production, directed by Mikhail Kalatozov. Screenplay by V. Rosov. Photographed by S. Urusevsky. Music by M. Vainberg. 92 minutes.

Starring Tatiana Samoilova, Alexei Batalov, A. Shvorin, Vasily Merkuryev, S. Kharitonova, V. Zubkov.

CRIES AND WHISPERS (Sweden)

Awards (2)

Best Film	New York Critics, 1972
Best Foreign Language Film	National Board of Review, 1973

A young woman (Harriet Andersson), dying slowly from cancer, is haunted by memories of her past life as she is cared for by her devoted maid (Kari Sylwan) and married sisters (Ingrid Thulin, Liv Ullmann) in the house where she was born. A harrowing Bergman exercise in love, pain and spiritual anguish; set in turn-of-the-century Sweden and marked by the uncompromising close-ups of Oscar-winning cameraman Sven Nykvist.

A Cinematograph Production/in co-operation with Svenska Filminstitutet. Written and directed by Ingmar Bergman. Photographed in Eastman Color by Sven Nykvist. 91 minutes.

Starring Harriet Andersson, Kari Sylwan, Ingrid Thulin, Liv Ullmann, Erland Josephson, Henning Moritzen, Georg Årlin, Anders Ek, Inga Gill.

CUL-DE-SAC (Britain)

Awards (1)
Golden Bear Berlin, 1966

Ghoulish black comedy by Roman Polanski about a bisexual businessman and his bored young wife who find their edgy relationship thrown off balance when they are visited at their Northumbrian castle by a couple of on-the-run gangsters. A bizarre study in the absurd that somehow emerged with best picture honours at the 1966 Berlin Festival. Donald Pleasence and Françoise Dorleac are the husband and wife, Lionel Stander and Jack MacGowran the gangsters. The film was shot on location on Northumberland's Holy Island.

Compton-Tekli Film Productions. Directed by Roman Polanski. Original screenplay by Roman Polanski and Gerard Brach. Photographed by Gilbert Taylor. Music by Christopher Komeda. 107 minutes.

Starring Donald Pleasence, Françoise Dorleac, Lionel Stander, Jack MacGowran, Iain Quarrier, Geoffrey Sumner, Renee Houston, William Franklyn.

DARLING (Britain)

Awards (1)
Best Film New York Critics, 1965

Julie Christie as an arrogant young model who rises to actress and socialite via the beds of Dirk Bogarde, Laurence Harvey *et al* and finishes up just as empty headed and unhappy as when she began. Told in flashback via a woman's magazine exposé, the film hits out savagely at the smart life and moneyed classes and captures all the frustrations of a young girl caught up in the empty glamour of the jet set life of the sixties. Britain's *La Dolce Vita*!

A Vic Film/Appia Film Production, directed by John Schlesinger. Screenplay by Frederic Raphael. Story by Frederic Raphael, John Schlesinger and Joseph Janni. Photographed by Ken Higgins. Music by John Dankworth. 127 minutes.

Starring Julie Christie, Dirk Bogarde, Laurence Harvey, Roland Curram, Alex Scott, Basil Henson, Helen Lindsay, Peter Bayliss.

DAVID (West Germany)

Awards (1)
Golden Bear Berlin, 1979

Drama of a teenage Jewish boy who escapes to Israel with forged papers after being trapped with his sister in Nazi Germany. The last Berlin prize-winner of the seventies and somewhat overshadowed by the row at the festival over the out-of-competition screening of *The Deer Hunter*, a row which resulted in Russia and other Communist countries walking out of the event.

Vietinghof Filmproduktion/Pro-Ject Film Produktion/Filmverlag Der Autoren/ZDF/Dedra Pictures Production. Directed by Peter Lilienthal. Screenplay by Jurek Becker, Ulla Zieman and Peter Lilienthal, based on the book by Joel Konig. Photographed in Eastman Color by Al Ruban. Music by Wojiech Kilar. 125 minutes.

Starring Walter Taub, Irena Vrkljan, Eva Mattes, Mario Fischel, Dominique Horwitz.

DAY FOR NIGHT (France/Italy)

Awards (3)

Best Foreign Language Film	American Academy Award, 1973
Best Film	New York Critics, 1973
Best Film	British Academy Award, 1973

François Truffaut as a fictional French film director, beset with problems — temperamental stars, impossible shooting schedules, financial trouble — as he tries to bring in his latest film on time and below budget. Shot in the Victorine Studio in Nice and arguably the most affectionate account of the making of a film ever put on celluloid. 'Day For Night' is the technical term for simulating night by the use of filters in daylight filming.

Les Films du Carrosse/P.E.C.F. (Paris)/P.I.C. (Rome). Directed by François Truffaut. Screenplay by François Truffaut, Jean-Louis Richard and Suzanne Schiffman. Photographed in Eastman Color by Pierre-William Glenn. Music by Georges Delerue. 116 minutes.

Starring Jacqueline Bisset, Valentina Cortese, Jean-Pierre Aumont, Jean-Pierre Léaud, Dani, Alexandra Stewart, Jean Champion, François Truffaut.

DAYS OF HEAVEN (USA)

Awards (1)

Best English Language Film	National Board of Review, 1978

Love, jealousy and death among a group of migrant workers on a Texas prairie farm just prior to America's entry into the First World War. Poetic camerawork of wheatfields, rainstorms and locust plagues earned Nestor Almendros a deserved Academy Award for cinematography; Terrence Malick's static direction won him a more debatable prize at Cannes in 1979.

An O.P. Production for Paramount, written and directed by Terrence Malick, Photographed in Metrocolor by Nestor Almendros. Music by Ennio Morricone. 94 minutes.

Starring Richard Gere, Brooke Adams, Sam Shepard, Linda Manz, Robert Wilke, Jackie Shultis, Stuart Margolin, Tim Scott.

THE DEER HUNTER (USA)

Awards (2)

Best Film	American Academy Award, 1978
Best Film	New York Critics, 1978

The effects of the Vietnam War on three young Pennsylvanian steel-workers who are deeply scarred by their experiences at the hands of the Vietcong. The most harrowing of the Vietnam pictures of the late seventies; unusual in its all-pervading optimism and unquestioning pro-American attitudes. A controversial non-competitive entry at Berlin where the Eastern bloc walked out in protest against the torture scenes.

An EMI Picture, directed by Michael Cimino. Screenplay by Deric Washburn. Story by Michael Cimino, Deric Washburn, Louis Garfinkle and Quinn K. Redeker. Photographed in Technicolor and Panavision by Vilmos Zsigmond. Music by Stanley Myers; main title theme performed by John Williams. 182 minutes.

Starring Robert De Niro, John Cazale, John Savage, Christopher Walken, Meryl Streep, George Dzundza, Chuck Aspegren, Shirley Stoler, Rutanya Alda.

THE DEFIANT ONES (USA)

Awards (1)

Best Film — New York Critics, 1958

One of Hollywood's most optimistic films about the problems of racial prejudice with Tony Curtis and Sidney Poitier as two chain gang convicts, shackled together by four feet of chain, and fleeing for their lives from police and tracker dogs in the American South. Boldly scripted and voted best of the year by the New York Critics who placed it ahead of *Separate Tables* by ten votes to five. *Gigi* earned the year's Oscar; *The Old Man And The Sea* the award of the National Board of Review.

A United Artists Picture, directed by Stanley Kramer. Screenplay by Nathan E. Douglas and Harold Jacob Smith. Photographed by Sam Leavitt. Music by Ernest Gold. 97 minutes.

Starring Tony Curtis, Sidney Poitier, Theodore Bikel, Charles McGraw, Lon Chaney, Jr, Cara Williams.

LE DÉPART (Belgium)

Awards (1)

Golden Bear — Berlin, 1967

Restless comedy about a young hairdresser's assistant who lives for only two things in life — driving fast cars and achieving success on the racetrack. Set in Brussels just prior to a big car rally, the film gradually links the boy's car mania with a sexual frustration that only becomes apparent at the film's close. Directed by Polish filmmaker Jerzy Skolimowski and visually a *tour-de-force*; below the surface less humorous and more ironic than it first appears.

Elisabeth Films. Directed by Jerzy Skolimowski. Screenplay by Jerzy Skolimowski and Andrzej Kostenko. Photographed by Willy Kurant. Music by Krzysztof Komeda. 89 minutes.

Starring Jean-Pierre Léaud, Catherine Duport, Léon Dony, Paul Roland, Jacqueline Bir, John Dobrynine, Georges Aubrey, Maxane.

DERSU UZALA (USSR/Japan)

Awards (2)

Best Foreign Language Film	American Academy Award, 1975
Grand Prix	Moscow, 1975

Akira Kurosawa's epic co-production, set at the turn-of-the-century, and concentrating on a Russian scientist-explorer and an aged Siberian trapper who form a deep inseparable friendship while surveying the unexplored forests of Russia's Pacific seaboard. Shot by Kurosawa in 70mm with a rescue from a treacherous river as a standout sequence.

A Mosfilm (Moscow)/Toho (Tokyo) Production, directed by Akira Kurosawa. Screenplay by Akira Kurosawa and Yuri Nagibin, based on the novels of Vladimir Klavdievic Arsenyev. Photographed in colour and Scope by Asakadzu Nakai, Yuri Gantman and Fyodor Dobronravov. Music by Isaak Shvartz. 141 minutes.

Starring Maksim Munzuk, Yuri Solomin, M. Bichkov, V. Khrulev, V. Lastochkin, S. Marin, I. Sikhra, V. Sergiyavov, Y. Yakobsons, V. Khlestov, G. Polunik, V. Koldin, M. Tetov, S. Sinyavsky, V. Sverba and V. Ignatov.

DESTINY OF A MAN (USSR)

Awards (1)

Grand Prix	Moscow, 1959

The tragic tale of a Russian carpenter who survives the horrors of a German concentration camp only to find that his wife and daughter have been killed in an air raid and his son at the front. At times, a quite overwhelming film, expressing all the enthusiasm of the Soviet new wave of the late fifties and ending on an optimistic note as the carpenter adopts a homeless orphan boy and starts his life anew. Director Sergei Bondarchuk, who was later responsible for the epic *War And Peace*, plays the carpenter. The film was the first Grand Prix winner of the newly-formed Moscow Film Festival.

A Mosfilm Production, directed by Sergei Bondarchuk. Screenplay by Yuri Lukin and Fyodor Shakhmagonov, based on a story by Mikhail Sholokhov. Photographed by Vladimir Monakhov. Music by Veniamin Basner. 100 minutes.

Starring Sergei Bondarchuk, Pavlik Boriskin, Zoya Kirienko, Pavel Volkov, Yuri Averin, K. Alekseyev.

LES DIABOLIQUES (France)

Awards (1)

Best Foreign Language Film	New York Critics, 1955

The headmaster of a Paris boarding school is murdered by his wife (Véra Clouzot) and mistress (Simone Signoret) but keeps mysteriously reappearing at windows and in darkened rooms, driving his already ailing wife to a fatal breakdown. A dark piece of *grand guignol* that finishes with all the nerve ends showing and includes one scene — when the 'dead' husband rises fully clothed from a bath and pops out his eyeballs — that remains a classic moment in screen terror. The film (known also as *The Fiends*) shared the 1955 New York Critics Award with the somewhat more humane *Umberto D.*

A Filmsonor Production, directed by Henri-Georges Clouzot. Screenplay by Henri-Georges Clouzot, Jérôme Géronimi, René Masson and Frédéric Grendel, based on the novel *Celle qui n'etait plus* by Boileau & Narcejac. Photographed by Armand Thirard. Music by Georges Van Parys. 114 minutes.

Starring Simone Signoret, Véra Clouzot, Paul Meurisse, Charles Vanel, Pierre Larquey.

IL DIAVOLO (Italy)

Awards (1)

Golden Bear	Berlin, 1963

The sexual misadventures of a small-town Italian businessman (Alberto Sordi) who gets the chance to live out his fantasies when he is sent on a long trip to Sweden. Hardly the stuff of which award movies are made but some ingenious playing by Sordi and several amusing highlights — an encounter with a suspicious hotel receptionist, an attempted seduction with the aid of VAT 69 and an exhausting session at a sauna. Co-winner, along with *Bushido*, of the 1963 Berlin Festival.

Dino De Laurentiis Cinematografica. Directed by Gian Luigi Polidoro. Story and screenplay by Rodolfo Sonego. Photographed by Aldo Tonti. Music by Piero Piccioni. 103 minutes.

Starring Alberto Sordi, Bernhard Tarschys, Inger Sjöstrand, Ulfe Palme, Ulla Smidje, Gunoild Gustavson, Barbro Wastenson.

THE DISCREET CHARM OF THE BOURGEOISIE (France)

Awards (1)

Best Foreign Language Film	American Academy Award, 1972

Six aristocrats try vainly to get through a sumptuous meal but find themselves constantly distracted by the erotic and bizarre events going on around them. During their abortive attempts to sample the food, master-satirist Luis Buñuel gets to work on his favourite targets — politics, bourgeois values, religion and the church. Fernando Rey, Delphine Seyrig, and Stéphane Audran lead the frustrated eaters in a film described by Buñuel himself as 'six characters in search of a hot dinner.'

Greenwich Film Production. Directed by Luis Buñuel. Screenplay by Luis Buñuel and Jean-Claude Carrière. Photographed in Eastman Color by Edmond Richard. 105 minutes.

Starring Fernando Rey, Delphine Seyrig, Stéphane Audran, Bulle Ogier, Jean-Pierre Cassel, Paul Frankeur, Julien Bertheau.

DISTANT THUNDER (India)

Awards (1)

Golden Bear	Berlin, 1973

The man-made famine of 1943 — caused by the diversion of rice for the war effort — chronicled in a story of two Bengali villagers whose lives are gradually affected by hunger and despair and whose values are eroded by events hopelessly out of their control. Among the most politically conscious of all Satyajit Ray's films and the picture that earned the director a much deserved first prize at Berlin. The 'distant thunder' of the film's title refers to World War II; the famine it created was responsible for the death of five million people in Bengal.

Produced by Mrs. Sarbani Bhattacharya. Written and directed by Satyajit Ray, based on the novel by Bibhuti Bhusan Bannerji. Photographed in Eastman Color by Soumendu Roy. Music by Satyajit Ray. 101 minutes.

Starring Soumitra Chatterjee, Babita, Romesh Mukerji, Chitra Bannerji, Gobinda Chakravarty, Sandhya Roy, Noni Ganguly, Sheli Pal, Suchita Roy.

DR. STRANGELOVE; OR, HOW I LEARNED TO STOP WORRYING AND LOVE THE BOMB (Britain)

Awards (1)

Best Film, Any Source	British Academy Award, 1964

A cigar-chomping American airforce general (Sterling Hayden) goes beserk when he believes the Commies have 'polluted his precious bodily fluids' and sends his B-52s to H-Bomb Russia. The result? The triggering of the Soviet Doomsday Device and the end of life on earth for a hundred years. A nightmare satire by Stanley Kubrick, given its just reward by the British Film Academy but overlooked at Oscar time when Hollywood opted for the somewhat gentler mood of Lerner and Loewe's *My Fair Lady*. Three roles for Peter Sellers — the US President, an RAF officer and the mad German scientist of the title; just one for George C. Scott who steals the whole thing as a hawkish general.

A Hawk Films Production (released by Columbia), directed by Stanley Kubrick. Screenplay by Stanley Kubrick, Terry Southern and Peter George, based on the novel 'Red Alert' by Peter George. Photographed by Gilbert Taylor. Music by Laurie Johnson. 93 minutes.

Starring Peter Sellers, George C. Scott, Sterling Hayden, Keenan Wynn, Slim Pickens, Peter Bull, Tracy Reed, James Earl Jones.

LA DOLCE VITA (Italy/France)

Awards (2)

Golden Palm	Cannes, 1960
Best Foreign Language Film	New York Critics, 1961

Fellini's three hour exposure of the decadent aspects of Roman café society centering on a gutter journalist (Marcello Mastroianni) who searches for material for his scandal sheet whilst on an endless round of parties and orgies. Sensationalised religion, fake intellectualism, the emptiness of the sweet life and the useless values of the film world all come under the Fellini microscope. From an all-star cast Anouk Aimée emerges with honors as a millionaire's daughter who gets her kicks from sleeping in a whore's bed.

Riama Film/Pathé Cinema/Gray Films. Directed by Federico Fellini. Screenplay by Federico Fellini, Ennio Flaiano, Tullio Pinelli and Brunello Rondi, based on a story by Fellini, Flaiano and Pinelli. Photographed in Totalscope by Otello Martelli. Art Direction by Piero Gherardi. Music by Nino Rota. 180 minutes.

Starring Marcello Mastroianni, Anita Ekberg, Anouk Aimée, Yvonne Furneaux, Magali Noël, Alain Cuny, Nadia Gray, Lex Barker, Annibale Ninchi, Walter Santesso, Jacques Sernas.

EARLY WORKS (Yugoslavia)

Awards (1)

Golden Bear	Berlin, 1969

Political allegory about four young revolutionaries — one girl (named Yugoslavia) and three boys — who wander the countryside preaching socialism to an indifferent populace. Result? Rape, arrests and brutalisations by peasants and police alike, plus numerous quotations from Karl Marx and Friedrich Engels.

Avala Film/Neoplanta Film. Directed by Želimir Žilnik. Screenplay by Želimir Žilnik and Branko Vučićević. Photographed by Karpo Aćimović Godina. 87 minutes.

Starring Milja Vujanović. Bogdan Tirnanić, Čedomir Rodović, Marko Nikolić, Slobodan Aligrudić, Želimira Žujović.

8½ (Italy)

Awards (4)

Best Foreign Language Film	American Academy Award, 1963
Best Foreign Language Film	New York Critics, 1963
Best Foreign Language Film	National Board of Review, 1963
Grand Prix	Moscow, 1963

The memories, fantasies and desires of an artistically exhausted Italian film director as he rests his mind and body at a spa and searches for a story for his new film. A complex self-portrait by Fellini with Marcello Mastroianni as the desperate film-maker, Anouk Aimée as his wife and Sandra Milo as his mistress. The film was the eighth full-length feature made by Fellini, the ½ referring to the episodes he directed in *Boccaccio 70* and *Amore in Citta*. It remains the most honoured of all his pictures, being named best of the year in America after its success at Moscow in the summer of 1963. *Amarcord* is the only other Fellini film to win the three major American awards.

An Angelo Rizzoli Production, directed by Federico Fellini. Screenplay by Federico Fellini, Ennio Flaiano, Tullio Pinelli and Brunello Rondi, based on a story by Fellini and Flaiano. Photographed by Gianni Di Venanzo. Music by Nino Rota. 138 minutes.

Starring Marcello Mastroianni, Claudia Cardinale, Anouk Aimée, Sandra Milo, Rossella Falk, Barbara Steele, Guido Alberti, Madeleine Lebeau, Jean Rougeul.

THE ELEANOR ROOSEVELT STORY (USA)

Awards (1)
Best English Language Film — National Board of Review, 1965

The life of the wife and widow of President Franklin Delano Roosevelt, told through still photographs and newsreel footage and linked by a commentary written by Archibald MacLeish. The film was the sixth of seven documentaries to receive the best picture award of the National Board of Review. Other pictures to have achieved the honour: *The True Glory* (45), *The Titan* (50), *A Queen Is Crowned* (53), *The Silent World* (56), *World Without Sun* (64) and *The Sorrow And The Pity* (72).

A Sidney Glazier Production, directed by Richard Kaplan. Screenplay by Archibald MacLeish. Edited by Miriam Arsham. Music by Ezra Laderman. Narration spoken by Eric Severeid, Archibald MacLeish and Mrs. Francis Cole. 90 minutes.

Note: The Eleanor Roosevelt Story was also awarded an Oscar as the best feature documentary of 1965.

ELVIRA MADIGAN (Sweden)

Awards (1)
Best Foreign Language Film — National Board of Review, 1967

Lyrical rendering of a real-life tragic romance between a circus tightrope performer and a married army officer who escape for one summer of happiness before dying together in a double suicide. A Mozart piano concerto accompanies the lovers' enchantment; the summer landscapes of trees, lakes and green meadows resemble a painting by Renoir. Set in late 19th century Denmark.

Europa Film/Janco Films. Written and directed by Bo Widerberg. Photographed in Eastman Color by Jörgen Persson. 90 minutes.

Starring Pia Degermark, Thommy Berggren, Lennart Malmer, Nina Widerberg, Cleo Jensen.

L'ENFANT SAUVAGE (France)

Awards (1)
Best Foreign Language Film — National Board of Review, 1970

The story of a dedicated French doctor who attempts to educate a wild boy who has spent his childhood living like an animal in a forest. Set in late eighteenth century France and based on a true incident, the film ends with the partly civilised boy seeking his freedom but eventually returning to the doctor's house. In real life the boy lived until he was forty when he was able to perform simple, menial tasks. Director François Truffaut also appears as the doctor.

Les Films du Carrosse/Les Productions Artistes Associés. Directed by François Truffaut. Screenplay by François Truffaut and Jean Grualt, based on *Memoire et Rapport sur Victor de l'Aveyron* by Jean Itard.

Photographed by Nestor Almendros. Music: Concerto for Mandolin and Concerto for Flautino by Antonio Vivaldi. 84 minutes.

Starring Jean-Pierre Cargol, François Truffaut, Jean Dasté, Françoise Seigner, Paul Villé, Claude Miler, Annie Miler, Pierre Fabre.

THE ETERNAL MASK (Austria/Switzerland)

Awards (1)

Best Foreign Film	National Board of Review, 1937

Adaptation of Leo Lapaire's novel about a young doctor who experiments with a meningitis serum then suffers a nervous breakdown and develops schizophrenia following the death of one of his patients. A rarely-seen film, vividly recording the meanderings of a disordered mind through Expressionist sets and bizarre camerawork.

Progress Films, directed by Werner Hochbaum. Screenplay by Leo Lapaire, based on his novel. Photographed by Oscar Schnirch. Music by Anton Profes. 88 minutes.

Starring Peter Petersen, Mathias Wieman, Olga Chechova, Tom Kraa, Thekla Ahrens.

Note: The Eternal Mask was first released in Austria in 1935.

THE FALL OF BERLIN (USSR)

Awards (1)
Grand Prix — Karlovy Vary, 1950

Russian follow up to Petrov's epic *The Battle Of Stalingrad* telling of the last days of the war through the eyes of a young Russian steelworker turned soldier and his part in the final onslaught on the German capital in 1945. Marred by pro-Stalin propaganda, saved by the sheer power of its massive war sequences. Highlight: the spectacular flooding of Berlin's underground railway.

A Mosfilm Production, directed by Mikhail Chiaureli. Screenplay by Pyotr Pavlenko and Mikhail Chiaureli. Photographed in Agfacolor by Leonid Kosmatov. Music by Dmitri Shostakovich. 120 minutes.

Starring Mikhail Gelovani, Boris Andreyev, Oleg Froelich, Victor Stanitsin, V. Savelyov, M. Kovaleva.

FAMILY CHRONICLE (Italy)

Awards (1)
Golden Lion — Venice, 1962

Two brothers, one raised in luxury, the other in poverty, are drawn together when the younger man is stricken by a fatal disease and his older brother tries desperately to save him. Moving performances by Jacques Perrin and Marcello Mastroianni; shot in muted colours and fashioned after the best-selling novel by Vasco Pratolini. Co-winner at Venice (see *The Childhood Of Ivan*) in 1962.

A Titanus Production, directed by Valerio Zurlini. Screenplay by Valerio Zurlini and Mario Missiroli, based on the novel by Vasco Pratolini. Photographed in Technicolor by Giuseppe Rotunno. Music by Goffredo Petrassi. 115 minutes.

Starring Marcello Mastroianni, Jacques Perrin, Sylvie, Salvo Randone, Valeria Ciangottini, Serena Vergano.

FAR FROM THE MADDING CROWD (Britain)

Awards (1)

Best English Language Film	National Board of Review, 1967

Julie Christie as Thomas Hardy's tempestuous nineteenth century Dorset girl Bathsheba Everdene who inherits a farm from her uncle and enslaves three men — a young cavalry officer (Terence Stamp), a wealthy landowner (Peter Finch) and a devoted herdsman (Alan Bates) — before settling down to a troubled happiness. Richly photographed West Country locations and a performance of some stature by Peter Finch as a man infatuated to the point of madness. Along with Lean's *Great Expectations* one of the most satisfying adaptations of a British classic novel yet put on screen — a fact recognised only by the National Board of Review in 1967.

Vic Films-Appia Films-Joseph Janni Productions. Directed by John Schlesinger. Screenplay by Frederic Raphael. Photographed in Metrocolor and Panavision by Nicolas Roeg. Music by Richard Rodney Bennett. 169 minutes.

Starring Julie Christie, Terence Stamp, Peter Finch, Alan Bates, Fiona Walker, Prunella Ransome, Alison Leggatt, Paul Dawkins, Julian Somers, John Barrett, Freddie Jones.

FATHER (Hungary)

Awards (1)

Grand Prix	Moscow, 1967

Hungarian film about a small boy whose father, a dedicated doctor, dies at the end of the war but who lives on in the uncertain boy's imagination, assuming different personalities — a partisan hero, a politician, a great surgeon — as the boy grows into adulthood. Only during the bewildering political upheavals of the fifties, when he becomes acquainted with the authentic personality of his father does the youth face up to reality and at last reach maturity. A strikingly original film, concerned, like many pictures from Eastern Europe, with adolescence and the problems of youth. *Father* shared the Moscow First Prize with the Russian production, *The Journalist*.

Mafilm Studios. Directed by István Szabó. Screenplay by János Herskó. Photographed by Sándor Sára. Music by János Gonda. 95 minutes.

Starring András Bálint, Miklós Gábor, Klári Tolnay, Dániel Erdélyi, Kati Sólyom, Zsuzsa Ráthonyi,

LA FEMME DU BOULANGER (France)

Awards (2)

Best Foreign Language Film	New York Critics, 1940
Best Foreign Film	National Board of Review, 1940

The problems and confusion caused in a Provençal village when the attractive young wife of the local baker runs off with a shepherd, and the baker, in his sorrow, refuses to bake any more bread until she's found. A rustic, satirical conversation piece by Marcel Pagnol, memorably performed by Raimu as the deceived husband, and winner of two foreign picture awards in America in 1940.

Films Marcel Pagnol, written and directed by Marcel Pagnol, based on a story by Jean Giono. Photographed by G. Benoit, R. Ledru and N. Daries. Music by Vincent Scotto. 119 minutes.

Starring Raimu, Ginette Leclerc, Charles Moulin, Robert Vattier, Charpin, Robert Barsac.

Note: La Femme Du Boulanger (known also as *The Baker's Wife*) was first released in France in 1938.

THE FIFTH SEAL (Hungary)

Awards (1)
Grand Prix — Moscow, 1977

Fascist oppression recalled by Zoltán Fábri in a drama about the moral choice facing those living under the Arrow Cross (Hungarian Nazi rule) in Budapest in the winter of 1944-45. The people singled out are five friends who are suddenly arrested and interrogated. The commandant states that each will be allowed to go free if they will slap a dying Communist prisoner hanging in the cells. Four refuse and are killed. Only one agrees. In the final scenes he is revealed to be sheltering ten Jewish orphans in his house. *The Fifth Seal* shared the Moscow Grand Prix with *The Long Weekend* and *Mimino*.

A Budapest Studio Production, directed by Zoltán Fábri. Screenplay by Zoltán Fábri, based on the novel by Ferenc Santa. Photographed in Eastman Color by György Illés. Music by György Vukán. 116 minutes.

Starring Lajos Öze, Sándor Horváth, László Márkus, Ferenc Benecze, Istvan Degi, Zoltán Latinovits.

FIVE EASY PIECES (USA)

Awards (1)
Best Film — New York Critics, 1970

Jack Nicholson as a middle-class dropout who rejects a career as a musician and drifts from job to job on the oil-rigs and construction sites of Northwest America. Basically, another 'road' movie in the mould of *Easy Rider* but a perceptive study of contemporary American values and one of the most accomplished of the realistic new wave films of the early seventies. Preferred by the New York Critics to Schaffner's Oscar-winning military biography, *Patton*.

A B.B.S. Production (released by Columbia), directed by Bob Rafelson. Screenplay by Adrien Joyce, from a story by Rafelson and Joyce. Photographed in Technicolor by Laszlo Kovaks. 98 minutes.

Starring Jack Nicholson, Karen Black, Lois Smith, Susan Anspach, Billy 'Green' Bush, Fannie Flagg, Ralph Waite.

THE FRENCH CONNECTION (USA)

Awards (1)

Best Film	American Academy Award, 1971

Two New York detectives (Gene Hackman and Roy Scheider) smash a thirty-two million dollar dope ring smuggling vast quantities of heroin into the USA. Tough, exciting thriller that scored at Oscar-time when many expected *A Clockwork Orange* to take the top prize. Highlight: a chase sequence in which Hackman drives in reckless pursuit of a train ripping non-stop through stations on an elevated railway.

A Twentieth Century-Fox Picture, directed by William Friedkin. Screenplay by Ernest Tidyman, based on the book by Robin Moore. Photographed in De Luxe Color by Owen Roizman. Music by Don Ellis. Edited by Jerry Greenberg. 104 minutes.

Starring Gene Hackman, Fernando Rey, Roy Scheider, Tony LoBianco, Marcel Bozzuffi, Frédéric de Pasquale, Bill Hickman, Ann Rebbot.

FRIENDLY PERSUASION (USA)

Awards (1)

Golden Palm	Cannes, 1957

Leisurely tale of a Quaker family living in Southern Indiana during the Civil War and of their spiritual struggles to reconcile their non-violent beliefs when the fighting threatens the peace of their home. Gary Cooper and Dorothy McGuire star as the Quaker farmer and his preacher wife, Anthony Perkins (in his first major role) as the eldest son who fears he might be hiding behind his religion to save his skin. A distinguished Wyler work, given its due recognition at Cannes some six months after its American premiere in November, 1956.

An Allied Artists Picture, directed by William Wyler. Screenplay (uncredited) by Michael Wilson, based on the novel by Jessamyn West. Photographed in De Luxe Color by Ellsworth Fredericks. Music by Dimitri Tiomkin. 139 minutes.

Starring Gary Cooper, Dorothy McGuire, Marjorie Main, Anthony Perkins, Mary Carr, Richard Eyer, Robert Middleton.

FROM HERE TO ETERNITY (USA)

Awards (2)

Best Film	American Academy Award, 1953
Best Film	New York Critics, 1953

The book they couldn't film but did! A seamy story of the experiences of American soldiers serving in Hawaii just prior to Pearl Harbour. Much, much better than it sounds, thanks to Fred Zinnemann's tasteful handling and a well tailored script by Daniel Taradash. Montgomery Clift and Frank Sinatra star as two G.I. buddies, Donna Reed as a 'professional hostess' in a whorehouse and Burt Lancaster as a sergeant who gets it together with Deborah Kerr on a damp beach in a scene much parodied in subsequent movies.

A Columbia Picture, directed by Fred Zinnemann. Screenplay by Daniel Taradash, based on the novel by James Jones. Photographed by Burnett Guffey. Music by George Duning. 118 minutes.

Starring Burt Lancaster, Montgomery Clift, Frank Sinatra, Deborah Kerr, Donna Reed, Philip Ober, Mickey Shaughnessy, Harry Bellaver, Ernest Borgnine.

THE GARDEN OF THE FINZI-CONTINIS (Italy/West Germany)

Awards (2)

Golden Bear	Berlin, 1971
Best Foreign Language Film	American Academy Award, 1971

The film that marked a return to top form for Vittorio De Sica; a chronicle of the downfall of an aristocratic Jewish family living on a luxurious estate in Mussolini's Italy in 1938. The film's story is told through the experiences of the young people who visit the estate in the summer months prior to the family's arrest and deportation. De Sica's first festival win since *Miracle In Milan* in 1951.

Documento Film (Rome)/CCC Filmkunst (Berlin). Directed by Vittorio De Sica. Screenplay by Tullio Pinelli, Valerio Zurlini, Franco Brusati, Ugo Pirro, Vittorio Bonicelli and Alain Katz, based on the novel by Giorgio Bassani. Photographed in Eastman Color by Ennio Guarnieri. Music by Manuel De Sica. 95 minutes.

Starring Dominique Sanda, Lino Capolicchio, Helmut Berger, Romolo Valli, Fabio Testi, Camillo Cesarei, Inna Alexeief, Barbara Pilavin.

GATE OF HELL (Japan)

Awards (3)

Grand Prix	Cannes, 1954
Best Foreign Language Film	American Academy Award, 1954
Best Foreign Language Film	New York Critics, 1954

A young Japanese wife, admired by a passionate medieval warrior, chooses death rather than submit to his desires and bring shame to her husband. An exquisite piece of film-making; the second Japanese picture to win a premier award at a post-war festival (see also *Rashomon*) and the first to employ a Western colour process.

A Daiei Production, directed by Teinosuke Kinugasa. Screenplay by Teinosuke Kinugasa, based on the novel by Kan Kikuchi. Photographed in Eastman Color by Kohei Sugiyama. Music by Yasushi Akutagawa. 90 minutes.

Starring Kazuo Hasegawa, Machiko Kyo, Isao Yamagata, Yataro Kurokawa, Kotaro Bando.

IL GENERALE DELLA ROVERE (Italy/France)

Awards (1)

Golden Lion	Venice, 1959

Confidence trickster Vittorio De Sica becomes a tool of the Germans when he is forced to impersonate a dead Italian general but then undergoes a change of heart and elects to die by firing squad rather than inform on the partisans. Based on a true story of World War II and descending slowly from ironic comedy into tragedy, the film re-established Roberto Rossellini as a major figure in the Italian cinema. It shared the Golden Lion of Venice with Mario Monicelli's not dissimilar film of World War I, *The Great War*.

Zebra Film (Rome)/SNE Gaumont (Paris). Directed by Roberto Rossellini. Screenplay by Sergio Amidei, Diego Fabbri, Indro Montanelli and Roberto Rossellini, based on a story by Montanelli. Photographed by Carlo Carlini. Music by Renzo Rossellini. 130 minutes.

Starring Vittorio De Sica, Hannes Messemer, Sandra Milo, Giovanna Ralli, Anne Vernon, Vittorio Caprioli, Ivo Garrani.

GENTLEMAN'S AGREEMENT (USA)

Awards (2)

Best Film	American Academy Award, 1947
Best Film	New York Critics, 1947

Among the first of Hollywood's fashionable crop of post-war 'message' pictures, focussing on the problems of a magazine journalist (Gregory Peck) when he poses as a Jew to write a series of articles about anti-Semitism in the United States. Courageous for its time and the film that raised Elia Kazan to major director status. John Garfield's minor performance as a returning Jewish ex-servicemen still stands it in good stead.

A Twentieth Century-Fox Picture, directed by Elia Kazan. Screenplay by Moss Hart, based on the novel by Laura Hobson. Photographed by Arthur Miller. Music by Alfred Newman. 118 minutes.

Starring Gregory Peck, Dorothy McGuire, John Garfield, Celeste Holm, Anne Revere, June Havoc, Albert Dekker, Jane Wyatt, Dean Stockwell.

GERVAISE (France)

Awards (2)

Best Foreign Language Film	New York Critics, 1957
Best Film, Any Source	British Academy Award, 1956

Maria Schell as a crippled laundress fighting desperately against her slum environment but sinking deeper and deeper into the drunken squalor of nineteenth century Paris. A grim study in human degradation, adapted from Emile Zola's novel *L'Assommoir* and named best picture of 1956 by the British Film Academy. By-passed the same year at the Venice festival where no first prize was presented. Director Réne Clément's only period film.

Agnès Delahaie Productions/Silver Films. Directed by Réne Clément. Screenplay by Jean Aurenche and Pierre Bost, based on the novel *L'Assommoir* by Emile Zola. Photographed by Robert Juillard. Music by Georges Auric. 114 minutes.

Starring Maria Schell, François Périer, Suzy Delair, Mathilde Casadessus, Armand Mestral, Jacques Harden.

Note: Gervaise was released in America a year after its European premiere at Venice.

GET OUT YOUR HANDKERCHIEFS (France/Belgium)

Awards (1)

Best Foreign Language Film	American Academy Award, 1978

Enigmatic French comedy about the experiences of a bored young wife, first with a potential lover (thoughtfully provided by her husband), then with a thirteen-year-old innocent who finally does the trick. A satirical comedy of situation; not unlike some of the lighter works of Luis Buñuel in its perverse and ironic attitudes.

Les Films Ariane/CAPAC Production, written and directed by Bertrand Blier. Photographed in Eastman Color by Jean Peuzer. Music by Georges Delerue. 108 minutes.

Starring Gerard Depardieu, Patrick Dewaere, Carole Laure, Riton, Michel Serrault, Eleonore Hirt, Sylvie Joly, Jean Rougerie.

GIGI (USA)

Awards (1)

Best Film	American Academy Award, 1958

Innocent young teenager Leslie Caron, schooled for the role of courtesan by her debauched aunt and grandmother, enslaves the bored society rake she has worshipped since childhood. A slight tale of turn-of-the-century Paris, enlivened by a tender Lerner and Loewe score and turned into a film of grace and elegance by veteran director Vincente Minnelli. Highspot: the gentle Maurice Chevalier-Hermione Gingold duet, 'I Remember It Well.' Honoured only by the American Oscar Academy as best picture of the year.

A Metro-Goldwyn-Mayer Picture, directed by Vincente Minnelli. Screenplay and lyrics by Alan Jay Lerner. Photographed in Metrocolor and CinemaScope by Joseph Ruttenberg. Costumes and Production Design by Cecil Beaton. Music by Frederick Loewe. Musical Direction by Andre Previn. 116 minutes.

Starring Leslie Caron, Maurice Chevalier, Louis Jourdan, Hermione Gingold, Eva Gabor, Jacques Bergerac, Isabel Jeans, John Abbott.

THE GIVEN WORD (Brazil)

Awards (1)
Golden Palm Cannes, 1962

A deeply religious farmer vows to carry a wooden cross into a church if the life of his ailing donkey is saved, but finds that his thirty-mile pilgrimage leads to riots, scandal and his own death as a martyr. The film was a Brazilian 'sleeper' of the early sixties and took the Cannes prize from such fancied contenders as Antonioni's *The Eclipse* and Bresson's *The Trial Of Joan Of Arc*. It was also nominated for an American Academy Award.

Oswaldo Massaini Productions. Written and directed by Anselmo Duarte, based on the play by Alfredo Dias Gomes. Photographed by Chick Fowle. Music by Gabriel Migliori. 98 minutes.

Starring Leonardo Vilar, Gloria Menezes, Dionísio Azevedo, Norma Bengell, Geraldo d'el Rey, Roberto Ferreira.

THE GO-BETWEEN (Britain)

Awards (1)
Golden Palm Cannes, 1971

A young boy unwittingly becomes the carrier of love notes between the daughter (Julie Christie) of an aristocratic family and the lower class worker (Alan Bates) who runs the neighbouring farm. A screen version of L. P. Hartley's novel, set during a languid Edwardian summer and probing into the moral corruption of an upper class society fraying at the edges and destined for oblivion. Joseph Losey's only festival success although he came close to the Cannes first prize with *Accident* in 1967.

MGM-EMI/World Film Services. Directed by Joseph Losey. Screenplay by Harold Pinter, based on the novel by L. P. Hartley. Photographed in Technicolor by Gerry Fisher. Art Direction by Carmen Dillon. Music by Richard Rodney Bennett. 116 minutes.

Starring Julie Christie, Alan Bates, Dominic Guard, Margaret Leighton, Michael Redgrave, Michael Gough, Edward Fox, Richard Gibson.

THE GODFATHER (USA)

Awards (1)
Best Film American Academy Award, 1972

A hundred and seventy-five-minute saga following the violent career of the New York Corleone family who rule supreme over other Mafia outfits, first under ageing chief Marlon Brando then under heir apparent Al Pacino. The action sequences are ferocious, the performances compelling and the bloodletting uncomfortably real. Yet only at Oscar time did the film come out ahead. Robert Duvall survives as the Corleone family lawyer; son James Caan exits in a hail of bullets at a toll gate.

An Alfran Production, distributed by Paramount. Directed by Francis Ford Coppola. Screenplay by Mario Puzo and Francis Ford Coppola, based on the novel by Puzo. Photographed in Technicolor by Gordon Willis. Music by Nino Rota. 175 minutes.

Starring Marlon Brando, Al Pacino, James Caan, Richard Castellano, Robert Duvall, Sterling Hayden, John Marley, Richard Conte, Diane Keaton, Al Lettieri, Abe Vigoda, Talia Shire, Gianni Russo, John Cazale.

THE GODFATHER PART II (USA)

Awards (1)

Best Film	American Academy Award, 1974

More of the same as Coppola traces not only Pacino's continuing rise to power (and journey into ultimate desolation) but also, in flashback, the story of his father's arrival in New York as an immigrant child and his gradual involvement in crime. Even more assured than Part One and deserving of that misused label 'masterpiece.' Robert De Niro appears as the Brando character in his younger days and Robert Duvall again survives the two hundred minutes; John Cazale, Lee Strasberg and Michael V. Gazzo are among those who fail to stay the course.

A Paramount/Coppola Company Picture. Directed by Francis Ford Coppola. Screenplay by Francis Ford Coppola and Mario Puzo, based on the novel *The Godfather* by Puzo. Photographed in Technicolor by Gordon Willis. Music by Nino Rota. Additional music and music direction by Carmine Coppola. 200 minutes.

Starring Al Pacino, Robert Duvall, Diane Keaton, Robert De Niro, John Cazale, Talia Shire, Lee Strasberg, Michael V. Gazzo.

GOING MY WAY (USA)

Awards (2)

Best Film	American Academy Award, 1944
Best Film	New York Critics, 1944

Bing Crosby, in holy orders for the first time, sorts out the problems of the poor community of St. Dominics by turning the local street gang into a sweet sounding choir. Just about perfect entertainment for wartime audiences who paid out well over six million dollars for the privilege of hearing Bing sing 'Swinging On A Star' and watching Barry Fitzgerald steal the picture with his portrait of an irascible old priest.

A Paramount Picture, directed by Leo McCarey. Screenplay by Frank Butler and Frank Cavett, based on an original story by Leo McCarey. Photographed by Lionel Lindon. Songs by James Van Heusen and Johnny Burke. 130 minutes.

Starring Bing Crosby, Barry Fitzgerald, Rise Stevens, James Brown, Jean Heather, Frank McHugh, Gene Lockhart.

GONE WITH THE WIND (USA)

Awards (1)
Best Film American Academy Award, 1939

Three and three quarter hours of passion, drama and spectacle as Southern belle Scarlett O'Hara wins then loses blockade runner Rhett Butler during the stormy days of the American Civil War. On one level, a stylish historical romance; on another a bitter illustration of the effects of war, both on the soldiers in battle and the civilian community caught in the crossfire. Most celebrated sequence: the long pull back shot which starts with a close-up of Scarlett and ends by revealing hundreds of dying soldiers at the railroad station at Atlanta.

A Selznick International/Metro-Goldwyn-Mayer Picture, directed by Victor Fleming. Screenplay by Sidney Howard, based on the novel by Margaret Mitchell. Photographed in Technicolor by Ernest Haller and Ray Rennahan. Music by Max Steiner. 219 minutes.

Starring Vivien Leigh, Clark Gable, Leslie Howard, Olivia de Havilland, Hattie McDaniel, Thomas Mitchell, Ona Munson, Victor Jory, Jane Darwell, Evelyn Keyes, Ann Rutherford.

THE GRADUATE (USA)

Awards (1)
Best Film British Academy Award, 1968

College graduate Dustin Hoffman, unable to communicate with his smug suburban parents, finds unexpected compensations when he is initiated into the pleasures of sex by the neurotic wife (Anne Bancroft) of one of his father's business associates. Hoffman, plus the 'generation gap theme', plus some trendy satire, equalled success at the box-office but not at the Oscar ceremonies when *In The Heat Of The Night* was preferred. Only in Britain was the film voted best of the year.

A Mike Nichols-Lawrence Turman Production, presented by Joseph E. Levine. Directed by Mike Nichols. Screenplay by Calder Willingham and Buck Henry, based on the novel by Charles Webb. Photographed in Technicolor and Panavision by Robert Surtees. Music by Paul Simon. Songs sung by Simon and Garfunkel. 105 minutes.

Starring Anne Bancroft, Dustin Hoffman, Katharine Ross, William Daniels, Murray Hamilton, Elizabeth Wilson, Brian Avery, Norman Fell, Buck Henry.

Note: The Graduate was first released in the USA in December, 1967.

GRAND HOTEL (USA)

Awards (1)
Best Film American Academy Award, 1931/32

Tragedy, greed, frustration, death and despair behind the plush doors of an expensive Berlin hotel in the early thirties. Stenographer Joan Crawford is on the make from the first reel; Lionel Barrymore's heart gives out in style; and Garbo says the immortal words, 'I want to be alone.' Also on hand: John Barrymore, Wallace Beery, Lewis Stone and Jean Hersholt. MGM's second best picture Oscar winner.

A Metro-Goldwyn-Mayer Picture, directed by Edmund Goulding. Adapted by Hans Kraly from the novel by Vicki Baum. Photographed by William Daniels. Art Direction by Cedric Gibbons. Costumes by Adrian. 112 minutes.

Starring Greta Garbo, John Barrymore, Joan Crawford, Wallace Beery, Lionel Barrymore, Lewis Stone, Jean Hersholt, Frank Conroy.

LA GRANDE ILLUSION (France)

Awards (2)

Best Foreign Language Film	New York Critics, 1938
Best Foreign Film	National Board of Review, 1938

Among the most profound of all anti- war films, set in a prison camp for French officers during World War I and focussing on the relationship between two men — the maimed Prussian camp commandant (Erich von Stroheim) and a French officer (Pierre Fresnay) — both of whom have seen their aristocratic way of life destroyed by the conflict. Passed over at Venice (see page 215) and banned by the Nazis because of its strong pacifist content, the film was based on Renoir's experiences as a prisoner-of-war in 1917. It was the first foreign language picture to earn a best picture nomination in Hollywood.

R.A.C. Production. Directed by Jean Renoir. Screenplay and dialogue by Charles Spaak and Jean Renoir. Photographed by Christian Matras. Art Direction by Eugène Lourié. Music by Joseph Kosma. 117 minutes.

Starring Jean Gabin, Pierre Fresnay, Erich von Stroheim, Dalio, Carette, Gaston Modot, Jean Dasté.

Note: La Grande Illusion was first shown in Paris in June, 1937.

THE GRAPES OF WRATH (USA)

Awards (2)

Best Film	New York Critics, 1940
Best American Film	National Board of Review, 1940

John Steinbeck's Depression story of the impoverished Joad family who are forced off their land in the Oklahoma Dust Bowl and head west in an old Ford to California where they begin a new life as fruit pickers. One of the very few occasions that a major novel has appeared equally as effective on screen as on the printed page and among the genuinely great films of American cinema. The New York Critics and National Board of Review named it best of the year; Oscars were awarded to director John Ford and supporting actress Jane Darwell.

A Twentieth Century-Fox Picture, directed by John Ford. Screenplay by Nunnally Johnson, based on the novel by John Steinbeck. Photographed by Gregg Toland. Music by Alfred Newman. 127 minutes.

Starring Henry Fonda, Jane Darwell, John Carradine, Charley Grapewin, Dorris Bowden, Russell Simpson, O. Z. Whitehead, John Qualen.

THE GREATEST SHOW ON EARTH (USA)

Awards (1)
Best Film — American Academy Award, 1952

DeMille hokum under the big top with circus manager Charlton Heston, trapeze artists Cornel Wilde and Betty Hutton, and mysterious clown James Stewart all experiencing love, hate and jealousy as they tour with the Ringling Brothers and Barnum and Bailey Circus. A cut above the usual DeMille production in its documentary-like observations of life behind the glamour of the sawdust ring and belonging very definitely in the category: 'They don't, in fact *can't* make 'em like that anymore!'

A Paramount Picture, directed by Cecil B. DeMille. Screenplay by Barre Lyndon and Theodore St. John, from a story by Frederic M. Frank and Frank Cavett. Photographed in Technicolor by George Barnes. Music by Victor Young. 153 minutes.

Starring Betty Hutton, Cornel Wilde, Charlton Heston, Dorothy Lamour, Gloria Grahame, James Stewart, Lyle Bettger, Henry Wilcoxon.

THE GREAT WAR (France/Italy)

Awards (1)
Golden Lion — Venice, 1959

The experiences of two reluctant Italian soldiers who use their wits to keep away from the front line during World War I but are eventually seized by the Austrians and choose an honourable death rather than betray their comrades. The anti-war sentiments eventually come through after much boisterous comedy from Vittorio Gassman and Alberto Sordi as the two garrulous soldiers. Along with *Il Generale Della Rovere*, the winner at Venice in 1959 but considered unworthy of the award by many of the festival critics.

Dino De Laurentiis Cinematografica/Gray Films. Directed by Mario Monicelli. Screenplay by Age and Scarpelli, Luciano Vincenzoni and Mario Monicelli. Story by Luciano Vincenzoni. Photographed in CinemaScope by Giuseppe Rotunno and Roberto Gerardi. Music by Nino Rota. 140 minutes.

Starring Vittorio Gassman, Alberto Sordi, Silvana Mangano, Folco Lulli, Bernard Blier, Romolo Valli, Vittorio Sanipoli, Nicola Arigliano.

THE GREAT ZIEGFELD

Awards (1)
Best Film American Academy Award, 1936

MGM's three-hour tribute to Florenz Ziegfeld with William Powell as the Broadway showman who became world famous for his lavish Follies Revues of the twenties. Co-starring with Mr. Powell: Luise Rainer as first wife, Anna Held, Myrna Loy as second wife Billie Burke, and hundreds of singing extras who revolve on a massive wedding cake to the tune of 'A Pretty Girl Is Like A Melody.' Capra's Depression comedy *Mr. Deeds Goes To Town* was preferred by the New York Critics and the National Board of Review.

A Metro-Goldwyn-Mayer Picture, directed by Robert Z. Leonard. Story and screenplay by William Anthony McGuire. Photographed by Oliver T. Marsh. 184 minutes.

Starring William Powell, Myrna Loy, Luise Rainer, Frank Morgan, Fanny Brice, Ray Bolger, Virginia Bruce, Nat Pendleton, Reginald Owen.

LA GUERRE EST FINIE (France/Sweden)

Awards (1)
Best Foreign Language Film New York Critics, 1967

Political melodrama by Alain Resnais about an ageing Spanish revolutionary (Yves Montand) who, after resisting the Franco regime for twenty-five years during his exile in Paris, suddenly finds himself being forced to re-examine his political ideals. Mistress Ingrid Thulin is on hand to relieve the Resnais intensity. The film was entered at Cannes in 1966 but withdrawn because of the possibility that its theme might offend the Spanish contingent.

Sofracima (Paris)/Europa Film (Stockholm). Directed by Alain Resnais. Screenplay by Jorge Semprun. Photographed by Sacha Vierny. Music by Giovanni Fusco. 121 minutes.

Starring Yves Montand, Ingrid Thulin, Geneviève Bujold, Jean Dasté, Jorge Semprun, Dominique Rozan, Jean-François Rèmi, Marie Mergey.

Note: La Guerre Est Finie (also known as *The War Is Over*) first opened in Paris in May, 1966.

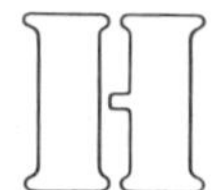

HAMLET (Britain)

Awards (3)

Best Film	American Academy Award, 1948
Best Film, Any Source	British Academy Award, 1948
International Grand Prix	Venice, 1948

Laurence Olivier as Shakespeare's doomed Danish prince who avenges his father's death amid the bleak interiors of Elsinore Castle. Less effective than it once appeared but invaluable as a record of a great actor at the height of his creative powers. The film was the first British production to win a prize at a post-war European festival and also the first British movie to receive a best picture Hollywood Oscar.

A Two Cities Film, directed by Laurence Olivier. Text adviser: Alan Dent. Photographed by Desmond Dickinson. Art Direction by Roger Furse and Carmen Dillon. Music by William Walton. 155 minutes.

Starring Laurence Olivier, Eileen Herlie, Basil Sydney, Norman Wooland, Felix Aylmer, Terence Morgan, Jean Simmons, Peter Cushing, Stanley Holloway, John Laurie, Anthony Quayle.

HANDS OVER THE CITY (Italy)

Awards (1)

Golden Lion	Venice, 1963

Rod Steiger in devastating form as a building tycoon who exploits a piece of land he has acquired cheaply and – despite a scandal and exposure of his methods by the Communists – is able to further his career by a swift change of political allegiances. Set in contemporary Naples and based on factual events, the film created a furore when first shown in Italy but deservedly won first prize at Venice even though the festival boasted three other potential winners – Alain Resnais' *Muriel*, Malle's *Le Feu Follet* and Britain's *Tom Jones*.

A Galatea (Lionello Santi) Production, directed by Francesco Rosi. Screenplay by Francesco Rosi, Raffaele La Capria, Enzo Provenzale and Enzo Forcella. Photographed by Gianni Di Venanzo. Music by Piero Piccioni. 105 minutes.

Starring Rod Steiger, Guido Alberti, Carlo Fermariello, Salvo Randone, Dany Paris, Angelo D'Alessandro.

HARVEST (France)

Awards (1)
Best Foreign Language Film New York Critics, 1939

Warm-hearted Marcel Pagnol fable about the rebirth of a deserted Provencal village, told through the love story of a poacher (Gabriel Gabrio) and an itinerant girl (Orane Demazis) who establish a new home in the village, sow the corn and set the land on a new road to life. Fernandel co-stars as a travelling knife-grinder. The New York Critics described the picture as 'an enduring work of art' and voted it best foreign film of 1939.

A Marcel Pagnol Production, written and directed by Pagnol. Based on the novel by Jean Giono. Photographed by Willy Sactorowitch. Music by Arthur Honegger. 122 minutes.

Starring Gabriel Gabrio, Orane Demazis, E. Delmont, Fernandel, Marguerite Moreno.

Note: Harvest (also known as *Regain*) was first released in France in 1937.

HEARTLAND (USA)

Awards (1)
Golden Bear Berlin, 1980

Anti-romantic look at the American West, set in a snowbound Wyoming in 1910 and centering on the hardships of a small family — a farmer, his wife and her ten-year-old son — as they battle against the rigours of a harsh winter. Something of a rarity in international competition, an American independent production (financed by the National Endowment for the Humanities) that shared the first prize at Berlin with the more ambitious West German production *Palermo Or Wolfsburg*. Total budget — just 600,000 dollars.

A Wilderness Womens Productions — Filmhaus Picture, directed by Richard Pearce. Screenplay by Beth Ferris based on the books and papers of Elinore Randall Stewart. Photographed in colour by Fred Murphy. Music by Charles Gross. 95 minutes.

Starring Conchata Ferrell, Rip Torn, Barry Primus, Lilia Skala, Megan Folsom.

HENRY V (Britain)

Awards (1)
Best Film National Board of Review, 1946

Laurence Olivier's version of Shakespeare's play about the coming of age of the young King Hal and his triumphs in battle against the French. Olivier features as Henry, Robert Newton as Ancient Pistol and Leslie Banks as the Chorus. The stirring Agincourt sequences were filmed in County Wicklow; the idea of framing the film by a typical performance at the Globe Theatre in Elizabethan times was suggested by Anthony Asquith.

A Two Cities Production, directed by Laurence Olivier. Text adviser: Alan Dent. Photographed in Technicolor by Robert Krasker. Art Direction by Paul Sheriff. Costumes by Roger Furse. Music by William Walton. 137 minutes.

Starring Laurence Olivier, Robert Newton, Leslie Banks, Rene Asherson, Esmond Knight, Leo Genn, Felix Aylmer, Ralph Truman.

Note: Henry V first opened in London late in 1944; it was one of nine international prize-winners at the Venice festival of 1946.

HIGH NOON (USA)

Awards (1)

Best Film	New York Critics, 1952

Classic western with lone marshal Gary Cooper searching desperately for help as he prepares to face a vengeful outlaw leader and his gang at noon. Seventy-five minutes of nail biting tension plus ten of blazing gunfire add up to a score of Gary Cooper three, Grace Kelly one, outlaws nil. The New York Critics went to six ballots before naming the film best of 1952 — by ten votes to five over *The African Queen*. DeMille's Oscar winner *The Greatest Show On Earth* and *The Quiet Man* were among the other films in contention.

A United Artists Picture, directed by Fred Zinnemann. Screenplay by Carl Foreman. Photographed by Floyd Crosby. Music by Dimitri Tiomkin. 85 minutes.

Starring Gary Cooper, Thomas Mitchell, Lloyd Bridges, Katy Jurado, Grace Kelly, Otto Kruger, Lon Chaney, Jr., Henry Morgan.

THE HIRELING (Britain)

Awards (1)

Golden Palm	Cannes, 1973

Sarah Miles as an upper-class woman suffering from deep mental depression following the death of her husband, and Robert Shaw as her chauffeur who helps her recover in the mistaken belief that she is attracted to him. A pessimistic little visit to L. P. Hartley country — Somerset in the years after World War I — that shared the first prize with *Scarecrow* at Cannes in 1973. Another Hartley novel, *The Go-Between*, formed the basis of the 1971 Cannes winner by Joseph Losey.

World Film Services/A Champion Production, released by Columbia and directed by Alan Bridges. Screenplay by Wolf Mankowitz, based on the novel by L. P. Hartley. Photographed in colour by Michael Reed. Music by Marc Wilkinson. 108 minutes.

Starring Robert Shaw, Sarah Miles, Peter Egan, Elizabeth Sellars, Caroline Mortimer, Patricia Lawrence, Petra Markham, Ian Hogg.

HIROSHIMA MON AMOUR (France/Japan)

Awards (1)
Best Foreign Language Film New York Critics, 1960

A French actress and a Japanese architect meet in modern day Hiroshima and remember back to the dropping of the atomic bomb and the girl's tragic affair with a young German soldier during the French occupation. Love, death, time and memory are all explored by Alain Resnais in a complex film that is either a celluloid landmark or pretentious hokum. The New York Critics leaned towards the former view by voting it best of 1960 ahead of *The Virgin Spring, Ballad Of A Soldier* and *The World Of Apu*; the Oscar Academy tended to the latter by ignoring it altogether in its list of foreign picture nominations.

Argos Films/Como Films/Daiei Motion Pictures/Pathé Overseas. Directed by Alain Resnais. Screenplay by Marguerite Duras. Photographed by Sacha Vierny and Michio Takahashi. Music by Giovanni Fusco and Georges Delerue. 91 minutes.

Starring Emmanuelle Riva, Eiji Okada, Bernard Fresson, Stella Dassas, Pierre Barbaud.

Note: Hiroshima Mon Amour was shown out of competition at Cannes in 1959.

HOBSON'S CHOICE (Britain)

Awards (1)
Golden Bear Berlin, 1954

Britain's only major prize-winner at Berlin in the festival's formative years; a version of Harold Brighouse's Lancashire comedy about the daughter of a tyrannical bootmaker who defies her father by marrying his humble boothand and turning him into a successful businessman. Rich in period flavour (Salford in the 1890s) and extravagantly played by Charles Laughton who is here given his head by director David Lean, notably in his drunken chase of the moon's reflection through a series of street puddles!

A London Films Production, directed by David Lean. Screenplay by David Lean, Norman Spencer and Wynyard Browne, based on the play by Harold Brighouse. Photographed by Jack Hildyard. Music by Malcolm Arnold. 107 minutes.

Starring Charles Laughton, John Mills, Brenda de Banzie, Daphne Anderson, Prunella Scales, Richard Wattis, Derek Blomfield, Helen Haye, Joseph Tomelty.

HOW GREEN WAS MY VALLEY (USA)

Awards (1)
Best Film American Academy Award, 1941

Richard Llewellyn's personal elegy to his youth in a Welsh mining town, centering on the everyday life and slow decline of the Morgan family living in a small coal-mining valley at the end of the last century. A poignant, sentimental film, made by John Ford at the height of his powers and Hollywood's answer to the New York Critics and National Board of Review that, in its opinion, *Citizen Kane* was *not* the best movie of 1941.

A Twentieth Century-Fox Picture, directed by John Ford. Screenplay by Philip Dunne, based on the novel by Richard Llewellyn. Photographed by Arthur Miller. Art Direction by Richard Day and Nathan Juran. Music by Alfred Newman. 118 minutes.

Starring Walter Pidgeon, Maureen O'Hara, Donald Crisp, Anna Lee, Roddy McDowall, John Loder, Sara Allgood, Barry Fitzgerald.

THE HUSTLER (USA)

Awards (1)

Best Film, Any Source — British Academy Award, 1961

Young pool shark Paul Newman learns about life the hard way as he shoots his way to the top and tries to wrest the championship from reigning pool king Minnesota Fats (Jackie Gleason). Robert Rossen's penultimate film and arguably the most accomplished movie yet made about American sport. A loser at Oscar time (to *West Side Story*), a winner in Britain where it shared top prize with the Russian *Ballad Of A Soldier*.

A Twentieth Century-Fox Picture, directed by Robert Rossen. Screenplay by Sidney Carroll and Robert Rossen, based on the novel by Walter S. Tevis. Photographed in CinemaScope by Eugen Shuftan. Music by Kenyon Hopkins. 133 minutes.

Starring Paul Newman, Jackie Gleason, Piper Laurie, George C. Scott, Myron McCormick, Murray Hamilton, Michael Constantine.

I

I AM A FUGITIVE FROM A CHAIN GANG (USA)

Awards (1)
Best American Film — National Board of Review, 1932

Paul Muni as an out-of-work ex-soldier, condemned first to hard labour on a Georgia chain gang for a robbery he did not commit, then, after his escape, to a fugitive life of petty crime. An early Hollywood 'social protest' film and the first to be named best of the year by the National Board of Review. The last scene in which Muni, when asked how he survives, whispers 'I steal' and retreats into the darkness, is justifiably one of the most famous closing scenes in movies.

A Warner Bros. Picture, directed by Mervyn LeRoy. Screenplay by Howard J. Green and Brown Holmes, based on the novel *I Am A Fugitive From A Georgia Chain Gang* by Robert E. Burns. Photographed by Sol Polito. 93 minutes.

Starring Paul Muni, Glenda Farrell, Preston Foster, Helen Vinson, David Landau, Sally Blane, Allen Jenkins, Edward Ellis, John Wray.

IF (Britain)

Awards (1)
Golden Palm — Cannes, 1969

Three public schoolboys rise up against the pressures of rigid discipline and lead an armed revolution against the masters and governors of their school. A piece of anti-establishment dynamite by Lindsay Anderson who uses the school as a microcosm of contemporary life and savagely attacks the outmoded rules of modern authoritarian society. The third British prize-winner at Cannes (see *The Third Man* and *The Knack* for earlier winners) and not dissimilar to Jean Vigo's pre-war *Zero de Conduite* in its surrealist attitudes.

A Memorial Enterprises Production (distributed by Paramount), directed by Lindsay Anderson. Screenplay by David Sherwin, based on the scenario *Crusaders* by Sherwin and John Howlett. Photographed in Eastman Color by Miroslav Ondricek. Music and music direction by Marc Wilkinson; *Sanctus* from the *Missa Luba* sung by Les Troubadours du Roi Baudoin. 111 minutes.

Starring Malcolm McDowell, David Wood, Richard Warwick, Robert Swann, Christine Noonan, Hugh Thomas, Rupert Webster, Peter Jeffrey, Anthony Nicholls, Arthur Lowe, Mona Washbourne.

THE INFORMER (USA)

Awards (2)

Best Film	New York Critics, 1935
Best American Film	National Board of Review, 1935

Liam O'Flaherty's tragedy of Dublin during the troubles with Victor McLaglen as a giant, slow-witted traitor who betrays a comrade to the police for the price of a boat ticket to America. Filmed by John Ford in under three weeks for just 200,000 dollars. The New York Critics and National Board of Review recognised the picture as best of the year; the Oscar Academy opted for *Mutiny On The Bounty*.

An RKO-Radio Picture, directed by John Ford. Screenplay by Dudley Nichols, based on the novel by Liam O'Flaherty. Photographed by Joseph H. August. Music by Max Steiner. 91 minutes.

Starring Victor McLaglen, Heather Angel, Preston Foster, Margot Grahame, Wallace Ford, Una O'Connor, J. M. Kerrigan, Joseph Sawyer.

IN THE HEAT OF THE NIGHT (USA)

Awards (2)

Best Film	American Academy Award, 1967
Best Film	New York Critics, 1967

Black homicide expert Sidney Poitier and slow-witted police chief Rod Steiger solve the murder of an industrialist in a small backwater town in Mississippi. A tense racial thriller that has stood the test of time better than most and preferred at the Oscar ceremonies to the more fancied *The Graduate* and *Bonnie And Clyde*. Despite its extensive publicity the latter movie failed to receive a best picture prize at any awards presentation or European festival.

A Mirisch/United Artists Picture, directed by Norman Jewison. Screenplay by Stirling Silliphant, based on the novel by John Ball. Photographed in De Luxe Color by Haskell Wexler. Music by Quincy Jones. 109 minutes.

Starring Rod Steiger, Sidney Poitier, Warren Oates, Quentin Dean, James Patterson, William Schallert, Lee Grant, Scott Wilson.

INVESTIGATION OF A CITIZEN ABOVE SUSPICION (Italy)

Awards (1)

Best Foreign Language Film	American Academy Award, 1970

Cleverly constructed film about a mentally unbalanced police chief who slashes the throat of his mistress then plants a series of clues that will lead his inferiors to discover his identity. A 1970 Oscar winner, strongly reminiscent at times of Dostoievsky's *Crime And Punishment* in its theme of a man believing that his moral superiority places him above the reaches of the law.

Vera Films. Directed by Elio Petri. Screenplay by Ugo Pirro and Elio Petri. Photographed in Technicolor by Luigi Kuveiller. Music by Ennio Morricone. 112 minutes.

Starring Gian Maria Volontè, Florinda Bolkan, Salvo Randone, Gianni Santuccio, Arturo Dominici, Orazio Orlando, Sergio Tramonti.

INVITATION TO THE DANCE (USA)

Awards (1)

Golden Bear	Berlin, 1956

Gene Kelly's long cherished dream project, an all-dancing film comprising three ballets of differing styles – 'Circus' with Kelly as an eighteenth century travelling clown, 'Ring Around The Rosy', a modern American ballet satirising *La Ronde*, and 'Sinbad The Sailor' in which Kelly romps his way through the pages of the Arabian Nights in the company of Hanna and Barbera cartoon characters. The film was the first to win a Jury Golden Bear at the Berlin Festival. In 1956 it shared the prize with *Vor Sonnenuntergang* which won the public vote.

A Metro-Goldwyn-Mayer Picture, written, directed and choreographed by Gene Kelly. Photographed in Technicolor by F. A. Young and Joseph Ruttenberg. Music by Jacques Ibert, Andre Previn and Rimsky-Korsakov. 93 minutes.

Starring Gene Kelly, Igor Youskevitch, Tommy Rall, Belita, Tamara Toumanova.

Note: Invitation To The Dance was filmed in Britain and the United States. Generally it ranks as a British film. At Berlin, however, it competed as an American entry.

IN WHICH WE SERVE (Britain)

Awards (2)

Best Film	New York Critics, 1942
Best English Language Film	National Board of Review, 1942

The story of a British destroyer and the men who served on her during the early days of World War II. The film is told in a series of flashbacks from the ship's sinking in the battle of Crete and concentrates on three survivors – captain Noel Coward, chief petty officer Bernard Miles and ordinary seaman John Mills – as they remember back to their domestic life and experiences on board ship. In 1942 it was either this film or *Mrs. Miniver* that were in line for the honours. *In Which We Serve* came out ahead, earning the awards of both the New York Critics and the National Board of Review. The Oscar went to *Mrs. Miniver*.

A Two Cities Film, directed by Noel Coward and David Lean. Screenplay by Noel Coward. Photographed by Ronald Neame. Music by Noel Coward. 115 minutes.

Starring Noel Coward, John Mills, Bernard Miles, Celia Johnson, Joyce Carey, Kay Walsh, Derek Elphinstone, Michael Wilding.

THE ISLAND (Japan)

Awards (1)

Grand Prix	Moscow, 1961

The daily struggles of a poor farming family living on a barren island off the coast of Japan — told without dialogue or commentary and with a poetic simplicity that marked such earlier films as Dovzhenko's *Earth* and Flaherty's *Man Of Aran*. The picture was made by just thirteen people (including director and cast) for a sixth of the cost of a normal Japanese feature film and shared the first prize with Russia's *Clear Skies* at the Moscow festival of 1961.

A Kindai Eiga Kyokai Production, written and directed by Kaneto Shindo. Photographed by Kiyoshi Kuroda. Music by Hikaru Hayashi. 96 minutes.

Starring Nobuko Otowa, Taiji Tonoyama, Shinji Tanaka, Masanori Horimoto.

IT HAPPENED ONE NIGHT (USA)

Awards (2)

Best Film	American Academy Award, 1934
Best American Film	National Board of Review, 1934

Claudette Colbert as a spoiled runaway heiress and Clark Gable as the hard-boiled newspaperman who pursues and woos her in a delightful journey across America. Frank Capra's first big success of the thirties (shot in four weeks on real locations) and, until *One Flew Over The Cuckoo's Nest*, the only movie to win all four major Academy Awards. Colbert's Oscar-winning role was turned down by Myrna Loy, Margaret Sullavan, Miriam Hopkins and Constance Bennett!

A Columbia Picture, directed by Frank Capra. Screenplay by Robert Riskin, based on *Night Bus* by Samuel Hopkins Adams. Photographed by Joseph Walker. Music Direction by Louis Silvers. 105 minutes.

Starring Claudette Colbert, Clark Gable, Walter Connolly Roscoe Karns, Alan Hale, Ward Bond, Jameson Thomas, Eddie Chandler.

(above) Broderick Crawford (left) as the dying Willie Stark in the final sequence from the Oscar-winning *All The King's Men* (Columbia)

(Below) Ingrid Bergman and Liv Ullmann in *Autumn Sonata* (ITC)

(Above) Martin Sheen on a journey into madness and (below) the special patrol mission caught up in battle in Coppola's Cannes prize-winner *Apocalypse Now* (EMI)

(Above) Marlon Brando as the renegade Colonel Kurtz in *Apocalypse Now*

(Above) Greta Garbo and Fredric March in *Anna Karenina* (MGM), award winner at Venice in 1935.

(Above) Jack Lemmon and Shirley MacLaine at the office Christmas party in Billy Wilder's *The Apartment* (United Artists)

(Below) Pre-war Fascism in Mussolini's Italy. A scene from Fellini's multi-award winner, *Amarcord* (Warner Bros.)

Catherine Deneuve enjoying sexual humiliation in Bunuel's *Belle De Jour* (Allied Artists), winner of the Golden Lion of St. Mark, Venice, 1967

(Above) Paul Newman demonstrates the art of bicycle riding in *Butch Cassidy And The Sundance Kid* (20th Century-Fox)

(Below) Ryan O'Neal at gunpoint in Stanley Kubrick's *Barry Lyndon* (Warner Bros.)

Ingrid Bergman and Humphrey Bogart in the 1943 Oscar winner *Casablanca* (Warner Bros.)

Paul Newman as an ageing William F. Cody in Robert Altman's Berlin award winner, *Buffalo Bill And The Indians, Or Sitting Bull's History Lesson* (EMI)

Lionel Stander and Jack MacGowran as two on-the-run gangsters in Polanski's *Cul-De-Sac* (Compton), winner of the Golden Bear at Berlin in 1966

Master of Ceremonies Joel Grey in the 1972 Bob Fosse musical *Cabaret* (Allied Artists)

(Above) Liv Ullman in Ingmar Bergman's *Cries And Whispers* (Gala)

(Below) Edward G. Robinson, pre-war Fascist hunter in *Confessions Of A Nazi Spy* (Warner Bros.), Best American Film of 1939 — National Board of Review

(Above) Fernando Rey practising the art of seduction in Buñuel's *The Discreet Charm Of The Bourgeoisie* (Greenwich Films)

Richard Gere in Terrence Malick's *Days Of Heaven* (Paramount), the National Board of Review's selection as the best film of 1978

Bed-hopping Julie Christie in John Schlesinger's *Darling* (Vic/Appia Films), Best Film, 1965 – New York Critics

(Above) George C. Scott, rarin' to go for world extermination in Kubrick's *Dr. Strangelove; Or, How I Learned To Stop Worrying And Love The Bomb* (Columbia)

(Below) Maksim Munzuk as the Siberian trapper *Dersu Uzala* (Curzon Films)

(Above) François Truffaut directs Jacqueline Bisset and Jean-Pierre Leaud in *Day For Night* (Warner Bros.)

(Below) Escaped convicts Sidney Poitier and Tony Curtis in Stanley Kramer's *The Defiant Ones* (United Artists), voted best film of 1958 by the New York Critics.

LES JEUX INTERDITS (France)

Awards (4)

Golden Lion	Venice, 1952
Best Foreign Language Film	American Academy Award, 1952
Best Foreign Language Film	New York Critics, 1952
Best Film, Any Source	British Academy Award, 1953

The effects of World War II on two French children – one a peasant boy, the other a five-year-old orphan girl – who create their own cemetery for dead animals and become obsessed, like their elders, with the ritual of death. The children's private fantasy world is explored with subtlety by René Clément in a film that remains one of the most moving ever made about the inhumanity of war. The film begins with the strafing of a refugee column on a road in Northern France. It ends with the girl, labelled and abandoned, alone at a Red Cross assembly point.

Robert Dorfmann/Silver Films. Directed by René Clément. Screenplay by Jean Aurenche, Pierre Bost, René Clément and Françoise Boyer, based on the novel by Boyer. Photographed by Robert Juilliard. Music by Narciso Yepes. 102 minutes.

Starring Brigitte Fossey, Georges Poujouly, Lucien Hubert, Suzanne Courtal, Jacques Marin, Laurence Badie, André Wasley.

THE JOURNALIST (USSR)

Awards (1)

Grand Prix	Moscow, 1967

Three and a half hour film by Sergei Gerasimov (director of the epic *Quiet Flows The Don*) concerning the experiences of a young newspaperman when he is sent on an assignment to a town in the Urals. To western eyes, an over-talkative production with nothing very new to offer; to Soviet audiences, frequently controversial in its presentation of a hero with dubious moral qualities and its unflattering portrait of Russian provincial life. Some lyrical moments though and an attractive warm blonde actress named Galina Polskik. Co-winner, with *Father*, of the 1967 Moscow Festival.

A Gorki Studio Production, written and directed by Sergei Gerasimov. Photographed by Vladimir Rapoport. Music by P. Checkalov. 205 minutes.

Starring Yuri Vasiliev, Galina Polskik, Ivan Lanikov, Sergei Nikonenko, Nadejda Fedosova, Sergei Gerasimov.

JULIA (USA)

Awards (1)

Best Film	British Academy Award, 1978

The lasting friendship between two women – American playwright Lillian Hellman (Jane Fonda) and her childhood friend, political activist Julia (Vanessa Redgrave) – in Europe and Nazi Germany during the thirties. Recalled in flashback and filmed by Fred Zinnemann with a classical elegance only rarely seen in modern day cinema. Jason Robards co-stars as Dashiell Hammett.

A Twentieth Century-Fox Picture, directed by Fred Zinnemann. Screenplay by Alvin Sargent, based on the story in the collection *Pentimento* by Lillian Hellman. Photographed in Technicolor (prints by DeLuxe) by Douglas Slocombe. Music by Georges Delerue. 117 minutes.

Starring Jane Fonda, Vanessa Redgrave, Jason Robards, Maximilian Schell, Hal Holbrook, Rosemary Murphy, Meryl Streep, Dora Doll.

Note: Julia first opened in the USA in 1977.

JULIET OF THE SPIRITS (France/Italy/West Germany)

Awards (2)

Best Foreign Language Film	New York Critics, 1965
Best Foreign Language Film	National Board of Review, 1965

Middle-aged Italian wife Giulietta Masina takes refuge in fantasies conjured up during spiritual seances when she learns that her husband has a mistress. Pretentious, tricksy Fellini movie, almost saved by the ravishing colourwork of Gianni Di Venanzo. Named best of the year by the New York Critics and National Board of Review; ignored at Oscar time when it was not included among the five best foreign picture nominations.

Federiz/Francoriz/Rizzoli Films/Eichberg Film. Directed by Federico Fellini. Screenplay by Federico Fellini, Tullio Pinelli, Ennio Flajano and Brunello Rondi, from a story by Fellini and Pinelli. Photographed in Technicolor by Gianni Di Venanzo. Music by Nino Rota. 148 minutes.

Starring Giulietta Masina, Alba Cancellieri, Mario Pisu, Caterina Boratto, Luisa Della Noce, Sylva Koscina, Sabrina Gigli, Rosella Di Sepio, Lou Gilbert, Valentina Cortese, Silvana Jachino, Elena Fondra, Sandra Milo.

JULIUS CAESAR (USA)

Awards (1)

Best American Film	National Board of Review, 1953

Power politics in Ancient Rome, centering on the assassination of Julius Caesar in 44 B.C. Austere, realistic Shakespeare (since acclaimed as the best ever filmed) with Marlon Brando as Marc Anthony, James Mason as Brutus and John Gielgud as arch-plotter Cassius. The National

Board of Review placed the picture ahead of *Shane* and *From Here To Eternity* in its ten best list of 1953; the Oscar Academy included it among its five best picture nominations.

A Metro-Goldwyn-Mayer Picture, adapted and directed by Joseph L. Mankiewicz. Based on the play by William Shakespeare. Photographed by Joseph Ruttenberg. Music by Miklos Rozsa. 121 minutes.

Starring Marlon Brando, James Mason, John Gielgud, Louis Calhern, Edmond O'Brien, Greer Garson, Deborah Kerr, George Macready.

JUSTICE EST FAITE (France)

Awards (2)

Golden Lion	Venice, 1950
Best Foreign Language Film	New York Critics, 1953

An examination of the preoccupations and prejudices of a French jury during the trial of a woman doctor accused of administering a fatal dose of morphine to her incurably ill lover. The woman claims her act was one of mercy; the prosecution alleges it was for monetary gain. The film follows the case through to the final verdict. *Justice Est Faite* triumphed at Venice over Huston's *The Asphalt Jungle*, Cocteau's *Orphée* and the Oscar-winning *All The King's Men*.

Silver Films. Directed by André Cayatte. Screenplay by André Cayatte and Charles Spaak. Photographed by Jean Bourgoin. Music by Raymond Legrand. 105 minutes.

Starring Claude Nollier, Balpêtre, Valentine Tessier, Raymond Bussières, Jacques Castelot, Jean Debucourt, Jean-Pierre Grenier.

Note: Justice Est Faite was also awarded a prize as the best criminal and adventure film at the 1951 Berlin festival. It was not released in the United States until 1953.

KAGEMUSHA (Japan)

Awards (1)
Golden Palm — Cannes, 1980

Kurosawa's return to the Samurai genre; an elaborate three hour spectacular set in 16th century Japan and centering on a petty thief who, because of his resemblance to the ailing warlord of a powerful clan, takes over as leader and gradually assumes the chieftain's dignity and character. Full of ferocious battle scenes, sweeping cavalry charges and stunning sunsets and co-winner of the Cannes prize with the musical *All That Jazz*. The film marked Kurosawa's first win at Cannes — some thirty years after his sensational *Rashomon* won at Venice in 1951.

A Toho/Twentieth Century Fox Release, directed by Akira Kurosawa. Screenplay by Akira Kurosawa and Mesata Ide. Photographed in Eastman Color by Kazuo Miyagawa and Asaichi Nakai. Music by Shinichiro Ikebe. 179 minutes.

Starring Tatsuya Nakadai, Tsutomu Yamazaki, Kenichi Hagiwara, Kota Yui, Hideji Otaki, Hideo Murata, Daisuke Ryu.

Note: The film is also known as *The Double*.

DER KAISER VON KALIFORNIEN (Germany)

Awards (1)
Mussolini Cup — Venice, 1936

Sombre German production, set in San Francisco in the pioneering days of the last century and following a Swiss immigrant who makes and loses a fortune in the land of plenty. Not especially memorable and now all but forgotten. Not so its competitors at Venice in 1936 — *The Story Of Louis Pasteur, Mr. Deeds Goes To Town, Show Boat, Mayerling*.

Luis Trenker Filmgesellschaft. Directed by Luis Trenker. Photographed by Albert Benitz. Music by Giuseppe Becce. 97 minutes.

Starring Luis Trenker, Victoria Von Ballasco, Werner Kung, Karli Zwingmann.

LA KERMESSE HEROIQUE (France)

Awards (2)

Best Foreign Language Film	New York Critics, 1936
Best Foreign Film	National Board of Review, 1936

Satirical French comedy, set in the early seventeenth century, about the women of a small Flemish town who give their menfolk a lesson in diplomacy by using their charm and sex appeal to disarm an army of Spanish invaders. Françoise Rosay as the burgomaster's wife and Louis Jouvet as a Dominican friar head the cast of a film justly famous for its visual qualities, notably Lazare Meerson's period sets and designs.

A Tobis Production, directed by Jacques Feyder. Screenplay by Bernard Zimmer, based on a story by Charles Spaak. Photographed by Harry Stradling. Music by Louis Beydts. 89 minutes.

Starring Françoise Rosay, Louis Jouvet, Jean Murat, Alerme, Lyne Clevers, Micheline Cheirel, Maryse Wendling.

Note: Le Kermesse Heroïque (known also as *Carnival In Flanders*) first opened in France in 1935.

KES (Britain)

Awards (1)

Grand Prix	Karlovy Vary, 1970

A fourteen-year-old boy finds temporary escape from his drab existence at home and at school when he captures and trains a kestrel hawk. A tender, often disturbing film that accurately reflects the bleak frustration and routine of working class life in the industrial North of England. The only British film to have triumphed at either the Moscow or Karlovy Vary festivals.

A Woodfall/Kestrel Films Production, released by United Artists. Directed by Ken Loach. Screenplay by Barry Hines, Ken Loach and Tony Garnett, based on the novel by Barry Hines. Photographed in Technicolor by Chris Menges. Music/music direction by John Cameron. 113 minutes.

Starring David Bradley, Lynne Perrie, Freddie Fletcher, Colin Welland, Brian Glover, Bob Bowes, Robert Naylor, Trevor Hesketh, Geoffrey Banks.

A KIND OF LOVING (Britain)

Awards (1)

Golden Bear	Berlin, 1962

Two young people — a draftsman (Alan Bates) and a girl from the typing pool (June Ritchie) — decide to wed after the girl becomes pregnant and make the best of the resulting unhappy marriage. An old, old story but given a fresh look by John Schlesinger's keen observations of the working class environment and life in a Northern industrial town. The film was Schlesinger's first feature and also the first British award winner at Berlin since *Hobson's Choice* nine years earlier.

Vic Films-Waterhall Productions. Directed by John Schlesinger. Screenplay by Willis Hall and Keith Waterhouse, based on the novel by Stan Barstow. Photographed by Denys Coop. Music by Ron Grainer. 112 minutes.

Starring Alan Bates, June Ritchie, Thora Hird, Bert Palmer, Gwen Nelson, Malcolm Patton, Pat Keen.

Note: A Kind Of Loving was first shown in Britain in April, 1961.

THE KNACK . . . AND HOW TO GET IT (Britain)

Awards (1)

Golden Palm	Cannes, 1965

A debunking of the British way of sex centering on the activities of three young men who practice their sexual art on an innocent young girl they befriend in London. Britain's first Grand Prix winner at Cannes since *The Third Man*; full of jump cuts, captions, speeded-up action and other fashionable new wave tricks of the sixties. Some Cannes 'also rans': Kobayashi's *Kwaidan*, Lumet's *The Hill* and Rosi's poetic bullfighting drama *The Moment Of Truth*.

Woodfall Film Productions. Directed by Richard Lester. Screenplay by Charles Wood, based on the play by Ann Jellicoe. Photographed by David Watkin. Music by John Barry. 84 minutes.

Starring Rita Tushingham, Ray Brooks, Michael Crawford, Donal Donnelly.

KRAMER VS. KRAMER (USA)

Awards (2)

Best Film	American Academy Award, 1979
Best Film	New York Critics, 1979

Superior tear-jerker from Robert Benton about an unhappy wife who walks out on her husband and six-year-old son but then returns eighteen months later to fight for custody of the child. Very much a movie of the seventies, probing into many areas of marriage and family life, and dealing with one of the most pertinent issues of modern times.

A Columbia Picture, written and directed by Robert Benton. Based on the novel by Avery Corman. Photographed in Technicolor by Nestor Almendros. 105 minutes.

Starring Dustin Hoffman, Meryl Streep, Jane Alexander, Justin Henry, Howard Duff, George Coe, Jobeth Williams, Bill Moor, Howland Chamberlain.

L

LACOMBE LUCIEN (France/Italy/West Germany)

Awards (1)

Best Film — British Academy Award, 1974

Louis Malle's portrait of a seventeen-year-old peasant boy who, more by accident than design, joins the French Gestapo workers and becomes a collaborator during the last months of World War II. A complex, many-layered film that argues that the dividing line between resistance hero and traitor in occupied France was a thin one and that the moral choice facing the French was far from being clear-cut.

NEF/UPF (Paris)/Vides Film (Rome)/Hallelujah Film (Munich). Directed by Louis Malle. Screenplay by Louis Malle and Patrick Modiano. Photographed in Eastman Color by Tonino Delli Colli. 137 minutes.

Starring Pierre Blaise, Aurore Clément, Holger Lowenadler, Thérèse Giehse, Stéphane Bouy, Loumi Jacobesco, René Bouloc.

THE LAST STAGE (Poland)

Awards (1)

Grand Prix — Karlovy Vary, 1948

The experiences of two Polish women who survived the horrors of Auschwitz concentration camp where millions were murdered by the Nazis in World War II. The two women wrote and directed the film which was the first to be awarded the Grand Prix at the Karlovy Vary festival. The 'last stage' of the film's title is the journey to the gas chamber.

A Film Polski Production. Written and directed by Wanda Jakubowska and Gerda Schneider. Photographed by Borys Monastyrski. Music by R. Palester. 110 minutes.

Starring Huguette Faget, W. Bartówna, T. Gorecka, A. Gorecka, N. W. Nogradowa.

LAST YEAR AT MARIENBAD (France/Italy)

Awards (1)
Golden Lion — Venice, 1961

The 'What's it all about movie?' of the early sixties. No-one seemed to know the answer in 1961 and no-one seems to know or care twenty years later. The only thing certain about the film is that it is set in a baroque hotel in Bavaria and centres on three people — a young man (Giorgio Albertazzi) trying to renew a love affair with a beautiful married woman, the woman (Delphine Seyrig) herself who remembers nothing of the affair, and a second, older man (Sacha Pitoëff) who is possibly the woman's husband. All three are referred to by letters of the alphabet — X, A and M respectively. Pretentious rubbish or a work of genius? Probably the former as no-one has yet unravelled its mysteries.

Terra Films/Societe Nouvelle des Films Cormoran/Como Films/ Précitel/Argos Films/Les Films Tamara/Cinétel/Silver Films/Cineriz. Directed by Alain Resnais. Screenplay and dialogue by Alain Robbe-Grillet. Photographed in Dyaliscope by Sacha Vierny. Music by Francis Seyrig. Edited by Henri Colpi. 100 minutes.

Starring Delphine Seyrig, Giorgio Albertazzi, Sacha Pitoëff, Pierre Barbaud, Francoise Bertin, Luce Garcia-Ville, Héléna Kornel, Jean Lanier.

LAWRENCE OF ARABIA (Britain)

Awards (2)
Best Film — American Academy Award, 1962
Best Film, Any Source — British Academy Award, 1962

Lavish two hundred and twenty-one-minute attempt to unravel the complex and enigmatic character of T. E. Lawrence who, during his two years in Arabia in the First World War, succeeded in uniting the Arab tribes against the Turks and became known as the legendary El Aurens. Thanks to a probing, intelligent script, inspired direction by David Lean and the luxurious desert camerawork of Freddie Young, the attempt succeeds. One of the few films to have cost several million dollars and be considered a work of art.

A Horizon Pictures-Columbia Production, directed by David Lean. Screenplay by Robert Bolt. Photographed in Technicolor and Super Panavision by Freddie Young. Music by Maurice Jarre. 221 minutes.

Starring Peter O'Toole, Alec Guinness, Anthony Quinn, Jack Hawkins, Jose Ferrer, Anthony Quayle, Claude Rains, Arthur Kennedy, Donald Wolfit, Omar Sharif.

LAZARILLO (Spain)

Awards (1)
Golden Bear — Berlin, 1960

The picaresque adventures of a small boy when he is sold by his widowed mother to a beggar and has to face up to the harsh realities of life in a series of encounters with priests, swindlers, actors, etc. Set in sixteenth century Spain and with some splendid landscapes of Castile, but a relatively minor work when compared with *The Angry Silence* which the Berlin audience felt should have taken the premier award.

Hesperia Films. Adapted and directed by César Ardavín, based on the anonymous novel *Lazarillo de Tormes*. Photographed by Manuel Berenguer. Music by Emilio Lehurberg. 100 minutes.

Starring Marco Paoletti, Juan José Menéndez, Carlos Casaravilla, Memmo Carotenuto, Margarita Lozano, Antonio Molino.

THE LEOPARD (France/Italy)

Awards (1)

Golden Palm	Cannes, 1963

Italy's *Gone With The Wind* as it was known in some quarters in the mid-sixties; a lavish adaptation of Lampedusa's novel about the decline and fall of an aristocratic Sicilian family during the Garibaldi uprising of the 1860s. For many critics an over indulgent, agonizingly long piece of celluloid. For others, a rich Visconti masterpiece that reflects the conflicts of the old and the new in a changing period of history. Cut from 205 minutes (its Cannes length) to 185 and finally 165.

Titanus/S.N.P.C./S.G.C. Directed by Luchino Visconti. Screenplay by Suso Cecchi D'Amico, Pasquale Festa Campanile, Enrico Medioli, Massimo Franciosa & Luchino Visconti, based on the novel by Giuseppe Tomasi di Lampedusa. Photographed in De Luxe Color and CinemaScope by Giuseppe Rotunno. Art Direction by Mario Garbuglia. Music by Nino Rota. 165 minutes.

Starring Burt Lancaster, Alain Delon, Claudia Cardinale, Rina Morelli, Paolo Stoppa, Romolo Valli, Lucilla Morlacchi, Serge Reggiani, Ida Galli.

THE LIFE OF EMILE ZOLA (USA)

Awards (2)

Best Film	American Academy Award, 1937
Best Film	New York Critics, 1937

Not so much a biography, more a reconstruction of the Dreyfus case, with crusading novelist Emile Zola coming to the aid of a French army officer unjustly accused of treason (because of anti-Semitic feeling) and condemned to imprisonment on Devil's Island. The Warner studio, wary of raising the subject of anti-Semitism in the thirties, opted instead for an attack on military and political corruption in late nineteenth century France. The result, although historically inaccurate, was no less effective.

A Warner Bros. Picture, directed by William Dieterle. Screenplay by Heinz Herald, Geza Herczeg and Norman Reilly Raine. Story by Heinz Herald and Geza Herczeg. Photographed by Tony Gaudio. Music by Max Steiner. 116 minutes.

Starring Paul Muni, Gale Sondergaard, Joseph Schildkraut, Gloria Holden, Donald Crisp, Erin O'Brien-Moore, John Litel, Henry O'Neill.

THE LION IN WINTER (Britain)

Awards (1)

Best Film	New York Critics, 1968

Christmas at Chinon Castle with the quarrelsome Plantagenets — Henry II (Peter O'Toole) and his estranged wife Eleanor of Aquitaine (Katharine Hepburn) — as they set about choosing a successor to the throne of England. Much shouting and snarling; one glorious moment when Hepburn, seated on a royal barge, is rowed slowly up river in the misty winter sunshine. The New York Critics voted the film best of the year by the narrow margin of thirteen votes to eleven for John Cassavetes' *Faces*.

A Haworth Production (released by Avco Embassy Pictures), directed by Anthony Harvey. Screenplay by James Goldman, based on his play. Photographed in Eastman Color and Panavision by Douglas Slocombe. Music by John Barry. 134 minutes.

Starring Peter O'Toole, Katharine Hepburn, Jane Merrow, John Castle, Timothy Dalton, Anthony Hopkins, Nigel Stock Nigel Terry.

LIVE TODAY, DIE TOMORROW (Japan)

Awards (1)

Grand Prix	Moscow, 1971

Powerful examination of the life and horrific childhood of a Japanese teenager who finds himself on-the-run for the murder of a policeman in contemporary Tokyo. Told in flashback and reputedly based on the true tale of a boy who wrote of his experiences while awaiting trial in jail. Co-winner, along with *White Bird With A Black Mark* and *Confessions Of A Police Inspector*, of the 1971 Moscow Grand Prix.

A Kindai Eiga Kyokai Production, written and directed by Kaneto Shindo. Photographed by Kiyomi Kuroda. Music by Hikaru Hayashi. 120 minutes.

Starring Daijiro Harada, Nobuko Otowa, Keiko Torii, Kiwako Taichi, Kei Sato, Taiji Tonoyama.

THE LONGEST DAY (USA)

Awards (1)

Best English Language Film	National Board of Review, 1962

Darryl F. Zanuck's all-star account of the Allied invasion of Normandy in June, 1944, recreated on the grand scale by three directors — Andrew Marton who handled the American sequences, Ken Annakin (the British scenes) and Bernhard Wicki (the German episodes) — plus

Zanuck himself, who frequently had a hand in things. Voted best film of 1962 by the National Board of Review who placed the year's other epic, *Lawrence Of Arabia*, fourth in its ten best list. Financially, one of the most successful war films ever made.

A Twentieth Century-Fox Picture, directed by Ken Annakin, Andrew Marton, Bernhard Wicki. Screenplay by Cornelius Ryan, based on his book. Photographed in CinemaScope by Jean Bourgoin and Walter Wottitz. Music by Maurice Jarre. 180 minutes.

Starring John Wayne, Rod Steiger, Robert Ryan, Peter Lawford, Henry Fonda, Red Buttons, Robert Mitchum, Richard Todd, Richard Beymer, Richard Burton and an all-star cast.

THE LONG WEEKEND (Spain)

Awards (1)

Grand Prix	Moscow, 1977

Left-wing allegory concerning a forty-year-old mechanic who makes a motor cycle trip from Madrid to a holiday resort in search of sex with foreign girls. Along the way he discovers the true nature of his country (past and present) and for the first time in his life develops a social conscience. The film was the first major festival success for Spanish director Juan Bardem and shared the 1977 Moscow prize with *Mimino* and *The Fifth Seal.* Sex comedy actor Alfredo Landa stars as the ageing 'easy rider.'

An Art 7 Production, directed by Juan A. Bardem. Photographed in colour by Jose Luis Alcaine. Music by Jose Nieto. 100 minutes.

Starring Alfredo Landa, Paco Algora, Victoria Abril, Mabel Escano, Pilar Bardem,

THE LOST WEEKEND (USA)

Awards (2)

Best Film	American Academy Award, 1945
Best Film	New York Critics, 1945

Three agonizing days in the life of dipsomaniac novelist Ray Milland as he pours out his shattered dreams to a New York bartender and drinks himself into a horrifying bout of the D.T.'s. The most famous 'binge' movie of all time and the first to confront the problem of alcoholism seriously on screen. Also the first award triumph for writer-director Billy Wilder.

A Paramount Picture, directed by Billy Wilder. Screenplay by Billy Wilder and Charles Brackett, based on the novel by Charles R. Jackson. Photographed by John F. Seitz. Music by Miklos Rozsa. 99 minutes.

Starring Ray Milland, Jane Wyman, Howard da Silva, Philip Terry, Doris Dowling, Frank Faylen, Mary Young.

Note: The Lost Weekend was one of eleven joint winners of the Grand Prix at the first Cannes Film Festival in 1946. (see page 226).

LUCIA (Cuba)

Awards (1)
Grand Prix Moscow, 1969

Three love stories in important periods of Cuban history, all told from the viewpoint of three women called Lucia. In 1895 she is an aristocrat who takes part in the war of independence against Spain; in 1932 she is a married factory worker involved in the overthrow of the Machado regime; and in 1960 she is a young bride experiencing marital problems shortly after the Castro revolution. The stories, all handled in different styles by director Humberto Solas, descend, in turn, from tragedy to irony to farce. Rapturously received in Moscow where the judges awarded it first prize, along with *See You Monday* and *Serafino*.

An I.C.A.I.C. Production, directed by Humberto Solas. Screenplay by Humberto Solas, Julio Garcia Espinosa and Nelson Rodriguez. Photographed by Jorge Herrera. Music by Leo Brouwer and Joseito Fernández. 161 minutes.

Starring Raquel Revuelta, Eslinda Nuñez, Adela Legra, Eduardo Moure, Ramon Brito, Adolfo Llaurado.

MACBETH (Britain)

Awards (1)

Best English Language Film — National Board of Review, 1971

Jon Finch as Shakespeare's Scots nobleman who is driven by the ambitions of his crazed wife to murder for the throne of Scotland. Strong, violent stuff, adapted by Roman Polanski and Kenneth Tynan and boasting a whole coven of naked witches. Oscar-winner *The French Connection* was placed fourth in the National Board of Review's ten best list of 1971.

Playboy Productions/Caliban Films. Directed by Roman Polanski. Screenplay by Roman Polanski and Kenneth Tynan, based on the play by William Shakespeare. Photographed in Todd-AO 35 and Technicolor by Gilbert Taylor. Production Design by Wilfrid Shingleton. Music by The Third Ear Band. 140 minutes.

Starring Jon Finch, Francesca Annis, Martin Shaw, Nicholas Selby, John Stride, Stephan Chase, Paul Shelley, Terence Bayler.

MADAME ROSA (France)

Awards (1)

Best Foreign Language Film — American Academy Award, 1977

An ailing Jewish prostitute (Simone Signoret) cares for the children of her younger colleagues and is eventually helped to die in peace and with dignity by a fourteen-year-old Arab boy in her charge. A film version of the prize-winning novel by Emile Ajar, set among the pimps and thieves of the Arab and Jewish worker sections of Paris. Preferred at Oscar time to Bunuel's *That Obscure Object Of Desire*.

Lira Films. Written and directed by Moshe Mizrahi, based on the novel by Emile Ajar. Photographed in Eastman Color by Nestor Almendros. Music by Philippe Sarde. 105 minutes.

Starring Simone Signoret, Claude Dauphin, Samy Ben Youb, Gabriel Jabbour, Michal Bat Adam, Costa-Gavras, Stella Annicette.

A MAN AND A WOMAN (France)

Awards (1)

Best Foreign Language Film	American Academy Award, 1966
Golden Palm	Cannes, 1966

The love affair between a racing car driver (Jean-Louis Trintignant) and a beautiful young script girl (Anouk Aimée) whose marriages have both ended in tragedy and who meet one Sunday while visiting their children at a boarding school at Deauville. Derided by many critics (except those at Cannes and in Hollywood) as being nothing more than a fairy story of two getaway people; enjoyed by millions who were carried along by the film's romanticism and the lush music score of Francis Lai. The film was photographed in colour and black and white and also included tinted sequences.

Les Films Treize. Directed by Claude Lelouch. Adaptation and dialogue by Claude Lelouch and Pierre Uytterhoeven, from a story by Lelouch. Photographed in Eastman Color by Claude LeLouch. Music by Francis Lai. 102 minutes.

Starring Anouk Aimée, Jean-Louis Trintignant, Pierre Barouh, Valérie Lagrange, Simone Paris, Antoine Sire, Souad Amidou.

Note: A Man And A Woman shared the Cannes Prize with *The Birds, The Bees And The Italians.*

A MAN FOR ALL SEASONS (Britain)

Awards (4)

Best Film	American Academy Award, 1966
Best Film	New York Critics, 1966
Best English Language Film	National Board of Review, 1966
Best Film, Any Source	British Academy Award, 1967

Immaculate version of Robert Bolt's play about the conflict of wills between Henry VIII (Robert Shaw) and Sir Thomas More (Paul Scofield) who refused, as a matter of conscience, to sign the Act of Succession which condoned the King's divorce from Catherine of Aragon and marriage to Anne Boleyn. A major award winner on both sides of the Atlantic. Only at Moscow where it was entered in competition in 1967 did it fail to take a best picture prize.

A Highland Films Production (released by Columbia), directed by Fred Zinnemann. Screenplay by Robert Bolt, based on his stage play. Photographed in Technicolor by Ted Moore. Music by Georges Delerue. Production Design by John Box. 120 minutes.

Starring Paul Scofield, Wendy Hiller, Leo McKern, Robert Shaw, Orson Welles, Susannah York, Nigel Davenport, John Hurt.

Note: A Man For All Seasons did not open in Britain until March, 1967.

MANHATTAN (USA)

Awards (2)

Best English Language Film	National Board of Review, 1979
Best Film	British Academy Award, 1979

More strained relationships, deep thinking and wisecracking from Woody Allen as he embarks on yet another complex love affair with Diane Keaton. The black and white camerawork, irresistible Gershwin score and the affection with which Allen pays homage to New York tend to make the film appear more substantial than it really is.

A United Artists Picture, directed by Woody Allen. Screenplay by Woody Allen and Marshall Brickman. Photographed in Panavision by Gordon Willis. Music by George Gershwin, adapted and arranged by Tom Pierson. 96 minutes.

Starring Woody Allen, Diane Keaton, Michael Murphy, Mariel Hemingway, Meryl Streep, Anne Byrne, Karen Ludwig, Michael O'Donoghue.

MAN OF ARAN (Britain)

Awards (2)

Mussolini Cup	Venice, 1934
Best Foreign Film	National Board of Review, 1934

Robert Flaherty documentary tracing the everyday life of a family – a man, his wife and their young son – as they struggle to earn a living on the isle of Aran off the west coast of Ireland. Flaherty spent two years on the project and lived for eighteen months among the islanders, using a cottage for the film's interiors and converting another into a cutting room. The film was the first major prize-winner at the newly formed Venice Festival, first held two years earlier.

Gainsborough/Gaumont British. Produced by Michael Balcon. Directed, written and photographed by Robert and Frances Flaherty. Music by John Greenwood. 75 minutes.

Starring Colman 'Tiger' King, Maggie Dirrane, Michael Dillane, Pat Mullen, Patch Ruadh, Patcheen Flaherty, Tommy O'Rourke.

MANON (France)

Awards (1)

Golden Lion	Venice, 1949

The life of a luxury-craving young whore who drags her enslaved lover through the brothels of post-war Paris, drives him to murder, and eventually flees with him to Palestine where she is slain by Arabs in the desert. An updating of Abbé Prévost's eighteenth century classic *Manon Lescaut* and France's first international success in post-war competition. Sixteen-year-old Cécile Aubry and Michael Auclair appear as the doomed lovers, Gabrielle Dorziat as a brothel madam.

An Alcina (Paul-Edmond Decharme) Production, directed by Henri-Georges Clouzot. Screenplay by Henri-Georges Clouzot and Jean Ferry, based on the novel by Abbé Prévost. Photographed by Armand Thirard. Music by Paul Misraki. 96 minutes.

Starring Cécile Aubry, Michael Auclair, Serge Reggiani, Gabrielle Dorziat, Henri Gilbert, Raymond Souplex.

DIE MARQUISE VON O. . . . (West Germany/France)

Awards (1)

Best Foreign Language Film	National Board of Review, 1976

Elegance and quiet eroticism from Eric Rohmer as he follows the fortunes of an Italian noblewoman who becomes pregnant while drugged and has to advertise for the unknown father of her child – conceived during the Russian invasion of Italy at the end of the eighteenth century. Like most Rohmer pictures, deceptively simple but visually one of the finest period pieces of the seventies. This was Rohmer's second award movie of the decade (see also *Claire's Knee*).

Janus-Film Produktion (Frankfurt)/Les Films du Losange (Paris). Written and directed by Eric Rohmer, based on the novels by Heinrich von Kleist. Photographed in Eastman Color by Nestor Almendros. Music by Roger Delmotte (improvisations on Prussian military tunes of 1804). 107 minutes.

Starring Edith Clever, Bruno Ganz, Peter Lühr, Edda Seippel, Otto Sander, Ezzo Huber, Bernhard Frey, Ruth Drexel, Eduard Linkers.

MARTY (USA)

Awards (4)

Best Film	American Academy Award, 1955
Best Film	New York Critics, 1955
Best American Film	National Board of Review, 1955
Golden Palm	Cannes, 1955

Small-scale movie about an ugly New York butcher who eventually finds happiness with a schoolteacher he meets at a Saturday night dance. Based on a TV play by Paddy Chayefsky and still the *only* American movie to have won all three U.S. awards and a first prize at a European festival. Delbert Mann's realistic depiction of working class life in the Bronx stand the film in good stead despite its soft centre.

Hecht-Lancaster Productions/United Artists. Directed by Delbert Mann. Screenplay by Paddy Chayefsky, based on his TV play. Photographed by Joseph La Shelle. Music by Roy Webb. 99 minutes.

Starring Ernest Borgnine, Betsy Blair, Joe Mantell, Esther Minciotti, Augusta Ciolli, Karen Steele, Jerry Paris, Frank Sutton.

M.A.S.H. (USA)

Awards (1)

Golden Palm	Cannes, 1970

Irreverent black comedy about an army medical team wisecracking its way through twelve-hour shifts in a mobile field hospital during the Korean War. Anti-war, anti-authority, just about anti-everything and a box-office smash (36 million dollars) for cult director Robert Altman. The movie began the American domination of the Cannes Festival during the seventies. The other U.S. winners: *Scarecrow, The Conversation, Taxi Driver, Apocalypse Now.*

An Aspen/Twentieth Century-Fox Picture, directed by Robert Altman. Screenplay by Ring Lardner, Jr., based on the novel by Richard Hooker. Photographed in De Luxe Color and Panavision by Harold E. Stine. Music by Johnny Mandel. 116 minutes.

Starring Donald Sutherland, Elliott Gould, Tom Skerritt, Sally Kellerman, Robert Duvall, Jo Ann Pflug, Rene Auberjonois, Roger Bowen.

THE MATTEI AFFAIR (Italy)

Awards (1)

Golden Palm — Cannes, 1972

Documentary styled investigation into the life of post-war Italian oil king Enrico Mattei, killed when his private plane mysteriously crashed in heavy rain in October, 1962. Framed in a *Citizen Kane* type structure, the film examines the pressures and pitfalls of Mattei's extraordinary power and hints that his death was the result of sabotage. In 1972 it brought director Francesco Rosi back to the forefront of world cinema and shared the Golden Palm at Cannes with another Italian film, *The Working Class Goes To Heaven.*

Vides-Verona. Directed by Francesco Rosi. Screenplay by Francesco Rosi and Tonino Guerra, with the collaboration of Nerio Munuzzo and Tito De Stefano. Photographed in Technicolor by Pasqualino De Santis. Music by Piero Piccioni. 118 minutes.

Starring Gian Maria Volonté, Luigi Squargina, Peter Baldwin, Franco Graziosi, Gianfranco Ombuen, Elio Jotta, Edda Ferronao.

MAYERLING (France)

Awards (1)

Best Foreign Language Film — New York Critics, 1937

Anatole Litvak's pre-war version of the tragic love affair between Archduke Rudolf of Austria (Charles Boyer) and a young baroness (Danielle Darrieux) and their double suicide at the hunting lodge of Mayerling. An elegant period romance and the film that established Boyer as the great continental screen lover of the 30s.

Pax Films, directed by Anatole Litvak. Screenplay by Joseph Kessel and J. V. Cube, based on the novel *Idyll's End* by Claude Anet. Photographed by Armand Thirard, Music by Arthur Honegger. 93 minutes.

Starring Charles Boyer, Danielle Darrieux, Suzy Prim, Jean Dax, Gabrielle Dorziat, Vladimir Sokoloff.

Note: Mayerling was first released in France in 1936.

MIDNIGHT COWBOY (USA)

Awards (2)

Best Film	American Academy Award, 1969
Best Film	British Academy Award, 1969

An excursion into loneliness, centering on two young losers — one a Texas stud (Jon Voight), the other a tubercular con man (Dustin Hoffman) — as they come to depend on each other in the unfriendly lower stratums of New York. John Schlesinger's first American film; named best picture at both the American and British Oscar ceremonies but overlooked by the New York Critics who preferred *Z* and the National Board of Review who favoured *They Shoot Horses, Don't They?*

A Jerome Hellman-John Schlesinger Production (released by United Artists), directed by John Schlesinger. Screenplay by Waldo Salt, based on the novel by James Leo Herlihy. Photographed in De Luxe Color by Adam Holender. Musical Supervision by John Barry. 113 minutes.

Starring Dustin Hoffman, Jon Voight, Sylvia Miles, John McGiver, Brenda Vaccaro, Barnard Hughes.

MIMINO (USSR)

Awards (1)

Grand Prix	Moscow, 1977

Soviet comedy about a daredevil helicopter pilot and his extraordinary adventures, first in the Caucasus where he delivers mail to outlying villages and airlifts a cow, then in Moscow where he achieves his long awaited ambition of becoming a transcontinental co-pilot. Consistently amusing, especially in its sight gags; along with Bardem's *The Long Weekend* and the sombre *The Fifth Seal*, winner of the 1977 Moscow Festival.

A Mosfilm Production, directed by Georgi Daneliya. Screenplay by Revaz Gabriadze, Victoria Tokareva and Georgi Daneliya. Photographed in colour by Anatoli Petritsky. 90 minutes.

Starring Vakhtang Kikabidze, Frunzik Mkrtchyan, Yelena Proklova, Yevgeny Leonov.

MIRACLE IN MILAN (Italy)

Awards (2)

Best Foreign Language Film	New York Critics, 1951
Grand Prix	Cannes, 1951

Vittorio De Sica's attempt to add a dash of fantasy to the uncompromising neo-realism of his post-war accomplishments, *Shoe-shine* and *Bicycle Thieves*. The chemistry doesn't always gel but the satire on the greed of wealthy industrialists is bitingly sharp and the ending when everyone flies off to heaven on broomsticks is sheer delight. The story concerns a young man who lives among the unemployed occupants of a Milan shanty town and, with the help of a magic dove, defends them from the rich when oil is discovered on their land.

A 'Societa' Produziona De Sica Film, in association with I.E.N.I.C. Directed by Vittorio De Sica. Photographed by Aldo Graziati. Music by Alessandro Cicognini. 101 minutes.

Starring Emma Gramatica, Francesco Golisano, Paolo Stoppa, Guglielmo Barnabo, Brunella Bovo, Anna Carena.

Note: Miracle In Milan shared the Cannes Festival Prize with Sjöberg's *Miss Julie*.

MISS JULIE (Sweden)

Awards (1)

Grand Prix	Cannes, 1951

Alf Sjöberg's extension of Strindberg's erotic one act play about the tragic love affair between a valet and a count's daughter in a class-ridden nineteenth century Sweden. Joint-winner with De Sica's *Miracle In Milan* at Cannes and, despite numerous entries by Ingmar Bergman (*Smiles Of A Summer Night, The Seventh Seal, Close To Life*, etc.), still the only Swedish film to take the first prize at the French festival.

Sandrew-Bauman (Rune Waldekranz) Production, directed by Alf Sjöberg. Screenplay by Alf Sjöberg, based on the play by August Strindberg. Photographed by Göran Strindberg. Music by Dag Wirén. 90 minutes.

Starring Anita Björk, Ulf Palme, Märta Dorff, Anders Henrikson, Lissie Alandh, Inger Norberg, Jan Hagerman, Ake Fridell.

Note: Miss Julie was first shown in Sweden in 1950.

MRS. MINIVER (USA)

Awards (1)

Best Film	American Academy Award, 1942

Greer Garson reads *Alice In Wonderland* to her children in an air raid shelter, waits for husband Walter Pidgeon to return from Dunkirk and captures a German paratrooper single-handed in her luxury garden. 'Never-never-land Britain' but just the ticket for 1942 and a popular best picture winner at Hollywood's Oscar ceremonies. The quiet sincerity of the piece still shines through the artificial MGM settings and the rose-coloured view of a typical English family in wartime.

A Metro-Goldwyn-Mayer Picture, directed by William Wyler. Screenplay by Arthur Wimperis, George Froeschel, James Hilton and Claudine West, based on the novel by Jan Struther. Photographed by Joseph Ruttenberg. Music by Herbert Stothart. 134 minutes.

Starring Greer Garson, Walter Pidgeon, Teresa Wright, Dame May Whitty, Henry Travers, Reginald Owen, Henry Wilcoxon, Richard Ney.

MR. DEED GOES TO TOWN (USA)

Awards (2)

Best Film	New York Critics, 1936
Best American Film	National Board of Review, 1936

Naïve country boy Longfellow Deeds (Gary Cooper) inherits a fortune from a playboy uncle then gives it all away when he discovers that his business associates are swindlers and crooks. Archetypal Capra Depression comedy, the second of the director's three award-winning movies of the thirties (see also *It Happened One Night* and *You Can't Take It With You*). Newspaper editor George Bancroft, crooked attorney Douglas Dumbrille and alcoholic author Walter Catlett head the supporting cast.

A Columbia Picture, directed by Frank Capra. Screenplay by Robert Riskin, based on a story by Clarence Budington Kelland. Photographed by Joseph Walker. Music direction by Howard Jackson. 115 minutes.

Starring Gary Cooper, Jean Arthur, George Bancroft, Lionel Stander, Douglas Dumbrille Raymond Walburn, H. B. Warner, Walter Catlett.

MON ONCLE (France/Italy)

Awards (2)

Best Foreign Language Film	American Academy Award, 1958
Best Foreign Language Film	New York Critics, 1958

Jacques Tati (second time out as Monsieur Hulot) tries to cope with the electronic mysteries of his sister's mechanized house and a factory that makes plastic hosepipes. He loses – the audience wins. Of the four Hulot films, *Mon Oncle* is the only one of the quartet to earn a best picture award.

Specta Films/Gray Film/Alter Film (Paris)/Film Del Centauro (Rome). Written and directed by Jacques Tati, with the collaboration of Jacques Lagrange and Jean L'Hôte. Photographed in Eastman Color by Jean Bourgoin. Music by Franck Barcellini and Alain Romans. 116 minutes.

Starring Jacques Tati, Jean-Pierre Zola, Alain Bécourt, Lucien Frégis, Dominique Marie, Betty Schneider, André Dino.

MONSIEUR VERDOUX (USA)

Awards (1)

Best Film	National Board of Review, 1947

The only Chaplin film to be named best of the year; a dark satire set in post-World War I Paris about a dapper Bluebeard who murders a number of rich widows in order to provide a comfortable life for his invalid wife and children. Chaplin's most ironic film, a bitter comment on the treacherous ethics of a warlike and money-mad world. Martha Raye adds moments of lunacy as a victim who refuses to die.

A United Artists Picture, written and directed by Charles Chaplin. Photographed by Rollie Totheroh. Music by Charles Chaplin. 125 minutes.

Starring Charles Chaplin, Mady Correll, Allison Roddan, Robert Lewis, Audrey Betz, Martha Raye, Isobel Elsom, Irving Bacon.

MONSIEUR VINCENT (France)

Awards (1)

Best Foreign Language Film	American Academy Award, 1948

Biography of the life and works of reforming priest Vincent de Paul who devoted his life to helping the poor and sick in seventeenth century France. Distinguished by a compelling central performance by Pierre Fresnay as the humble cleric; awarded an honorary Oscar by the Academy of Motion Picture Arts and Sciences.

A EDIC/UGC Production, directed by Maurice Cloche. Screenplay by Jean Bernard Luc and Jean Anouilh. Photographed by Claude Renoir. Music by J. J. Grunenwald. 113 minutes.

Starring Pierre Fresnay, Aimé Clariond, Jean Debucourt, Lise Delamare, Germaine Dermoz, Yvonne Godeau, Gabrielle Dorziat.

Note: Monsieur Vincent was first released in France in 1947.

MUTINY ON THE BOUNTY (USA)

Awards (1)

Best Film	American Academy Award, 1935

The Oscar winner of 1935, a year when most critical bodies favoured John Ford's *The Informer* as the best film of the year. Charles Laughton features as the sadistic Captain Bligh, Clark Gable as the noble Fletcher Christian who rises up against his tyranny and sets him adrift in an open boat. Described by MGM as 'A story of brutality, fierce courage, unquenchable hope and powerful drama, against a wide sweep of sea and sky,' the film finished with a gross of four and a half million dollars – the biggest take by a movie since *Ben-Hur* in 1926.

A Metro-Goldwyn-Mayer Picture, directed by Frank Lloyd. Screenplay by Talbot Jennings, Jules Furthman and Carey Wilson, based on the novel by Charles Nordhoff and James Norman Hall. Photographed by Arthur Edeson. Music by Herbert Stothart. 132 minutes.

Starring Clark Gable, Charles Laughton, Franchot Tone, Dudley Digges, DeWitt Jennings, Movita, Mamo, Herbert Mundin, Eddie Quillan, Donald Crisp, Henry Stephenson.

MY FAIR LADY (USA)

Awards (3)

Best Film	American Academy Award, 1964
Best Film	New York Critics, 1964
Best Film, Any Source	British Academy Award, 1965

Straightforward adaptation of Lerner and Loewe's musical version of 'Pygmalion' with Rex Harrison repeating his stage success as Professor Higgins and Audrey Hepburn replacing Julie Andrews as Eliza Doolittle, the cockney flower girl he turns into a well-spoken lady of society. A built-in award winner before a camera turned on the Burbank lot although, in view of the conventional and somewhat uninspired treatment, a rather lucky one. Harrison and the lyrics just see it through.

A Warner Bros. Picture, directed by George Cukor. Screenplay by Alan Jay Lerner, based on the musical by Lerner and Frederick Loewe. Photographed in Technicolor and Super Panavision 70 by Harry Stradling. Music and Lyrics by Alan Jay Lerner and Frederick Loewe. Production Design by Cecil Beaton. 170 minutes.

Starring Audrey Hepburn, Rex Harrison, Stanley Holloway, Wilfrid Hyde-White, Gladys Cooper, Jeremy Brett, Theodore Bikel, Mona Washbourne.

Note: My Fair Lady was not released in Britain until 1965.

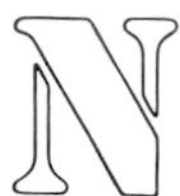

NASHVILLE (USA)

Awards (2)

Best Film	New York Critics, 1975
Best English Language Film	National Board of Review, 1975

Epic Robert Altman movie centering on twenty-four Nashville residents and visitors during the preparations for a concert being held in the city to aid the campaign of a leading presidential candidate. No story, just a series of soft, despairing impressions of modern American life in 'The Country Music Capital of the World.' A standout performance by Ronee Blakley as a singer driven first to a nervous breakdown, then to a violent death.

An American Broadcasting Companies Production for Paramount, directed by Robert Altman. Screenplay by Joan Tewkesbury. Photograhed in colour (MGM Film Laboratories) and Panavision by Paul Lohmann. Music arranged by Richard Baskin. 161 minutes.

Starring David Arkin, Barbara Baxley, Ned Beatty, Karen Black, Ronee Blakley, Timothy Brown, Keith Carradine, Geraldine Chaplin, Robert Doqui, Shelley Duvall, Allen Garfield, Henry Gibson, Scott Glenn, Jeff Goldblum, Barbara Harris, David Hayward, Michael Murphy, Allan Nicholls, Dave Peel, Christina Raines, Bert Remsen, Lily Tomlin, Gwen Welles, Keenan Wynn.

Note: Nashville shared the award of the National Board of Review with Stanley Kubrick's *Barry Lyndon.*

NIGHT MUST FALL (USA)

Awards (1)

Best American Film	National Board of Review, 1937

Robert Montgomery as an innocent-looking young waiter who spends his out-of-work hours hacking women to pieces with an axe and keeping their heads in hat boxes. Hypochondriac invalid Dame May Whitty is one of his victims; Rosalind Russell a lucky survivor. An ugly psychological shocker from the stage play by Emlyn Williams, voted best of 1937 ahead of *The Life Of Emile Zola* by the National Board of Review.

A Metro-Goldwyn-Mayer Picture, directed by Richard Thorpe. Screenplay by John Van Druten, based on the play by Emlyn Williams. Photographed by Ray June. Music by Edward Ward. 117 minutes.

Starring Robert Montgomery, Rosalind Russell, Dame May Whitty, Alan Marshal, Merle Tottenham, Kathleen Harrison, Matthew Boulton.

THE NIGHTS OF CABIRIA (Italy/France)

Awards (1)
Best Foreign Language Film American Academy Award, 1957

Giulietta Masina as a happy-go-lucky prostitute forever suffering setbacks in life but always searching for the dream man she is sure is just around the corner. The smiling innocence of Masina lights up a moving Fellini film that was the second in his quartet of Oscar winners. The others: *La Strada, 8½* and *Amarcord*. The Shirley MacLaine musical *Sweet Charity* was based on *The Nights Of Cabiria*.

A Dino de Laurentiis/Films Marceau Production, directed by Federico Fellini. Screenplay by Federico Fellini, Ennio Flaiano and Tullio Pinelli. Photographed by Aldo Tonti. Music by Nino Rota. 110 minutes.

Starring Giulietta Masina, François Perier, Amadeo Nazzari, Franca Marzi, Dorian Gray, Aldo Silvana, Mario Passante, Pina Gualandri.

NINE DAYS OF ONE YEAR (USSR)

Awards (1)
Grand Prix Karlovy Vary, 1962

Nine key days in the life of a young thermo-nuclear physicist who is severely injured when he is exposed to radiation but carries on with his work despite the risk to his health and marriage. Sombre, over-talkative but minus the usual flag-waving excesses and refreshing in its probes into the conflict of ideas and man and woman relationships.

A Mosfilm Production, directed by Mikhail Romm. Screenplay by Mikhail Romm and Daniel Chrabrovicky. Photographed by German Lavrov. Music by D. Ter-Tatevosyan. 107 minutes.

Starring Aleksei Batalov, Innokenti Smoktunovsky, Tatiana Lavrova, Nikolai Plotnikov.

NONE BUT THE LONELY HEART (USA)

Awards (1)
Best English Language Film National Board of Review, 1944

An interesting experiment from the imaginative RKO lot of the mid-forties with Cary Grant as a young cockney tramp who struggles to find a more noble life in London's East End slums just prior to World War II. Ethel Barrymore as Grant's poverty-stricken mother dying of cancer earned a supporting actress Oscar; the film itself the accolade of the National Board of Review as the best of 1944.

An RKO-Radio Picture, directed by Clifford Odets. Screenplay by Clifford Odets, based on the novel by Richard Llewellyn. Photographed by George Barnes. Music by Hans Eisler. 113 minutes.

Starring Cary Grant, Ethel Barrymore, Jane Wyatt, June Duprez, Barry Fitzgerald, George Coulouris, Roman Bohnen, Konstantin Shayne, Dan Duryea.

LA NOTTE (Italy/France)

Awards (1)
Golden Bear Berlin, 1961

Bleak Antonioni portrait of a rich young Milanese couple (Jeanne Moreau and Marcello Mastroianni) who are observed in the final stages of their disintegrating marriage. A slow, literary, depressing work, concentrated into just twenty-four hours; received rather restlessly by the Berlin audience who were expecting something more akin to *La Dolce Vita*. The jury, however, found it to their liking.

Nepi Film/Silva Film (Rome)/Sofitedip (Paris). Directed by Michelangelo Antonioni. Story and screenplay by Michelangelo Antonioni, Ennio Flajano and Tonino Guerra. Photographed by Gianni Di Venanzo. Music by Giorgio Gaslini. 120 minutes.

Starring Jeanne Moreau, Marcello Mastroianni, Monica Vitti, Bernhard Wicki, Rosi Mazzacurati, Maria Pia Luzi, Vincenzo Corbella.

THE NUN'S STORY (USA)

Awards (1)
Best American Film National Board of Review, 1959

The spiritual struggles of a young Belgian nun (Audrey Hepburn) whose desire to nurse the sick and learn more about medicine conflicts with the grim discipline of her religious order. A Hollywood rarity – a religious film that is both tasteful and sincere. In a vintage year the National Board of Review named it best picture ahead of *Ben-Hur, Anatomy Of A Murder, The Diary Of Anne Frank, Some Like It Hot* and *North By Northwest*.

A Warner Bros. Picture, directed by Fred Zinnemann. Screenplay by Robert Anderson, based on a book by Kathryn C. Hulme. Photographed in Technicolor by Franz Planer. Music by Franz Waxman. 151 minutes.

Starring Audrey Hepburn, Peter Finch, Edith Evans, Peggy Ashcroft, Dean Jagger, Mildred Dunnock, Niall MacGinnis, Patricia Collinge, Eva Kotthaus.

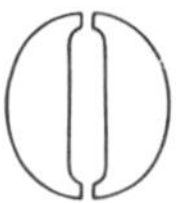

OKLAHOMA CRUDE (USA)

Awards (1)
Grand Prix — Moscow, 1973

The only American movie to win first prize at the Moscow festival, a cynical tale of the Oklahoma oilfields of 1913 with small-time prospectors Faye Dunaway, George C. Scott and John Mills battling to run a wildcat oil rig against the opposition of ruthless capitalists. A parable of human greed that greatly appealed to the Moscow jury who adjudged it, along with the Bulgarian *Affection* and *That Sweet Word Liberty*, as best of the 1973 festival. The most convincing of Stanley Kramer's recent films despite the curious casting of John Mills as an ageing, footloose opportunist who, somewhere along the way, fathered Faye Dunaway!

A Columbia Picture, directed by Stanley Kramer. Screenplay by Marc Norman. Photographed in Technicolor and Panavision by Robert Surtees. Music by Henry Mancini. 111 minutes.

Starring George C. Scott, Faye Dunaway, John Mills, Jack Palance, William Lucking, Harvey Jason, Ted Gehring, Cliff Osmond.

THE OLD MAN AND THE SEA (USA)

Awards (1)
Best American Film — National Board of Review, 1958

Hemingway parable about an aged Cuban fisherman who catches his first fish for three months — a huge marlin — then has to watch as the sharks strip it clean on his journey back to shore. Spencer Tracy stars as Hemingway's lone hero, speaking many of the author's lines off screen during the long scenes at sea. The film was named best of the year by the National Board of Review who thought it worked. Most other critics didn't.

A Warner Bros. Picture, directed by John Sturges. Screenplay by Peter Viertel, based on the novel by Ernest Hemingway. Photographed in WarnerColor by James Wong Howe. Additional photography by Floyd Crosby and Tom Tutwiler. Music by Dimitri Tiomkin. 86 minutes.

Starring Spencer Tracy, Felipe Pazes, Harry Bellaver, Donald Diamond, Don Blackman, Joey Ray, Richard Alameda, Tony Rosa.

OLE DOLE DOFF (Sweden)

Awards (1)
Golden Bear — Berlin, 1968

Uncompromising portrait of a Swedish schoolmaster (Per Oscarsson) whose mind is on the brink of collapse and who is unable to maintain discipline among his pupils. Authentic classroom scenes (filmed by Jan Troell in his home town of Malmo) and a brilliant use of the soundtrack emphasise the desk-slamming nightmare of the teacher's day. The third Swedish success at the Berlin festival (see also *One Summer Of Happiness* and *Wild Strawberries*).

A Svensk Filmindustri Production, directed by Jan Troell. Screenplay by Claes Engström, Bengt Forslund and Jan Troell, based on the novel *On Sjunker* by Engström. Photographed and edited by Jan Troell. Music by Erik Nordgren. 110 minutes.

Starring Per Oscarsson, Kerstin Tidelius, Ann-Marie Gyllenspetz, Bengt Ekerot, Harriet Forssell, Per Sjöstrand, Georg Oddner, Catharina Edfeldt, Bo Malmqvist.

OLIVER! (Britain)

Awards (1)
Best Film — American Academy Award, 1968

Lavish production of Lionel Bart's stage musical with Ron Moody (Fagin) teaching his young charges to 'Pick A Pocket Or Two', Mark Lester as the orphan boy who falls into his clutches and Oliver Reed as burglar Bill Sikes. One of four musical Oscar winners of the sixties (*West Side Story, My Fair Lady, The Sound Of Music* were the others) but the last of its genre to win an Academy Award. No musical has won since.

Warwick Film Productions-Romulus Films (released by Columbia). Directed by Carol Reed. Screenplay by Vernon Harris, based on Lionel Bart's stage musical and Charles Dickens' novel, *Oliver Twist*. Photographed in Technicolor and Panavision by Oswald Morris. Art Direction by Terence Marsh. Music, Lyrics and Book by Lionel Bart. 153 minutes.

Starring Ron Moody, Shani Wallis, Oliver Reed, Harry Secombe, Mark Lester, Jack Wild, Hugh Griffith, Joseph O'Connor, Peggy Mount, Leonard Rossiter.

OLYMPIA (Germany)

Awards (1)
Mussolini Cup — Venice, 1938

Leni Riefenstahl's record of the 1936 Berlin Olympics; remarkable as a poetic monument to sport, frightening in its observations of the mood of hysterical nationalism in which the games were conducted. The picture was the last to win the Mussolini Cup at the pre-war Venice

Festival. British and American delegations expressed anger that the prize had been presented to a film that glorified the Nazi regime as much as sport. Britain participated at Venice the following year, the United States not until after World War II.

Leni Riefenstahl/Tobis-Filmkunst. Produced, directed and edited by Leni Riefenstahl. Photographed by Hans Ertl, Walter Frentz, Guzzi Lantschner, Kurt Neubert, Hans Scheib, Willy Zielke and others. Music by Herbert Windt. 220 minutes.

ONE FLEW OVER THE CUCKOO'S NEST (USA)

Awards (2)

Best Film	American Academy Award, 1975
Best Film	British Academy Award, 1976

Misfit prisoner Jack Nicholson inspires the patients of a mental hospital to rise up against the tyranny of nurse Louise Fletcher but is himself finally defeated by 'the system.' Harrowing stuff at the final count but for the most part wildly comic and accomplished enough to become the first movie to win all four major Oscars — best film, actor, actress, director — since *It Happened One Night*. The New York Critics opted for *Nashville*; the National Board of Review divided the best picture honours between *Nashville* and Kubrick's *Barry Lyndon*.

A Fantasy Films Production (released by United Artists), directed by Milos Forman. Screenplay by Lawrence Hauben and Bo Goldman, based on the novel by Ken Kesey. Photographed in De Luxe Color by Haskell Wexler. Additional photography by Bill Butler and William A. Fraker. Music by Jack Nitzsche. 134 minutes.

Starring Jack Nicholson, Louise Fletcher, William Redfield, Will Sampson, Brad Dourif, Sydney Lassick, Christopher Lloyd, Danny De Vito.

Note: One Flew Over The Cuckoo's Nest was not released in Britain until 1976.

ONE SUMMER OF HAPPINESS (Sweden)

Awards (1)

Golden Bear	Berlin, 1952

Swedish film of the early fifties about a young country girl who enjoys a brief summer of happiness with her student lover before meeting her death in a motor cycle accident. A variation of the Romeo and Juliet theme that examines the conflict between a strict, narrow-minded church community and a younger generation seeking to break free from old fashioned values. Set in rural Sweden and the first of three Swedish winners of the Berlin Golden Bear (see also *Wild Strawberries* and *Ole Dole Doff*).

A Nordisk Tonefilm Production, directed by Arne Mattsson. Screenplay by W. Semitjov, based on the novel by Per Olof Ekström. Photographed by Göran Strindberg. Music by Sven Sköld. 93 minutes.

Starring Folke Sundquist, Ulla Jacobsson, Edvin Adolphson, Irma Christenson, Gösta Gustavsson, Berta Hall, John Elfström, Erik Hell, Nils Hallberg.

Note: One Summer Of Happiness was first shown in Sweden in 1951.

ON THE WATERFRONT (USA)

Awards (3)

Best Film	American Academy Award, 1954
Best Film	New York Critics, 1954
Best American Film	National Board of Review, 1954

Corruption and racketeering on New York's waterfront with Marlon Brando as a punch-drunk ex-boxer who takes up the cause of the longshoremen and destroys the stranglehold of the scab union bosses led by Lee J. Cobb. Sheer dynamite as a film and the first to be named best of the year by all three major American Award organizations. Only five other movies have achieved the distinction; *Marty, Around The World In 80 Days, The Bridge On The River Kwai, Tom Jones* and *A Man For All Seasons.*

A Horizon Picture (released by Columbia), directed by Elia Kazan. Story and screenplay by Budd Schulberg. Photographed by Boris Kaufman. Music by Leonard Bernstein. 107 minutes.

Starring Marlon Brando, Rod Steiger, Karl Malden, Lee J. Cobb, Eva Marie Saint, Leif Erickson, Pat Henning, James Westerfield.

OPEN CITY (Italy)

Awards (1)

Best Foreign Language Film	New York Critics, 1946

Rossellini's first international success, a newsreel-type account of the Italian Resistance in Rome during the Nazi occupation, shot partly with concealed cameras while the German army was still in the city. A defiant protest against Fascism, played by both non-professional and professional actors. Among the latter: Aldo Fabrizi as a priest who dies for his beliefs and Anna Magnani as a fierce widow who is shot down in the streets by the Germans.

Excelsa Film. Directed by Roberto Rossellini. Screenplay by Sergio Amidei, Federico Fellini and Roberto Rossellini, from a story by Sergio Amidei and Alberto Consiglio. Photographed by Ubaldo Arata. Music by Renzo Rossellini. 100 minutes.

Starring Anna Magnani, Aldo Fabrizi, Marcello Pagliero, Maria Michi, Harry Feist, Francesco Grandjacquet, Giovanna Galletti, Vito Annichiarico.

Note: Open City (known also as *Rome, Open City*) was first shown in Italy in 1945. It was one of eleven films to share the collective best picture award at Cannes in 1946.

ORDET (Denmark)

Awards (2)

Golden Lion	Venice, 1955
Best Foreign Film	National Board of Review, 1957

The only Carl Dreyer film to achieve success at a major European festival; a profound study of spiritual faith centering on the death in childbirth of a village girl and her miraculous resurrection by a young farmer. The Venice award of 1955 was presented 'for the work and artistic life of Carl Dreyer, associated with the showing of *Ordet*.'

A Palladium Film Production. Written and directed by Carl Dreyer, based on the play by Kaj Munk. Photographed by Henning Bendtsen. Music by Poul Schierbeck. 126 minutes.

Starring Henrik Malberg, Emil Hass Christensen, Preben Lerdorff Rye, Cay Kristiansen, Birgitte Federspiel, Ejner Federspiel.

OTHELLO (Morocco)

Awards (1)

Grand Prix	Cannes, 1952

Shakespeare's tragedy of the noble Moor who loved not wisely but too well, revamped in exciting fashion by Orson Welles who filmed the play on a shoestring budget in Venice, Rome and the old Arab citadels of French Morocco. The film was adjudged co-winner of the 1952 Cannes Festival (see also *Two Pennyworth Of Hope*) and, apart from *Citizen Kane*, remains the only Welles production to be honoured with a major award. The murder of Roderigo was staged in a turkish bath because the costumes had failed to turn up from Rome!

A Mercury Production, released by Films Marceau and United Artists. Directed by Orson Welles. Script by Orson Welles, from the play by William Shakespeare. Photographed by Anchise Brizzi, G. R. Aldo, George Fanto, with Obadan Troiani and Roberto Fusi. Art Direction by Alexander Trauner. Music by Francesco Lavagnino and Alberto Barberis. 91 minutes.

Starring Orson Welles, Michael MacLiammoir, Suzanne Cloutier, Robert Coote, Hilton Edwards, Michael Lawrence, Fay Compton, Nicholas Bruce, Jean Davis, Doris Dowling.

THE OX-BOW INCIDENT (USA)

Awards (1)

Best English Language Film	National Board of Review, 1943

Mob hysteria examined in chilling fashion in a western drama of Nevada in the 1880s where three cowboys are lynched for a murder they did not commit. Dana Andrews, Anthony Quinn and Francis Ford play the three victims, Henry Fonda a helpless onlooker unable to prevent the execution. The National Board of Review placed the film top of its ten best list of 1943, in retrospect something of an inspired decision. Oscar-winner *Casablanca* was placed sixth.

A Twentieth Century-Fox Picture, directed by William A. Wellman. Screenplay by Lamar Trotti, based on the novel by Walter Van Tilburg Clark. Photographed by Arthur Miller. Music by Cyril J. Mockridge. 75 minutes.

Starring Henry Fonda, Dana Andrews, Mary Beth Hughes, Anthony Quinn, William Eythe, Henry Morgan, Jane Darwell, Francis Ford, Victor Kilian, Matt Briggs, Harry Davenport, Marc Lawrence.

PADRE, PADRONE (Italy)

Awards (1)

Golden Palm	Cannes, 1977

The true story of a six-year-old Sardinian boy who is compelled by his patriarchal father to sacrifice his childhood and adolescence for a lonely life as a sheepherder in the high country. The boy's mental tortures during his extended solitude and his final escape and transformation into a man of letters are recalled in a manner that owes much to the post-war neo-realist traditions of De Sica and Rossellini. The film was originally made for TV and was the surprise winner at Cannes in 1977.

RAI-Radiotelevisione Italiana. Directed by Paolo Taviani and Vittorio Taviani. Screenplay by Paolo Taviani and Vittorio Taviani, based on the autobiographical novel by Gavino Ledda. Photographed in Eastman Color by Mario Masini. Music by Egisto Macchi. 113 minutes.

Starring Omero Antonutti, Saverio Marconi, Marcella Michelangeli, Fabrizio Forte, Marino Cenna, Nanni Moretti, Stanko Molnar.

PAISA (Italy)

Awards (2)

Best Foreign Language Film	New York Critics, 1948
Best Film	National Board of Review, 1948

Six separate episodes concerning the Americans in Italy during the invasion of Sicily and the Italian mainland in World War II. The film was the second of Rossellini's two pictures about the impact of the war on Italian life; it was shot against real backgrounds (including the newly liberated Naples), performed mostly by non-professionals and, together with *Open City*, helped introduce neo-realism to post-war audiences.

OFI/Foreign Film Production, Inc./Capitani Film. Directed by Roberto Rossellini. Screenplay by Federico Fellini and Roberto Rossellini, based on stories by Victor Haines, Marcello Pagliero, Sergio Amidei, Federico Fellini, Roberto Rossellini and (uncredited) Vasco Pratolini. Photographed by Otello Martelli. Music by Renzo Rossellini. 124 minutes.

Starring Carmela Sazio, Robert Vanloon, Dots M. Johnson, Alfonsini, Maria Michi, Gar Moore, Harriet White, Renzo Avanzo, Bill Tubbs. Dale Edmunds, Cigolani.

Note: Paisa (known also as *Paisan*) was premiered in Italy in 1946. It was one of nine films to earn a collective international prize at Venice.

PALERMO OR WOLFSBURG (West Germany)

Awards (1)

Golden Bear	Berlin, 1980

The bitter experiences of a young Sicilian factory worker as he tries to come to terms with life in a remote German industrial town near the East German border. Described by one critic as 'an essay in operatic neo realism', the film follows the worker from his life in a poverty-stricken Sicily to his murder trial in a German court. It shared the 1980 Berlin prize with *Heartland* and was the third West German success in the 1979/80 period (see also *David* and *The Tin Drum*).

A Thomas Mauch Film Production, Berlin. Written and directed by Werner Schroeter. Photographed in colour by Thomas Mauch. Edited by Werner Schroeter. 180 minutes.

Starring Nicola Zarbo, Calogero Arancio, Padre Pace, Cavaliere Comparato, Brigitte Tilg, Gisela Hahn, Antonio Orlando.

LE PASSAGE DU RHIN (France/Italy/West Germany)

Awards (1)

Golden Lion	Venice, 1960

The fortunes of two prisoners-of-war — one a journalist (Georges Rivière) who escapes to become a Resistance hero, the other a simple baker (Charles Aznavour) who serves out his time and settles down happily with a German girl after the conflict. The picture raises some important questions about the motives and principles of people in wartime and marked the only occasion that a director had won two Golden Lions at Venice. André Cayatte's previous award was for *Justice Est Faite* made ten years earlier.

Franco London Film-Gibé-Jonia Film-UFA. Directed by André Cayatte. Screenplay by André Cayatte and Armand Jammot. Adaptation by André Cayatte and Pascal Jardin. Dialogue by Maurice Aubergé. Photographed by Roger Fellous. Music by Louiguy. 124 minutes.

Starring Charles Aznavour, Nicole Courcel, Georges Rivière, Cordula Trantow, Betty Schneider, Georges Chamarat, Alfred Schieske.

PATHER PANCHALI (India)

Awards (1)

Best Foreign Film	National Board of Review, 1958

Study of a poor Indian scholar and his family suffering the hardships of everyday existence in a small Bengali village. The film, the first in a trilogy, earned critical recognition at Cannes in 1956 and brought the Indian cinema and director Satyajit Ray to world prominence. Two years after its Cannes showing it was released in America and named best foreign film by the National Board of Review. See also: *Aparajito* and *The World Of Apu*.

Government of West Bengal, written and directed by Satyajit Ray. Based on the novel by Bidhutibhustan Bandapadhaya. Photographed by Subrata Mitra. Music by Ravi Shankar. 115 minutes.

Starring Kanu Banerjee, Karuna Banerjee, Subir Banerjee, Uma Das Gupta, Chunibala Devi.

PATTON (USA)

Awards (2)

Best Film	American Academy Award, 1970
Best English Language Film	National Board of Review, 1970

The final years (1943-45) in the turbulent career of General George S. Patton (George C. Scott), one of the most outspoken and controversial American commanders of World War II. The film was something of a watershed in American movie history in that it marked the first occasion that a biographical picture was crafted with imagination and a perceptive understanding of its subject. The New York Critics named Scott best actor but favoured *Five Easy Pieces* as top film.

A Twentieth Century-Fox Picture, directed by Franklin J. Schaffner. Screenplay by Francis Ford Coppola and Edmund H. North, based on material from the books *Patton: Ordeal And Triumph* by Ladislas Farago and *A Soldier's Story* by Omar N. Bradley. Photographed in De Luxe Color and Dimension 150 by Fred Koenekamp. Music by Jerry Goldsmith. 171 minutes.

Starring George C. Scott, Karl Malden, Michael Bates, Stephen Young, Michael Strong, Cary Loftin, Albert Dumortier, Frank Latimore.

PEPE-LE-MOKO (France)

Awards (1)

Best Foreign Film	National Board of Review, 1941

Jean Gabin as one of the most famous criminals in movie history, a French thief who finds temporary safety from the police in the Algerian Casbah but is eventually lured to his doom by his love for a beautiful woman. The film established Gabin as an international star and was named by the National Board of Review as best foreign picture of 1941 — the year of its American release.

Paris Film Productions, directed by Julien Duvivier. Screenplay by Julien Duvivier and Henri Jeanson, based on the detective novel by Roger Ashelbé. Photographed by J. Kruger and M. Fossard. Music by Vincent Scotto and Mohamed Yguerbuchen. 90 minutes.

Starring Jean Gabin, Mireille Balin, Gabriel Gabrio, Lucas Gridoux, Marcel Dalio, Saturnin Fabre, Charpin.

Note: Pepe-Le-Moko was first released in France in 1937.

A PLACE IN THE SUN (USA)

Awards (1)

Best American Film	National Board of Review, 1951

Young factory worker Montgomery Clift finds himself hopelessly trapped — with murder as the only solution — between the working class girl (Shelley Winters) he has made pregnant and the society beauty

(Elizabeth Taylor) whose luxury world he craves. Stylish updating of Theodore Dreiser's book *An American Tragedy*, voted best of 1951 by the National Board of Review in a year when the American awards were split three ways — the Oscar going to *An American In Paris* and the New York Critics prize to *A Streetcar Named Desire*.

A Paramount Picture, directed by George Stevens. Screenplay by Michael Wilson and Harry Brown, based on the novel by Theodore Dreiser. Photographed by William C. Mellor. Music by Franz Waxman. 122 minutes.

Starring Montgomery Clift, Elizabeth Taylor, Shelley Winters, Anne Revere, Raymond Burr, Herbert Heyes, Keefe Brasselle.

THE PRISONER (Britain)

Awards (1)

Best Foreign Film	National Board of Review, 1955

Alec Guinness as an East European cardinal (formerly a resistance leader during the enemy occupation) who is brainwashed into a confession of treason because he is a menace to the new regime. Adapted by Bridget Boland from her stage play about the clash of church and state in the shadow of modern dictatorship and loosely based on the real life case of Cardinal Mindszenty. Jack Hawkins as the state interrogator matches Guinness scene for scene.

A Columbia Picture, directed by Peter Glenville. Screenplay by Bridget Boland, based on her play. Photographed by Reg Wyer. Music by Benjamin Frankel. 94 minutes.

Starring Alec Guinness, Jack Hawkins, Wilfrid Lawson, Kenneth Griffith, Jeanette Sterke, Ronald Lewis, Raymond Huntley.

THE PROMISED LAND (Poland)

Awards (1)

Grand Prix	Moscow, 1975

Social unrest in late nineteenth century Poland observed by Andrezj Wajda in a turbulent saga of business corruption and worker revolt in the factory town of Lodz. Epic in proportion, baroque and flamboyant in style; adapted from the prophetic novel by Wladyslaw Reymont. Together with *Dersu Uzala* and *Those Were The Years*, the joint winner of the 1975 Moscow Festival.

A Film Polski Release of X Film Unit Production, directed by Andrezj Wajda. Screenplay by Andrezj Wajda, based on the novel by Wladyslaw Reymont. Photographed in Eastman Color by Witold Sobociński, Edward Klosiński and Waclaw Dybowski. Music by Wojiech Kilar. 165 minutes.

Starring Daniel Ollbrychski, Wojciech Pszoniak, Andrej Seweryn, Anna Nehrebecka.

Note: This picture is also known under the title *Land Of Promise*.

QUAI DES BRUMES (France)

Awards (1)
Best Foreign Film — National Board of Review, 1939

Disillusioned army deserter Jean Gabin wanders the port of Le Havre searching for a ship to take him to South America but becomes involved instead with a lovely raincoated waif (Michèle Morgan) and the gangsters ultimately responsible for his death. A sordid tale, perfectly evoking the pessimism of the French cinema of the late thirties and given a melancholy beauty by Schuftan's lensing of drab misty factories, docks and working class streets.

A Gregor Rabinovitch Production, directed by Marcel Carné. Screenplay by Jacques Prévert, based on the novel by Pierre MacOrlan. Photographed by Eugène Schuftan. Art Direction by Alexandre Trauner. Music by Maurice Jaubert. 89 minutes.

Starring Jean Gabin, Michel Simon, Michèle Morgan, Aimos, René Génin, Pierre Brasseur.

Note: Quai Des Brumes (known also as *Port Of Shadows*) was first released in France in 1938.

LES QUATRE CENTS COUPS (France)

Awards (1)
Best Foreign Language Film — New York Critics, 1959

The film that brought François Truffaut international fame, derived from his memories of life in a reform school and following the experiences of a twelve-year-old boy (Jean-Pierre Léaud) as he wanders across Paris to escape from his preoccupied parents and the dismal school that represses him. Truffaut, who received the director's prize at the 1959 Cannes Festival, has since followed the life of the same boy in early manhood in a series of films that includes *Love At Twenty* (62), *Stolen Kisses* (68), *Bed And Board* (70) and *Love On The Run* (79).

Les Films du Carrosse/SEDIF. Written and directed by François Truffaut. Photographed in Dyaliscope by Henri Decaë. Music by Jean Constantin. 94 minutes.

Starring Jean-Pierre Léaud, Albert Rémy, Claire Maurier, Patrick Auffay, Georges Flamant, Yvonne Claudie, Robert Beauvais.

A QUEEN IS CROWNED (Britain)

Awards (1)
Best Foreign Film — National Board of Review, 1953

Feature colour documentary of the Coronation of Elizabeth II including scenes of the ceremony in Westminster Abbey and the pageantry in the rain-filled streets of London. Christopher Fry's narration was spoken by Laurence Olivier, the film released just seventy-two hours after the event – and also seventy-two hours after the whole thing had been covered live on British TV.

A J. Arthur Rank Production, produced by Castleton Knight. Narration written by Christopher Fry and spoken by Laurence Olivier. Photographed in Technicolor. Music by Guy Warrack. Musical Adviser: Malcolm Sargent. 89 minutes.

QUESTION 7 (USA/West Germany)

Awards (1)
Best American Film — National Board of Review, 1961

A Lutheran minister, sent from West Germany to become the pastor of a small East German town, finds that he cannot come to terms with the Communist doctrine and, together with his student son, finishes in open conflict with the authorities. Based on actual events and filmed in semi-documentary style by Stuart Rosenberg whose first solo screen credit this was. The National Board of Review voted the picture best of the year ahead of *The Hustler* and *West Side Story*.

Louis de Rochemont Associates-Lutheran Film Associates – Luther Film. Directed by Stuart Rosenberg. Screenplay by Allan Sloane. Photographed by Günter Senftleben. Music by Hans-Martin Majewski. 107 minutes.

Starring Michael Gwynn, Margaret Jahnen, Christian de Bresson, Almut Eggert, Erik Schuman, Max Buchsbaum, John Ruddock.

QUIET FLOWS THE DON (USSR)

Awards (1)
Grand Prix — Karlovy Vary, 1958

The third part of Gerasimov's trilogy about a passionate young Cossack living in Russia in the turbulent years leading up to the Revolution. The three films (totalling six hours) follow the Cossack from youth to early middle age when he loses the woman he loves and becomes disillusioned with everything he ever fought for. Part three of the trilogy (120 minutes) shared the Karlovy Vary prize with Japan's *The Stepbrothers*.

A Gorki Film Production, directed by Sergei Gerasimov. Screenplay by Sergei Gerasimov, based on the novel by Michal Sholokhov. Photographed in Sovcolor by Vladimir Rapoport. Music by Yuri Levitin. 120 minutes.

Starring Peter Glebov, Elina Bystricka, Zinaida Kiriyenkova, Daniel Ilchenko, A. Filippova.

THE QUIET MAN (USA)

Awards (1)
Best American Film National Board of Review, 1952

John Ford in 'never-never Ireland' with ex-prizefighter John Wayne returning to his native Galway to court fiery redhead Maureen O'Hara and defeat her bullying brother Victor McLaglen. Very much a director's home movie and a little fortunate to achieve best picture success in a year which also saw *High Noon, Limelight, Five Fingers, The Bad And The Beautiful* and *Singin' In The Rain* in the top ten list of the National Board of Review. Oscars to Ford and cameramen Winton C. Hoch and Archie Stout for their colourwork.

Argosy Pictures/Republic. Directed by John Ford. Screenplay by Frank S. Nugent, based on a story by Maurice Walsh. Photographed in Technicolor by Winton C. Hoch and Archie Stout. Music by Victor Young. 129 minutes.

Starring John Wayne, Maureen O'Hara, Barry Fitzgerald, Ward Bond, Victor McLaglen, Mildred Natwick, Francis Ford, Eileen Crowe, May Craig, Arthur Shields.

A RACE FOR LIFE (France)

Awards (1)

Grand Prix	Karlovy Vary, 1956

A race against time to get a serum to a French trawler whose crew members are slowly dying from the deadly disease of botulism. Awarded first prize at Karlovy Vary primarily because of its argument that international brotherhood — symbolised by the co-operative efforts of dedicated radio amateurs all over the world — is preferable to the useless fetters of international officialdom. A point well worth making.

Ariane/Filmsonor/Francinex. Directed by Christian-Jaque. Screenplay by Jacques Remy. Adaptation by Henri-Georges Clouzot, Jean Ferry and Christian-Jaque. Photographed by Armand Thirard. Music by Georges Van Parys. 110 minutes.

Starring André Valmy, Jean Gaven, Doudou-Babet, Marc Cassot, Hélène Perdière.

RASHOMON (Japan)

Awards (3)

Golden Lion	Venice, 1951
Best Foreign Language Film	American Academy Award, 1951
Best Foreign Film	National Board of Review, 1951

Four versions of the murder of a nobleman and the rape of his wife in eighth century Japan. The murder is recalled by a woodcutter, the dead nobleman (whose thoughts are reflected through a medium representing the dead man's spirit), his wife, and the bandit who supposedly committed the crime. Each version of the story is distorted and the complete truth is never uncovered. The film awakened post-war audiences to the potential of the Japanese cinema and was based on two stories by Ryunosuke Akutagawa, one of the foremost names in modern Japanese literature.

Daiei (Jingo Minoru/Masaichi Nagata). Directed by Akira Kurosawa. Screenplay by Shinobu Hashimoto and Akira Kurosawa, based on stories by Ryunosuke Akutagawa. Photographed by Kazuo Miyagawa. Music by Fumio Hayasaka. 88 minutes.

Starring Toshiro Mifune, Masayuki Mori, Takashi Shimura, Machiko Kyo, Minoru Chiaki.

DIE RATTEN (West Germany)

Awards (1)
Golden Bear — Berlin, 1955

A homeless girl from Germany's Soviet Zone gives her newly-born baby to a woman who has long been wanting a child. Her reward is a fake passport to West Berlin; the reward for the childless woman is a chance to retain her husband's love. A Golden Bear winner at Berlin but grim, depressing stuff that parallels the actions of its characters with the rats of the film's title, shown gnawing ferociously at furniture and other objects. Not nearly as much fun as number three on the public's list, *Carmen Jones*.

A CCC Production, directed by Robert Siodmak. Screenplay by Jochen Huth, based on the stage play by Gerhart Hauptmann. Photographed by Goeran Strindberg. Music by Werner Eisbrenner. 97 minutes.

Starring Curt Jürgens, Maria Schell, Gustav Knuth, Heidemarie Hatheyer, Isle Steppat, Fritz Rémond, Barbara Rost, Lou Seitz.

REBECCA (USA)

Awards (1)
Best Film — American Academy Award, 1940

Timid newly-wed Joan Fontaine gets more than she bargains for when she joins husband Laurence Olivier in his huge Cornish mansion and has to cope with both a new way of life and the spirit of her husband's mysteriously deceased first spouse. Hitchcock's first American movie, a broody, uncharacteristic melodrama, adapted from the novel by Daphne du Maurier. Preferred at Oscar time to Ford's masterwork *The Grapes Of Wrath*.

A David O. Selznick Production (released by United Artists), directed by Alfred Hitchcock. Screenplay by Robert E. Sherwood and Joan Harrison, based on the novel by Daphne du Maurier. Photographed by George Barnes. Music by Franz Waxman. 130 minutes.

Starring Laurence Olivier, Joan Fontaine, George Sanders, Judith Anderson, Nigel Bruce, C. Aubrey Smith, Reginald Denny, Gladys Cooper, Leo G. Carroll.

THE RED DESERT (Italy/France)

Awards (1)
Golden Lion — Venice, 1964

Antonioni study of an acutely depressed married woman (Monica Vitti) whose neurosis stems both from the mental effects of a car accident and her inability to adapt to the pressures of modern industrial society. A prime example of the 'form over content movie' of the early sixties, adjudged best of Venice ahead of Pasolini's *The Gospel According To St. Matthew* which shared the Jury Prize with Kozintsev's Russian *Hamlet*. Antonioni's first film in colour.

Film Duemila/Cinematografica Federiz (Rome)/Francoriz (Paris). Directed by Michelangelo Antonioni. Screenplay by Michelangelo Antonioni and Tonino Guerra. Photographed in Eastman Color by Carlo Di Palma. Music by Giovanni Fusco. 120 minutes.

Starring Monica Vitti, Richard Harris, Carlo Chionetti, Xenia Valderi, Rita Renoir, Aldo Grotti, Valerio Bartoleschi.

RICHARD III (Britain)

Awards (1)

Best Film, Any Source	British Academy Award, 1955

Laurence Olivier as Shakespeare's hunchback Duke of Gloucester who woos, schemes and murders his way to the throne in fifteenth century England. A Who's Who of British Theatre – including the luckless John Gielgud who finishes drowned headfirst in a barrel of wine – aid and abet his rise to power. The third of Olivier's Shakespearean adaptations and preferred by the voters of the British Academy to the American 'sleeper' *Marty* which swept the board in the States and won first prize at Cannes.

A London Films Production (released by British Lion), directed by Laurence Olivier. Text adviser: Alan Dent. Photographed in Technicolor and VistaVision by Otto Heller. Production Design by Roger Furse. Music by William Walton. 161 minutes.

Starring Laurence Olivier, John Gielgud, Ralph Richardson, Claire Bloom, Cedric Hardwicke, Mary Kerridge, Pamela Brown, Alec Clunes, Michael Gough, Stanley Baker, Laurence Naismith.

THE RICKSHAW MAN (Japan)

Awards (1)

Golden Lion	Venice, 1958

The moving tale of a rickshaw man who selflessly devotes his life to the happiness of a young widow and her small son but whose deeply affectionate love for the woman is only revealed after his tragic death. Lovely colour effects and a *tour-de-force* from Toshiro Mifune in the title role. Preferred at Venice to Louis Malle's *Les Amants* which shared the Silver Lion award with Francesco Rosi's *La Sfida*.

A Toho Company Production, directed by Hiroshi Inagaki. Screenplay by Mansaku Itami and Hiroshi Inagaki. Story by Shunsaku Iwashita. Photographed in Agfacolor and Tohoscope by Kazuo Yamada. Music by Ikuma Dan. 104 minutes.

Starring Toshiro Mifune, Hideko Takamine, Hiroshi Akutagawa, Kenji Kasahara, Kaoru Matsumoto, Chishu Ryu.

ROCKY (USA)

Awards (1)
Best Film — American Academy Award, 1976

The surprise Oscar winner of the seventies, a heroic tale of a battered young boxer (Sylvester Stallone) who gets a lucky, million-to-one shot at the heavyweight title and proves to himself that he isn't 'just another bum from the neighbourhood.' Beneath the modern trappings, strictly B picture stuff, enlivened by fine performances from Talia Shire as Rocky's shy girl friend and Burgess Meredith as his trainer. The New York Critics and National Board of Review both opted for *All The President's Men.*

A United Artists Picture, directed by John G. Avildsen. Screenplay by Sylvester Stallone. Photographed in Technicolor (prints by DeLuxe) by James Crabe. Music by Bill Conti. 119 minutes.

Starring Sylvester Stallone, Talia Shire, Burt Young, Carl Weathers, Burgess Meredith, Thayer David, Joe Spinell, Jimmy Gambina.

ROMANCE OF LOVERS (USSR)

Awards (1)
Grand Prix — Karlovy Vary, 1974

Fragile romance about a young girl who marries another man when her lover is reported killed during military service then has to face up to the problems of divided loyalties when he unexpectedly returns. Hollywood usually played this sort of thing for laughs, e.g. *My Favourite Wife* and *Move Over Darling*; Russia opts for drama as the returning soldier cracks up in despair, marries without love and is left remembering his idyllic first romance at a party to celebrate the birth of his child.

A Mosfilm Production, directed by Andrei Mikhalkov-Konchalovsky. Screenplay by Yevgeny Grigoryev. Photographed in Sovcolor and 70mm by Levan Paatashvili. Music by Alexander Gradsky. 129 minutes.

Starring Yevgeny Kindinov, Yalena Koreneva, Innokenti Smoktunovsky, Irina Kupchenko, Yesesaveta Solodva, Iya Saavina.

ROMEO AND JULIET (Britain/Italy)

Awards (2)
Golden Lion — Venice, 1954
Best Foreign Film — National Board of Review, 1954

Elegant screen version of Shakespeare's tragedy about star-cross'd lovers in sixteenth century Italy, photographed against the courtyards, churches, piazzas, palaces and ancient walls of Verona and Venice. A feast for the eye but, in retrospect, something of a surprise winner at the 1954 Venice festival considering the quality of the four films that shared the runner-up award — *Seven Samurai, On The Waterfront, La Strada* and Mizoguchi's *Sansho Dayu.*

A Universalcine-Verona Production. Directed and adapted by Renato Castellani. Photographed in Technicolor by Robert Krasker. Costumes by Leonor Fini. Music by Roman Vlad. 138 minutes.

Starring Laurence Harvey, Susan Shentall, Flora Robson, Mervyn Johns, Bill Travers, Enzo Fiermonte, Aldo Zollo, Sebastian Cabot, Lydia Sherwood, Norman Wooland.

LA RONDE (France)

Awards (1)

Best Film, Any Source — British Academy Award, 1951

Max Ophuls film consisting of a series of episodes about the nature of physical love. The episodes are linked by a cynical Anton Walbrook who presides over a roundabout of love in turn-of-the-century Vienna and introduces the amours of first a soldier and a streetwalker, then the soldier and a housemaid, then the housemaid and the son of the house, and so on until, having ranged from top to bottom in Viennese society, the circle is completed and the film ends with the same soldier hurrying in the direction of the original streetwalker. Sophisticated and near perfect yet only the British Academy recognized its virtues in 1951.

A Sacha Gordine Production, directed by Max Ophuls. Screenplay by Jacques Natanson and Max Ophuls, based on the play *Reigen* by Arthur Schnitzler. Photographed by Christian Matras. Music by Oscar Strauss and Joe Hajos. 97 minutes.

Starring Anton Walbrook, Simone Signoret, Serge Reggiani, Simone Simon, Daniel Gélin, Danielle Darrieux, Fernand Gravey, Odette Joyeux, Jean-Louis Barrault, Isa Miranda, Gérard Philipe.

Note: La Ronde was premiered in Monte Carlo in September, 1950.

ROOM AT THE TOP (Britain)

Awards (1)

Best Film, Any Source — British Academy Award, 1958

Laurence Harvey as a young man on the make who bounces to the top via the seduction of an industrialist's daughter and the suicide of his ageing mistress. Simone Signoret's performance in the latter role earned acclaim the world over although only in Britain did the film earn best picture honours, winning out over the Cannes prize-winner *The Cranes Are Flying* and Ingmar Bergman's Berlin triumph *Wild Strawberries*. Filmed partly on location in Bradford, the movie kicked off the British 'new wave movement' of the late fifties.

A Remus Production, directed by Jack Clayton. Screenplay by Neil Paterson, based on the novel by John Braine. Photographed by Freddie Francis. Music by Mario Nascimbene. 117 minutes.

Starring Laurence Harvey, Simone Signoret, Heather Sears, Donald Wolfit, Ambrosine Philpotts, Donald Houston, Raymond Huntley.

SALT OF THE EARTH (USA)

Awards (1)
Grand Prix — Karlovy Vary, 1954

Much publicised though now rarely seen movie about a real-life strike for better pay and working conditions in a New Mexico zinc mine. The film was written, directed and filmed by technicians blacklisted in Hollywood for refusing to co-operate with the McCarthy witch hunts of the early fifties. It was denounced by American 'patriotic' groups who attempted to stop its distribution, but awarded the Grand Prix at Karlovy Vary where it shared the top prize with *Close Friends*.

An Independent Productions Corporation Picture, directed by Herbert J. Biberman. Screenplay by Michael Wilson. Photographed by Simon Lazarus. Music by Sol Kaplan. 94 minutes.

Starring Rosaura Revueltas, Juan Chacon, Will Geer, David Wolfe, Mervin Williams, David Sarvis, Henrietta Williams.

SAMURAI (Japan)

Awards (1)
Best Foreign Language Film — American Academy Award, 1955

Story of a young villager who leaves home seeking to elevate himself from low-caste to the high ranks of the samurai, powerful warriors who are masters of the sword. Based on the experiences of a legendary figure in seventeenth century Japan and the last film to win an honorary foreign language Oscar. Not to be confused with Kurosawa's more famous *Seven Samurai* which failed to win a prize in any form of competition.

A Kazuo Takimura (Toho Co. Ltd) Production, directed by Hiroshi Inagaki. Screenplay by Tokuhei Wakao and Hiroshi Inagaki. Adapted by Hideji Hojo from the novel by Eiji Yoshikawa. Photographed in Eastman Color by Jun Yasumoto. Music by Ikuma Dan. 92 minutes.

Starring Toshiro Mifune, Kaoru Yachigusa, Rentaro Mikuni, Mariko Okada, Kuroemon Onoe, Mitsuko Mito.

SCARECROW (USA)

Awards (1)
Golden Palm Cannes, 1973

A kind of seventies version of Steinbeck's *Of Mice And Men* with George and Lennie replaced by Max and Lion — the former an ex-jail bird who wants to start his own car-wash business, the latter a drifter who accompanies him on his cross-country journey from California to Pittsburgh. Striking performances by Gene Hackman and Al Pacino and some moody landscapes by cameraman Vilmos Zsigmond but, in the end, just another contemporary 'road' picture from the American new wave. Crosby, Hope and Lamour used to do them better! The film shared the 1973 Cannes prize with *The Hireling*.

A Warner Bros. Picture, directed by Jerry Schatzberg. Story and screenplay by Garry Michael White. Photographed in Technicolor and Panavision by Vilmos Zsigmond. Music by Fred Myrow. 112 minutes.

Starring Gene Hackman, Al Pacino, Dorothy Tristan, Ann Wedgeworth, Richard Lynch, Eileen Brennan, Penny Allen, Richard Hackman.

SEE YOU MONDAY (USSR)

Awards (1)
Grand Prix Moscow, 1969

Soviet school drama, referred to by some critics as a Russian *Up The Down Staircase*; an insight into Soviet school life that skilfully integrates a developing love affair between a young headmistress and a progressive schoolmaster with staff room struggles over new and old established teaching methods. A slow, gentle picture that caused some controversy among Russian educationalists and parents when first released. Co-winner, along with the Cuban *Lucia* and the Italian *Serafino*, of the 1969 Moscow Festival.

A Gorki Studios Production, directed by Stanislav Rostotsky. Screenplay by Georgi Polonsky. 105 minutes.

Starring Irina Pechernikova, Nina Menzhikova, Vyacheslav Tikhonov, Olga Zhizneva.

SERAFINO (France/Italy)

Awards (1)
Grand Prix Moscow, 1969

Tale of a lusty shepherd boy who makes nightly visits to the beds of local village beauties (including his seventeen-year-old cousin and a popular prostitute) before being left a small fortune by his eccentric aunt. Marriage and money hold no attractions for him and he eventually returns to his simple ways as a shepherd in the hills. A rollicking pastoral comedy by Pietro Germi whose fame rested on his work in post-war Italian neo-realism (*The Road To Hope*) and on his satirical comedies of the sixties — *Divorce, Italian Style* and *Seduced And Abandoned.* Co-winner of the 1969 Moscow Film Festival. See also *Lucia* and *See You Monday.*

R.P.A.-Rizzoli Films-Francoriz. Directed by Pietro Germi. Screenplay by Leo Benvenuti, Piero De Bernardi, Tullio Pinelli & Pietro Germi. Photographed in Technicolor by Aiace Parolin. Music by Carlo Rustichelli. 94 minutes.

Starring Adriano Celentano, Ottavia Piccolo, Saro Urzi, Francesca Romana Coluzzi, Benjamin Lev, Nazareno Natale.

SERYOZHA (USSR)

Awards (1)
Grand Prix — Karlovy Vary, 1960

A five-year-old Russian boy, living alone with his mother on a farm, finds that the simple pleasures of childhood are suddenly overshadowed when he has to accept a stepfather into the family. A gentle, psychological insight into the mind of a child; based on a work by Vera Panova, a well-known Soviet writer of children's books who also collaborated on the screenplay. Little known in the West but a prize-winner at Karlovy Vary in 1960.

A Mosfilm Production, directed by G. Danieli and I. Talankin. Screenplay by Vera Panova, G. Danieli and I. Talankin, based on the novel by Panova. Photographed by A. Nitochkin. Music by B. Chaikovsky. 80 minutes.

Starring Boria Barchatov, Sergei Bondarchuk, Irina Skobtseva, Natasha Chechetkina, Seryosha Metelitsin.

SEVEN DAYS IN JANUARY (Spain)

Awards (1)
Grand Prix — Moscow, 1979

Based-on-fact drama about the shooting of four Communist lawyers by right wing militants in Madrid in January, 1977. A part-fiction, part-documentary reconstruction that earned Juan Bardem his second, consecutive win at the Moscow Film Festival (see also *The Long Weekend*). The film shared first prize with the Polish comedy *Camera Buff* and Rosi's *Christ Stopped At Eboli.*

A Goya Films and Les Films des Deux Mondes Production, directed by Juan A. Bardem. Screenplay by Juan A. Bardem and Gregorio Moron. Photographed in Eastman Color by Leopoldo Villasenor. Music by Nicolas Peyrac. 130 minutes.

Starring Manuel Egea Martinez, Fernando Sanchez Pollack, Virginia Gonzalez Mataix, Madeleine Robinson, Jack Francois, Alberto Alonso Lopez.

SHADOWS OF A HOT SUMMER (Czechoslovakia)

Awards (1)
Grand Prix Karlovy Vary, 1978

Harrowing film about a gentle sheep farmer and his family who are terrorized by a group of German soldiers stranded in Eastern Europe after the Second World War. Referred to by some as the Czechoslovakian *Straw Dogs* and, in its final bloodbath, certainly brutal enough to be deserving of the label. Co-winner, along with *White Bim With A Black Ear*, of the 1978 Karlovy Vary festival.

A Czechoslovak, Studio Barrandov, Film Production, Prague. Directed by František Vláčil. Screenplay by Jiři Křižan. Photographed in colour by Ivan Šlapeta. Music by Zdenek Liška. 90 minutes.

Starring Juraj Kukura, Marta Vančurová, Gustáv Valach, Karel Chromik, Zdeněk Kutil, Jiři Bartoška, Augustin Kuban, Gustav Opecensky.

SHAME (Sweden)

Awards (1)
Best Foreign Language Film National Board of Review, 1969

Max von Sydow and Liv Ullmann as two concert violinists whose lives are shattered when the civil war that is ravaging the mainland engulfs the remote island on which they live. A major Bergman work about the degrading effect of war on human existence; voted best of the year by the National Board of Review, narrowly defeated by *War And Peace* in the vote of the New York Critics.

A Svensk Filmindustri Production, directed by Ingmar Bergman. Screenplay by Ingmar Bergman. Photographed by Sven Nykvist. 103 minutes.

Starring Liv Ullmann, Max von Sydow, Gunnar Björnstrand, Sigge Fürst, Birgitta Valberg, Hans Alfredson, Ingvar Kjellson.

Note: Shame first opened in Stockholm in September, 1968.

SHOE-SHINE (Italy)

Awards (1)
Best Foreign Language Film American Academy Award, 1947

Vittorio De Sica movie about two street urchins who work as shoe-shine boys in order to ward off starvation but become involved instead in a black market racket and finish up in the grim Regina Coeli prison. The film spotlighted the plight of hundreds of boys in war-shattered Europe and was shot by De Sica in the streets of Rome. It was the first picture to be awarded a foreign language Oscar.

Alfa Cinematografica (W. Tamburella). Directed by Vittorio De Sica. Screenplay by Cesare Zavattini. Photographed by Anchise Brizzi. Music by Alessandro Cicognini. 90 minutes.

Starring Rinaldo Smordoni, Franco Interlenghi, Aniello Mele, Bruno Ortensi, Claudio Ermelli, Emilio Cigoli, Maria Campi.

Note: Shoe-Shine was first released in Italy in 1946.

THE SHOES OF THE FISHERMAN (USA)

Awards (1)

Best English Language Film	National Board of Review, 1968

Screen version of Morris West's best-seller with Anthony Quinn as the first Russian pope trying to promote world peace, fend off atomic war and save millions from starving in China. Most critics regarded this one as ponderous and uninspired. Not so the National Board of Review who voted it 'best of 68' ahead of *Romeo And Juliet, Yellow Submarine* and *Charly*. The year's Oscar winner, *Oliver!* was placed ninth, Kubrick's *2001: A Space Odyssey*, tenth.

A Metro-Goldwyn-Mayer Picture, directed by Michael Anderson. Screenplay by John Patrick and James Kennaway, based on the novel by Morris West. Photographed in Metrocolor and Panavision by Erwin Hillier. Music by Alex North. 155 minutes.

Starring Anthony Quinn, Laurence Olivier, Oskar Werner, David Janssen, Vittorio De Sica, Leo McKern, John Gielgud, Barbara Jefford, Rosemarie Dexter, Frank Finlay, Paul Rogers.

THE SHOP ON MAIN STREET (Czechoslovakia)

Awards (2)

Best Foreign Language Film	American Academy Award, 1965
Best Foreign Language Film	New York Critics, 1966

The first Czech film to win an Academy Award, set in a sleepy provincial town in occupied Czechoslovakia and focussing on a simple carpenter who tries to protect an old Jewish lady from the Nazis and the gas chamber. A moving, tragi-comic tale; the forerunner of several distinguished Czech films of the sixties e.g. *A Blonde In Love, Closely Observed Trains, Capricious Summer.*

Barrandov Film Studio, for Československý Film. Directed by Ján Kadár and Elmar Klos. Screenplay by Ladislav Grosman, Ján Kadár and Elmar Klos, based on the novel by Grosman. Photographed by Vladimìr Novotný. Music by Zdeněk Liška. 128 minutes.

Starring Jozef Króner, Ida Kaminska, Hana Slivková, František Zvarík, Elena Zvaríková, Martin Hollý, Martin Gregor, Adam Matejka.

THE SILENT WORLD (France)

Awards (2)

Golden Palm	Cannes, 1956
Best Foreign Film	National Board of Review, 1956

The only documentary feature ever to win the first prize at Cannes; a Jacques Cousteau/Louis Malle production about the work of Cousteau's boat *The Calypso* in charting life below the surface for world museums. Among the highlights: a shark carnage on a whale being towed by the boat, a turtle laying her large crop of eggs and the behaviour of a trained fish which eats from a diver's hand. Filmed in the biggest set in the world – the Mediterranean, the Red Sea, the Indian Ocean and the Persian Gulf!

Filmad-F.S.J.Y.C. Directed by Jacques Cousteau and Louis Malle. Photographed in Technicolor by Edmond Séchan. Underwater photography by Jacques-Yves Cousteau, Louis Malle, Frédéric Dumas and Albert Falco. Music by Yves Baudrier. 82 minutes.

With Captain Cousteau and divers and crew of *The Calypso*.

SIRÉNA (Czechoslovakia)

Awards (1)

International Grand Prix	Venice, 1947

Czech drama of a working class family and their tragic involvement in a miner's strike that was quelled with considerable bloodshed towards the end of the nineteenth century. A surprise winner at the 1947 Venice festival – it was not included in the official calendar and was screened without prior notice – the film triumphed over several more fancied contenders, e.g. Clouzot's *Quai Des Orfevres*, Carol Reed's *Odd Man Out* and Sjoberg's *Hets*.

A Czech State Enterprise Production, directed by Karel Steklý. Screenplay by Karel Steklý and Jiri Weiss, based on the novel by Marie Majerova. Photographed by O. Payer. Music by E. F. Burian. 80 minutes.

Starring Marie Vašová, Boháč, Majerova, Rief, Sucha Bek, Karen, Nedbal.

THE SLEEPING CAR MURDERS (France)

Awards (1)

Best Foreign Language Film	National Board of Review, 1966

Or, 'Murder on the Marseilles-Paris Express' with sardonic police inspector Yves Montand investigating the death of a young woman found murdered in a sleeping car on the overnight train. The tension mounts when Montand realises that five other passengers might finish up the same way or that one of the five might be the killer. A classy thriller by Costa-Gavras who later directed the award-winning *Z*.

P.E.C.F. Written and directed by Costa-Gavras. Based on the novel *Compartiment Tueurs* by Sébastien Japrisot. Photographed in CinemaScope by Jean Tournier. Music by Michel Magne. 92 minutes.

Starring Yves Montand, Simone Signoret, Pierre Mondy, Catherine Allégret, Pascale Roberts, Jacques Perrin, Michel Piccoli, Jean-Louis Trintignant, Charles Denner, Claude Mann.

Note: The Sleeping Car Murders first opened in Paris in November, 1965.

SONS AND LOVERS (Britain)

Awards (2)

Best Film	New York Critics, 1960
Best American Film	National Board of Review, 1960

D.H.Lawrence's autobiographical saga of a young man (Dean Stockwell) struggling to break free from his coal-mining environment and start a career as an artist. Wendy Hiller as his dominating mother, Trevor Howard as his drunken father and Heather Sears and Mary Ure as the two women in his life are among those who stand in his way before he can take the train out of Nottingham and head for London. Highly regarded in the United States where it won two major awards; not so in Britain where it failed to win even the Best British Film prize of 1960. The New York Critics Award was shared with *The Apartment.*

A Twentieth Century-Fox Picture, directed by Jack Cardiff. Screenplay by Gavin Lambert and T. E. B. Clarke, based on the novel by D. H. Lawrence. Photographed in CinemaScope by Freddie Francis. Music by Lambert Williamson. 100 minutes.

Starring Trevor Howard, Dean Stockwell, Wendy Hiller, Mary Ure, Heather Sears, William Lucas, Donald Pleasence, Ernest Thesiger.

Note: Sons And Lovers is generally referred to as a British production, financed by Twentieth Century-Fox. The National Board of Review, however, selected it as an American picture in its ten best list.

THE SORROW AND THE PITY (Switzerland)

Awards (1)

Best Foreign Language Film	National Board of Review, 1972

Two hundred and sixty-minute documentary about life in occupied France during World War II, concentrating on the occupation of Clermont Ferrand, an industrial city in central France where the Vichy regime was based and collaboration was prevalent. An emotional subject handled shrewdly and with insight by director Marcel Ophuls (son of Max) who combined extensive interview material with original French newsreel footage of the time.

A TV Recontre Production, directed by Marcel Ophuls — as conceived by Ophuls and André Harris. Photographed by André Juraz. Edited by Claude Vadja. 260 minutes.

Note: The Sorrow And The Pity which was premiered in Europe in 1969, was named as the best documentary of 1972 by the New York Critics.

THE SOUND BARRIER (Britain)

Awards (2)

Best Foreign Film	National Board of Review, 1952
Best Film, Any Source	British Academy Award, 1952

Terence Rattigan original about a wealthy aircraft manufacturer (Ralph

Richardson) and two pilots (Nigel Patrick and John Justin) who risk their lives and reputations as they try to produce a jet plane that will fly faster than sound. The handsomely photographed aerial scenes (notably a spectacular pre-credit sequence in which an out-of-control Spitfire sweeps low over the Dover cliffs) helped earn the film a British Oscar as best of the year. David Lean remains the only director to have been honoured with three 'best film' awards by the British Academy (see also *The Bridge On The River Kwai* and *Lawrence Of Arabia*).

A London Films Production (released by British Lion), directed by David Lean. Story and screenplay by Terence Rattigan. Photographed by Jack Hildyard. Music by Malcolm Arnold. 118 minutes.

Starring Ralph Richardson, Ann Todd, Nigel Patrick, John Justin, Dinah Sheridan, Joseph Tomelty, Denholm Elliott.

Note: The film was released as *Breaking The Sound Barrier* in the United States.

THE SOUND OF MUSIC (USA)

Awards (1)

Best Film	American Academy Award, 1965

Julie Andrews as an orphan governess (straight from a convent) who teaches her charges to sing, marries their stern father Christopher Plummer and finally escapes with them all from a Nazi dominated Austria to America and world fame. A three hour musical trifle that eventually ended *Gone With The Wind's* twenty-five year reign as the most financially successful film of all time. Apart from the Nazis just about everyone in the picture sings.

A Twentieth Century-Fox Picture, directed by Robert Wise. Screenplay by Ernest Lehman, based on the Broadway musical of Richard Rodgers and Oscar Hammerstein II. Photographed in De Luxe Color and Todd-AO by Ted McCord. 174 minutes.

Starring Julie Andrews, Christopher Plummer, Eleanor Parker, Richard Haydn, Peggy Wood.

THE SOUTHERNER (USA)

Awards (1)

International Prize	Venice, 1946

Zachary Scott as a young farmer who leaves his sharecropping cabin to go it alone and, together with his family, struggles to earn a modest living from growing cotton on a derelict Texas farm. The third and most accomplished of Renoir's five American films, not unlike *The Grapes Of Wrath* in its affinity with the men who work the soil. The film's prize at the first post-war Venice festival was the only major award ever won by a Renoir film in European competition.

A United Artists Picture, directed by Jean Renoir. Screenplay and dialogue by Jean Renoir, based on the novel *Hold Autumn In Your Hand* by George Perry. Photographed by Lucien Andriot. Music by Werner Janssen. 91 minutes.

Starring Zachary Scott, Betty Field, J. Carroll Naish, Beulah Bondi, Percy Kilbride, Blanche Yurka, Charles Kemper, Norman Lloyd.

Note: The Southerner was first shown in the United States in 1945.

THE STEPBROTHERS (Japan)

Awards (1)

Grand Prix	Karlovy Vary, 1958

A Japanese wife, long treated as a servant by her soldier husband, eventually rises up against his rigid discipline and takes her rightful place in the household. A now all-but-forgotten production, set before, during and after World War II, which won the 1958 prize at Karlovy Vary for 'its clear and impressive revelation of the inhumanity of militarism.' The film shared the top award with the Russian *Quiet Flows The Don.*

A Nikkatsu Production, directed by Mioji Iyeki. Screenplay by Y. Yoda and N. Terada. Photographed by Yoshio Miyajima. Edited by Y. Akutagawa. 95 minutes.

Starring Rentaro Mikuni, Kinuyo Tanaka.

THE STING (USA)

Awards (2)

Best Film	American Academy Award, 1973
Best English Language Film	National Board of Review, 1973

The most successful of the 'buddy, buddy' films so popular in America in the early seventies with the *Butch Cassidy* team, Paul Newman and Robert Redford, reunited as two con-men who swindle New York gangster Robert Shaw out of a small fortune. One of the most elaborate of all heist films, linked by the piano rags of Scott Joplin and affectionately in period thanks to the sets and costumes of Chicago in the Depression thirties.

A Universal Picture, directed by George Roy Hill. Screenplay by David S. Ward. Photographed in Technicolor by Robert Surtees. Art Direction by Henry Bumstead. Costumes by Edith Head. 129 minutes.

Starring Paul Newman, Robert Redford, Robert Shaw, Charles Durning, Ray Walston, Eileen Brennan, Harold Gould, John Heffernan.

THE STORY OF ADÈLE H (France)

Awards (1)

Best Foreign Language Film	National Board of Review, 1975

The love of the youngest daughter of Victor Hugo for an English army officer, an all-consuming passion that resulted in her following him half-way round the world and degenerating into madness. A disturbing, uncharacteristic Truffaut movie that earned Isabelle Adjani best actress awards from the New York Critics and the National Board of Review, plus an Oscar nomination in Hollywood.

Les Films Du Carrosse/Les Artistes Associés. Directed by François Truffaut. Screenplay by François Truffaut, Jean Gruault and Suzanne Schiffman; with the collaboration of Frances V. Guille, editor of *The Journal Of Adéle Hugo*. Photographed in Eastman Color by Nestor Almendros. Music by Maurice Jaubert. 98 minutes.

Starring Isabelle Adjani, Bruce Robinson, Sylvia Marriott, Joseph Blatchley, Reubin Dorey, M. White, Carl Hathwell, Ivry Gitlis.

LA STRADA (Italy)

Awards (2)

Best Foreign Language Film	American Academy Award, 1956
Best Foreign Language Film	New York Critics, 1956

Giulietta Masina as a tragic little waif who is sold by her mother to brutish strongman Anthony Quinn and assists him in his act as he tours from town to town across Italy. Fellini's first great international success; a desolate tale, told against bleak, rain-filled landscapes and with a haunting score by Nino Rota. A double award winner in America in 1956. First shown at Venice in 1954.

A Ponti/De Laurentiis Production, directed by Federico Fellini. Screenplay by Fellini, Ennio Flaiano and Tullio Pinelli, based on a story by Fellini and Pinelli. Photographed by Otello Martelli. Music by Nino Rota. 115 minutes.

Starring Giulietta Masina, Anthony Quinn, Richard Basehart, Aldo Silvani, Marcella Rovena, Lidia Venturina.

A STREETCAR NAMED DESIRE (USA)

Awards (1)

Best Film	New York Critics, 1951

The final degradation of faded Southern belle Blanche du Bois (Vivien Leigh) who ends her days an alcoholic slut in her sister's sleazy apartment in the slum district of New Orleans. Sordid, high voltage cinema but a near perfect adaptation of Tennessee Williams' 1947 stage play. Sharing in the general misery: Marlon Brando as Blanche's brutal Polish-American brother-in-law, Kim Hunter as her sister and Karl Malden as her middle-aged beau.

A Warner Bros. Picture, directed by Elia Kazan. Screenplay by Tennessee Williams, based on his stage play. Adaptation by Oscar Saul. Photographed by Harry Stradling. Music by Alex North. 125 minutes.

Starring Vivien Leigh, Marlon Brando, Kim Hunter, Karl Malden, Rudy Bond, Nick Dennis.

SUNDAY, BLOODY SUNDAY (Britain)

Awards (1)

Best Film	British Academy Award, 1971

The last few days of the relationship between a young sculptor (Murray Head) and his two lovers — an older, divorced woman (Glenda Jackson) and a middle-aged homosexual doctor (Peter Finch) — as they come to terms with the break-up of their involvement. A risqué theme but a warm, very honest film considered by many critics to be John Schlesinger's most accomplished work. Overlooked in Hollywood's list of five best picture Oscar nominees; named best film of the year by the British Film Academy.

A Vectia Film (released by United Artists), directed by John Schlesinger. Screenplay by Penelope Gilliatt. Photographed in De Luxe Color by Billy Williams. 110 minutes.

Starring Glenda Jackson, Peter Finch, Murray Head, Peggy Ashcroft, Maurice Denham, Vivian Pickles, Frank Windsor, Tony Britton.

SUNDAYS AND CYBÈLE (France)

Awards (2)

Best Foreign Language Film	American Academy Award, 1962
Best Foreign Language Film	National Board of Review, 1962

The friendship between a shell-shocked ex-pilot (Hardy Krüger) whose experiences in the French-Indochina war have driven him close to madness and a twelve-year-old convent girl who has been deserted by her parents and whom he takes out on Sunday afternoons. A much admired prize-winner in 1962; less highly regarded by contemporary critics, although the tragic climax remains deeply moving and the film visually enchanting.

Terra Films/Fidès/Orsay Films/Les Films du Trocadéro. Directed by Serge Bourguignon. Screenplay by Serge Bourguignon and Antoine Tudal. Dialogue by Bourguignon and Bernard Eschassériaux, based on the novel by Eschassériaux. Photographed in Franscope by Henri Decaë. Music by Maurice Jarre. 110 minutes.

Starring Hardy Krüger, Patricia Gozzi, Nicole Courcel, Daniel Ivernel, Michel de Ré, André Oumansky.

SUNSET BOULEVARD (USA)

Awards (1)

Best American Film	National Board of Review, 1950

Still the most penetrating of all Hollywood exposés with Gloria Swanson as a faded silent movie queen and William Holden as the struggling writer she hires to script her comeback picture. Lending support: Erich von Stroheim as Miss Swanson's butler, Cecil B. DeMille (seen as himself directing *Samson And Delilah*) and Fred Clark as an ulcerated producer. Probably the unluckiest Oscar loser of all time, although the National Board of Review went some way to making amends by placing it ahead of its main rival, *All About Eve*.

A Paramount Picture, directed by Billy Wilder. Screenplay by Charles Brackett, Billy Wilder and D. M. Marshman, Jr. Photographed by John F. Seitz. Music by Franz Waxman. 110 minutes.

Starring Gloria Swanson, William Holden, Erich von Stroheim, Nancy Olson, Fred Clark, Lloyd Gough, Jack Webb, Cecil B. DeMille.

T

THE TAMING OF FIRE (USSR)

Awards (1)
Grand Prix Karlovy Vary, 1972

Hollywood style Russian 'bio-pic' about a Soviet scientist who worked on the Atomic Bomb in the war and later helped develop the sputniks and rockets in his country's exploration of space. The film parallels the man's scientific accomplishments with his less than happy personal life with a woman who always takes second place to his work. Directed by Daniel Chrabrovicky, scriptwriter on Romm's *Nine Days Of One Year*, and based on the career of rocket builder Sergei Korolyov.

A Mosfilm Production, written and directed by Daniel Chrabrovicky. Photographed in Sovcolor by Sergei Bronsky. Music by Andrei Petrov. 140 minutes.

Starring Kiril Lavov, Ada Regonceva, Igor Gerbachev, Igor Vladimirov, Innokenti Smoktunovsky.

TAXI DRIVER (USA)

Awards (1)
Golden Palm Cannes, 1976

A nightmare of a film with a young Vietnam war veteran at its centre, a man cruising with his taxi cab through the streets of New York and viewing the city through his distorted mind as an open sewer spewing forth pimps, whores and criminals. Rated highly in 1976 when it was described as 'unsettling' and a 'scorching experience' and given sensational qualities by the performance of the young Jodie Foster as a twelve-year-old hooker. Robert De Niro stars in the title role.

An Italo-Judeo Production (released by Columbia) directed by Martin Scorsese. Screenplay by Paul Schrader. Photographed in MGM Color by Michael Chapman. Music by Bernard Herrmann. 114 minutes.

Starring Robert De Niro, Cybill Shepherd, Jodie Foster, Peter Boyle, Leonard Harris, Harvey Keitel, Martin Scorsese, Steven Prince.

THAT MAN FROM RIO (France/Italy)

Awards (1)
Best Foreign Language Film — New York Critics, 1964

Enjoyable chase thriller by Philippe de Broca with on-leave airman Jean-Paul Belmondo indulging in some extravagant acrobatics as he becomes involved in an international heist that takes him from Paris to South America. An engaging spoof of the Bond-type movies, preferred by the New York Critics to Pietro Germi's *Seduced And Abandoned*, De Sica's two comedies, *Marriage, Italian Style* and *Yesterday, Today And Tomorrow*, and the 1964 Cannes winner, *The Umbrellas Of Cherbourg*.

Ariane-Les Productions Artistes Associés-Dear Film. Directed by Philippe de Broca. Screenplay by de Broca, Jean-Paul Rappeneau, Ariane Mnouchkine and Daniel Boulanger. Photographed in Eastman Color by Edmond Séchan. Music by Georges Delerue. 114 minutes.

Starring Jean-Paul Belmondo, Françoise Dorleac, Jean Servais, Simone Renant, Milton Ribeiro.

THAT OBSCURE OBJECT OF DESIRE (France/Spain)

Awards (1)
Best Foreign Language Film — National Board of Review, 1977

Adaptation of Pierre Louÿs' novel about a middle-aged Parisian (Fernando Rey) who is driven to despair by a man-destroying servant girl who continually teases him but refuses to submit to his sexual desires. Luis Buñuel as ambiguous as ever (two actresses play the role of the servant girl) and near to top form even though he was in his late seventies when he made the film. The picture was named the year's best by the National Board of Review, voted second to *Annie Hall* by the New York Critics and nominated for a foreign language Oscar.

Greenwich Film Production/Les Films Galaxie (Paris)/In Cine (Madrid). Directed by Luis Buñuel. Screenplay by Luis Buñuel and Jean-Claude Carrière, based on the novel *La Femme et le Pantin* by Pierre Louÿs. Photographed in Eastman Color by Edmond Richard. 103 minutes.

Starring Fernando Rey, Carole Bouquet, Angela Molina, Julien Bertheau, André Weber, Piéral.

THAT SWEET WORD – LIBERTY (USSR)

Awards (1)
Grand Prix — Moscow, 1973

Tense Soviet thriller, set in South America, about three Communist senators who are arrested and held in prison without trial. One of the three secures his release by claiming to leave the Party; shortly afterwards, he sets up a cafe opposite the prison and masterminds a tunnel escape plot from cell to cafe and freedom. Directed by the Lithuanian film-maker V. Zhalakyavichus, the picture was based on a true life escape in Venezuela and shared the Moscow Grand Prix with *Affection* and *Oklahoma Crude*.

A Mosfilm Production with the Lithuania Film Studio. Directed by V. Zhalakyavichus. Screenplay by V. Zhalakyavichus and V. Ezhov. Photographed in colour and black and white by V. Nachabtsev. 190 minutes.

Starring R. Adomaytis, I. Miroshnichenko, I. Unguryanu, B. Babkauskas.

THEY SHOOT HORSES, DON'T THEY? (USA)

Awards (1)

Best English Language Film	National Board of Review, 1969

The hopes, fears and disillusionments of the contestants in one of the infamous American dance marathons of the Depression years. In charge of the fearsome event: master of ceremonies Gig Young. Among those fighting for the 1500 dollar prize and a better life: embittered loser Jane Fonda, middle-aged sailor Red Buttons, Hollywood hopeful Susannah York and impoverished farm worker Bruce Dern.

A Palomar Pictures International Production, directed by Sydney Pollack. Screenplay by James Poe and Robert E. Thompson, based on the novel by Horace McCoy. Photographed in De Luxe Color and Panavision by Philip H. Lathrop. Music by John Green. 129 minutes.

Starring Jane Fonda, Michael Sarrazin, Susannah York, Gig Young, Red Buttons, Bonnie Bedelia, Michael Conrad, Bruce Dern.

THE THIRD MAN (Britain)

Awards (1)

Grand Prix	Cannes, 1949

Orson Welles as a penicillin racketeer on the run in the ruins of post-war Vienna, Valli as his devoted mistress and Joseph Cotten as the boyhood friend who eventually destroys him. A classic Carol Reed thriller and the first British picture to earn the Grand Prix at the Cannes Festival. Robert Krasker's filming of a once proud city littered with bombed streets and half empty cafes earned him an American Academy Award; Anton Karas' unique zither score became famous the world over.

A London Films Production, directed by Carol Reed. Screenplay by Graham Greene. Photographed by Robert Krasker. Music by Anton Karas. 104 minutes.

Starring Joseph Cotten, Trevor Howard, Valli, Orson Welles, Bernard Lee, Wilfrid Hyde White, Paul Hoerbiger, Annie Rosar, Ernst Deutsch, Erich Ponto, Siegfried Breuer.

THOSE WERE THE YEARS (Italy)

Awards (1)
Grand Prix Moscow, 1975

The lives of three wartime resistance friends as they struggle to adjust to the problems of post-war Italy. One, a politically conscious hospital attendant, retains his optimism; the others — a film critic who records milestones in Italian cinema, and an opportunist who marries a millionaire's daughter — become disillusioned. Through their interweaving stories, Ettore Scola offers a pessimistic commentary on the social history and lost opportunities of his country over the last thirty years. Dedicated to neo-realist pioneer Vittorio De Sica and co-winner of the 1975 Moscow Grand Prix. See also *Dersu Uzala* and *The Promised Land.*

A Dean Cinematografica & Delta Production, directed by Ettore Scola. Photographed in Technicolor by Claudio Cirillo. Music by Armando Trovajoli. 136 minutes.

Starring Nino Manfredi, Vittorio Gassman, Stefania Sandrelli, Stefano Satta Flores, Giovanna Ralli, Aldo Fabrizi.

THROUGH A GLASS DARKLY (Sweden)

Awards (1)
Best Foreign Language Film American Academy Award, 1961

Ingmar Bergman in his most pessimistic mood as he probes into the lives of four people — a just-released mental patient living in a twilight world between sanity and madness, her doctor husband, and her father and younger brother — when they spend one summer of misery on a desolate island in the Baltic. Harriet Andersson features as the schizophrenic who finally declines into permanent insanity when 'God reveals himself to her' in the form of a giant black spider.

Svensk Filmindustri Production. Written and directed by Ingmar Bergman. Photographed by Sven Nykvist. 91 minutes.

Starring Harriet Andersson, Gunnar Björnstrand, Max von Sydow, Lars Passgard.

THE TIN DRUM (West Germany/France/Yugoslavia/Poland)

Awards (2)
Golden Palm Cannes, 1979
Best Foreign Language Film American Academy Award, 1979

The symbolic adventures of a young boy who decides to remain at the age of three and accompany, on his tin drum, the history of the troubled years of twentieth century Germany. Masterly, expressionistic West German production, co-winner at Cannes (see also *Apocalypse Now*) and based on the 1959 bestseller by Guenter Grass. Twelve-year-old David Bennent, a boy hindered in his own growth, appears as the precocious drummer.

A Franz Seitz Film/Bioskop-Film/Artemis Film/Hallelujah-Film/ GGB 14. KG/Argos Films Paris Production in collaboration with Jadran Film Zagreb and Film Polski Warsaw. Directed by Volker Schlöendorff. Screenplay by Jean-Claude Carrière, Franz Seitz and Volker Schlöendorff, based on the novel by Guenter Grass. Extra dialogue by Guenter Grass. Photographed in Eastman Color by Igor Luther. Music by Friedrich Meyer. 150 minutes.

Starring Mario Adorf, Angela Winkler, David Bennent, Daniel Olbrychski,, Katharina Thalbach, Heinz Bennent, Fritz Hakl, Mariella Oliveri.

THE TITAN: STORY OF MICHELANGELO (Italy)

Awards (1)
Best Foreign Film — National Board of Review, 1950

Documentary tracing Michelangelo's life through his paintings and sculptures and concentrating on the places in Rome and Florence where he lived and worked. The 1950 film shown in America was twenty-five minutes shorter than the original version made by Curt Oertel in Italy before the war. Music, sound effects and a narration by Fredric March were added to the post-war version which the National Board of Review placed ahead of *Whisky Galore, The Third Man* and *Kind Hearts And Coronets* as the best foreign film of 1950.

Classics Pictures Inc. Presented by Robert Flaherty. Written by Norman Borisoff; adapted from Curt Oertel's film *Michelangelo: Life Of A Titan*. Directed and edited by Richard Lyford. Narrated by Fredric March. 70 minutes.

Note: The Titan was also awarded an Oscar as the best feature documentary of 1950.

TO LIVE IN PEACE (Italy)

Awards (1)
Best Foreign Language Film — New York Critics, 1947

Tragi-comedy by Luigi Zampa about the moral responsibilities facing a group of Italian villagers when they find themselves hiding two escaped Americans from the sole Nazi guard in their village. Aldo Fabrizi (of *Open City* fame) heads the cast; the New York Critics adjudged the film best foreign picture ahead of De Sica's *Shoe-shine,* Carné's *Les Enfants Du Paradis* and Duvivier's thriller *Panique*.

A Lux Pao Production, directed by Luigi Zampa. Screenplay by Suso Cecchi D'Amico, Aldo Fabrizi and Piero Tellini. Photographed by Carlo Montuori. 89 minutes.

Starring Aldo Fabrizi, Gar Moore, Mirella Monti, John Kitzmiller, Heinrich Bode, Ave Ninchi.

TOM JONES (Britain)

Awards (4)	
Best Film	American Academy Award, 1963
Best Film	New York Critics, 1963
Best English Language Film	National Board of Review, 1963
Best Film, Any Source	British Academy Award, 1963

The film that just about everyone loved back in 1963, Henry Fielding's rollicking, bawdy tale of an eighteenth century country boy (Albert Finney) who wenches his way to success during a series of amorous escapades in the West Country and London. An over-dinner seduction at a wayside inn and, on a different level, a realistic stag hunt sequence, remain the highlights. The audience at Venice was the only one the film didn't conquer (*Hands Over The City* was awarded the Golden Lion) although Finney did receive the actor's prize at the festival.

A Woodfall Film (released by United Artists), directed by Tony Richardson. Screenplay by John Osborne, based on the novel by Henry Fielding. Photographed in Eastman Color by Walter Lassally. Music by John Addison. 131 minutes.

Starring Albert Finney, Susannah York, Hugh Griffith, Edith Evans, Joan Greenwood, Diane Cilento, George Devine, David Tomlinson, Joyce Redman.

TOPAZE (USA)

Awards (1)	
Best American Film	National Board of Review, 1933

John Barrymore as a timid, scrupulously honest schoolteacher who finds that honesty is not always the best policy in life and that double dealing in big business can lead to wealth and extreme comfort. The second of five screen versions of Marcel Pagnol's satirical stage play, named best of the year by the National Board of Review who placed it ahead of such formidable contenders as *Berkeley Square, Little Women* and the year's Oscar winner, *Cavalcade*. The film was not listed among the ten best picture Oscar nominations of 1932/33.

An RKO Radio Picture, directed by Harry d'Abbadie d'Arrast. Screenplay by Benn W. Levy, based on the play by Marcel Pagnol. Photographed by Lucien Andriot. Music by Max Steiner. 78 minutes.

Starring John Barrymore, Myrna Loy, Albert Conti, Luis Alberni, Reginald Mason, Jobyna Howland, Jackie Searl.

THE TREASURE OF THE SIERRA MADRE (USA)

Awards (1)	
Best Film	New York Critics, 1948

Near classic John Huston movie about the effects of gold on three men — Humphrey Bogart, Walter Huston and Tim Holt — as they risk danger both from marauding bandits and each other while prospecting in the Mexican hills of the Sierra Madre. A loser at Academy Award time but a winner at the New York Critics' prize-giving when it came out ahead of the Oscar-winning *Hamlet* by the slender margin of nine votes to eight. *The Snake Pit* and *The Search* were the other two films in contention.

A Warner Bros. Picture, directed by John Huston. Screenplay by John Huston, based on the novel by B. Traven. Photographed by Ted McCord. Music by Max Steiner. 126 minutes.

Starring Humphrey Bogart, Walter Huston, Tim Holt, Bruce Bennett, Barton MacLane, Alfonso Bedoya, A. Soto Rangel, Manuel Donde, John Huston, Jack Holt.

THE TREE OF WOODEN CLOGS (Italy)

Awards (2)

Golden Palm	Cannes, 1978
Best Foreign Language Film	New York Critics, 1979

One hundred and eighty-seven-minute evocation of peasant life following the experiences of four families living on a vast estate in Lombardy at the end of the nineteenth century. Days of labour and hardship within an unremitting feudal system are observed by director Olmi in a manner that frequently conjures up memories of the post-war triumphs of the neo-realists. Beautifully photographed; gently underlined throughout with dark political undertones, and performed by an entirely non-professional cast.

RAI-Radiotelevisione Italiana/Italnoleggio Cinematografico. A GPC (Milan) Production. Written and directed by Ermanno Olmi. Photographed in Gevacolor by Ermanno Olmi. 187 minutes.

Starring Luigi Ornaghi, Francesca Moriggi, Omar Brignoli, Antonio Ferrari, Teresa Brescianini, Giuseppe Brignoli, Carlo Rota, Pasqualina Brolis, Massimo Fratus, Francesca Villa.

THE TROUT (Spain)

Awards (1)

Golden Bear	Berlin, 1978

The chaotic progress of a wealthy fishing club's annual banquet at which the trout — caught in a local sewer — infects everyone with disastrous results. The club members are cast as establishment figures blind to the fact that their society is crumbling and who carry on eating the infected fish simply because it has been caught at their club! Not a Buñuel film although heavily influenced by him and bearing a strong resemblance to several of his satirical works. Co-winner, along with *What Max Said*, of the 1978 Berlin Festival.

A Cinema 2000 S.A. Release produced by Luis Megino for Arandano S.A. Directed by Luis Garcia Sánchez. Screenplay by Manuel Gutiérrez Aragón, Luis Garcia Sánchez and Luis Megino Grande. Photographed

in colour by Magi Torruella. Music by Victor Manuel. 99 minutes.
Starring Héctor Alterio, Walter Vidarte, Carla Cristi, Lautaro Murúa, Juan Amigo, Ofelia Angelica, Maria Carmen Arevalo, Norma Bacaicoa.

THE TRUE GLORY (Britain/USA)

Awards (1)

Best Film	National Board of Review, 1945

Account of the Allied invasion of Europe from its early planning stages to the meeting of the Western and Eastern armies on the banks of the River Elbe. Co-directed by Carol Reed and Garson Kanin who edited 6½ million feet of celluloid – shot by 1400 cameramen – down to 84 minutes of film. The picture was named best of the year by the National Board of Review who, in 1945, combined both documentaries and features in their best film award. *The Lost Weekend, The Southerner* and *The Story Of G.I. Joe* earned the next three places in the top ten.

Produced by the US Office of War Information and the Ministry of Information. Directed by Carol Reed and Garson Kanin. Script by Eric Maschwitz, Arthur Macrae, Jenny Nicholson, Gerald Kersh, Guy Trosper, Harry Brown and Peter Ustinov. Music by William Alwyn. 84 minutes.

Note: The True Glory was awarded an Oscar as the best feature documentary of 1945 and earned a special award of the New York Critics.

THE TURNING POINT (USA)

Awards (1)

Best English Language Film	National Board of Review, 1977

An *All About Eve* of the ballet world with Shirley MacLaine as a dancer who gave it all up to raise a family and Anne Bancroft as a principal ballerina who sacrificed everything for her career and has to face the daunting prospect of approaching middle-age. High-powered performances from the two stars helped earn the film the National Board of Review's vote as best of the year. At Oscar time, however, the picture ended up without a single award despite receiving eleven nominations.

A Twentieth Century-Fox Picture, directed by Herbert Ross. Screenplay by Arthur Laurents. Photographed in De Luxe Color by Robert Surtees. 119 minutes.

Starring Shirley MacLaine, Anne Bancroft, Mikhail Baryshnikov, Leslie Browne, Tom Skerritt, Martha Scott, Antoinette Sibley.

TWELVE ANGRY MEN (USA)

Awards (1)

Golden Bear	Berlin, 1957

Ninety-five nail-biting minutes in the company of dedicated juror Henry

Fonda as he tries to convince his eleven colleagues of the innocence of a black youth accused of murder. Set in a sweltering New York jury room and shot by Sidney Lumet (first film) in twenty days for just 340,000 dollars. The first solo winner of the Jury Golden Bear at the Berlin festival.

A United Artists (Orion-Nova) Picture, directed by Sidney Lumet. Screenplay by Reginald Rose, based on his TV play. Photographed by Boris Kaufman. Music by Kenyon Hopkins. 95 minutes.

Starring Henry Fonda, Lee J. Cobb, E. G. Marshall, Jack Warden, Ed Begley, Martin Balsam, John Fiedler, Jack Klugman, George Voskovec, Robert Webber, Edward Binns, Joseph Sweeney.

TWENTY HOURS (Hungary)

Awards (1)

Grand Prix	Moscow, 1965

Hungarian film that tackles a previously taboo subject — the uprising of 1956 — through a story of the disintegrating relationship of four former friends in the years leading up to the revolution. The film hinges superficially on a murder investigation by a young reporter; beneath the surface it illustrates the turning points in the life of the Hungarian peasantry in the post-war years and shows how a new brand of Communism emerged in Hungary. A carefully structured Zoltán Fábri film, too measured for some and something of a surprise winner when it shared the Moscow Grand Prix with *War And Peace* in 1965.

Studio I, Mafilm. Directed by Zoltán Fábri. Screenplay by Miklós Kollo, based on the reportage/novel by Ferenc Sánta. Photographed by György Illés. 112 minutes.

Starring Antal Páger, János Görbe, Adám Szirtes, László György, Emil Keres, Károly Kovács, Gyula Bodrogi, Ferenc Kiss.

TWO PENNYWORTH OF HOPE (Italy)

Awards (1)

Grand Prix	Cannes, 1952

Renato Castellani comedy about a young ex-soldier who returns to his small village on the slopes of Vesuvius and attempts to hold down a series of jobs that will enable him to save enough money to marry his fiery girl friend. An exuberant, optimistic slice of Italian country life, acted out, as was the vogue in many post-war Italian films, by a mostly non-professional cast. Joint winner at Cannes in 1952, sharing the premier award with Orson Welles' *Othello*.

Universalcine. Directed by Renato Castellani. Screenplay by Renato Castellani and Titina De Filippo, from a story by Castellani and M. Margadonna. Photographed by Arturo Gallea. Music by Alessandro Cicognini. 98 minutes.

Starring Vincenzo Musolino, Maria Fiore, Filomeno Russo, Luigi Astarita, Luigi Barone.

UMBERTO D (Italy)

Awards (1)

Best Foreign Language Film — New York Critics, 1955

The loneliness of old age reflected in a story of a retiring government official who finds it impossible to exist on his meagre pension and is driven to the verge of suicide. An impassioned work of protest, performed mostly by non-professional actors and the third in a trio of neo-realist masterpieces begun by Vittorio De Sica with *Shoe-shine* and *Bicycle Thieves*. First shown in Italy in 1952, the film was co-winner (along with *Les Diaboliques*) of the 1955 New York Critics Award. The hero of the film is based on De Sica's father, to whom the picture is dedicated.

A Rizzoli/De Sica/Amato Production, directed by Vittorio De Sica. Screenplay by Cesare Zavattini. Photographed by G. R. Aldo. Music by Alessandro Cicognini. 88 minutes.

Starring Carlo Battisti, Maria Pia Casilio, Ileana Simova, Lina Gennari, Elena Rea, Memmo Cartenuto.

THE UMBRELLAS OF CHERBOURG (France/West Germany)

Awards (1)

Golden Palm — Cannes, 1964

All singing operetta about a young girl from an umbrella shop in Cherbourg who marries another man for security while her lover (the father of her unborn child) is serving in the army in Algeria. A lush score by Michel Legrand, elegant colourwork and the exquisite beauty of Catherine Deneuve combine to make the first out-and-out musical entertainment to win the main prize at Cannes.

Parc Film/Madeleine Film (Paris)/Beta Films (Munich)/Mag Bodard. Written and directed by Jacques Demy. Photographed in Eastman Color by Jean Rabier. Art Direction by Bernard Evein. Music by Michel Legrand. 90 minutes.

Starring Anne Vernon, Catherine Deneuve, Marc Michel, Nino Castelnovo, Mireille Perry, Ellen Farner, Dorothée Blank.

UNDER THE CLOAK OF NIGHT (India)

Awards (1)
Grand Prix — Karlovy Vary, 1957

Allegorical tale of a poor villager who finds himself branded as a thief and caught up in the intrigues of modern civilization when he arrives thirsty in a large Indian city and attempts to find water. An uneven combination of raw slapstick, satire and tragedy with strong echoes of Chaplin and Clair in its plea for social equality. The film was the third non East European picture to win first prize at the Karlovy Vary festival. Earlier winners: *Salt Of The Earth* (USA) and *A Race For Life* (France).

A Raj Kapoor Production, written and directed by Shanbhu Mitre and Amit Maitra. Photographed by Radhu Karmakar. Music by Salil Chaudhuri. 115 minutes.

Starring Raj Kapoor, Rana Sahib, Pradip Kumar, Sumitra Devi.

THE UNFORGETTABLE YEAR 1919 (USSR)

Awards (1)
Grand Prix — Karlovy Vary, 1952

A glorification of Stalin's role in the Communist uprising at Kronstadt naval base in Petrograd in 1919. Super-hero Stalin, then Lenin's deputy, saves Petrograd not only from enemies within Russia but also from British warships sent by Churchill. The Soviet dictator is reported to have viewed the film many times, relishing in the sequences showing him on the steps of an armoured train and practically vanquishing his enemies single-handed with his sabre.

A Mosfilm Production, directed by Mikhail Chiaureli. Screenplay by Vsevolod Vishnevsky, Mikhail Chiaureli and A. Filimonov, based on the play by Vishnevsky. Photographed in colour by Leonid Kosmatov and V. Nikolayev. Music by Dmitri Shostakovich. 11 reels.

Starring I. Molchanov, Mikhail Gelovani, Boris Andreyev, M. Kovaleva, Yevgeni Samoilov, Sergei Lukyanov, Victor Stanitsin, V. Koltsov.

VAGHE STELLE DELL'ORSA (Italy)

Awards (1)
Golden Lion Venice, 1965

The Electra legend updated to post-war Italy where a young Jewish girl (Claudia Cardinale) returns to her decaying family mansion to investigate the killing of her father by the Nazis. Stylish black and white camerawork plus lavish helpings of guilt, corruption and incest helped earn the film the Venice prize of 1965 – the first time that a Luchino Visconti picture had been so honoured. Visconti had been runner-up on three previous occasions – in 1948 with *La Terra Trema*, 1957 with *White Nights* and 1960 with *Rocco And His Brothers*.

Vides. Directed by Luchino Visconti. Screenplay by Suso Cecchi D'Amico, Luchino Visconti and Enrico Medioli. Photographed by Armando Nannuzzi. Art Direction by Mario Garbuglia. 100 minutes.

Starring Claudia Cardinale, Jean Sorel, Michael Craig, Marie Bell, Renzo Ricci.

Note: In the United States the film was known under the more manageable title of *Sandra*.

THE VIRGIN SPRING (Sweden)

Awards (1)
Best Foreign Language Film American Academy Award, 1960

Stark Ingmar Bergman morality tale based on a fourteenth century Swedish ballad about a father's vengeance on three swineherds who rape and murder his innocent daughter. Superstition, witchcraft, lust, man's suffering on earth and doubts about faith are additional ingredients. Max von Sydow suffers for most of the 88 minutes as the vengeful father.

A Svensk Filmindustri Production, directed by Ingmar Bergman. Screenplay by Ulla Isaksson, based on the 14th century ballad *Tores Dotter I Vänge*. Photographed by Sven Nykvist. Music by Erik Nordgren. 88 minutes.

Starring Max von Sydow, Birgitta Valberg, Gunnel Lindblom, Birgitta Pettersson, Axel Düberg, Tor Isedal.

VIRIDIANA (Mexico/Spain)

Awards (1)
Golden Palm Cannes, 1961

The experiences of a young novice who makes a last excursion into the outside world before taking her final vows. Her eagerness to do good results not in happiness but the death of her elderly uncle, the ruination of his estate when she converts it into a rest home for beggars, and her own rape and degradation. A savage attack on religious bigotry, Christian myths and outworn social patterns; also the film which earned Luis Buñuel belated recognition at the Cannes Festival.

Uninci, S.A.-Films 59-Gustavo Alatriste. Directed by Luis Buñuel. Screenplay by Luis Buñuel and Julio Alejandro. Photographed by José F. Aguayo. Music Direction by Gustavo Pitaluga. 90 minutes.

Starring Silvia Pinal, Francisco Rabal, Fernando Rey, Margarita Lozano, Victoria Zinny, Teresa Rabal.

Note: Viridiana shared the Cannes prize with *Une Aussi Longue Absence.*

VOR SONNENUNTERGANG (West Germany)

Awards (1)
Golden Bear Berlin, 1956

The last movie to be awarded the public vote Golden Bear at Berlin, a sentimental tearjerker by Gottfried Reinhardt about the May/December romance between a young girl and an ageing industrialist. Highly popular with the public but not the festival critics who regarded it as thirties style soap opera treated with 'a maximum of clichés' and 'a minimum of taste.' The jury winner at Berlin in 1956 was *Invitation To The Dance.*

CCC (Arthur Brauner) Production. Directed by Gottfried Reinhardt. Screenplay by Jochen Huth, based on the play by Gerhart Hauptmann. Photographed by Kurt Hasse. Music by Werner Eisbrenner. 102 minutes.

Starring Hans Albers, Annemarie Düringer, Martin Held, Hannelore Schroth, Claus Biederstaedt, Maria Becker, Erich Schellow, Inge Langen.

THE WAGES OF FEAR (France/Italy)

Awards (3)

Golden Palm	Cannes, 1953
Golden Bear	Berlin, 1953
Best Film, Any Source	British Film Academy, 1954

Gripping thriller about four stranded Europeans who, in order to escape from their desperate existence in a squalid South American oil town, drive two trucks of nitroglycerine over 300 miles of treacherous roads to a burning oil well. The 'wages of fear' are 2000 dollars for each man — if he makes it. Director Henri-Georges Clouzot ensures that none of them does, screwing every ounce of tension from the journey and stripping away the outward veneer of civilised behaviour as his four characters react to stress and fear. Yves Montand, Charles Vanel, Folco Lulli and Peter Van Eyck star as the four drivers.

C.I.C.C./Filmsonor/Vera Films/Fono Roma. Directed by Henri-Georges Clouzot. Screenplay by Henri-Georges Clouzot and Jérôme Géronimi, based on the novel by Georges Arnaud. Photographed by Armand Thirard. Music by Georges Auric. 153 minutes.

Starring Yves Montand, Charles Vanel, Folco Lulli, Peter Van Eyck, Véra Clouzot.

THE WALLS OF MALAPAGA (France/Italy)

Awards (1)

Best Foreign Language Film	American Academy Award, 1950

Fatalistic melodrama with Jean Gabin cast once more as a doomed hero figure — an on-the-run murderer who is sheltered by waitress Isa Miranda in Genoa before being finally trapped and caught by the police. An early co-production, filmed by French director René Clément in the crowded streets of Genoa with a predominantly Italian cast. Isa Miranda (best actress) and Clément (best director) were both award winners at Cannes in 1949.

A Guarini/Francinex Production, directed by René Clément. Screenplay by Cesare Zavattini and Suso Cecchi d'Amico. Adaptation and dialogue by Jean Aurenche and Pierre Bost. Photographed by Louis Page. Music by Roman Vlad. 90 minutes.

Starring Jean Gabin, Isa Miranda, Andréa Cecchi, Vera Talchi, Robert Dalban.

Note: The film (also known as *Au Dela Des Grilles*) was first released in 1949.

WAR AND PEACE (USSR)

Awards (4)

Best Foreign Language Film	American Academy Award, 1968
Best Foreign Language Film	New York Critics, 1968
Best Foreign Language Film	National Board of Review, 1968
Grand Prix	Moscow, 1965

Sergei Bondarchuk's massive adaptation of Tolstoy's classic novel, following the fortunes of four aristocratic families during the period of Napoleon's invasion and subsequent retreat from Moscow. Life, death, love and war, plus lavish settings and incomparable spectacle are just some of the ingredients in a film lasting 8 hours 27 minutes. The Moscow Festival prize (shared with *Twenty Hours*) was awarded for the first part only (3 hours 40 minutes), the rest of the picture still being filmed at the time of the festival. The American awards three years later were for the complete version, reduced for English language audiences to 357 minutes in two 3-hour parts. Complicated, but great stuff whichever way you look at it!

A Mosfilm Studios Production, directed by Sergei Bondarchuk. Screenplay by Sergei Bondarchuk and Vasily Solovyov, based on the novel by Leo Tolstoy. Photographed in Sovcolor and 70mm by Anatoly Petritsky, Dmitri Korzhikin and A. Zenyan. Music by Vyacheslav Ovchinnikov. 507 minutes.

Starring Ludmila Savelyeva, Sergei Bondarchuk, Vyacheslav Tikhonov, Anastasia Vertinskaya, Vasily Lanovoi, Viktor Stanitsin, Oleg Tabakov, Anatoly Ktorov.

WATCH ON THE RHINE (USA)

Awards (1)

Best Film	New York Critics, 1943

Straight adaptation of Lillian Hellman's distinguished play about a German underground leader (Paul Lukas) and his family who find themselves harried and blackmailed by the Nazis even in the comparative safety of Washington, D.C. One of the most probing examinations of the nature of Fascism ever put on screen and, on a less important level, the only Warner film of the forties in which Bette Davis (as Lukas' wife) subdued herself to a secondary role. A New York Critics best film winner by eleven votes to six for *The Human Comedy*.

A Warner Bros. Picture, directed by Herman Shumlin. Screenplay by Dashiell Hammett, with additional scenes and dialogue by Lillian Hellman, based on the play by Hellman. Photographed by Merritt Gerstad and Hal Mohr. Music by Max Steiner. 114 minutes.

Starring Bette Davis, Paul Lukas, Geraldine Fitzgerald, Lucile Watson, Beulah Bondi, George Coulouris, Donald Woods, Henry Daniell.

WATERLESS SUMMER (Turkey)

Awards (1)
Golden Bear Berlin, 1964

Turkish film about the violent emotions that erupt when a wealthy landowner refuses to share his water supply with his fellow farmers during a severe drought. The Berlin jury regarded the film as a work about honour, tradition and loyalty and referred to it as 'a primitive story told in a clear and simple style, with humour and power.' One German newspaper called the film's Golden Bear Award 'the disgrace of Berlin.'

Hitit Filim. Directed by Metin Erksan. Screenplay by Metin Erksan, Ismet Saydan and Kemal Inci. Story by Necati Cumali. Photographed by Ali Uğur. 90 minutes.

Starring Ulvi Doğan, Erol Taş, Hülya Koçyiğit, Hakki Haktan, Yavuz Yalinkiliç, Zeki Tüney.

WAYS OF LOVE (France/Italy)

Awards (1)
Best Foreign Language Film New York Critics, 1950

A trio of short features from different periods of film history, each linked by their interpretations of the word 'love': Pagnol's *Jofroi* (34); Renoir's unfinished *Une Partie De Campagne* (36) and Rossellini's *The Miracle* (48). A controversial winner of the New York Critics, rating more a best omnibus prize than a best picture award!

A Joseph Burstyn Release of three features compiled into a full-length film:

Jofroi (France), directed by Marcel Pagnol and starring Vincent Scotto, Annie Toinon, Tyrand. 40 minutes.

Une Partie De Campagne (France), directed by Jean Renoir and starring Sylvia Bataille, Georges Saint-Saëns, Jacques Borel, Jeanne Marken. 37 minutes.

The Miracle (Italy), directed by Roberto Rossellini and starring Anna Magnani and Federico Fellini — who also wrote the original story. 41 minutes.

WEST SIDE STORY (USA)

Awards (2)
Best Film American Academy Award, 1961
Best Film New York Critics, 1961

An updated, musical 'Romeo And Juliet', set in the slums of Manhattan's Upper West Side where the rival street gangs of the native New Yorkers (the Jets) and the immigrant Puerto Ricans (the Sharks) battle for supremacy. Caught tragically in the crossfire: Jet boy Richard Beymer and lovely Puerto Rican girl Natalie Wood. High on the list of most people's favourite musicals of all time but overlooked in Britain where it lost to Lean's *Lawrence Of Arabia* in the 1962 awards of the British Film Academy.

A Mirisch-Seven Arts Production (released by United Artists), directed by Robert Wise and Jerome Robbins. Screenplay by Ernest Lehman, based on the Broadway musical by Arthur Laurents (book), Leonard Bernstein (music) and Stephen Sondheim (lyrics). Photographed in Technicolor and Panavision 70 by Daniel L. Fapp. Production Design by Boris Leven. Choreography by Jerome Robbins. 155 minutes.

Starring Natalie Wood, Richard Beymer, Russ Tamblyn, Rita Moreno, George Chakiris, Simon Oakland.

WHAT MAX SAID (Spain)

Awards (1)
Golden Bear — Berlin, 1978

Disquieting portrait of loneliness and isolation, concentrating on a middle-aged man (Fernández de Castro) who has reached a crisis point in his domestic life and tries unsuccessfully to reassemble his past. The film shared the Berlin prize with *The Trout* (see page 128) and the short, *The Lift*. The 1978 award marked the first occasion that the Golden Bear had been presented to a country for 'the total of its contribution.'

An Elias Querejeta P.C. Production, directed by Emilio Martinez Lázaro. Screenplay by Elias Querejeta and Emilio Martinez Lazáro. Photographed in colour by Teo Escamilla. Music by Luis de Pablo. 97 minutes.

Starring Fernández de Castro, Gracia Querejeta, Miriam Maeztu, Cecilia Villarean, Héctor Alterio, Raul Sender, Maria de la Riva.

WHITE BIM WITH A BLACK EAR (USSR)

Awards (1)
Grand Prix — Karlovy Vary, 1978

Intriguingly titled little movie about the relationship between an ageing ex-soldier and a white puppy dog (with one black ear) that grows up to become the man's faithful companion. Essentially a Russian equivalent to a Disney family picture although its less than sympathetic observations of small town life often raise it above that level. Produced by the Gorky Film Studios which specialise in children's and youth pictures; co-winner (see also *Shadows Of A Hot Summer*) of the 1978 Karlovy Vary Festival.

A Gorky Film Studios Production, written and directed by Stanislav Rostotsky. Photographed in colour by Vyacheslav Shumsky. Music by Andrei Petrov. 90 minutes.

Starring Viatcheslav Tikhonov.

WHITE BIRD WITH A BLACK MARK (USSR)

Awards (1)
Grand Prix — Moscow, 1971

Russian spectacular about a peasant family living on the Rumanian border that finds itself bitterly divided into two factions — one supporting the partisans for the Nazis, the other the partisans for the Communists — when the region is united to the Soviet Ukraine just before World War II. Full of adventure and feats of derring do; more serious issues about divided loyalties are cast into the background along with the beautiful forests and mountains of the Transcarpathian Ukraine. A Moscow prize-winner in 1971 when it shared the top award with *Live Today, Die Tomorrow* and *Confessions Of A Police Inspector*.

A Studio Alexandre Dovzhenko Production, directed by Yuri Ilyenko. Screenplay by Yuri Ilyenko and Ivan Mikolaitchouk. Photographed in Sovcolor by Vilen Kaluta. 100 minutes.

Starring Larissa Kadochnikova, Alexandre Plotnikov, Natalie Naoum, Ivan Mikolaitchouk, Yuri Mikolaitchouk, Mikhail Ilyenko.

WHO'S AFRAID OF VIRGINIA WOOLF? (USA)

Awards (1)
Best Film, Any Source — British Academy Award, 1966

Film version of Edward Albee's play about the ceaseless verbal conflict between a middle-aged college professor (Richard Burton) and his frumpy, foul-mouthed wife (Elizabeth Taylor) who almost destroy a young faculty couple (George Segal and Sandy Dennis) during one of their vicious, no-holds-barred evenings of drunken fun and games. A *tour-de-force* of powerhouse acting and one of four sixties American pictures — *The Hustler, The Graduate* and *Butch Cassidy And The Sundance Kid* were the others — to be acclaimed in Britain but not in its country of origin.

A Warner Bros. Picture, directed by Mike Nichols. Screenplay by Ernest Lehman, based on the play by Edward Albee. Photographed by Haskell Wexler. Music by Alex North. 131 minutes.

Starring Elizabeth Taylor, Richard Burton, George Segal, Sandy Dennis.

WILD STRAWBERRIES (Sweden)

Awards (2)
Golden Bear — Berlin, 1958
Best Foreign Film — National Board of Review, 1959

An elderly Stockholm professor (Victor Sjöström) recollects his past life as he travels by car to receive an honorary degree at his old university and becomes aware for the first time of his failings and the reasons for his wretched loneliness. The film combines flashbacks, dream sequences and reality and reveals, with each new character it introduces — the professor's son, his daughter-in-law, a young girl hitchhiker, etc. — a new side to the old man's personality. The only Ingmar Bergman film to win Grand Prix recognition at a European festival.

A Svensk Filmindustri Production, written and directed by Ingmar Bergman. Photographed by Gunnar Fischer. Music by Erik Nordgren. 90 minutes.

Starring Victor Sjöström, Ingrid Thulin, Bibi Andersson, Gunnar Björnstrand, Folke Sundquist, Björn Bjelvenstam, Naima Wifstrand.

Note: Wild Strawberries was first shown in Sweden in December, 1957.

WINGS (USA)

Awards (1)

Best Film	American Academy Award, 1927/28

The World War I experiences of two American pilots (Charles 'Buddy' Rogers and Richard Arlen) who flirt with death and the affections of small-town gals Clara Bow and Jobyna Ralston in war-shattered France. Spectacular flying sequences, plus a memorable four-minute appearance by Gary Cooper as a doomed pilot, helped the film become the first ever best picture Oscar winner.

A Paramount Picture, directed by William A. Wellman. Screenplay by Hope Loring and Louis D. Lighton. Story by John Monk Saunders. Photographed by Harry Perry. Edited by Lucien Hubbard. 13 reels.

Starring Charles 'Buddy' Rogers, Clara Bow, Richard Arlen, Gary Cooper, Jobyna Ralston, El Brendel, Richard Tucker.

THE WORKING CLASS GOES TO HEAVEN (Italy)

Awards (1)

Golden Palm	Cannes, 1972

The life of a middle-aged Italian metal worker who slowly comes apart at the seams because of the pressures on the assembly line and his fears that, like his uncle before him, he will finish up in a psychiatric ward. Strong stuff, brutally realistic in its observations of the lives of modern Italian factory workers but summarily dismissed by many critics even though it shared the 1972 Cannes prize with Rosi's *The Mattei Affair*. Gian Maria Volonté appeared in both Grand Prix winners but failed to take the best actor award which went to Jean Yanne in *Break Up*.

Euro International. Directed by Elio Petri. Screenplay by Ugo Pirro and Elio Petri. Photographed in Eastman Color by Luigi Kuveiller. Music by Ennio Morricone. 120 minutes.

Starring Gian Maria Volonté, Salvo Randone, Mariangela Melato, Mietta Albertini, Gino Pernice, Luigi Diberti.

THE WORLD OF APU (India)

Awards (1)
Best Foreign Film National Board of Review, 1960

The final chapter of Satyajit Ray's acclaimed trilogy about the life of a Bengali peasant from childhood to maturity. This third part of the story, set in Calcutta, concentrates on the now grown up son, his attempts to earn a living as a writer, his idyllic marriage which ends tragically with his wife's death in childbirth and his eventual reconciliation with the son he has refused to love. *Pather Panchali* and *Aparajito* were the earlier films in the trilogy.

Satyajit Ray Productions, Calcutta, directed by Satyajit Ray. Screenplay by Ray, based on the novel by Bidhutibhustan Bandapadhaya. Photographed by Subrata Mitra. Music by Ravi Shankar. 106 minutes.

Starring Soumitra Chatterjee, Sharmila Tagore, Shapan Mukherjee, S. Aloke Chakraverty.

Note: The World Of Apu was first shown in India in 1958.

WORLD WITHOUT SUN (France/Italy)

Awards (1)
Best Foreign Language Film National Board of Review, 1964

A photographic record of the exploration of the Red Sea, 'starring' Jacques Cousteau and his oceanauts who lived for a month in a five-room underwater house and probed to depths of 1000 ft. The film was Cousteau's second prize-winning documentary (see also *The Silent World*) and revealed for the first time the corals, weeds and fantastic fish of the sea bed.

Filmad/Les Requins Associés/Orsay Films/C.E.I.A.P. Produced and directed by Jacques-Yves Cousteau. Photographed in Eastman Color (by Pathé) by Pierre Goupil. Music by Serge Baudo. 93 minutes.

With oceanauts André Falco, Pierre Guilbert, Raymond Kientzy, Raymond Vaissière, André Portelatine, Pierre Vannoni, Claude Wesly, Antoine Lopez, Jacques-Yves Cousteau, Simone Cousteau.

Note: World Without Sun was also awarded an Oscar as the best feature documentary of 1964.

WUTHERING HEIGHTS (USA)

Awards (1)
Best Film New York Critics, 1939

Goldwyn's much simplified version of Emily Bronte's sombre love story of the Yorkshire moors with Laurence Olivier as the passionate Heathcliff and Merle Oberon as his tragic love Cathy. A 'compromise' best picture winner of the New York Critics who failed to agree as to whether *Gone With The Wind* or *Mr. Smith Goes To Washington* was the best film of 1939. So they chose *Wuthering Heights* instead!

A Samuel Goldwyn Production (released by United Artists), directed by William Wyler. Screenplay by Ben Hecht and Charles MacArthur. based on the novel by Emily Bronte. Photographed by Gregg Toland. Music by Alfred Newman. 103 minutes.

Starring Laurence Olivier, Merle Oberon, David Niven, Flora Robson, Donald Crisp, Hugh Williams, Geraldine Fitzgerald, Leo G. Carroll.

YESTERDAY, TODAY AND TOMORROW (Italy)

Awards (1)
Best Foreign Language Film American Academy Award, 1964

Omnibus comedy about Italian morality with beautiful Sophia Loren giving full rein to her talents in three differing roles — as a slum black marketeer who finds she can escape the penalties of the law by remaining pregnant, the flirtacious wife of a rich industrialist and a prostitute having an affair with a playboy. Marcello Mastroianni co-stars in all three stories which are set in Naples, Milan and Rome respectively. Directed by Vittorio De Sica but light years away from the post-war world of *Shoe-shine* and *Bicycle Thieves*.

C.C. Champion-Les Films Concordia. Directed by Vittorio De Sica. Screenplay by Eduardo De Filippo, Isabella Quarantotti (Naples), Cesare Zavattini, Billa Billa Zanuso (Milan), Cesare Zavattini (Rome). Photographed in Technicolor and Techniscope by Giuseppe Rotunno. Music by Armando Trovajoli. 119 minutes.

Starring Sophia Loren, Marcello Mastroianni, Aldo Giuffrè, Agostino Salvietti, Armando Trovajoli, Tina Pica, Giovanni Ridolfi.

Note: Yesterday, Today And Tomorrow was first shown in Rome in December, 1963.

YOU CAN'T TAKE IT WITH YOU (USA)

Awards (1)
Best Film American Academy Award, 1938

Screen version of the Moss Hart/George Kaufman stage hit about a blissfully happy family doing its own thing in a fun-loving household in pre-war America. A wild, zany movie that gibes at big business and blows sky-high the myth that the self-made businessman should be regarded as an American hero figure. Frank Capra's last award success of the thirties.

A Columbia Picture, directed by Frank Capra. Screenplay by Robert Riskin, based on the stage play by Moss Hart and George S. Kaufman. Photographed by Joseph Walker. Music by Dimitri Tiomkin. 127 minutes.

Starring Lionel Barrymore, Jean Arthur, James Stewart, Spring Byington, Ann Miller, Mischa Auer, Edward Arnold, Halliwell Hobbes, Samuel S. Hinds.

Z

Z (France/Algeria)

Awards (2)

Best Foreign Language Film	American Academy Award, 1969
Best Film	New York Critics, 1969

Political thriller based on the assassination of a left wing Greek deputy in Greece in 1963. The chilling aftermath when a young district magistrate investigates the killing and uncovers evidence that the murder has been engineered by police officials, makes for a strong attack on totalitarianism. *Z* was the foreign language Oscar winner of 1969 and also the choice of the New York Critics who, for the first time since they initiated their awards in 1935, combined their best film and best foreign film prizes into a simple best film vote!

Reggane Film (Paris)/O.N.C.I.C. (Algiers). Directed by Costa-Gavras. Screenplay by Costa-Gavras and Jorge Semprun, based on the novel by Vassili Vassilikos. Photographed in Eastman Color (print by Technicolor) by Raoul Coutard. Music by Mikis Theodorakis. 127 minutes.

Starring Yves Montand, Jean-Louis Trintignant, Jacques Perrin, François Périer, Irene Papas, Georges Gerét, Charles Denner, Bernard Fresson.

Part Two

THE AWARDS

This section presents a history of each award organization and festival, and details all the leading prizewinners — best film, actor, actress, director, etc. — in year order.

The awards are listed as follows: The American Academy Awards; the New York Critics Awards; The Ten Best Lists of The National Board of Review; The British Academy Awards; and the festivals at Venice, Cannes, Berlin, Karlovy Vary and Moscow.

American Academy Awards

The American Academy Awards, or 'Oscars' as they are more affectionately known, remain the most famous of all film awards and make headlines the world over when they are announced each spring.

The awards ceremonies (first staged in May, 1929) were initially held at banquets but were eventually moved to cinemas and larger auditoriums when the event grew in popularity. In 1953 the awards were televised for the first time and since that year the 'Oscarcast' has figured regularly in the top ten ratings on American television.

Awards in all categories – acting, writing, cinematography, etc. – are decided by the votes of the 3000-plus members of the Academy of Motion Picture Arts and Sciences. Nominations in the various categories are made by the respective members of each creative branch of the Academy. Results are secret and never made public.

The 13½ inch high statuette, covered with 14 carat gold and weighing 8lbs, was designed by MGM's art director Cedric Gibbons and presented at the first prize-giving ceremony. It remained nameless until 1931 when Margaret Herrick, late president director of the Academy, remarked that it looked like her 'Uncle Oscar.'

During the early history of the awards, the Academy voters were often accused of neglecting less ambitious films and showing bias towards the commercially successful pictures. In recent years, however, such winners as *One Flew Over The Cuckoo's Nest, Rocky, Annie Hall* and *The Deer Hunter* – have tended to disprove this theory.

At a time of perpetual uncertainty in the movie business, the Oscars remain as popular as ever and are still Hollywood's most valuable public asset.

1927/28

Best Film — *Wings* (USA)
Best Actor — Emil Jannings in *The Way Of All Flesh* (USA) & *The Last Command* (USA)
Best Actress — Janet Gaynor in *Seventh Heaven* (USA), *Street Angel* (USA) & *Sunrise* (USA)
Best Direction — Frank Borzage for *Seventh Heaven* (USA)

Best Film nominations: *The Last Command* (USA); *The Racket* (USA); *Seventh Heaven* (USA); *The Way Of All Flesh* (USA); *Wings* (USA).

1928/29

Best Film — *The Broadway Melody* (USA)
Best Actor — Warner Baxter in *In Old Arizona* (USA)
Best Actress — Mary Pickford in *Coquette* (USA)
Best Direction — Frank Lloyd for *The Divine Lady* (USA)

Best Film nominations: *Alibi* (USA); *The Broadway Melody* (USA); *Hollywood Revue* (USA); *In Old Arizona* (USA); *The Patriot* (USA).

1929/30

Best Film — *All Quiet On The Western Front* (USA)
Best Actor — George Arliss in *Disraeli* (USA)
Best Actress — Norma Shearer in *The Divorcee* (USA)
Best Direction — Lewis Milestone for *All Quiet On The Western Front* (USA)

Best Film nominations: *All Quiet On The Western Front* (USA); *The Big House* (USA); *Disraeli* (USA); *The Divorcee* (USA); *The Love Parade* (USA).

1930/31

Best Film — *Cimarron* (USA)
Best Actor — Lionel Barrymore in *A Free Soul* (USA)
Best Actress — Marie Dressler in *Min And Bill* (USA)
Best Direction — Norman Taurog for *Skippy* (USA)

Best Film nominations: *Cimarron* (USA); *East Lynne* (USA); *The Front Page* (USA); *Skippy* (USA); *Trader Horn* (USA).

1931/32

Best Film — *Grand Hotel* (USA)
Best Actor — Fredric March in *Dr. Jekyll & Mr Hyde* (USA) & Wallace Beery in *The Champ* (USA)
Best Actress — Helen Hayes in *The Sin Of Madelon Claudet* (USA)
Best Direction — Frank Borzage for *Bad Girl* (USA)

Best Film nominations: *Arrowsmith* (USA); *Bad Girl* (USA); *The Champ* (USA); *Five Star Final* (USA); *Grand Hotel* (USA); *One Hour With You* (USA); *Shanghai Express* (USA); *The Smiling Lieutenant* (USA).

1932/33

Best Film	*Cavalcade* (USA)
Best Actor	Charles Laughton in *The Private Life Of Henry VIII* (Britain)
Best Actress	Katharine Hepburn in *Morning Glory* (USA)
Best Direction	Frank Lloyd for *Cavalcade* (USA)

Best Film nominations: *Cavalcade* (USA); *A Farewell To Arms* (USA); *42nd Street* (USA); *I Am A Fugitive From A Chain Gang* (USA); *Lady For A Day* (USA); *Little Women* (USA); *The Private Life Of Henry VIII* (Britain); *She Done Him Wrong* (USA); *Smilin' Thru* (USA); *State Fair* (USA).

1934

Best Film	*It Happened One Night* (USA)
Best Actor	Clark Gable in *It Happened One Night*
Best Actress	Claudette Colbert in *It Happened One Night*
Best Direction	Frank Capra for *It Happened One Night*

Best Film nominations: *The Barretts Of Wimpole Street* (USA); *Cleopatra* (USA); *Flirtation Walk* (USA); *The Gay Divorcee* (USA); *Here Comes The Navy* (USA); *The House Of Rothschild* (USA); *Imitation Of Life* (USA); *It Happened One Night* (USA); *One Night Of Love* (USA); *The Thin Man* (USA); *Viva Villa* (USA); *The White Parade* (USA).

1935

Best Film	*Mutiny On The Bounty* (USA)
Best Actor	Victor McLaglen in *The Informer* (USA)
Best Actress	Bette Davis in *Dangerous* (USA)
Best Direction	John Ford for *The Informer* (USA)

Best Film nominations: *Alice Adams* (USA); *The Broadway Melody Of 1936* (USA); *Captain Blood* (USA); *David Copperfield* (USA); *The Informer* (USA); *Les Miserables* (USA); *Lives Of A Bengal Lancer* (USA); *A Midsummer Night's Dream* (USA); *Mutiny On The Bounty* (USA); *Naughty Marietta* (USA); *Ruggles Of Red Gap* (USA); *Top Hat* (USA).

1936

Best Film	*The Great Ziegfeld* (USA)
Best Actor	Paul Muni in *The Story Of Louis Pasteur* (USA)
Best Actress	Luise Rainer in *The Great Ziegfeld* (USA)
Best Supporting Actor	Walter Brennan in *Come And Get It* (USA)
Best Supporting Actress	Gale Sondergaard in *Anthony Adverse* (USA)
Best Direction	Frank Capra for *Mr. Deeds Goes To Town* (USA)

Best Film nominations: *Anthony Adverse* (USA); *Dodsworth* (USA); *The Great Ziegfeld* (USA); *Libeled Lady* (USA); *Mr. Deeds Goes To Town* (USA); *Romeo And Juliet* (USA); *San Francisco* (USA); *The Story*

Of Louis Pasteur (USA); *A Tale Of Two Cities* (USA); *Three Smart Girls* (USA).

1937

Best Film	*The Life Of Emile Zola* (USA)
Best Actor	Spencer Tracy in *Captains Courageous* (USA);
Best Actress	Luise Rainer in *The Good Earth* (USA)
Best Supporting Actor	Joseph Schildkraut in *The Life Of Emile Zola* (USA)
Best Supporting Actress	Alice Brady in *In Old Chicago* (USA)
Best Direction	Leo McCarey for *The Awful Truth* (USA)

Best Film nominations: *The Awful Truth* (USA); *Captains Courageous* (USA); *Dead End* (USA); *The Good Earth* (USA); *In Old Chicago* (USA); *The Life Of Emile Zola* (USA); *Lost Horizon* (USA); *One Hundred Men And A Girl* (USA); *Stage Door* (USA); *A Star Is Born* (USA).

1938

Best Film	*You Can't Take It With You* (USA);
Best Actor	Spencer Tracy in *Boys Town* (USA)
Best Actress	Bette Davis in *Jezebel* (USA)
Best Supporting Actor	Walter Brennan in *Kentucky* (USA)
Best Supporting Actress	Fay Bainter in *Jezebel* (USA)
Best Direction	Frank Capra for *You Can't Take It With You* (USA)

Best Film nominations: *The Adventures Of Robin Hood* (USA); *Alexander's Ragtime Band* (USA); *Boys Town* (USA); *The Citadel* (Britain); *Four Daughters* (USA); *La Grande Illusion* (France); *Jezebel* (USA); *Pygmalion* (Britain); *Test Pilot* (USA); *You Can't Take It With You* (USA).

1939

Best Film	*Gone With The Wind* (USA)
Best Actor	Robert Donat in *Goodbye Mr. Chips* (Britain)
Best Actress	Vivien Leigh in *Gone With The Wind* (USA)
Best Supporting Actor	Thomas Mitchell in *Stagecoach* (USA)
Best Supporting Actress	Hattie McDaniel in *Gone With The Wind* (USA)
Best Direction	Victor Fleming for *Gone With The Wind* (USA)

Best Film nominations: *Dark Victory* (USA); *Gone With The Wind* (USA); *Goodbye Mr. Chips* (Britain); *Love Affair* (USA); *Mr. Smith Goes To Washington* (USA); *Ninotchka* (USA); *Of Mice And Men* (USA); *Stagecoach* (USA); *The Wizard Of Oz* (USA); *Wuthering Heights* (USA).

1940

Best Film	*Rebecca* (USA)
Best Actor	James Stewart in *The Philadelphia Story* (USA)
Best Actress	Ginger Rogers in *Kitty Foyle* (USA)
Best Supporting Actor	Walter Brennan in *The Westerner* (USA)

Best Supporting Actress	Jane Darwell in *The Grapes Of Wrath* (USA)
Best Direction	John Ford for *The Grapes of Wrath* (USA)

Best Film nominations: *All This, And Heaven Too* (USA); *Foreign Correspondent* (USA); *The Grapes Of Wrath* (USA); *The Great Dictator* (USA); *Kitty Foyle* (USA); *The Letter* (USA); *The Long Voyage Home* (USA); *Our Town* (USA); *The Philadelphia Story* (USA); *Rebecca* (USA).

1941

Best Film	*How Green Was My Valley* (USA)
Best Actor	Gary Cooper in *Sergeant York* (USA)
Best Actress	Joan Fontaine in *Suspicion* (USA)
Best Supporting Actor	Donald Crisp in *How Green Was My Valley* (USA)
Best Supporting Actress	Mary Astor in *The Great Lie* (USA)
Best Direction	John Ford for *How Green Was My Valley* (USA)

Best Film nominations: *Blossoms In The Dust* (USA); *Citizen Kane* (USA); *Here Comes Mr. Jordan* (USA); *Hold Back The Dawn* (USA); *How Green Was My Valley* (USA); *The Little Foxes* (USA); *The Maltese Falcon* (USA); *One Foot In Heaven* (USA); *Sergeant York* (USA); *Suspicion* (USA).

1942

Best Film	*Mrs. Miniver* (USA)
Best Actor	James Cagney in *Yankee Doodle Dandy* (USA)
Best Actress	Greer Garson in *Mrs. Miniver* (USA)
Best Supporting Actor	Van Heflin in *Johnny Eager* (USA)
Best Supporting Actress	Teresa Wright in *Mrs. Miniver* (USA)
Best Direction	William Wyler for *Mrs. Miniver* (USA)

Best Film nominations: *The 49th Parallel* (Britain); *Kings Row* (USA); *The Magnificent Ambersons* (USA); *Mrs. Miniver* (USA); *The Pied Piper* (USA); *The Pride Of The Yankees* (USA); *Random Harvest* (USA); *The Talk Of The Town* (USA); *Wake Island* (USA); *Yankee Doodle Dandy* (USA).

1943

Best Film	*Casablanca* (USA)
Best Actor	Paul Lukas in *Watch On The Rhine* (USA)
Best Actress	Jennifer Jones in *The Song Of Bernadette* (USA)
Best Supporting Actor	Charles Coburn in *The More The Merrier* (USA)
Best Supporting Actress	Katina Paxinou in *For Whom The Bell Tolls* (USA)
Best Direction	Michael Curtiz for *Casablanca* (USA)

Best Film nominations: *Casablanca* (USA); *For Whom The Bell Tolls* (USA); *Heaven Can Wait* (USA); *The Human Comedy* (USA); *In Which*

We Serve (Britain); *Madame Curie* (USA); *The More The Merrier* (USA); *The Ox-Bow Incident* (USA); *The Song Of Bernadette* (USA); *Watch On The Rhine* (USA).

1944

Best Film	*Going My Way* (USA)
Best Actor	Bing Crosby in *Going My Way* (USA)
Best Actress	Ingrid Bergman in *Gaslight* (USA)
Best Supporting Actor	Barry Fitzgerald in *Going My Way* (USA)
Best Supporting Actress	Ethel Barrymore in *None But The Lonely Heart* (USA)
Best Direction	Leo McCarey for *Going My Way* (USA)

Best Film nominations: *Double Indemnity* (USA); *Gaslight* (USA); *Going My Way* (USA); *Since You Went Away* (USA); *Wilson* (USA).

1945

Best Film	*The Lost Weekend* (USA)
Best Actor	Ray Milland in *The Lost Weekend* (USA)
Best Actress	Joan Crawford in *Mildred Pierce* (USA)
Best Supporting Actor	James Dunn in *A Tree Grows In Brooklyn* (USA)
Best Supporting Actress	Anne Revere in *National Velvet* (USA)
Best Direction	Billy Wilder for *The Lost Weekend* (USA)

Best Film nominations: *Anchors Aweigh* (USA); *The Bells Of St. Mary's* (USA); *The Lost Weekend* (USA); *Mildred Pierce* (USA); *Spellbound* (USA).

1946

Best Film	*The Best Years Of Our Lives* (USA)
Best Actor	Fredric March in *The Best Years Of Our Lives* (USA)
Best Actress	Olivia de Havilland in *To Each His Own* (USA)
Best Supporting Actor	Harold Russell in *The Best Years Of Our Lives* (USA)
Best Supporting Actress	Anne Baxter in *The Razor's Edge* (USA)
Best Direction	William Wyler for *The Best Years Of Our Lives* (USA)

Best Film nominations: *The Best Years Of Our Lives* (USA); *Henry V* (Britain); *It's A Wonderful Life* (USA); *The Razor's Edge* (USA); *The Yearling* (USA):

1947

Best Film	*Gentleman's Agreement* (USA)
Best Actor	Ronald Colman in *A Double Life* (USA)
Best Actress	Loretta Young in *The Farmer's Daughter* (USA)
Best Supporting Actor	Edmund Gwenn in *Miracle On 34th Street* (USA)

Best Supporting Actress	Celeste Holm in *Gentleman's Agreement* (USA)
Best Direction	Elia Kazan for *Gentleman's Agreement* (USA)

Best Film nominations: *The Bishop's Wife* (USA); *Crossfire* (USA); *Gentleman's Agreement* (USA); *Great Expectations* (Britain); *Miracle On 34th Street* (USA).

Note: The Italian production *Shoe Shine* was voted a special award for its high quality.

1948

Best Film	*Hamlet* (Britain)
Best Actor	Laurence Olivier in *Hamlet* (Britain)
Best Actress	Jane Wyman in *Johnny Belinda* (USA)
Best Supporting Actor	Walter Huston in *The Treasure Of The Sierra Madre* (USA)
Best Supporting Actress	Claire Trevor in *Key Largo* (USA)
Best Direction	John Huston for *The Treasure Of The Sierra Madre* (USA)

Best Film nominations: *Hamlet* (Britain); *Johnny Belinda* (USA); *The Red Shoes* (Britain); *The Snake Pit* (USA); *The Treasure Of The Sierra Madre* (USA).

Note: Monsieur Vincent (France) was voted by the Academy Board of Governors as the most outstanding foreign language film of the year.

1949

Best Film	*All The King's Men* (USA)
Best Actor	Broderick Crawford in *All The King's* Men (USA)
Best Actress	Olivia de Havilland in *The Heiress* (USA)
Best Supporting Actor	Dean Jagger in *Twelve O'Clock High* (USA)
Best Supporting Actress	Mercedes McCambridge in *All The King's Men* (USA)
Best Direction	Joseph L. Mankiewicz for *A Letter To Three Wives* (USA)

Best Film nominations: *All The King's Men* (USA); *Battleground* (USA); *The Heiress* (USA); *A Letter To Three Wives* (USA); *Twelve O'Clock High* (USA).

Note: Bicycle Thieves (Italy) was voted by the Academy Board of Governors as the most outstanding foreign language film of the year.

1950

Best Film	*All About Eve* (USA)
Best Actor	Jose Ferrer in *Cyrano de Bergerac* (USA)
Best Actress	Judy Holliday in *Born Yesterday* (USA)
Best Supporting Actor	George Sanders in *All About Eve* (USA)

Best Supporting Actress — Josephine Hull in *Harvey* (USA)
Best Direction — Joseph L. Mankiewicz for *All About Eve* (USA)
Best Film nominations: *All About Eve* (USA); *Born Yesterday* (USA); *Father Of The Bride* (USA); *King Solomon's Mines* (USA); *Sunset Boulevard* (USA).

Note: The Walls Of Malapaga (France/Italy) was voted by the Academy Board of Governors as the most outstanding foreign language film of the year.

1951

Best Film	*An American In Paris* (USA)
Best Actor	Humphrey Bogart in *The African Queen* (Britain)
Best Actress	Vivien Leigh in *A Streetcar Named Desire* (USA)
Best Supporting Actor	Karl Malden in *A Streetcar Named Desire* (USA)
Best Supporting Actress	Kim Hunter in *A Streetcar Named Desire* (USA)
Best Direction	George Stevens for *A Place In The Sun* (USA)

Best Film nominations: *An American In Paris* (USA); *Decision Before Dawn* (USA); *A Place In The Sun* (USA); *Quo Vadis* (USA); *A Streetcar Named Desire* (USA).

Note: Rashomon (Japan) was voted by the Academy Board of Governors as the most outstanding foreign language film of the year.

1952

Best Film	*The Greatest Show On Earth* (USA)
Best Actor	Gary Cooper in *High Noon* (USA)
Best Actress	Shirley Booth in *Come Back Little Sheba* (USA)
Best Supporting Actor	Anthony Quinn in *Viva Zapata!* (USA)
Best Supporting Actress	Gloria Grahame in *The Bad And The Beautiful* (USA)
Best Direction	John Ford for *The Quiet Man* (USA)

Best Film nominations: *The Greatest Show On Earth* (USA); *High Noon* (USA); *Ivanhoe* (Britain); *Moulin Rouge* (Britain); *The Quiet Man* (USA).

Note: Les Jeux Interdits (France) was voted by the Academy Board of Governors as the most outstanding foreign language film of the year.

1953

Best Film	*From Here To Eternity* (USA)
Best Actor	William Holden in *Stalag 17* (USA)
Best Actress	Audrey Hepburn in *Roman Holiday* (USA)
Best Supporting Actor	Frank Sinatra in *From Here To Eternity* (USA)

Best Supporting Actress	Donna Reed in *From Here To Eternity* (USA)
Best Direction	Fred Zinnemann for *From Here To Eternity* (USA)

Best Film nominations: *From Here To Eternity* (USA); *Julius Caesar* (USA); *The Robe* (USA); *Roman Holiday* (USA), *Shane* (USA).

Note: The Academy Board of Governors made no award to a foreign language picture in 1953.

1954

Best Film	*On The Waterfront* (USA)
Best Actor	Marlon Brando in *On The Waterfront* (USA)
Best Actress	Grace Kelly in *The Country Girl* (USA)
Best Supporting Actor	Edmond O'Brien in *The Barefoot Contessa* (USA)
Best Supporting Actress	Eva Marie Saint in *On The Waterfront* (USA)
Best Direction	Elia Kazan for *On The Waterfront* (USA)

Best Film nominations: *The Caine Mutiny* (USA); *The Country Girl* (USA); *On The Waterfront* (USA); *Seven Brides For Seven Brothers* (USA); *Three Coins In The Fountain* (USA).

Note: Gate Of Hell (Japan) was voted by the Academy Board of Governors as the most outstanding foreign language film of the year.

1955

Best Film	*Marty* (USA)
Best Actor	Ernest Borgnine in *Marty* (USA)
Best Actress	Anna Magnani in *The Rose Tattoo* (USA)
Best Supporting Actor	Jack Lemmon in *Mister Roberts* (USA)
Best Supporting Actress	Jo Van Fleet in *East Of Eden* (USA)
Best Direction	Delbert Mann for *Marty* (USA)

Best Film nominations: *Love Is A Many-Splendoured Thing* (USA); *Marty* (USA); *Mister Roberts* (USA); *Picnic* (USA); *The Rose Tattoo* (USA).

Note: Samurai (Japan) was voted by the Academy Board of Governors as the most outstanding foreign language film of the year.

1956

Best Film	*Around The World In 80 Days* (USA)
Best Actor	Yul Brynner in *The King And I* (USA)
Best Actress	Ingrid Bergman in *Anastasia* (USA)
Best Supporting Actor	Anthony Quinn in *Lust For Life* (USA)
Best Supporting Actress	Dorothy Malone in *Written On The Wind* (USA)
Best Direction	George Stevens for *Giant* (USA)

Best Film nominations: *Around The World In 80 Days* (USA); *Friendly Persuasion* (USA); *Giant* (USA); *The King And I* (USA); *The Ten Commandments* (USA).

La Strada (Italy) was named best foreign language film of the year. This marked the first occasion that the full Academy membership had voted in this category.

Other foreign language film nominations: *The Captain Of Kopenick* (Germany); *Gervaise* (France); *The Burmese Harp* (Japan); *Qivitoq* (Denmark).

1957

Best Film	*The Bridge On The River Kwai* (Britain)
Best Actor	Alec Guinness in *The Bridge On The River Kwai* (Britain)
Best Actress	Joanne Woodward in *The Three Faces Of Eve* (USA)
Best Supporting Actor	Red Buttons in *Sayonara* (USA)
Best Supporting Actress	Miyoshi Umeki in *Sayonara* (USA)
Best Direction	David Lean for *The Bridge On The River Kwai* (Britain)

Best Film nominations: *The Bridge On The River Kwai* (Britain); *Peyton Place* (USA); *Sayonara* (USA); *Twelve Angry Men* (USA); *Witness For The Prosecution* (USA);

The Nights Of Cabiria (Italy/France) was named best foreign language film of the year. Other foreign film nominations: *The Devil Came At Night* (Germany); *Gates Of Paris* (France); *Mother India* (India); *Nine Lives* (Norway).

1958

Best Film	*Gigi* (USA)
Best Actor	David Niven in *Separate Tables* (USA)
Best Actress	Susan Hayward in *I Want To Live* (USA)
Best Supporting Actor	Burl Ives in *The Big Country* (USA)
Best Supporting Actress	Wendy Hiller in *Separate Tables* (USA)
Best Direction	Vincente Minnelli for *Gigi* (USA)

Best Film nominations: *Auntie Mame* (USA); *Cat On A Hot Tin Roof* (USA); *The Defiant Ones* (USA); *Gigi* (USA); *Separate Tables* (USA).

Mon Oncle (France/Italy) was named best foreign language film of the year. Other foreign film nominations: *Arms And The Man* (Germany); *La Venganza* (Spain); *The Road A Year Long* (Yugoslavia); *The Usual Unidentified Thieves* (Italy).

1959

Best Film	*Ben-Hur* (USA)
Best Actor	Charlton Heston in *Ben-Hur* (USA)
Best Actress	Simone Signoret in *Room At The Top* (Britain)
Best Supporting Actor	Hugh Griffith in *Ben-Hur* (USA)
Best Supporting Actress	Shelley Winters in *The Diary Of Anne Frank* (USA)
Best Direction	William Wyler for *Ben-Hur* (USA)

Best Film nominations: *Anatomy Of A Murder* (USA); *Ben-Hur* (USA); *The Diary Of Anne Frank* (USA); *The Nun's Story* (USA); *Room At The Top* (Britain).

Black Orpheus (France/Italy) was named best foreign language film of the year. Other foreign film nominations: *The Bridge* (West Germany); *The Great War* (France/Italy); *Paw* (Denmark); *The Village On The River* (Holland).

1960

Best Film	*The Apartment* (USA)
Best Actor	Burt Lancaster in *Elmer Gantry* (USA)
Best Actress	Elizabeth Taylor in *Butterfield 8* (USA)
Best Supporting Actor	Peter Ustinov in *Spartacus* (USA)
Best Supporting Actress	Shirley Jones in *Elmer Gantry* (USA)
Best Direction	Billy Wilder for *The Apartment* (USA)

Best Film nominations: *The Alamo* (USA); *The Apartment* (USA); *Elmer Gantry* (USA); *Sons And Lovers* (Britain); *The Sundowners* (Britain).

The Virgin Spring (Sweden) was named best foreign language film of the year. Other foreign film nominations: *Kapo* (Italy); *La Vérité* (France); *Macario* (Mexico); *The Ninth Circle* (Yugoslavia).

1961

Best Film	*West Side Story* (USA)
Best Actor	Maximilian Schell in *Judgment At Nuremberg* (USA)
Best Actress	Sophia Loren in *Two Women* (France/Italy)
Best Supporting Actor	George Chakiris in *West Side Story* (USA)
Best Supporting Actress	Rita Moreno in *West Side Story* (USA)
Best Direction	Robert Wise and Jerome Robbins for *West Side Story* (USA)

Best Film nominations: *Fanny* (USA); *The Guns Of Navarone* (Britain); *The Hustler* (USA); *Judgment At Nuremberg* (USA); *West Side Story* (USA).

Through A Glass Darkly (Sweden) was named best foreign language film of the year. Other foreign film nominations: *Harry And The Butler* (Denmark); *Immortal Love* (Japan); *The Important Man* (Mexico); *Placido* (Spain).

1962

Best Film	*Lawrence Of Arabia* (Britain)
Best Actor	Gregory Peck in *To Kill A Mockingbird* (USA)
Best Actress	Anne Bancroft in *The Miracle Worker* (USA)
Best Supporting Actor	Ed Begley in *Sweet Bird Of Youth* (USA)
Best Supporting Actress	Patty Duke in *The Miracle Worker* (USA)
Best Direction	David Lean for *Lawrence Of Arabia* (Britain)

Best Film nominations: *Lawrence Of Arabia* (Britain); *The Longest Day* (USA); *The Music Man* (USA); *Mutiny On The Bounty* (USA); *To Kill A Mockingbird* (USA).

Sundays And Cybèle (France) was named best foreign language film of the year. Other foreign film nominations: *Electra* (Greece); *The Four Days Of Naples* (Italy); *The Given Word* (Brazil); *Tlayucan* (Mexico).

1963

Best Film	*Tom Jones* (Britain)
Best Actor	Sidney Poitier in *Lilies Of The Field* (USA)
Best Actress	Patricia Neal in *Hud* (USA)
Best Supporting Actor	Melvyn Douglas in *Hud* (USA)
Best Supporting Actress	Margaret Rutherford in *The V.I.P.s* (Britain)
Best Direction	Tony Richardson for *Tom Jones* (Britain)

Best Film nominations: *America, America* (USA); *Cleopatra* (USA); *How The West Was Won* (USA); *Lilies Of The Field* (USA); *Tom Jones* (Britain).

8½ (Italy) was named best foreign language film of the year. Other foreign film nominations: *Knife In The Water* (Poland); *Los Tarantos* (Spain); *The Red Lanterns* (Greece); *Twin Sisters Of Kyoto* (Japan).

1964

Best Film	*My Fair Lady* (USA)
Best Actor	Rex Harrison in *My Fair Lady* (USA)
Best Actress	Julie Andrews in *Mary Poppins* (USA)
Best Supporting Actor	Peter Ustinov in *Topkapi* (USA)
Best Supporting Actress	Lila Kedrova in *Zorba The Greek* (USA/Greece)
Best Direction	George Cukor for *My Fair Lady* (USA)

Best Film nominations: *Becket* (Britain); *Dr. Strangelove, Or How I Learned To Stop Worrying And Love The Bomb* (Britain); *Mary Poppins* (USA); *My Fair Lady* (USA); *Zorba The Greek* (USA/Greece).

Yesterday, Today And Tomorrow (Italy) was named best foreign language film of the year. Other foreign film nominations: *Raven's End* (Sweden); *Sallah* (Israel); *The Umbrellas Of Cherbourg* (France/West Germany); *Woman Of The Dunes* (Japan).

1965

Best Film	*The Sound Of Music* (USA)
Best Actor	Lee Marvin in *Cat Ballou* (USA)
Best Actress	Julie Christie in *Darling* (Britain)
Best Supporting Actor	Martin Balsam in *A Thousand Clowns* (USA)
Best Supporting Actress	Shelley Winters in *A Patch Of Blue* (USA)
Best Direction	Robert Wise for *The Sound Of Music* (USA)

Best Film nominations: *Darling* (Britain); *Doctor Zhivago* (USA);

Ship Of Fools (USA); *The Sound Of Music* (USA); *A Thousand Clowns* (USA).

The Shop On Main Street (Czechoslovakia) was named best foreign language film of the year. Other foreign film nominations: *Blood On The Land* (Greece); *Dear John* (Sweden); *Kwaidan* (Japan); *Marriage, Italian Style* (Italy).

1966

Best Film	*A Man For All Seasons* (Britain)
Best Actor	Paul Scofield in *A Man For All Seasons* (Britain)
Best Actress	Elizabeth Taylor in *Who's Afraid Of Virginia Woolf?* (USA)
Best Supporting Actor	Walter Matthau in *The Fortune Cookie* (USA)
Best Supporting Actress	Sandy Dennis in *Who's Afraid Of Virginia Woolf?* (USA)
Best Direction	Fred Zinnemann for *A Man For All Seasons* (Britain)

Best Film nominations: *Alfie* (Britain); *A Man For All Seasons* (Britain); *The Russians Are Coming, The Russians Are Coming* (USA); *The Sand Pebbles* (USA); *Who's Afraid Of Virginia Woolf?* (USA).

A Man And A Woman (France) was named best foreign language film of the year. Other foreign film nominations: *The Battle Of Algiers* (Algeria/Italy); *A Blonde In Love* (Czechoslovakia); *Pharaoh* (Poland); *Three* (Yugoslavia).

1967

Best Film	*In The Heat Of The Night* (USA)
Best Actor	Rod Steiger in *In The Heat Of The Night* (USA)
Best Actress	Katharine Hepburn in *Guess Who's Coming To Dinner?* (USA)
Best Supporting Actor	George Kennedy in *Cool Hand Luke* (USA)
Best Supporting Actress	Estelle Parsons in *Bonnie And Clyde* (USA)
Best Direction	Mike Nichols for *The Graduate* (USA)

Best Film nominations: *Bonnie And Clyde* (USA); *Doctor Dolittle* (USA); *The Graduate* (USA); *Guess Who's Coming To Dinner?* (USA); *In The Heat Of The Night* (USA).

Closely Observed Trains (Czechoslovakia) was named best foreign language film of the year. Other foreign film nominations: *El Amor Brujo* (Spain); *I Even Met Happy Gypsies* (Yugoslavia); *Live For Life* (France); *Portrait Of Chieko* (Japan).

1968

Best Film	*Oliver!* (Britain)
Best Actor	Cliff Robertson in *Charly* (USA)
Best Actress	Barbra Streisand in *Funny Girl* (USA) and Katharine Hepburn in *The Lion In Winter* (Britain)
Best Supporting Actor	Jack Albertson in *The Subject Was Roses* (USA)
Best Supporting Actress	Ruth Gordon in *Rosemary's Baby* (USA)
Best Direction	Carol Reed for *Oliver!* (Britain)

Best Film nominations: *Funny Girl* (USA); *The Lion In Winter* (Britain); *Oliver!* (Britain); *Rachel, Rachel* (USA); *Romeo And Juliet* (Britain).

War And Peace (USSR) was named best foreign language film of the year. Other foreign film nominations: *The Boys Of Paul Street* (Hungary); *The Fireman's Ball* (Czechoslovakia); *The Girl With The Pistol* (Italy); *Stolen Kisses* (France).

1969

Best Film	*Midnight Cowboy* (USA)
Best Actor	John Wayne in *True Grit* (USA)
Best Actress	Maggie Smith in *The Prime Of Miss Jean Brodie* (Britain)
Best Supporting Actor	Gig Young in *They Shoot Horses, Don't They?* (USA)
Best Supporting Actress	Goldie Hawn in *Cactus Flower* (USA)
Best Direction	John Schlesinger for *Midnight Cowboy* (USA)

Best Film nominations: *Anne Of The Thousand Days* (Britain); *Butch Cassidy And The Sundance Kid* (USA); *Hello, Dolly!* (USA); *Midnight Cowboy* (USA); *Z* (France/Algeria).

Z (France/Algeria) was named best foreign language film of the year. Other foreign film nominations: *Adalen '31* (Sweden); *The Battle Of Neretva* (Yugoslavia); *The Brothers Karamazov* (USSR); *My Night At Maud's* (France).

1970

Best Film	*Patton* (USA)
Best Actor	George C. Scott in *Patton* (USA)
Best Actress	Glenda Jackson in *Women In Love* (Britain)
Best Supporting Actor	John Mills in *Ryan's Daughter* (Britain)
Best Supporting Actress	Helen Hayes in *Airport* (USA)
Best Direction	Franklin J. Schaffner for *Patton* (USA)

Best Film nominations: *Airport* (USA); *Five Easy Pieces* (USA); *Love Story* (USA); *M.A.S.H.* (USA); *Patton* (USA).

Investigation Of A Citizen Above Suspicion (Italy) was named best foreign language film of the year. Other foreign film nominations: *First Love* (Switzerland); *Hoa-Binh* (France); *Paix Sur Les Champs* (Belgium; *Tristana* (Spain).

1971

Best Film — *The French Connection* (USA)
Best Actor — Gene Hackman in *The French Connection* (USA)
Best Actress — Jane Fonda in *Klute* (USA)
Best Supporting Actor — Ben Johnson in *The Last Picture Show* (USA)
Best Supporting Actress — Cloris Leachman in *The Last Picture Show* (USA)
Best Direction — William Friedkin for *The French Connection* (USA)

Best Film nominations: *A Clockwork Orange* (Britain); *Fiddler On The Roof* (USA); *The French Connection* (USA); *The Last Picture Show* (USA); *Nicholas And Alexandra* (USA).

The Garden Of The Finzi-Continis (Italy/West Germany) was named best foreign language film of the year. Other foreign film nominations: *Dodes'ka-Den* (Japan); *The Emigrants* (Sweden); *The Policeman* (Israel); *Tchaikovsky* (USSR).

1972

Best Film — *The Godfather* (USA)
Best Actor — Marlon Brando in *The Godfather* (USA)
Best Actress — Liza Minnelli in *Cabaret* (USA)
Best Supporting Actor — Joel Grey in *Cabaret* (USA)
Best Supporting Actress — Eileen Heckart in *Butterflies Are Free* (USA)
Best Direction — Bob Fosse for *Cabaret* (USA)

Best Film nominations: *Cabaret* (USA); *Deliverance* (USA); *The Emigrants* (Sweden); *The Godfather* (USA); *Sounder* (USA).

The Discreet Charm Of The Bourgeoisie (France) was named best foreign language film of the year. Other foreign film nominations: *The Dawns Here Are Quiet* (USSR); *I Love You Rosa* (Israel); *My Dearest Senorita* (Spain); *The New Land* (Sweden).

1973

Best Film — *The Sting* (USA)
Best Actor — Jack Lemmon in *Save The Tiger* (USA)
Best Actress — Glenda Jackson in *A Touch Of Class* (Britain)
Best Supporting Actor — John Houseman in *The Paper Chase* (USA)
Best Supporting Actress — Tatum O'Neal in *Paper Moon* (USA)
Best Direction — George Roy Hill for *The Sting* (USA)

Best Film nominations: *American Graffiti* (USA); *Cries And Whispers* (Sweden); *The Exorcist* (USA); *The Sting* (USA); *A Touch Of Class* (Britain).

Day For Night (France/Italy) was named best foreign language film of the year. Other foreign film nominations: *The House On Chelouche Street* (Israel); *The Invitation* (Switzerland); *The Pedestrian* (West Germany); *Turkish Delight* (Holland).

1974

Best Film	*The Godfather Part II* (USA)
Best Actor	Art Carney in *Harry And Tonto* (USA)
Best Actress	Ellen Burstyn in *Alice Doesn't Live Here Anymore* (USA)
Best Supporting Actor	Robert De Niro in *The Godfather Part II* (USA)
Best Supporting Actress	Ingrid Bergman in *Murder On The Orient Express* (Britain)
Best Direction	Francis Ford Coppola for *The Godfather Part II* (USA)

Best Film nominations: *Chinatown* (USA); *The Conversation* (USA); *The Godfather Part II* (USA); *Lenny* (USA); *The Towering Inferno* (USA).

Amarcord (Italy/France) was named best foreign language film of the year. Other foreign film nominations: *Catsplay* (Hungary); *The Deluge* (Poland); *Lacombe Lucien* (France/Italy/West Germany); *The Truce* (Argentina).

1975

Best Film	*One Flew Over The Cuckoo's Nest* (USA)
Best Actor	Jack Nicholson in *One Flew Over The Cuckoo's Nest* (USA)
Best Actress	Louise Fletcher in *One Flew Over The Cuckoo's Nest* (USA)
Best Supporting Actor	George Burns in *The Sunshine Boys* (USA)
Best Supporting Actress	Lee Grant in *Shampoo* (USA)
Best Direction	Milos Forman for *One Flew Over The Cuckoo's Nest* (USA)

Best Film nominations: *Barry Lyndon* (Britain); *Dog Day Afternoon* (USA); *Jaws* (USA); *Nashville* (USA); *One Flew Over The Cuckoo's Nest* (USA).

Dersu Uzala (USSR/Japan) was named best foreign language film of the year. Other foreign film nominations: *The Promised Land* (Poland); *Letters From Marusia* (Mexico); *Sandakan No. 8* (Japan); *Scent Of A Woman* (Italy).

1976

Best Film	*Rocky* (USA)
Best Actor	Peter Finch in *Network* (USA)
Best Actress	Faye Dunaway in *Network* (USA)
Best Supporting Actor	Jason Robards in *All The President's Men* (USA)
Best Supporting Actress	Beatrice Straight in *Network* (USA)
Best Direction	John G. Avildsen for *Rocky* (USA)

Best Film nominations: *All The President's Men* (USA); *Bound For Glory* (USA); *Network* (USA); *Rocky* (USA); *Taxi Driver* (USA).

Black And White In Colour (France/Switzerland/Ivory Coast) was named best foreign language film of the year. Other foreign film nominations: *Cousin Cousine* (France); *Jacob, The Liar* (East Germany); *Nights And Days* (Poland; *Seven Beauties* (Italy).

1977

Best Film	*Annie Hall* (USA)
Best Actor	Richard Dreyfuss in *The Goodbye Girl* (USA)
Best Actress	Diane Keaton in *Annie Hall* (USA)
Best Supporting Actor	Jason Robards in *Julia* (USA)
Best Supporting Actress	Vanessa Redgrave in *Julia* (USA)
Best Direction	Woody Allen for *Annie Hall* (USA)

Best Film nominations: *Annie Hall* (USA); *The Goodbye Girl* (USA); *Julia* (USA); *Star Wars* (USA); *The Turning Point* (USA).

Madame Rosa (France) was named best foreign language film of the year. Other foreign film nominations: *Iphigenia* (Greece); *Operation Thunderbolt* (Israel); *A Special Day* (Italy); *That Obscure Object Of Desire* (France/Spain).

1978

Best Film	*The Deer Hunter* (USA)
Best Actor	Jon Voight in *Coming Home* (USA)
Best Actress	Jane Fonda in *Coming Home* (USA)
Best Supporting Actor	Christopher Walken in *The Deer Hunter* (USA)
Best Supporting Actress	Maggie Smith in *California Suite* (USA)
Best Direction	Michael Cimino for *The Deer Hunter* (USA)

Best Film nominations: *Coming Home* (USA); *The Deer Hunter* (USA); *Heaven Can Wait* (USA); *Midnight Express* (Britain); *An Unmarried Woman* (USA).

Get Out Your Handkerchiefs (France/Belgium) was named best foreign language film of the year. Other foreign film nominations: *The Glass Cell* (West Germany); *Hungarians* (Hungary); *Viva Italia* (Italy); *White Bim With A Black Ear* (USSR).

1979

Best Film	*Kramer vs. Kramer* (USA)
Best Actor	Dustin Hoffman in *Kramer vs. Kramer* (USA)
Best Actress	Sally Field in *Norma Rae* (USA)
Best Supporting Actor	Melvyn Douglas in *Being There* (USA)
Best Supporting Actress	Meryl Streep in *Kramer vs. Kramer* (USA)
Best Direction	Robert Benton for *Kramer vs. Kramer* (USA)

Best Film nominations: *All That Jazz* (USA); *Apocalypse Now* (USA); *Breaking Away* (USA); *Kramer vs. Kramer* (USA); *Norma Rae* (USA).

The Tin Drum (West Germany) was voted best foreign language film of the year. Other foreign film nominations: *The Maids Of Wilko* (Poland); *Mama Turns A Hundred* (Spain); *A Simple Story* (France); *To Forget Venice* (Italy).

New York Film Critics

The New York Film Critics Circle was the third major organization to present best film and performance awards in the United States. The Circle was inaugurated in 1935 and its awards presented to signify the recognition of the highest creative achievements in motion pictures and to uphold the dignity and significance of film criticism.

In the early years, the awards were made by the 17 or 18 critics of the New York papers. In the eighties the number has grown to over 30 and includes critics from magazines and journals as well as newspapers.

Balloting has always been secret although the Circle frequently makes public the number of votes each film or performer receives.

Voting systems have changed since the awards began in 1935. In the first few years, a two-thirds majority was required for a film or performer to be named best of the year. On one occasion this necessitated as many as 14 ballots before a decision was reached. In the forties and throughout the fifties and sixties, the same procedure was streamlined so that if the two-thirds majority was not achieved on the first 5 ballots a straight vote on the sixth and final ballot decided the winner.

In 1969, when the best film and best foreign film awards were combined into a single best picture prize, the votes were cast on a points system with each critic allocating 3, 2 and 1 for the top three pictures respectively. The total number of points decided the year's best.

Best film, actor, actress and direction awards have been presented since the first annual banquet. Supporting actor and actress awards were added in 1969.

The New York Critics Awards are held in high esteem and are often a guide to those presented at the subsequent Oscar ceremonies in April.

1935

Best Film	*The Informer* (USA)
Best Actor	Charles Laughton in *Mutiny On The Bounty* (USA) & *Ruggles Of Red Gap* (USA)
Best Actress	Greta Garbo in *Anna Karenina* (USA)
Best Direction	John Ford for *The Informer* (USA)

Note: The Informer was the unanimous choice on the first ballot.

1936

Best Film	*Mr. Deeds Goes To Town* (USA)
Best Actor	Walter Huston in *Dodsworth* (USA)
Best Actress	Luise Rainer in *The Great Ziegfeld* (USA)
Best Direction	Rouben Mamoulian for *The Gay Desperado* (USA)

Five movies were considered for the best film award: Frank Capra's *Mr. Deeds Goes To Town* (USA), *Fury* (USA), *Winterset* (USA), *These Three* (USA) and *Dodsworth* (USA). The Capra picture won on the second ballot by 11 votes to 4 for *Fury*.

La Kermesse Heroïque (France) was named best foreign language film.

1937

Best Film	*The Life Of Emile Zola* (USA)
Best Actor	Paul Muni in *The Life Of Emile Zola* (USA)
Best Actress	Greta Garbo in *Camille* (USA)
Best Direction	Gregory La Cava for *Stage Door* (USA)

The Life Of Emile Zola was named best picture on the second ballot. *Captains Courageous* (USA) and *The Good Earth* (USA) were the runners-up.

Mayerling (France) was voted best foreign language film.

1938

Best Film	*The Citadel* (Britain)
Best Actor	James Cagney in *Angels With Dirty Faces* (USA)
Best Actress	Margaret Sullavan in *Three Comrades* (USA)
Best Direction	Alfred Hitchcock for *The Lady Vanishes* (Britain)

The Citadel won the best picture award on the fourth ballot. *The Lady Vanishes* (Britain), *To The Victor* (Britain), *Sing You Sinners* (USA), *In Old Chicago* (USA), *Blockade* (USA) and *Bank Holiday* (Britain) were the other films considered. 18 critics voted.

Jean Renoir's *La Grande Illusion* (France) was named best foreign language film; Walt Disney received a special award for his *Snow White And The Seven Dwarfs* (USA).

1939

Best Film	*Wuthering Heights* (USA)
Best Actor	James Stewart in *Mr. Smith Goes To Washington* (USA)
Best Actress	Vivien Leigh in *Gone With The Wind* (USA)
Best Direction	John Ford for *Stagecoach* (USA)

Wuthering Heights was a compromise best picture winner. It was selected after 14 ballots and eventually preferred to the two favourites for the award — *Gone With The Wind* and *Mr. Smith Goes To Washington.*

Harvest (France) was voted best foreign language film ahead of Julien Duvivier's *La Fin Du Jour* (France).

1940

Best Film	*The Grapes Of Wrath* (USA)
Best Actor	Charles Chaplin in *The Great Dictator* (USA)
Best Actress	Katharine Hepburn in *The Philadelphia Story* (USA)
Best Direction	John Ford for *The Grapes Of Wrath* (USA) & *The Long Voyage Home* (USA)

Marcel Pagnol's *La Femme Du Boulanger* (France) was named best foreign language film; Walt Disney and Leopold Stokowski were presented with a special award for *Fantasia* (USA); Charles Chaplin refused his acting prize for *The Great Dictator*.

1941

Best Film	*Citizen Kane* (USA)
Best Actor	Gary Cooper in *Sergeant York* (USA)
Best Actress	Joan Fontaine in *Suspicion* (USA)
Best Direction	John Ford for *How Green Was My Valley* (USA)

Citizen Kane won on the sixth ballot defeating *How Green Was My Valley* by 10 votes to 7. Howard Hawks' *Sergeant York* was also a contender in the early voting.

The critics abandoned their foreign language award because of the war. They also streamlined their voting system to a maximum of six ballots. A two-thirds majority was required for a film to win during the first five ballots; only a simple majority verdict was needed to win if the voting went to a sixth and final ballot.

1942

Best Film	*In Which We Serve* (Britain)
Best Actor	James Cagney in *Yankee Doodle Dandy* (USA)
Best Actress	Agnes Moorehead in *The Magnificent Ambersons* (USA)
Best Direction	John Farrow for *Wake Island* (USA)

In Which We Serve (with 11 votes on the fifth ballot) was named best film ahead of *Wake Island* (7 votes) and *The Moon And Sixpence* (USA).

1943

Best Film — *Watch On The Rhine* (USA)
Best Actor — Paul Lukas in *Watch On The Rhine* (USA)
Best Actress — Ida Lupino in *The Hard Way* (USA)
Best Direction — George Stevens for *The More The Merrier* (USA)

Watch On The Rhine won on the sixth ballot, defeating *The Human Comedy* (USA) by 11 votes to 5.

Also considered: *Hangmen Also Die* (USA); *Mission To Moscow* (USA); *Corvette K-225* (USA); *Claudia* (USA); *Action In The North Atlantic* (USA); *This Is The Army* (USA); *Holy Matrimony* (USA); *Air Force* (USA).

1944

Best Film — *Going My Way* (USA)
Best Actor — Barry Fitzgerald in *Going My Way* (USA)
Best Actress — Tallulah Bankhead in *Lifeboat* (USA)
Best Direction — Leo McCarey for *Going My Way* (USA)

Three ballots were needed before the critics selected *Going My Way* as best film. Final voting figures – *Going My Way*, 11 votes; *Hail The Conquering Hero* (USA), 3 votes; *Wilson* (USA), 2 votes.

Billy Wilder's *Double Indemnity* (USA) and Britain's *Thunder Rock* were also in contention.

1945

Best Film — *The Lost Weekend* (USA)
Best Actor — Ray Milland in *The Lost Weekend* (USA)
Best Actress — Ingrid Bergman in *Spellbound* (USA) & *The Bells Of St. Mary's* (USA)
Best Direction — Billy Wilder for *The Lost Weekend* (USA)

The Lost Weekend narrowly defeated *The Story Of G.I. Joe* (USA) by 9 votes to 8. Voting went to the sixth and final ballot. The Powell/Pressburger production *The Life And Death Of Colonel Blimp* (Britain) and the musical *State Fair* (USA) were other best picture contenders.

1946

Best Film — *The Best Years Of Our Lives* (USA)
Best Actor — Laurence Olivier in *Henry V* (Britain)
Best Actress — Celia Johnson in *Brief Encounter* (Britain)
Best Direction — William Wyler for *The Best Years Of Our Lives* (USA)

Three movies were considered for the best film award: *The Best Years Of Our Lives, Henry V* and *A Matter Of Life And Death* (Britain). Wyler's picture came out ahead on the second ballot, defeating *Henry V* by 12 votes to 6.

The foreign language award was re-instated in 1946. Rossellini's *Open City* (Italy) was named best of the year ahead of Marcel Pagnol's *The Well-Digger's Daughter* (France).

1947

Best Film	*Gentleman's Agreement* (USA)
Best Actor	William Powell in *Life With Father* (USA) & *The Senator Was Indiscreet* (USA)
Best Actress	Deborah Kerr in *Black Narcissus* (Britain) & *I See A Dark Stranger* (Britain)
Best Direction	Elia Kazan for *Gentleman's Agreement* (USA) & *Boomerang* (USA)

Gentleman's Agreement won on the sixth ballot, defeating David Lean's *Great Expectations* by 9 votes to 7.

Five other films merited consideration: *Odd Man Out* (Britain); *Crossfire* (USA); *Miracle On 34th Street* (USA); *The Fugitive* (USA); and *Boomerang* (USA).

To Live In Peace (Italy) was named best foreign language film on the fourth ballot. De Sica's *Shoe-Shine* (Italy), Duvivier's *Panique* (France) and Marcel Carné's *Les Enfants Du Paradis* (France) were other candidates for the award.

1948

Best Film	*The Treasure Of The Sierra Madre* (USA)
Best Actor	Laurence Olivier in *Hamlet* (Britain)
Best Actress	Olivia de Havilland in *The Snake Pit* (USA)
Best Direction	John Huston for *The Treasure Of The Sierra Madre* (USA)

The Treasure Of The Sierra Madre (9 votes) won on the sixth ballot. Runners-up: *Hamlet* (8 votes) and *The Snake Pit*. Fred Zinnemann's *The Search* (USA/Switzerland) was also a contender in the early balloting.

Rossellini's *Paisa* (Italy) was selected as the best foreign language film on the third ballot. Also considered: *Monsieur Vincent* (France); *La Symphonie Pastorale* (France); *Four Steps In The Clouds* (Italy); *Farrebique* (France); *Fanny* (France); and *Day Of Wrath* (Denmark).

1949

Best Film	*All The King's Men* (USA)
Best Actor	Broderick Crawford in *All The King's Men* (USA)
Best Actress	Olivia de Havilland in *The Heiress* (USA)
Best Direction	Carol Reed for *The Fallen Idol* (Britain)

Voting went to the sixth ballot. Final voting figures: *All The King's Men*, 9 votes; *Intruder In The Dust* (USA), 5 votes; *The Fallen Idol* (Britain), 3 votes.

Britain's *Quartet* and *Fame Is The Spur*; *Lost Boundaries* (USA) and Wellman's *Battleground* (USA) were among the other films considered for the award.

Bicycle Thieves (Italy) — with 13 votes — was named best foreign language film on the first ballot. *Le Diable Au Corps* (France), *The Last Stage* (Poland) and *Affaire Blum* (Germany) were runners-up.

1950

Best Film	*All About Eve* (USA)
Best Actor	Gregory Peck in *Twelve O'Clock High* (USA)
Best Actress	Bette Davis in *All About Eve* (USA)
Best Direction	Joseph L. Mankiewicz for *All About Eve* (USA)

All About Eve won on the first ballot, defeating its nearest rival *Sunset Boulevard* (USA) by 11 votes to 3. Two other films were nominated: *The Asphalt Jungle* (USA) with 2 votes and *Devil's Doorway* (USA) with 1 vote.

The compilation film *Ways Of Love* (France/Italy) was voted best foreign language picture.

1951

Best Film	*A Streetcar Named Desire* (USA)
Best Actor	Arthur Kennedy in *Lights Out* (USA)
Best Actress	Vivien Leigh in *A Streetcar Named Desire* (USA)
Best Direction	Elia Kazan for *A Streetcar Named Desire* (USA)

A Streetcar Named Desire won on the sixth ballot, narrowly defeating Renoir's *The River* (India) by 8 votes to 7. The Oscar-winning *An American In Paris* (USA), *A Place In The Sun* (USA) and *Death Of A Salesman* (USA) also figured in the voting.

Five films were nominated for the best foreign language picture: — *Rashomon* (Japan); *Miracle In Milan* (Italy); *La Marie Du Port* (France); *The Secret Of Mayerling* (France); and *Passion For Life* (France).

De Sica's *Miracle In Milan* won on the fourth ballot defeating *Rashomon* by 10 votes to 5.

1952

Best Film	*High Noon* (USA)
Best Actor	Ralph Richardson in *The Sound Barrier* (Britain)
Best Actress	Shirley Booth in *Come Back, Little Sheba* (USA)
Best Direction	Fred Zinnemann for *High Noon* (USA)

High Noon was named on the sixth and final ballot, defeating the *1951* Oscar contender *The African Queen* by 10 votes to 5.

Seven other films were in contention: *The Quiet Man* (USA); *The Greatest Show On Earth* (USA); *The Man In The White Suit* (Britain); *Come Back, Little Sheba* (USA); *The Sound Barrier* (Britain); *Hans Christian Andersen* (USA); *Singin' In The Rain* (USA).

Les Jeux Interdits (France) was voted best foreign language film of the year.

1953

Best Film	*From Here To Eternity* (USA)
Best Actor	Burt Lancaster in *From Here To Eternity* (USA)
Best Actress	Audrey Hepburn in *Roman Holiday* (USA)
Best Direction	Fred Zinnemann for *From Here To Eternity* (USA)

Just two ballots were required to select *From Here To Eternity* as the year's best. Zinnemann's film won with 11 votes. *Conquest Of Everest* (Britain), *Roman Holiday* (USA), *Moulin Rouge* (Britain) and the first CinemaScope feature, *The Robe* (USA) were also considered.

Justice Est Faite (France) was named best foreign language film.

1954

Best Film	*On The Waterfront* (USA)
Best Actor	Marlon Brando in *On The Waterfront* (USA)
Best Actress	Grace Kelly in *The Country Girl* (USA), *Rear Window* (USA) & *Dial M For Murder* (USA)
Best Direction	Elia Kazan for *On The Waterfront* (USA)

On The Waterfront (with 12 of a possible 16 votes) was named best film on the first ballot. *The Country Girl* (USA), 2 votes; *Romeo And Juliet* (Britain/Italy), 1 vote; and *Carmen Jones* (USA), 1 vote, were the runners-up.

Three films were nominated for the foreign language award — *Gate Of Hell* (Japan), *Monsieur Hulot's Holiday* (France) and *Bread, Love And Dreams* (Italy). *Gate Of Hell* won on the second ballot, defeating *Monsieur Hulot's Holiday* by 11 votes to 5.

1955

Best Film	*Marty* (USA)
Best Actor	Ernest Borgnine in *Marty* (USA)
Best Actress	Anna Magnani in *The Rose Tattoo* (USA)
Best Direction	David Lean for *Summertime* (USA)

Marty (12 votes) was selected on the third ballot. *Mister Roberts* (USA), with 4 votes, *Summertime, The Rose Tattoo* and *Oklahoma!* (USA) also figured in the voting.

The foreign language prize was tied for the first time in the history of the awards, De Sica's *Umberto D* (Italy) and Clouzot's thriller *Les Diaboliques* (France) each sharing 5 votes.

1956

Best Film	*Around The World In 80 Days* (USA)
Best Actor	Kirk Douglas in *Lust For Life* (USA)
Best Actress	Ingrid Bergman in *Anastasia* (USA)
Best Direction	John Huston for *Moby Dick* (Britain)

Only two ballots were needed to name *Around The World In 80 Days* best picture of the year. *Giant* (USA), *The King And I* (USA), *Lust For Life* (USA) and *Moby Dick* (Britain) were the main competitors.

La Strada (Italy) — with 12 votes on the first ballot — was named best foreign language film.

1957

Best Film	*The Bridge On The River Kwai* (Britain)
Best Actor	Alec Guinness in *The Bridge On The River Kwai* (Britain)
Best Actress	Deborah Kerr in *Heaven Knows, Mr. Allison* (USA)
Best Direction	David Lean for *The Bridge On The River Kwai* (Britain)

The Bridge On The River Kwai was named best film on the second ballot. Final voting figures: *The Bridge On The River Kwai*, 13 votes; *Twelve Angry Men* (USA), 2 votes; *Sayonara* (USA), 1 vote.

Zinnemann's *A Hatful Of Rain* (USA) and Huston's *Heaven Knows, Mr. Allison* (USA) were considered on the first ballot. 16 critics voted.

René Clément's *Gervaise* (France) earned the foreign language award, defeating Albert Lamorisse's *The Red Balloon* (France) by 8 votes to 5 on the sixth ballot. *Ordet* (Denmark) with 3 votes was placed third.

The Gold Of Naples (Italy); *Nous Sommes Tous Des Assassins* (France); *The Devil's General* (Germany); *The Nights Of Cabiria* (Italy/France); *The Last Bridge* (Austria) and *Torero!* (Mexico) were also considered.

1958

Best Film	*The Defiant Ones* (USA)
Best Actor	David Niven in *Separate Tables* (USA)
Best Actress	Susan Hayward in *I Want To Live* (USA)
Best Direction	Stanley Kramer for *The Defiant Ones* (USA)

The Defiant Ones defeated *Separate Tables* (USA) by 10 votes to 5 on the third ballot.

The Horse's Mouth (Britain), *The Last Hurrah* (USA), *Gigi* (USA), *Hot Spell* (USA) and *The Big Country* (USA) were also in contention during the early balloting.

Jacques Tati's *Mon Oncle* (France/Italy) was named best foreign language picture after six ballots. Dassin's *He Who Must Die* (France) and *Pather Panchali* (India) were runners-up.

1959

Best Film	*Ben-Hur* (USA)
Best Actor	James Stewart in *Anatomy Of A Murder* (USA)
Best Actress	Audrey Hepburn in *The Nun's Story* (USA)
Best Direction	Fred Zinnemann for *The Nun's Story* (USA)

Ben-Hur defeated *Room At The Top* (Britain) by 10 votes to 5. Voting went to the fifth ballot.

Stanley Kramer's *On The Beach* (USA); *Anatomy Of A Murder*; *The Nun's Story*; *Suddenly, Last Summer* (Britain); *Career* (USA); *The Last Angry Man* (USA) and *The Diary Of Anne Frank* (USA) were other best picture contenders.

Les Quatre Cents Coups (France) was named best foreign language picture and defeated the Cannes winner *Black Orpheus* (France/Italy) by 12 votes to 3 on the third ballot. Also considered: *Wild Strawberries* (Sweden), *Aparajito* (India), *The Face* (Sweden) and *Ivan The Terrible Part II* (USSR).

1960

Best Film	*The Apartment* (USA) & *Sons And Lovers* (Britain)
Best Actor	Burt Lancaster in *Elmer Gantry* (USA)
Best Actress	Deborah Kerr in *The Sundowners* (Britain/Australia)
Best Direction	Billy Wilder for *The Apartment* (USA) & Jack Cardiff for *Sons And Lovers* (Britain)

The Apartment and *Sons And Lovers* shared the first-ever tie in the best picture category. *Elmer Gantry* (USA), *Sunrise At Campobello* (USA), *Exodus* (USA), *Inherit The Wind* (USA), *Psycho* (USA) and *Tunes Of Glory* (Britain) were also in contention.

Alain Resnais' *Hiroshima, Mon Amour* (France/Japan) was named best foreign language film.

Runners-up: *Il Generale Della Rovere* (Italy/France); *The Virgin Spring* (Sweden); *Never On Sunday* (Greece); *The Big Deal* (Italy); *Ikuru* (Japan); *Ballad Of A Soldier* (USSR); and *The World Of Apu* (India).

1961

Best Film	*West Side Story* (USA)
Best Actor	Maximilian Schell in *Judgment At Nuremberg* (USA)
Best Actress	Sophia Loren in *Two Women* (France/Italy)
Best Direction	Robert Rossen for *The Hustler* (USA)

West Side Story won on the third ballot, defeating *Judgment At Nuremberg* by 11 votes to 5. Five other films merited consideration: *The Greengage Summer* (Britain); *The Guns Of Navarone* (Britain); *A Raisin In The Sun* (USA); *Saturday Night And Sunday Morning* (Britain); and *The Mark* (Britain).

La Dolce Vita (Italy/France) was named best foreign language picture ahead of *Two Women* and Antonioni's *L'Avventura* (Italy). Voting went to the third ballot.

1962

The Awards were not presented in 1962 because of a New York newspaper strike.

1963

Best Film	*Tom Jones* (Britain)
Best Actor	Albert Finney in *Tom Jones* (Britain)
Best Actress	Patricia Neal in *Hud* (USA)
Best Direction	Tony Richardson for *Tom Jones* (Britain)

Tom Jones was voted best picture ahead of *Hud* (USA), *To Kill A Mockingbird* (USA), *It's A Mad, Mad, Mad, Mad World* (USA) and Hitchcock's *The Birds* (USA).

Fellini's *8½* (Italy) was named the year's best foreign language film.

1964

Best Film	*My Fair Lady* (USA)
Best Actor	Rex Harrison in *My Fair Lady* (USA)
Best Actress	Kim Stanley in *Seance On A Wet Afternoon* (Britain)
Best Direction	Stanley Kubrick for *Dr. Strangelove; or, How I Learned To Stop Worrying And Love The Bomb* (Britain)

My Fair Lady won on the fourth ballot, defeating *Dr. Strangelove* by 8 votes to 5. Votes were also cast for *The Servant* (Britain), *Zorba The Greek* (USA/Greece) and *Becket* (Britain).

That Man From Rio (France/Italy) took the foreign language honours against strong opposition i.e. *Seduced And Abandoned* (France/Italy); *The Organizer* (France/Italy/Yugoslavia); *The Umbrellas Of Cherbourg* (France/West Germany); *Marriage — Italian Style* (Italy); and *Yesterday, Today And Tomorrow* (Italy).

1965

Best Film	*Darling* (Britain)
Best Actor	Oskar Werner in *Ship Of Fools* (USA)
Best Actress	Julie Christie in *Darling* (Britain)
Best Direction	John Schlesinger for *Darling* (Britain)

Voting went to the sixth ballot. Final tally: *Darling*, 8 votes; *The Pawnbroker* (USA), 5 votes; *Those Magnificent Men In Their Flying Machines* (Britain), 3 votes.

A Thousand Clowns (USA), *The Knack* (Britain), *Doctor Zhivago* (USA), *Ship Of Fools* (USA) and *The Collector* (USA) were also in the running.

Fellini's *Juliet Of The Spirits* (France/Italy/West Germany) was named best foreign language film ahead of Antonioni's *The Red Desert* (Italy/France)

1966

Best Film	*A Man For All Seasons* (Britain)
Best Actor	Paul Scofield in *A Man For All Seasons* (Britain)
Best Actress	Lynn Redgrave in *Georgy Girl* (Britain) & Elizabeth Taylor in *Who's Afraid Of Virginia Woolf?* (USA)
Best Direction	Fred Zinnemann for *A Man For All Seasons* (Britain)

A Man For All Seasons was selected on the first ballot ahead of *Who's Afraid Of Virginia Woolf?* (USA) and *Blow-Up* (Britain/Italy).

The Shop On Main Street (Czechoslovakia) won the foreign language film award with 11 votes. Pasolini's *The Gospel According To St. Matthew* (France/Italy) and Lelouch's *A Man And A Woman* (France) were runners-up.

1967

Best Film	*In The Heat Of The Night* (USA)
Best Actor	Rod Steiger in *In The Heat Of The Night* (USA)
Best Actress	Edith Evans in *The Whisperers* (Britain)
Best Direction	Mike Nichols for *The Graduate* (USA)

In The Heat Of The Night was named best picture on the sixth ballot. *Bonnie And Clyde* (USA); *Ulysses* (USA/Britain); *In Cold Blood* (USA); *The Graduate* (USA); and *Guess Who's Coming To Dinner?* (USA) were the other 'best film' contenders.

Alain Resnais' *La Guerre Est Finie* (France/Sweden) was voted best foreign language film.

Runners-up: *Elvira Madigan* (Sweden), *The Battle Of Algiers* (Algeria/Italy), *The Hunt* (Spain) and *Closely Observed Trains* (Czechoslovakia).

1968

Best Film	*The Lion In Winter* (Britain)
Best Actor	Alan Arkin in *The Heart Is A Lonely Hunter* (USA)
Best Actress	Joanne Woodward in *Rachel, Rachel* (USA)
Best Direction	Paul Newman for *Rachel, Rachel* (USA)

The Lion In Winter won on the sixth ballot, narrowly defeating John Cassavetes *Faces* (USA) by 13 votes to 11. The year's Oscar winner *Oliver!* (Britain), *2001: A Space Odyssey* (Britain), *Rachel, Rachel* (USA), *The Seagull* (USA/Britain), *The Fixer* (USA) and *Secret Ceremony* (Britain) also figured in the voting.

The foreign language award went to a seventh exceptional ballot after *War And Peace* (USSR) and *Shame* (Sweden) had tied with 11 votes each. *War And Peace* eventually won by 12 votes to 11.

Also in contention: Buñuel's *Belle De Jour* (France/Italy), *Weekend* (France/Italy) and Ingmar Bergman's *Hour Of The Wolf* (Sweden).

1969

Best Film	*Z* (France/Algeria)
Best Actor	Jon Voight in *Midnight Cowboy* (USA)
Best Actress	Jane Fonda in *They Shoot Horses, Don't They?* (USA)
Best Supporting Actor	Jack Nicholson in *Easy Rider* (USA)
Best Supporting Actress	Dyan Cannon in *Bob And Carol And Ted And Alice* (USA)
Best Direction	Costa-Gavras for *Z* (France/Algeria)

The voting rules were changed in 1969 and a points system — 3 points for a critic's first selection, 2 for his second, 1 for his third — was introduced.

The best film award was combined to include English speaking and foreign language pictures. Supporting acting awards were introduced for the first time.

Z (France/Algeria) received 39 points, *Oh! What A Lovely War* (Britain) 18, *The Damned* (Italy/West Germany) 17 and *Midnight Cowboy* (USA) 15.

1970

Best Film	*Five Easy Pieces* (USA)
Best Actor	George C. Scott in *Patton* (USA)
Best Actress	Glenda Jackson in *Women In Love* (Britain)
Best Supporting Actor	Chief Dan George in *Little Big Man* (USA)
Best Supporting Actress	Karen Black in *Five Easy Pieces* (USA)
Best Direction	Bob Rafelson for *Five Easy Pieces* (USA)

1971

Best Film	*A Clockwork Orange* (Britain)
Best Actor	Gene Hackman in *The French Connection* (USA)
Best Actress	Jane Fonda in *Klute* (USA)
Best Supporting Actor	Ben Johnson in *The Last Picture Show* (USA)
Best Supporting Actress	Ellen Burstyn in *The Last Picture Show* (USA)
Best Direction	Stanley Kubrick for *A Clockwork Orange* (Britain)

A Clockwork Orange (Britain) received 31 points, *The Last Picture Show* (USA) 24, *The French Connection* (USA) 11 and *Sunday, Bloody Sunday* (Britain) 8.

1972

Best Film	*Cries And Whispers* (Sweden)
Best Actor	Laurence Olivier in *Sleuth* (Britain)
Best Actress	Liv Ullmann in *Cries And Whispers* (Sweden)
Best Supporting Actor	Robert Duvall in *The Godfather* (USA)
Best Supporting Actress	Jeannie Berlin in *The Heartbreak Kid* (USA)
Best Direction	Ingmar Bergman for *Cries And Whispers* (Sweden)

1973

Best Film	*Day For Night* (France/Italy)
Best Actor	Marlon Brando in *Last Tango In Paris* (France/Italy/USA)
Best Actress	Joanne Woodward in *Summer Wishes, Winter Dreams* (USA)
Best Supporting Actor	Robert De Niro in *Bang The Drum Slowly* (USA)
Best Supporting Actress	Valentina Cortese in *Day For Night* (France/Italy)
Best Direction	François Truffaut for *Day For Night* (France/Italy)

Day For Night was voted best picture ahead of *Last Tango In Paris* (France/Italy/USA), *Mean Streets* (USA) and *American Graffiti* (USA).

1974

Best Film	*Amarcord* (Italy/France)
Best Actor	Jack Nicholson in *Chinatown* (USA) & *The Last Detail* (USA)
Best Actress	Liv Ullmann in *Scenes From A Marriage* (Sweden)
Best Supporting Actor	Charles Boyer in *Stavisky* (France/Italy)
Best Supporting Actress	Valerie Perrine in *Lenny* (USA)
Best Direction	Federico Fellini for *Amarcord* (Italy/France)

Amarcord (Italy/France) received 43 points, *Scenes From A Marriage* (Sweden) 38, *The Godfather Part II* (USA) 17 and *The Conversation* (USA) 12.

1975

Best Film	*Nashville* (USA)
Best Actor	Jack Nicholson in *One Flew Over The Cuckoo's Nest* (USA)
Best Actress	Isabelle Adjani in *The Story Of Adele H* (France)
Best Supporting Actor	Alan Arkin in *Hearts Of The West* (USA)
Best Supporting Actress	Lily Tomlin in *Nashville* (USA)
Best Direction	Robert Altman for *Nashville* (USA)

1976

Best Film	*All The President's Men* (USA)
Best Actor	Robert De Niro in *Taxi Driver* (USA)
Best Actress	Liv Ullmann in *Face To Face* (Sweden)
Best Supporting Actor	Jason Robards in *All The President's Men* (USA)
Best Supporting Actress	Talia Shire in *Rocky* (USA)
Best Direction	Alan Pakula for *All The President's Men* (USA)

1977

Best Film	*Annie Hall* (USA)
Best Actor	John Gielgud in *Providence* (France/Switzerland)
Best Actress	Diane Keaton in *Annie Hall* (USA)
Best Supporting Actor	Maximilian Schell in *Julia* (USA)
Best Supporting Actress	Sissy Spacek in *3 Women* (USA)
Best Direction	Woody Allen for *Annie Hall* (USA)

Annie Hall (USA) received 46 points, *That Obscure Object Of Desire* (France/Spain) 28 and Steven Spielberg's *Close Encounters Of The Third Kind* (USA) 12.

1978

Best Film	*The Deer Hunter* (USA)
Best Actor	Jon Voight in *Coming Home* (USA)
Best Actress	Ingrid Bergman in *Autumn Sonata* (West Germany)
Best Supporting Actor	Christopher Walken in *The Deer Hunter* (USA)
Best Supporting Actress	Maureen Stapleton in *Interiors* (USA)
Best Direction	Terrence Malick for *Days Of Heaven* (USA)

The award for the best foreign language film was re-introduced in 1978 and presented to director Franco Brusati for his *Bread And Chocolate* (Italy).

1979

Best Film	*Kramer vs. Kramer* (USA)
Best Actor	Dustin Hoffman in *Kramer vs. Kramer* (USA)
Best Actress	Sally Field in *Norma Rae* (USA)
Best Supporting Actor	Melvyn Douglas in *Being There* (USA)
Best Supporting Actress	Meryl Streep in *Kramer vs. Kramer* (USA) & *The Seduction Of Joe Tynan* (USA)
Best Direction	Woody Allen for *Manhattan* (USA)

Olmi's *The Tree Of Wooden Clogs* (Italy) was named the year's best foreign language film.

Gene Hackman as hard-nosed New York cop 'Popeye' Doyle in William Friedkin's Oscar-winning thriller *The French Connection* (20th Century-Fox)

Escape from a Vietnam river in Michael Cimino's *The Deer Hunter* (EMI), American Academy Award, 1978

(Above) Christopher Walken suffering Russian Roulette torture and (below) Robert De Niro reunited with Meryl Streep in *The Deer Hunter* (EMI)

(Above) Deborah Kerr and Burt Lancaster in the beach scene and (below) Montgomery Clift and Frank Sinatra in Fred Zinnemann's Oscar-winning version of *From Here To Eternity* (Columbia)

(Above) Marcello Mastroianni as the exhausted film director in Fellini's *8½* (Embassy Pictures)

(Below) Dominic Guard and Alan Bates in *The Go-Between* (EMI), Golden Palm, Cannes, 1971

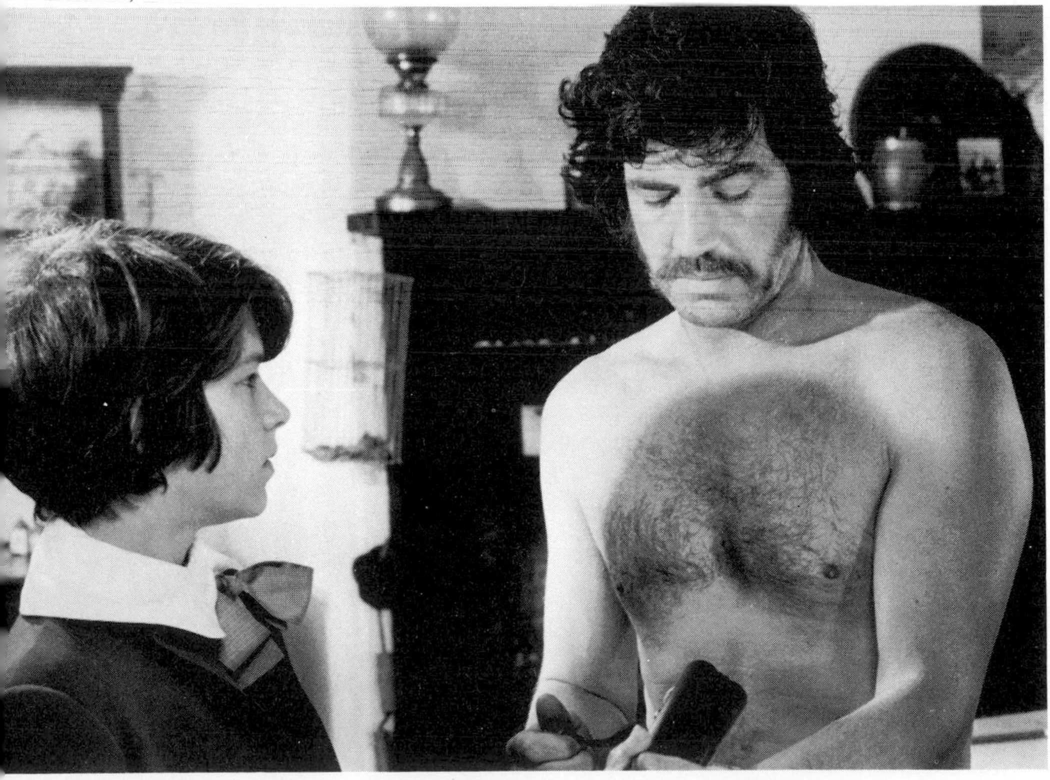

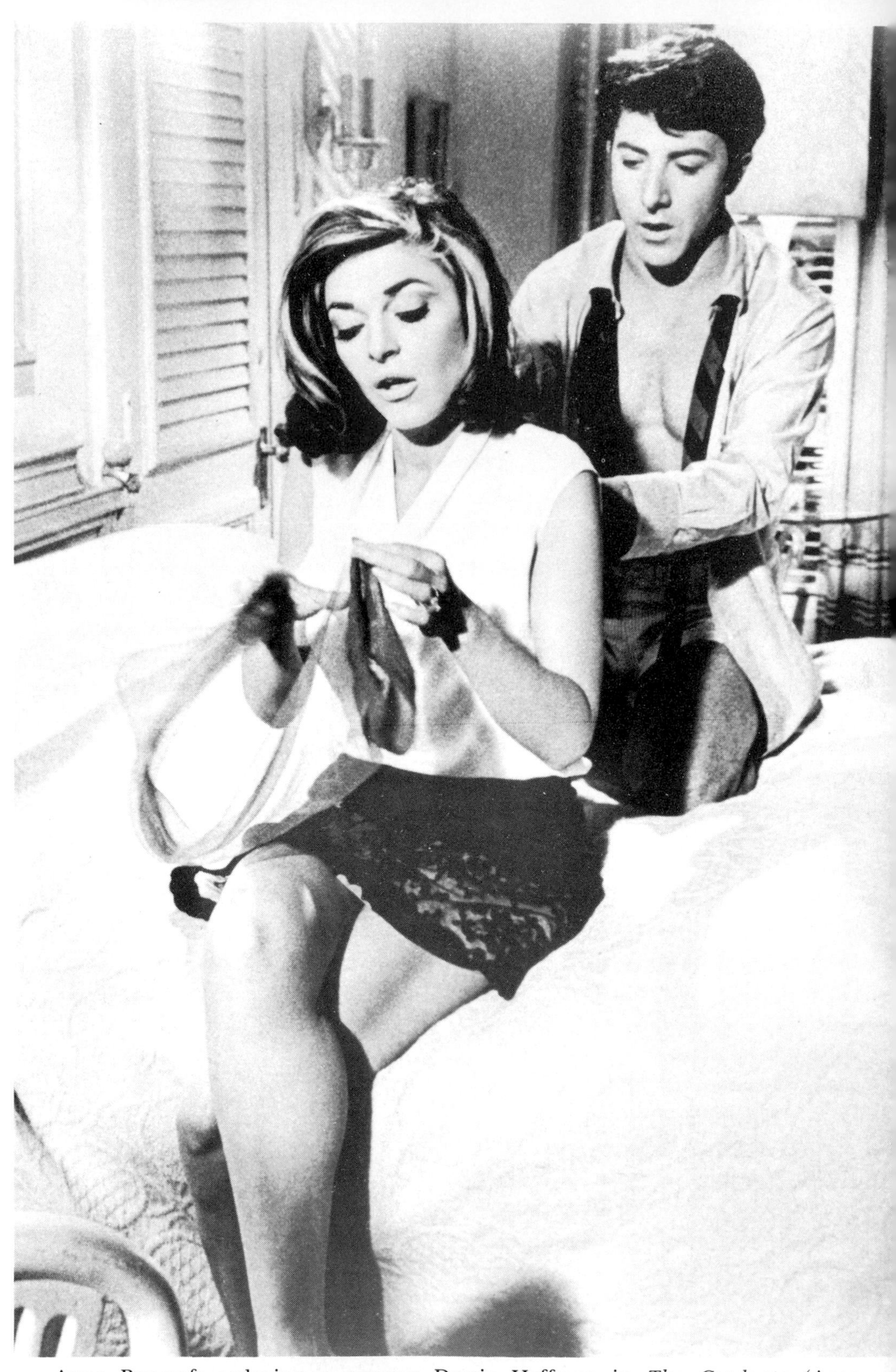

Anne Bancroft seducing a nervous Dustin Hoffman in *The Graduate* (Avco Embassy), best film, British Academy Award, 1968

The Godfather Parts I & II (Paramount)
(Above) Marlon Brando as Don Corleone, (Below) assassination in Sicily

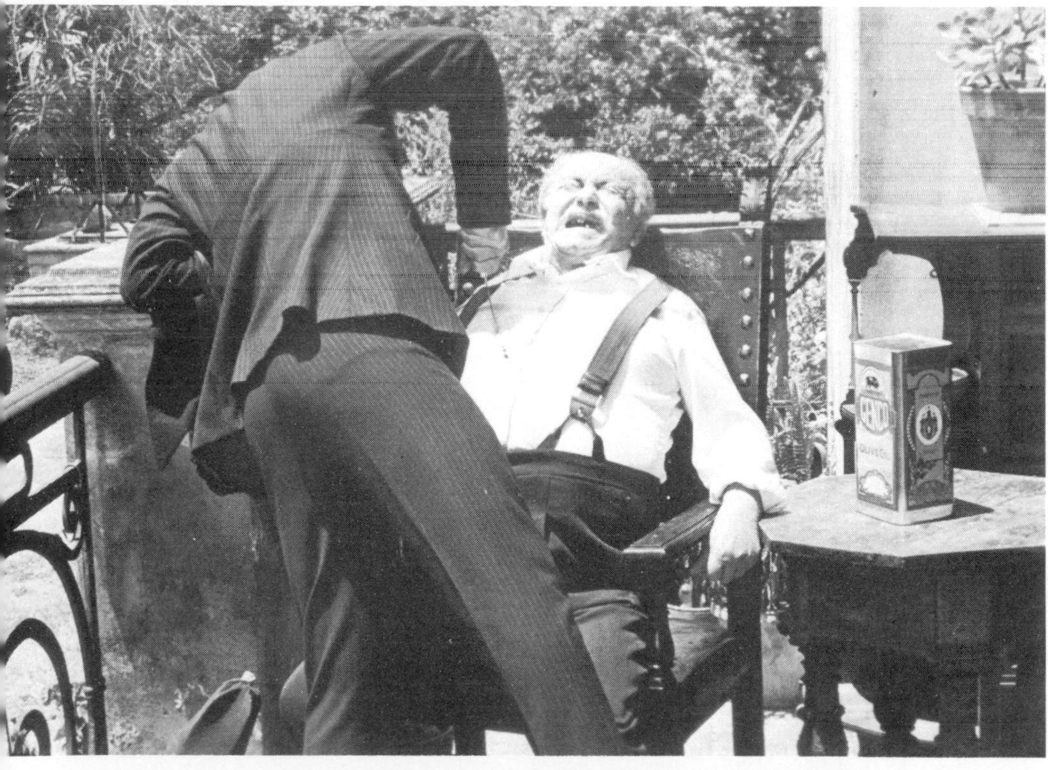

Murder in Ancient Rome in Mankiewicz's *Julius Caesar* (MGM), best film 1953, National Board of Review

Murder in the Old West in Zinnemann's *High Noon* (United Artists), best film, New York Critics, 1952

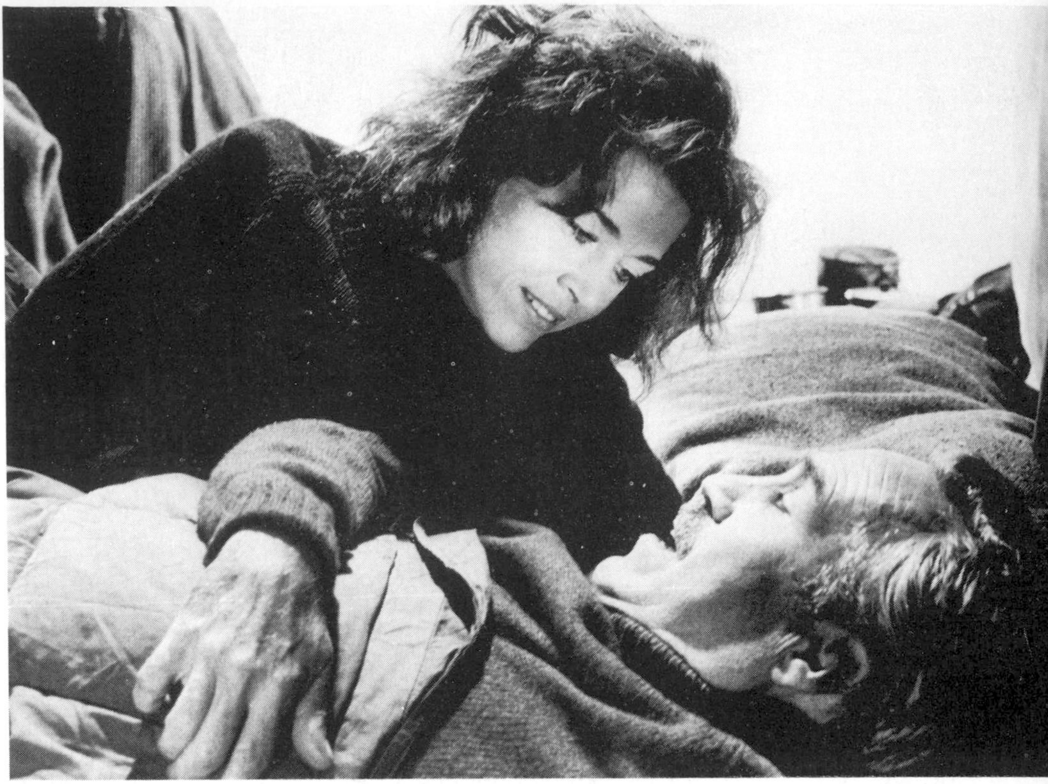

(Above) Jane Fonda and Jason Robards and (Below) Fonda and Vanessa Redgrave in *Julia* (20th Century-Fox), voted best film of 1978 by the British Film Academy

(Above) Rod Steiger in his Academy Award winning role in *In The Heat Of The Night* (United Artists), directed by Norman Jewison in 1967.

(Below) Dustin Hoffman and six-year-old Justin Henry in *Kramer vs. Kramer* (Columbia).

(Above) Peter O'Toole's first encounter with Omar Sharif and (Below) with a dying Arab boy in David Lean's Oscar-winning *Lawrence Of Arabia* (Columbia)

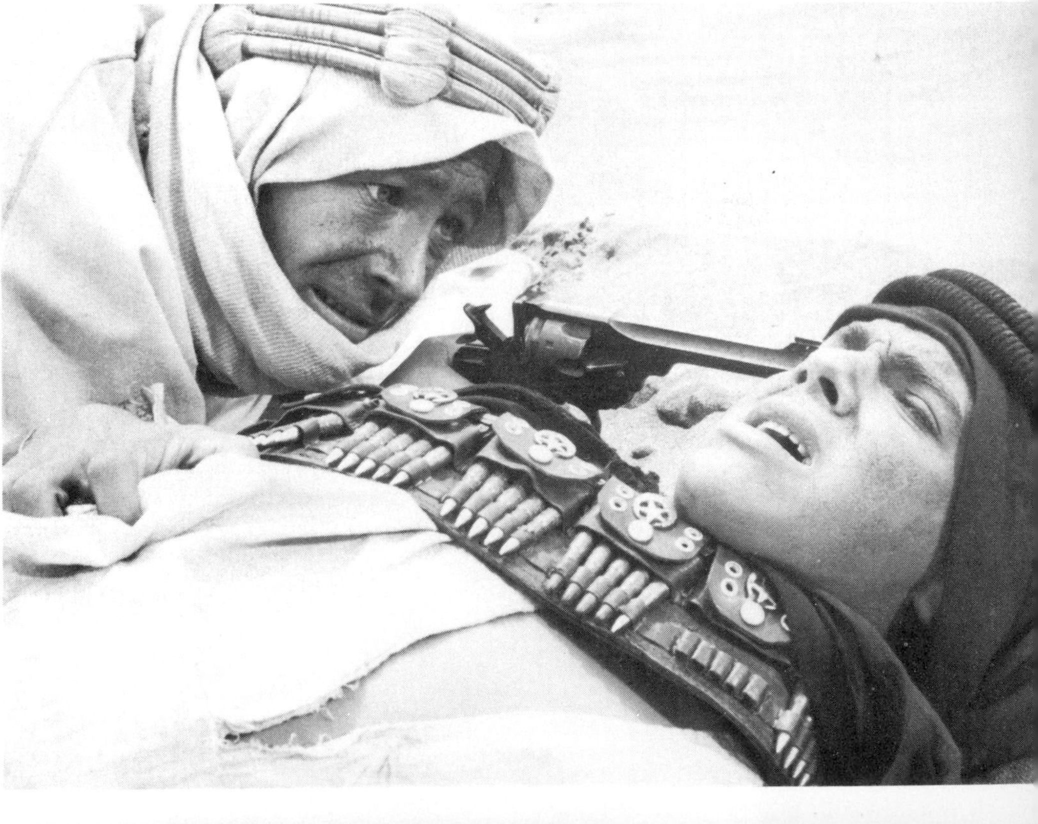

Anthony Quinn and Arthur Kennedy in *Lawrence Of Arabia* (Columbia)

The invasion of Europe — by air — in Zanuck's all-star war epic *The Longest Day* (20th Century-Fox)

The invasion of Korea — by helicopter — in Robert Altman's war comedy *M.A.S.H.* (20th Century-Fox), prize-winner at Cannes in 1970

Rex Harrison and Audrey Hepburn in George Cukor's version of the musical *My Fair Lady* (Warner Bros.)

National Board of Review

Together with the Academy of Motion Picture Arts and Sciences and the New York Critics Circle, the National Board of Review is one of the three major award organizations in the United States.

It consists of some 175 public-spirited men and women with an interest in motion pictures and a mature sense of social responsibility. It was the first and is still the foremost public organization devoted to the movies as an entertainment, an art and a social force.

The National Board of Review was the first body to present 'ten best lists', a practice it began in 1930 and continues to this day. It is invariably the first to announce the best movie achievements of the calendar year and presents ten best selections of both English and Foreign Language pictures, as well as acting and direction awards.

Like the prizes of the New York Critics, the awards are made by men and women with critical experience and flair and are often a pointer to the Oscar winners announced every April.

Joint acting awards were introduced in 1937, individual acting and direction awards in 1945 and prizes for supporting acting in 1954. During the war and post-war years the Board abandoned its policy of distinguishing between documentary and fiction films and combined them in its ten best lists. Towards the end of the war and for a few years after it, the Board did not use separate categories for American and Foreign Language films.

In 1979 the awards were named for the first time and presented as the David Wark Griffith Awards. The first presentations were made at Luchow's (across the street from Griffith's original Biograph Studio) on February 10, 1980.

1930
Ten Best: alphabetical order
American: (1) *All Quiet On The Western Front*; (2) *Holiday*; (3) *Laughter*; (4) *The Man From Blankley's*; (5) *Men Without Women* (6) *Morocco*; (7) *Outward Bound*; (8) *Romance*; (9) *The Street Of Chance*; (10) *Tol'able David.*

Foreign: (1) *High Treason* (Germany); (2) *Old And New* (USSR); (3) *Earth* (USSR); (4) *Storm Over Asia* (USSR); (5) *Zwei Herzen Im ¾ Takt* (Germany).

1931
Ten Best: alphabetical order
American: (1) *Cimarron*; (2) *City Lights*; (3) *City Streets*; (4) *Dishonored*; (5) *The Front Page*; (6) *The Guardsman*; (7) *Quick Millions*; (8) *Rango*; (9) *Surrender*; (10) *Tabu.*

Foreign: (1) *Die Dreigroschenoper* (Germany); (2) *Das Lied Vom Leben* (Germany); (3) *Le Million* (France); (4) *Sous Les Toits De Paris* (France); (5) *Vier Von Der Infanterie* (Germany).

1932
Ten Best: One 'best film' then nine pictures in alphabetical order (Foreign films all listed in alphabetical order).
American: (1) *I Am A Fugitive From A Chain Gang*; (2) *As You Desire Me*; (3) *A Bill Of Divorcement*; (4) *A Farewell To Arms*; (5) *Madame Racketeer*; (6) *Payment Deferred*; (7) *Scarface*; (8) *Tarzan, The Ape Man*; (9) *Trouble In Paradise*; (10) *Two Seconds.*

Foreign: (1) *A Nous La Liberté* (France); (2) *Der Andere* (Germany); (3) *The Battle Of Gallipoli* (Britain); (4) *Golden Mountains* (USSR); (5) *Kameradschaft* (Germany); (6) *Mädchen In Uniform* (Germany); (7) *Der Raub Der Mona Lisa* (Germany); (8) *Reserved For Ladies* (Britain); (9) *Road To Life* (USSR); (10) *Zwei Menschen* (Germany).

Note: The Battle Of Gallipoli was released in Britain as *Tell England*; *Reserved For Ladies* as *Service For Ladies.*

1933
Ten Best: One 'best American film' then nine pictures in alphabetical order (the Foreign 'ten best' listed entirely in alphabetical order).
American: (1) *Topaze*; (2) *Berkeley Square*; (3) *Cavalcade*; (4) *Little Women*; (5) *Mama Loves Papa*; (6) *The Pied Piper* (cartoon); (7) *She Done Him Wrong*; (8) *State Fair*; (9) *Three Cornered Moon*; (10) *Zoo In Budapest.*

Foreign: (1) *Hertha's Erwachen* (Germany); (2) *Ivan* (USSR); (3) *M* (Germany); (4) *Morgenrot* (Germany); (5) *Niemandsland* (Germany); (6) *Poil De Carotte* (France); (7) *The Private Life Of Henry VIII* (Britain); (8) *Quatorze Juillet* (France); (9) *Rome Express* (Britain); (10) *Le Sang D'un Poète* (France).

1934

Ten Best: One 'best film' then remaining pictures in alphabetical order (same rules for American and Foreign films).
American: (1) *It Happened One Night*; (2) *The Count Of Monte Cristo*; (3) *Crime Without Passion*; (4) *Eskimo*; (5) *The First World War*; (6) *The Lost Patrol*; (7) *Lot In Sodom* (a non-theatrical short); (8) *No Greater Glory*; (9) *The Thin Man*; (10) *Viva Villa!*

Foreign: (1) *Man Of Aran* (Britain); (2) *The Blue Light* (Germany); (3) *Catherine The Great* (Britain); (4) *The Constant Nymph* (Britain); (5) *Madame Bovary* (France).

1935

Ten Best: One 'best American film' then nine pictures in alphabetical order (the Foreign 'ten best' listed entirely in alphabetical order).
American: (1) *The Informer*; (2) *Alice Adams*; (3) *Anna Karenina*; (4) *David Copperfield*; (5) *The Gilded Lily*; (6) *Les Miserables*; (7) *Lives Of A Bengal Lancer*; (8) *Mutiny On The Bounty*; (9) *Ruggles Of Red Gap*; (10) *Who Killed Cock Robin?* (cartoon).

Foreign: (1) *Chapayev* (USSR); (2) *Crime And Punishment* (France); (3) *Le Dernier Milliardaire* (France); (4) *The Man Who Knew Too Much* (Britain); (5) *Marie Chapdelaine* (France); (6) *La Maternelle* (France); (7) *The New Gulliver* (USSR); (8) *Peasants* (USSR); (9) *Thunder In The East* (France); (10) *The Youth Of Maxim* (USSR).

1936

Ten Best: From this year onwards both American and foreign films were placed in order of merit.
American: (1) *Mr. Deeds Goes To Town*; (2) *The Story Of Louis Pasteur*; (3) *Modern Times*; (4) *Fury*; (5) *Winterset*; (6) *The Devil Is A Sissy*; (7) *Ceiling Zero*; (8) *Romeo And Juliet*; (9) *The Prisoner Of Shark Island*; (10) *The Green Pastures*.

Foreign: (1) *La Kermesse Heroïque* (France); (2) *The New Earth* (Holland); (3) *Rembrandt* (Britain); (4) *The Ghost Goes West* (Britain); (5) *Tudor Rose* (Britain); (6) *We Are From Kronstadt* (USSR); (7) *Son Of Mongolia* (USSR); (8) *The Yellow Cruise* (France); (9) *Les Miserables* (France); (10) *The Secret Agent* (Britain).

1937

Ten Best:
American: (1) *Night Must Fall*; (2) *The Life Of Emile Zola*; (3) *Black Legion*; (4) *Camille*; (5) *Make Way For Tomorrow*; (6) *The Good Earth*; (7) *They Won't Forget*; (8) *Captains Courageous*; (9) *A Star Is Born*; (10) *Stage Door*.

Foreign: (1) *The Eternal Mask* (Austria/Switzerland); (2) *The Lower Depths* (France); (3) *Baltic Deputy* (USSR); (4) *Mayerling* (France);

(5) *The Spanish Earth* (Spain); (6) *Golgotha* (France); (7) *Elephant Boy* (Britain); (8) *Rembrandt* (Britain); (9) *Janosik* (Czechoslovakia); (10) *The Wedding Of Palo* (Greenland/Denmark).

Best Acting (alphabetical): Harry Baur in *The Golem* (France); Humphrey Bogart in *Black Legion* (USA); Charles Boyer in *Conquest* (USA); Nikolai Cherkassov in *Baltic Deputy* (USSR); Danielle Darrieux in *Mayerling* (France); Greta Garbo in *Camille* (USA); Robert Montgomery in *Night Must Fall* (USA); Maria Ouspenskaya in *Conquest* (USA); Luise Rainer in *The Good Earth* (USA); Joseph Schildkraut in *The Life Of Emile Zola* (USA); Mathias Wieman in *The Eternal Mask* (Austria/ Switzerland); Dame May Whitty in *Night Must Fall* (USA).

1938

Ten Best:

English Language: (1) *The Citadel* (Britain); (2) *Snow White And The Seven Dwarfs* (USA); (3) *The Beachcomber* (Britain); (4) *To The Victor* (Britain); (5) *Sing You Sinners* (USA); (6) *The Edge Of The World* (Britain); (7) *Of Human Hearts* (USA); (8) *Jezebel* (USA); (9) *South Riding* (Britain); (10) *Three Comrades* (USA).

Foreign: (1) *La Grande Illusion* (France); (2) *Ballerina* (France); (3) *Un Carnet De Bal* (France); (4) *Generals Without Buttons* (France); (5) *Peter The First* (USSR).

Best Acting (alphabetical): Lew Ayres in *Holiday* (USA); Pierre Blanchar, Harry Baur, Louis Jouvet and Raimu in *Un Carnet De Bal* (France); James Cagney in *Angels With Dirty Faces* (USA); Joseph Calleia in *Algiers* (USA); Chico in *The Adventures Of Chico* (USA); Robert Donat in *The Citadel* (Britain); Will Fyffe in *To The Victor* (Britain); Pierre Fresnay, Jean Gabin, Dita Parlo and Erich von Stroheim in *La Grande Illusion* (France); John Garfield in *Four Daughters* (USA); Wendy Hiller in *Pygmalion* (Britain); Charles Laughton and Elsa Lanchester in *The Beachcomber* (Britain); Robert Morley in *Marie Antoinette* (USA); Ralph Richardson in *South Riding* (Britain) and *The Citadel* (Britain); Margaret Sullavan in *Three Comrades* (USA), Spencer Tracy in *Boys Town* (USA).

1939

Ten Best:

English Language: (1) *Confessions Of A Nazi Spy* (USA); (2) *Wuthering Heights* (USA); (3) *Stagecoach* (USA); (4) *Ninotchka* (USA); (5) *Young Mr. Lincoln* (USA); (6) *Crisis* (Czechoslovakian documentary, English narration); (7) *Goodbye Mr. Chips* (Britain); (8) *Mr. Smith Goes To Washington* (USA); (9) *The Roaring Twenties* (USA); (10) *U-Boat 29* (Britain).

Foreign: (1) *Quai Des Brumes* (France); (2) *Harvest* (France); (3) *Alexander Nevsky* (USSR); (4) *La Fin Du Jour* (France); (5) *Robert Koch* (Germany).

Best Acting (alphabetical): James Cagney in *The Roaring Twenties* (USA); Bette Davis in *Dark Victory* (USA) and *The Old Maid* (USA); Geraldine Fitzgerald in *Dark Victory* (USA) and *Wuthering Heights* (USA); Henry Fonda in *Young Mr. Lincoln* (USA); Jean Gabin in *Quai Des Brumes* (France); Greta Garbo in *Ninotchka* (USA); Francis Lederer in *Confessions Of A Nazi Spy* (USA); Paul Lukas in *Confessions Of A Nazi Spy* (USA); Thomas Mitchell in *Stagecoach* (USA); Laurence Olivier in *Wuthering Heights* (USA); Flora Robson in *We Are Not Alone* (USA); Michel Simon in *Quai Des Brumes* and *La Fin Du Jour* (France).

1940
Ten Best:
American: (1) *The Grapes Of Wrath*; (2) *The Great Dictator*; (3) *Of Mice And Men*; (4) *Our Town*; (5) *Fantasia*; (6) *The Long Voyage Home*; (7) *Foreign Correspondent*; (8) *The Biscuit Eater*; (9) *Gone With The Wind*; (10) *Rebecca*.

Foreign: *La Femme Du Boulanger* (France).

Best Acting (alphabetical): Jane Bryan in *We Are Not Alone* (USA); Charles Chaplin in *The Great Dictator* (USA); Jane Darwell in *The Grapes Of Wrath* (USA); Betty Field in *Of Mice And Men* (USA); Henry Fonda in *The Grapes Of Wrath* (USA); and *The Return Of Frank James* (USA); Joan Fontaine in *Rebecca* (USA); Greer Garson in *Pride And Prejudice* (USA); William Holden in *Our Town* (USA); Vivien Leigh in *Gone With The Wind* (USA) and *Waterloo Bridge* (USA); Thomas Mitchell in *The Long Voyage Home* (USA); Raimu in *La Femme Du Boulanger* (France); Ralph Richardson in *On The Night Of The Fire* (Britain); Ginger Rogers in *The Primrose Path* (USA); George Sanders in *Rebecca* (USA); Martha Scott in *Our Town* (USA); James Stewart in *The Shop Around The Corner* (USA); Conrad Veidt in *Escape* (USA).

1941
Ten Best:
American: (1) *Citizen Kane*; (2) *How Green Was My Valley*; (3) *The Little Foxes*; (4) *The Stars Look Down*; (5) *Dumbo*; (6) *High Sierra*; (7) *Here Comes Mr. Jordan*; (8) *Tom, Dick And Harry*; (9) *The Road To Zanzibar*; (10) *The Lady Eve*.

Foreign: *Pépé-Le-Moko* (France).

Best Acting (alphabetical): Sara Allgood in *How Green Was My Valley* (USA); Mary Astor in *The Great Lie* (USA) and *The Maltese Falcon* (USA); Ingrid Bergman in *Rage In Heaven* (USA); Humphrey Bogart in *High Sierra* (USA) and *The Maltese Falcon* (USA); Gary Cooper in *Sergeant York* (USA); Donald Crisp in *How Green Was My Valley* (USA); Bing Crosby in *The Road To Zanzibar* (USA) and *The Birth Of The Blues* (USA); George Coulouris in *Citizen Kane* (USA); Patricia Collinge in *The Little Foxes* (USA); Bette Davis in *The Little Foxes* (USA); Isobel Elsom in *Ladies In Retirement* (USA); Joan Fontaine in *Suspicion* (USA); Greta Garbo in *Two-Faced Woman* (USA); James Gleason in *Meet John*

Doe (USA) and *Here Comes Mr. Jordan* (USA); Walter Huston in *All That Money Can Buy* (USA); Ida Lupino in *High Sierra* (USA) and *Ladies in Retirement* (USA); Roddy McDowall in *How Green Was My Valley* (USA); Robert Montgomery in *Rage In Heaven* (USA) and *Here Comes Mr. Jordan* (USA); Ginger Rogers in *Kitty Foyle* (USA) and *Tom, Dick And Harry* (USA); James Stephenson in *The Letter* (USA) and *Shining Victory* (USA); Orson Welles in *Citizen Kane* (USA).

1942
Ten Best:
English Language: (1) *In Which We Serve* (Britain); (2) *One Of Our Aircraft Is Missing* (Britain); (3) *Mrs. Miniver* (USA); (4) *Journey For Margaret* (USA); (5) *Wake Island* (USA); (6) *The Male Animal* (USA); (7) *The Major And The Minor* (USA); (8) *Sullivan's Travels* (USA); (9) *The Moon And Sixpence* (USA); (10) *The Pied Piper* (USA).

Foreign: None cited.

Best Acting (alphabetical): Ernest Anderson in *In This Our Life* (USA); Florence Bates in *The Moon And Sixpence* (USA); James Cagney in *Yankee Doodle Dandy* (USA); Charles Coburn in *H. M. Pulham, Esq.* (USA), *In This Our Life* (USA) and *King's Row* (USA); Jack Carson in *The Male Animal* (USA); Greer Garson in *Mrs. Miniver* (USA) and *Random Harvest* (USA); Sydney Greenstreet in *Across The Pacific* (USA); William Holden in *The Remarkable Andrew* (USA); Tim Holt in *The Magnificent Ambersons* (USA); Glynis Johns in *The Forty-Ninth Parallel* (Britain); Gene Kelly in *For Me And My Gal* (USA); Diana Lynn in *The Major And The Minor* (USA); Ida Lupino in *Moontide* (USA); Bernard Miles in *In Which We Serve* (Britain); John Mills in *In Which We Serve* (Britain); Agnes Moorehead in *The Magnificent Ambersons* (USA); Hattie McDaniel in *In This Our Life* (USA); Thomas Mitchell in *Moontide* (USA); Margaret O'Brien in *Journey For Margaret* (USA); Susan Peters in *Random Harvest* (USA); Edward G. Robinson in *Tales Of Manhattan* (USA); Ginger Rogers in *Roxy Hart* (USA) and *The Major And The Minor* (USA); George Sanders in *The Moon And Sixpence* (USA); Ann Sheridan in *King's Row* (USA); William Severn in *Journey For Margaret* (USA); Rudy Vallee in *The Palm Beach Story* (USA); Anton Walbrook in *The Forty-Ninth Parallel* (Britain); Googie Withers in *One Of Our Aircraft Is Missing* (Britain); Monty Woolley in *The Pied Piper* (USA); Teresa Wright in *Mrs. Miniver* (USA); Robert Young in *H. M. Pulham, Esq.* (USA), *Joe Smith, American* (USA) and *Journey For Margaret* (USA).

1943
Ten Best:
English Language: (1) *The Ox-Bow Incident* (USA); (2) *Watch On The Rhine* (USA); (3) *Air Force* (USA); (4) *Holy Matrimony* (USA); (5) *The Hard Way* (USA); (6) *Casablanca* (USA); (7) *Lassie Come Home* (USA); (8) *Bataan* (USA); (9) *The Moon Is Down* (USA); (10) *The Next Of Kin* (Britain).

Foreign: None cited.

Best Direction: William A. Wellman for *The Ox-Bow Incident* (USA); Tay Garnett for *Bataan* (USA) and *The Cross Of Lorraine* (USA); Michael Curtiz for *Casablanca* (USA) and *This Is The Army* (USA).

Best Actresses: Gracie Fields in *Holy Matrimony* (USA); Katina Paxinou in *For Whom The Bell Tolls* (USA); Teresa Wright in *Shadow Of A Doubt* (USA).

Best Actors: Paul Lukas in *Watch On The Rhine* (USA); Henry Morgan in *The Ox-Bow Incident* (USA) and *Happy Land* (USA); Cedric Hardwicke in *The Moon Is Down* (USA) and *The Cross Of Lorraine* (USA).

1944

Ten Best:

English Language: (1) *None But The Lonely Heart* (USA); (2) *Going My Way* (USA); (3) *The Miracle Of Morgan's Creek* (USA); (4) *Hail The Conquering Hero* (USA); (5) *The Song Of Bernadette* (USA); (6) *Wilson* (USA); (7) *Meet Me In St. Louis* (USA); (8) *Thirty Seconds Over Tokyo* (USA); (9) *Thunder Rock* (Britain); (10) *Lifeboat* (USA).

Foreign: None cited.

Best Acting (alphabetical): Ethel Barrymore in *None But The Lonely Heart* (USA); Ingrid Bergman in *Gaslight* (USA); Eddie Bracken in *Hail The Conquering Hero* (USA); Humphrey Bogart in *To Have And Have Not* (USA); Bing Crosby in *Going My Way* (USA); June Duprez in *None But The Lonely Heart* (USA); Barry Fitzgerald in *Going My Way* (USA); Betty Hutton in *The Miracle Of Morgan's Creek* (USA); Margaret O'Brien in *Meet Me In St. Louis* (USA); Franklin Pangborn in *Hail The Conquering Hero* (USA).

1945

Ten Best:

(Including documentaries as well as feature films, and British as well as American).

(1) *The True Glory* (Britain/USA); (2) *The Lost Weekend* (USA); (3) *The Southerner* (USA); (4) *The Story Of G.I. Joe* (USA); (5) *The Last Chance* (Switzerland); (6) *The Life And Death Of Colonel Blimp* (Britain); (7) *A Tree Grows In Brooklyn* (USA); (8) *The Fighting Lady* (USA); (9) *The Way Ahead* (Britain); (10) *The Clock* (USA).

Foreign: None cited.

Best Actor	Ray Milland in *The Lost Weekend* (USA)
Best Actress	Joan Crawford in *Mildred Pierce* (USA)
Best Direction	Jean Renoir for *The Southerner* (USA)

1946

Ten Best:

(1) *Henry V* (Britain); (2) *Open City* (Italy); (3) *The Best Years Of Our Lives* (USA); (4) *Brief Encounter* (Britain); (5) *A Walk In The Sun* (USA); (6) *It Happened At The Inn* (France); (7) *My Darling Clementine* (USA); (8) *The Diary Of A Chambermaid* (USA); (9) *The Killers* (USA); (10) *Anna And The King Of Siam* (USA).

Best Actor	Laurence Olivier in *Henry V* (Britain)
Best Actress	Anna Magnani in *Open City* (Italy)
Best Direction	William Wyler for *The Best Years Of Our Lives* (USA)

1947

Ten Best:

(1) *Monsieur Verdoux* (USA); (2) *Great Expectations* (Britain); (3) *Shoe-Shine* (Italy); (4) *Crossfire* (USA); (5) *Boomerang* (USA); (6) *Odd Man Out* (Britain); (7) *Gentleman's Agreement* (USA); (8) *To Live In Peace* (Italy); (9) *It's A Wonderful Life* (USA); (10) *The Overlanders* (Britain).

Best Actor	Michael Redgrave in *Mourning Becomes Electra* (USA)
Best Actress	Celia Johnson in *This Happy Breed* (Britain)
Best Direction	Elia Kazan for *Boomerang* (USA) and *Gentleman's Agreement* (USA)

1948

Ten Best:

(1) *Paisa* (Italy); (2) *Day Of Wrath* (Denmark); (3) *The Search* (USA/Switzerland); (4) *The Treasure Of The Sierra Madre* (USA); (5) *Louisiana Story* (USA); (6) *Hamlet* (Britain); (7) *The Snake Pit* (USA); (8) *Johnny Belinda* (USA); (9) *Joan Of Arc* (USA); (10) *The Red Shoes* (Britain).

Best Actor	Walter Huston in *The Treasure Of The Sierra Madre* (USA)
Best Actress	Olivia de Havilland in *The Snake Pit* (USA)
Best Direction	Roberto Rossellini for *Paisa* (Italy)

1949

Ten Best:

(1) *Bicycle Thieves* (Italy); (2) *The Quiet One* (USA); (3) *Intruder In The Dust* (USA); (4) *The Heiress* (USA); (5) *Le Diable Au Corps* (France); (6) *Quartet* (Britain); (7) *Germany, Year Zero* (France/Italy); (8) *Home Of The Brave* (USA); (9) *A Letter To Three Wives* (USA); (10) *The Fallen Idol* (Britain).

Best Actor	Ralph Richardson in *The Heiress* (USA) and *The Fallen Idol* (Britain)

Best Actress	Not Awarded
Best Direction	Vittorio De Sica for *Bicycle Thieves* (Italy)

1950

Ten Best:

American: (1) *Sunset Boulevard*; (2) *All About Eve*; (3) *The Asphalt Jungle*; (4) *The Men*; (5) *Edge Of Doom*; (6) *Twelve O'Clock High*; (7) *Panic In The Streets*; (8) *Cyrano de Bergerac*; (9) *No Way Out*; (10) *Stage Fright*.

Foreign: (1) *The Titan* (Italy); (2) *Whisky Galore* (Britain); (3) *The Third Man* (Britain); (4) *Kind Hearts And Coronets* (Britain); (5) *Paris 1900* (France).

Best Actor	Alec Guinness in *Kind Hearts And Coronets* (Britain)
Best Actress	Gloria Swanson in *Sunset Boulevard* (USA)
Best Direction	John Huston for *The Asphalt Jungle* (USA)

1951

Ten Best:

American: (1) *A Place In The Sun*; (2) *The Red Badge Of Courage*; (3) *An American In Paris*; (4) *Death Of A Salesman*; (5) *Detective Story*; (6) *A Streetcar Named Desire*; (7) *Decision Before Dawn*; (8) *Strangers On A Train*; (9) *Quo Vadis*; (10) *Fourteen Hours*.

Foreign: (1) *Rashomon* (Japan); (2) *The River* (India); (3) *Miracle In Milan* (Italy); (4) *Kon Tiki* (Norway/Sweden); (5) *The Browning Version* (Britain).

Best Actor	Richard Basehart in *Fourteen Hours* (USA)
Best Actress	Jan Sterling in *Ace In The Hole* (USA)
Best Direction	Akira Kurosawa for *Rashomon* (Japan)

1952

Ten Best:

American: (1) *The Quiet Man*; (2) *High Noon*; (3) *Limelight*; (4) *Five Fingers*; (5) *The Snows Of Kilimanjaro*; (6) *The Thief*; (7) *The Bad And The Beautiful*; (8) *Singin' In The Rain*; (9) *Above And Beyond*; (10) *My Son John*.

Foreign: (1) *The Sound Barrier* (Britain); (2) *The Man In The White Suit* (Britain); (3) *Les Jeux Interdits* (France); (4) *La Beauté Du Diable* (Italy/France); (5) *Where No Vultures Fly* (Britain).

Best Actor	Ralph Richardson in *The Sound Barrier* (Britain)
Best Actress	Shirley Booth in *Come Back, Little Sheba* (USA)
Best Direction	David Lean for *The Sound Barrier* (Britain)

1953

Ten Best:

American: (1) *Julius Caesar*; (2) *Shane*; (3) *From Here To Eternity*; (4) *Martin Luther*; (5) *Lili*; (6) *Roman Holiday*; (7) *Stalag 17*; (8) *The Little Fugitive*; (9) *Mogambo*; (10) *The Robe*.

Foreign: (1) *A Queen Is Crowned* (Britain); (2) *Moulin Rouge* (Britain); (3) *The Little World Of Don Camillo* (France/Italy); (4) *Il Christo Proibito* (Italy); (5) *Conquest Of Everest* (Britain).

Best Actor	James Mason in *Face To Face* (USA), *The Desert Rats* (USA), *The Man Between* (Britain) & *Julius Caesar* (USA)
Best Actress	Jean Simmons in *Young Bess* (USA), *The Robe* (USA) & *The Actress* (USA)
Best Direction	George Stevens for *Shane* (USA)

1954

Ten Best:

American: (1) *On The Waterfront*; (2) *Seven Brides For Seven Brothers*; (3) *The Country Girl*; (4) *A Star Is Born*; (5) *Executive Suite*; (6) *The Vanishing Prairie*; (7) *Sabrina*; (8) *20,000 Leagues Under The Sea*; (9) *The Unconquered*; (10) *Beat The Devil*.

Foreign: *Romeo And Juliet* (Britain/Italy); (2) *The Heart Of The Matter* (Britain); (3) *Gate Of Hell* (Japan); (4) *The Diary Of A Country Priest* (France); (5) *The Kidnappers* (Britain); (6) *Genevieve* (Britain); (7) *Les Belles De Nuit* (France/Italy); (8) *Monsieur Hulot's Holiday* (France); (9) *Father Brown* (Britain); (10) *Bread, Love And Dreams* (Italy).

Best Actor	Bing Crosby in *The Country Girl* (USA)
Best Actress	Grace Kelly in *The Country Girl* (USA), *Dial M For Murder* (USA) & *Rear Window* (USA)
Best Supporting Actor	John Williams in *Sabrina* (USA) & *Dial M For Murder* (USA)
Best Supporting Actress	Nina Foch in *Executive Suite* (USA)
Best Direction	Renato Castellani for *Romeo And Juliet* (Britain/Italy)

1955

Ten Best:

American: (1) *Marty*; (2) *East Of Eden*; (3) *Mister Roberts*; (4) *Bad Day At Black Rock*; (5) *Summertime*; (6) *The Rose Tattoo*; (7) *A Man Called Peter*; (8) *Not As A Stranger*; (9) *Picnic*; (10) *The African Lion*.

Foreign: (1) *The Prisoner* (Britain); (2) *The Great Adventure* (Sweden); (3) *The Divided Heart* (Britain); (4) *Les Diaboliques* (France); (5) *The End Of The Affair* (Britain).

Best Actor	Ernest Borgnine in *Marty* (USA)
Best Actress	Anna Magnani in *The Rose Tattoo* (USA)
Best Supporting Actor	Charles Bickford in *Not As A Stranger* (USA)
Best Supporting Actress	Majorie Rambeau in *A Man Called Peter* (USA) & *The View From Pompey's Head* (USA)
Best Direction	William Wyler for *The Desperate Hours* (USA)

1956

Ten Best:

American: (1) *Around The World In 80 Days;* (2) *Moby Dick*; (3) *The King And I*; (4) *Lust For Life*; (5) *Friendly Persuasion*; (6) *Somebody Up There Likes Me*; (7) *The Catered Affair*; (8) *Anastasia*; (9) *The Man Who Never Was*; (10) *Bus Stop*.

Foreign: (1) *The Silent World* (France); (2) *War And Peace* (USA/Italy); (3) *Richard III* (Britain); (4) *La Strada* (Italy); (5) *Rififi* (France).

Best Actor	Yul Brynner in *The King And I* (USA), *Anastasia* (USA) & *The Ten Commandments* (USA)
Best Actress	Dorothy McGuire in *Friendly Persuasion* (USA)
Best Supporting Actor	Richard Basehart in *Moby Dick* (USA)
Best Supporting Actress	Debbie Reynolds in *The Catered Affair* (USA)
Best Direction	John Huston for *Moby Dick* (USA)

1957

Ten Best:

American: (1) *The Bridge On The River Kwai*; (2) *Twelve Angry Men*; (3) *The Spirit Of St. Louis*; (4) *The Rising Of The Moon*; (5) *Albert Schweitzer*; (6) *Funny Face*; (7) *The Bachelor Party*; (8) *The Enemy Below*; (9) *A Hatful Of Rain*; (10) *A Farewell To Arms*.

Foreign: (1) *Ordet* (Denmark); (2) *Gervaise* (France); (3) *Torero!* (Mexico); (4) *The Red Balloon* (France); (5) *A Man Escaped* (France).

Best Actor	Alec Guinness in *The Bridge On The River Kwai* (Britain)
Best Actress	Joanne Woodward in *The Three Faces Of Eve* (USA) & *No Down Payment* (USA)
Best Supporting Actor	Sessue Hayakawa in *The Bridge On The River Kwai* (Britain)
Best Supporting Actress	Sybil Thorndike in *The Prince And The Showgirl* (Britain)
Best Direction	David Lean for *The Bridge On The River Kwai* (Britain)

Note: The Bridge On The River Kwai was generally classed as a British film made with American finance; The National Board of Review selected it as the best American picture of the year.

1958

Ten Best:

American: (1) *The Old Man And The Sea*; (2) *Separate Tables*; (3) *The Last Hurrah*; (4) *The Long Hot Summer*; (5) *Windjammer*; (6) *Cat On A Hot Tin Roof*; (7) *The Goddess*; (8) *The Brothers Karamazov*; (9) *Me And The Colonel*; (10) *Gigi*.

Foreign: (1) *Pather Panchali* (India); (2) *Le Rouge Et Le Noir* (France/Italy); (3) *The Horse's Mouth* (Britain); (4) *Mon Oncle* (France/Italy); (5) *A Night To Remember* (Britain).

Best Actor	Spencer Tracy in *The Old Man And The Sea* (USA) & *The Last Hurrah* (USA)
Best Actress	Ingrid Bergman in *The Inn Of The Sixth Happiness* (Britain)
Best Supporting Actor	Albert Salmi in *The Brothers Karamazov* (USA) & *The Bravados* (USA)
Best Supporting Actress	Kay Walsh in *The Horse's Mouth* (Britain)
Best Direction	John Ford for *The Last Hurrah* (USA)

1959

Ten Best:

American: (1) *The Nun's Story*; (2) *Ben-Hur*; (3) *Anatomy Of A Murder*; (4) *The Diary Of Anne Frank*; (5) *Middle Of The Night*; (6) *The Man Who Understood Women*; (7) *Some Like It Hot*; (8) *Suddenly, Last Summer*; (9) *On The Beach*; (10) *North By Northwest*.

Foreign: (1) *Wild Strawberries* (Sweden); (2) *Room At The Top* (Britain); (3) *Aparajito* (India); (4) *The Roof* (Italy); (5) *Look Back In Anger* (Britain).

Best Actor	Victor Sjöström in *Wild Strawberries* (Sweden)
Best Actress	Simone Signoret in *Room At The Top* (Britain)
Best Supporting Actor	Hugh Griffith in *Ben-Hur* (USA)
Best Supporting Actress	Edith Evans in *The Nun's Story* (USA)
Best Direction	Fred Zinnemann for *The Nun's Story* (USA)

1960

Ten Best:

American: (1) *Sons And Lovers*; (2) *The Alamo*; (3) *The Sundowners*; (4) *Inherit The Wind*; (5) *Sunrise At Campobello*; (6) *Elmer Gantry*; (7) *Home From The Hill*; (8) *The Apartment*; (9) *Wild River*; (10) *The Dark At The Top Of The Stairs*.

Foreign: (1) *The World Of Apu* (India); (2) *Il Generale Della Rovere* (Italy/France); (3) *The Angry Silence* (Britain); (4) *I'm All Right Jack* (Britain); (5) *Hiroshima Mon Amour* (France/Japan)

Best Actor	Robert Mitchum in *Home From The Hill* (USA) & *The Sundowners* (USA)
Best Actress	Greer Garson in *Sunrise At Campobello* (USA)
Best Supporting Actor	George Peppard in *Home From The Hill* (USA)
Best Supporting Actress	Shirley Jones in *Elmer Gantry* (USA)
Best Direction	Jack Cardiff for *Sons And Lovers* (Britain)

Note: Sons And Lovers was generally classed as a British film made with American finance; The National Board of Review selected it as the best American picture of the year.

1961

Ten Best:

American: (1) *Question 7*; (2) *The Hustler*; (3) *West Side Story*; (4) *The Innocents*; (5) *The Hoodlum Priest*; (6) *Summer And Smoke*; (7) *The Young Doctors*; (8) *Judgment At Nuremberg*; (9) *One, Two, Three*; (10) *Fanny*.

Foreign: (1) *The Bridge* (West Germany); (2) *La Dolce Vita* (Italy/France); (3) *Two Women* (France/Italy); (4) *Saturday Night And Sunday Morning* (Britain); (5) *Seryozha* (USSR).

Best Actor	Albert Finney in *Saturday Night And Sunday Morning* (Britain)
Best Actress	Geraldine Page in *Summer And Smoke* (USA)
Best Supporting Actor	Jackie Gleason in *The Hustler* (USA)
Best Supporting Actress	Ruby Dee in *A Raisin In The Sun* (USA)
Best Direction	Jack Clayton for *The Innocents* (Britain)

Note: The Innocents, a British film made with American finance, was classed as an American picture by the National Board of Review.

1962

Ten Best:

In English: (1) *The Longest Day* (USA); (2) *Billy Budd* (Britain); (3) *The Miracle Worker* (USA); (4) *Lawrence Of Arabia* (Britain); (5) *Long Day's Journey Into Night* (USA); (6) *Whistle Down The Wind* (Britain); (7) *Requiem For A Heavyweight* (USA); (8) *A Taste Of Honey* (Britain); (9) *Birdman Of Alcatraz* (USA); (10) *War Hunt* (USA).

In Foreign Languages: (1) *Sundays And Cybèle* (France); (2) *Barabbas* (Italy); (3) *Divorce — Italian Style* (Italy); (4) *The Island* (Japan); (5) *Through A Glass Darkly* (Sweden).

Best Actor	Jason Robards, Jr. in *Long Day's Journey Into Night* (USA) and *Tender Is The Night* (USA)
Best Actress	Anne Bancroft in *The Miracle Worker* (USA)

Best Supporting Actor	Burgess Meredith in *Advise And Consent* (USA)
Best Supporting Actress	Angela Lansbury in *The Manchurian Candidate* (USA) and *All Fall Down* (USA)
Best Direction	David Lean for *Lawrence Of Arabia* (Britain)

1963

Ten Best:

In English: (1) *Tom Jones* (Britain); (2) *Lilies Of The Field* (USA); (3) *All The Way Home* (USA); (4) *Hud* (USA); (5) *This Sporting Life* (Britain); (6) *Lord Of The Flies* (Britain); (7) *The L-Shaped Room* (Britain); (8) *The Great Escape* (USA); (9) *How The West Was Won* (USA); (10) *The Cardinal* (USA).

In Foreign Languages: (1) *8½* (Italy); (2) *The Four Days Of Naples* (USA/Italy); (3) *Winter Light* (Sweden); (4) *The Leopard* (France/Italy); (5) *Any Number Can Win* (France/Italy).

Best Actor	Rex Harrison in *Cleopatra* (USA)
Best Actress	Patricia Neal in *Hud* (USA)
Best Supporting Actor	Melvyn Douglas in *Hud* (USA)
Best Supporting Actress	Margaret Rutherford in *The V.I.P.s* (Britain)
Best Direction	Tony Richardson for *Tom Jones* (Britain)

1964

Ten Best:

In English: (1) *Becket* (Britain); (2) *My Fair Lady* (USA); (3) *Girl With Green Eyes* (Britain); (4) *The World Of Henry Orient* (USA); (5) *Zorba The Greek* (USA/Greece); (6) *Topkapi* (USA); (7) *The Chalk Garden* (Britain); (8) *The Finest Hours* (Britain); (9) *Four Days In November* (USA); (10) *Seance On A Wet Afternoon* (Britain).

In Foreign Languages: (1) *World Without Sun* (France/Italy); (2) *The Organizer* (France/Italy/Yugoslavia); (3) *Anatomy Of A Marriage* (France/Italy); (4) *Seduced And Abandoned* (France/Italy); (5) *Yesterday, Today And Tomorrow* (Italy).

Best Actor	Anthony Quinn in *Zorba The Greek* (USA/Greece)
Best Actress	Kim Stanley in *Seance On A Wet Afternoon* (Britain)
Best Supporting Actor	Martin Balsam in *The Carpetbaggers* (USA)
Best Supporting Actress	Edith Evans in *The Chalk Garden* (Britain)
Best Direction	Desmond Davis for *Girl With Green Eyes* (Britain)

1965
Ten Best:
In English: (1) *The Eleanor Roosevelt Story* (USA); (2) *The Agony And The Ecstasy* (USA); (3) *Doctor Zhivago* (USA); (4) *Ship Of Fools* (USA); (5) *The Spy Who Came In From The Cold* (Britain); (6) *Darling* (Britain); (7) *The Greatest Story Ever Told* (USA); (8) *A Thousand Clowns* (USA); (9) *The Train* (USA/France/Italy); (10) *The Sound Of Music* (USA).

In Foreign Languages: (1) *Juliet Of The Spirits* (France/Italy/West Germany); (2) *The Overcoat* (USSR); (3) *La Bohème* (Switzerland); (4) *La Tia Tula* (Spain); (5) *Gertrud* (Denmark).

Best Actor	Lee Marvin in *Cat Ballou* (USA) and *Ship Of Fools* (USA)
Best Actress	Julie Christie in *Darling* (Britain) and *Doctor Zhivago* (USA)
Best Supporting Actor	Harry Andrews in *The Agony And The Ecstasy* (USA) and *The Hill* (Britain)
Best Supporting Actress	Joan Blondell in *The Cincinnati Kid* (USA)
Best Direction	John Schlesinger for *Darling* (Britain)

1966
Ten Best:
In English: (1) *A Man For All Seasons* (Britain); (2) *Born Free* (Britain); (3) *Alfie* (Britain); (4) *Who's Afraid Of Virginia Woolf?* (USA); (5) *The Bible* (USA/Italy); (6) *Georgy Girl* (Britain); (7) *Years Of Lightning, Day Of Drums* (USA); (8) *It Happened Here* (Britain); (9) *The Russians Are Coming, The Russians Are Coming* (USA); (10) *Shakespeare Wallah* (India).

In Foreign Languages: (1) *The Sleeping Car Murders* (France); (2) *The Gospel According To St. Matthew* (France/Italy); (3) *The Shameless Old Lady* (France); (4) *A Man And A Woman* (France); (5) *Hamlet* (USSR).

Best Actor	Paul Scofield in *A Man For All Seasons* (Britain)
Best Actress	Elizabeth Taylor in *Who's Afraid Of Virginia Woolf?* (USA)
Best Supporting Actor	Robert Shaw in *A Man For All Seasons* (Britain)
Best Supporting Actress	Vivien Merchant in *Alfie* (Britain)
Best Direction	Fred Zinnemann for *A Man For All Seasons* (Britain)

1967
Ten Best:
In English: (1) *Far From The Madding Crowd* (Britain); (2) *The Whisperers* (Britain); (3) *Ulysses* (USA/Britain); (4) *In Cold Blood* (USA); (5) *The Family Way* (Britain); (6) *The Taming Of The Shrew* (USA/Italy); (7) *Doctor Dolittle* (USA); (8) *The Graduate* (USA); (9) *The Comedians* (USA/Bermuda/France); (10) *Accident* (Britain).

In Foreign Languages: (1) *Elvira Madigan* (Sweden); (2) *The Hunt* (Spain); (3) *Africa Addio* (Italy); (4) *Persona* (Sweden); (5) *The Great British Train Robbery* (West Germany).

Best Actor	Peter Finch in *Far From The Madding Crowd* (Britain)
Best Actress	Edith Evans in *The Whisperers* (Britain)
Best Supporting Actor	Paul Ford in *The Comedians* (USA/Bermuda/France)
Best Supporting Actress	Marjorie Rhodes in *The Family Way* (Britain)
Best Direction	Richard Brooks for *In Cold Blood* (USA)

1968

Ten Best:

In English: (1) *The Shoes Of The Fisherman* (USA); (2) *Romeo And Juliet* (Britain/Italy); (3) *Yellow Submarine* (Britain); (4) *Charly* (USA); (5) *Rachel, Rachel* (USA); (6) *The Subject Was Roses* (USA); (7) *The Lion In Winter* (Britain); (8) *Planet Of The Apes* (USA); (9) *Oliver!* (Britain); (10) *2001: A Space Odyssey* (Britain).

In Foreign Languages: (1) *War And Peace* (USSR); (2) *Hagbard And Signe* (Denmark/Iceland/Sweden); (3) *Hunger* (Denmark/Norway/Sweden); (4) *The Two Of Us* (France); (5) *The Bride Wore Black* (France/Italy).

Best Actor	Cliff Robertson in *Charly* (USA)
Best Actress	Liv Ullmann in *Hour Of The Wolf* (Sweden) and *Shame* (Sweden)
Best Supporting Actor	Leo McKern in *The Shoes Of The Fisherman* (USA)
Best Supporting Actress	Virginia Maskell in *Interlude* (Britain)
Best Direction	Franco Zeffirelli for *Romeo And Juliet* (Britain/Italy)

1969

Ten Best:

In English: (1) *They Shoot Horses, Don't They?* (USA); (2) *Ring Of Bright Water* (Britain); (3) *Topaz* (USA); (4) *Goodbye, Mr. Chips* (Britain); (5) *Battle Of Britain* (Britain); (6) *Isadora* (Britain); (7) *The Prime Of Miss Jean Brodie* (Britain); (8) *Support Your Local Sheriff* (USA); (9) *True Grit* (USA); (10) *Midnight Cowboy* (USA).

In Foreign Languages: (1) *Shame* (Sweden); (2) *Stolen Kisses* (France); (3) *The Damned* (Italy/West Germany); (4) *La Femme Infidèle* (France/Italy); (5) *Adalen '31* (Sweden).

Best Actor	Peter O'Toole in *Goodbye, Mr. Chips* (Britain)
Best Actress	Geraldine Page in *Trilogy* (USA)
Best Supporting Actor	Philippe Noiret in *Topaz* (USA)

Best Supporting Actress	Pamela Franklin in *The Prime Of Miss Jean Brodie* (Britain)
Best Direction	Alfred Hitchcock for *Topaz* (USA)

1970

Ten Best:

In English: (1) *Patton* (USA); (2) *Kes* (Britain); (3) *Women In Love* (Britain); (4) *Five Easy Pieces* (USA); (5) *Ryan's Daughter* (Britain); (6) *I Never Sang For My Father* (USA); (7) *Diary Of A Mad Housewife* (USA); (8) *Love Story* (USA); (9) *The Virgin And The Gypsy* (Britain); (10) *Tora! Tora! Tora!* (USA/Japan).

In Foreign Languages: (1) *L'Enfant Sauvage* (France); (2) *My Night At Maud's* (France); (3) *A Passion* (Sweden); (4) *The Confession* (France/Italy); (5) *This Man Must Die* (France/Italy).

Best Actor	George C. Scott in *Patton* (USA)
Best Actress	Glenda Jackson in *Women In Love* (Britain)
Best Supporting Actor	Frank Langella in *Diary Of A Mad Housewife* (USA) and *The Twelve Chairs* (USA)
Best Supporting Actress	Karen Black in *Five Easy Pieces* (USA)
Best Direction	François Truffaut for *L'Enfant Sauvage* (France)

1971

Ten Best:

In English: (1) *Macbeth* (Britain); (2) *The Boy Friend* (Britain); (3) *One Day In The Life Of Ivan Denisovich* (Britain); (4) *The French Connection* (USA); (5) *The Last Picture Show* (USA); (6) *Nicholas And Alexandra* (USA); (7) *The Go-Between* (Britain); (8) *King Lear* (Britain/Denmark); (9) *Tales Of Beatrix Potter* (Britain); (10) *Death In Venice* (Italy).

In Foreign Languages: (1) *Claire's Knee* (France); (2) *Bed And Board* (France/Italy); (3) *The Clowns* (Italy/France/West Germany); (4) *The Garden Of The Finzi-Continis* (Italy/West Germany); (5) *The Conformist* (Italy/France/West Germany).

Best Actor	Gene Hackman in *The French Connection* (USA)
Best Actress	Irene Papas in *The Trojan Women* (USA)
Best Supporting Actor	Ben Johnson in *The Last Picture Show* (USA)
Best Supporting Actress	Cloris Leachman in *The Last Picture Show* (USA)
Best Direction	Ken Russell for *The Devils* (Britain) and *The Boy Friend* (Britain)

1972

Ten Best:

In English: (1) *Cabaret* (USA); (2) *Man Of La Mancha* (USA); (3) *The Godfather* (USA); (4) *Sounder* (USA); (5) *1776* (USA); (6) *The Effect Of*

Gamma Rays On Man-In-The-Moon Marigolds (USA); (7) *Deliverance* (USA); (8) *The Ruling Class* (Britain); (9) *The Candidate* (USA); (10) *Frenzy* (Britain).

In Foreign Languages: (1) *The Sorrow And The Pity* (Switzerland); (2) *The Emigrants* (Sweden); (3) *The Discreet Charm Of The Bourgeoisie* (France); (4) *Love In The Afternoon* (France); (5) *Uncle Vanya* (USSR).

Best Actor	Peter O'Toole in *The Ruling Class* (Britain) & *Man Of La Mancha* (USA)
Best Actress	Cicely Tyson in *Sounder* (USA)
Best Supporting Actor	Al Pacino in *The Godfather* (USA) & Joel Grey in *Cabaret* (USA)
Best Supporting Actress	Marisa Berenson in *Cabaret* (USA)
Best Direction	Bob Fosse for *Cabaret* (USA)

1973
Ten Best:
In English: (1) *The Sting* (USA); (2) *Paper Moon* (USA); (3) *The Homecoming* (USA); (4) *Bang The Drum Slowly* (USA); (5) *Serpico* (USA); (6) *O Lucky Man* (Britain); (7) *The Last American Hero* (USA); (8) *The Hireling* (Britain); (9) *The Day Of The Dolphin* (USA); (10) *The Way We Were* (USA).

In Foreign Languages: (1) *Cries And Whispers* (Sweden); (2) *Day For Night* (France/Italy); (3) *The New Land* (Sweden); (4) *The Tall Blond Man With One Black Shoe* (France); (5) *Alfredo, Alfredo* (Italy) and *Traffic* (France/Italy).

Best Actor	Al Pacino in *Serpico* (USA) and Robert Ryan in *The Iceman Cometh* (USA)
Best Actress	Liv Ullmann in *The New Land* (Sweden)
Best Supporting Actor	John Houseman in *The Paper Chase* (USA)
Best Supporting Actress	Sylvia Sidney in *Summer Wishes, Winter Dreams* (USA)
Best Direction	Ingmar Bergman for *Cries And Whispers* (Sweden)

1974
Ten Best:
In English: (1) *The Conversation* (USA); (2) *Murder On The Orient Express* (Britain); (3) *Chinatown* (USA); (4) *The Last Detail* (USA); (5) *Harry And Tonto* (USA); (6) *A Woman Under The Influence* (USA); (7) *Thieves Like Us* (USA); (8) *Lenny* (USA); (9) *Daisy Miller* (USA); (10) *The Three Musketeers* (Panama).

In Foreign Languages: (1) *Amarcord* (Italy/France); (2) *Lacombe Lucien* (France/Italy/West Germany); (3) *Scenes From A Marriage* (Sweden); (4) *The Phantom Of Liberté* (France); (5) *The Pedestrian* (West Germany).

Best Actor	Gene Hackman in *The Conversation* (USA)
Best Actress	Gena Rowlands in *A Woman Under The Influence* (USA)
Best Supporting Actor	Holger Lowenadler in *Lacombe Lucien* (France/Italy/West Germany)
Best Supporting Actress	Valerie Perrine in *Lenny* (USA)
Best Direction	Francis Ford Coppola for *The Conversation* (USA)

1975

Ten Best:

In English: (1) *Barry Lyndon* (Britain) and *Nashville* (USA); (2) *Conduct Unbecoming*; (3) *One Flew Over The Cuckoo's Nest* (USA); (4) *Lies My Father Told Me* (USA); (5) *Dog Day Afternoon* (USA); (6) *The Day Of The Locust* (USA); (7) *The Passenger* (Italy/France/Spain); (8) *Hearts Of The West* (USA); (9) *Farewell My Lovely* (USA); (10) *Alice Doesn't Live Here Anymore* (USA).

In Foreign Languages: (1) *The Story Of Adèle H* (France); (2) *Brief Vacation* (Italy); (3) *Section Spéciale* (France/Italy/West Germany); (4) *Stavisky* (France/Italy); (5) *Swept Away* (Italy).

Best Actor	Jack Nicholson in *One Flew Over The Cuckoo's Nest* (USA)
Best Actress	Isabelle Adjani in *The Story Of Adele H* (France)
Best Supporting Actor	Charles Durning in *Dog Day Afternoon* (USA)
Best Supporting Actress	Ronee Blakely in *Nashville* (USA)
Best Direction	Stanley Kubrick for *Barry Lyndon* (Britain) & Robert Altman for *Nashville* (USA)

1976

Ten Best:

In English: (1) *All The President's Men* (USA); (2) *Network* (USA); (3) *Rocky* (USA); (4) *The Last Tycoon* (USA); (5) *The Seven-Per-Cent Solution* (Britain); (6) *The Front* (USA); (7) *The Shootist* (USA); (8) *Family Plot* (USA); (9) *Silent Movie* (USA); (10) *Obsession* (USA).

In Foreign Languages: (1) *Die Marquise Von O* (West Germany/France); (2) *Face To Face* (Sweden); (3) *Pocket Money* (France); (4) *Cousin, Cousine* (France); (5) *The Clockmaker* (France).

Best Actor	David Carradine in *Bound For Glory* (USA)
Best Actress	Liv Ullmann in *Face To Face* (Sweden)
Best Supporting Actor	Jason Robards in *All The President's Men* (USA)
Best Supporting Actress	Talia Shire in *Rocky* (USA)
Best Direction	Alan Pakula for *All The President's Men* (USA)

1977
Ten Best:
In English: (1) *The Turning Point* (USA); (2) *Annie Hall* (USA); (3) *Julia* (USA); (4) *Star Wars* (USA); (5) *Close Encounters Of The Third Kind* (USA); (6) *The Late Show* (USA); (7) *Saturday Night Fever* (USA); (8) *Equus* (USA); (9) *The Picture Show Man* (Australia); (10) *Harlan County, USA* (USA).

In Foreign Languages: (1) *That Obscure Object Of Desire* (France/Spain); (2) *The Man Who Loved Women* (France); (3) *A Special Day* (Italy/Canada); (4) *Cria!* (Spain); (5) *The American Friend* (West Germany/France).

Best Actor	John Travolta in *Saturday Night Fever* (USA)
Best Actress	Anne Bancroft in *The Turning Point* (USA)
Best Supporting Actor	Tom Skerritt in *The Turning Point* (USA)
Best Supporting Actress	Diane Keaton in *Annie Hall* (USA)
Best Direction	Luis Buñuel for *That Obscure Object Of Desire* (France/Spain)

1978
Ten Best:
In English: (1) *Days Of Heaven* (USA); (2) *Coming Home* (USA); (3) *Interiors* (USA); (4) *Superman* (USA); (5) *Movie, Movie* (USA); (6) *Midnight Express* (Britain); (7) *An Unmarried Woman* (USA); (8) *Pretty Baby* (USA); (9) *Girlfriends* (USA); (10) *Comes A Horseman* (USA).

In Foreign Languages: (1) *Autumn Sonata* (West Germany); (2) *Dear Detective* (France); (3) *Madame Rosa* (France); (4) *A Slave Of Love* (USSR); (5) *Bread And Chocolate* (Italy).

Best Actor	Jon Voight in *Coming Home* (USA) & Laurence Olivier in *The Boys From Brazil* (USA)
Best Actress	Ingrid Bergman in *Autumn Sonata* (West Germany)
Best Supporting Actor	Richard Farnsworth in *Comes A Horseman* (USA)
Best Supporting Actress	Angela Lansbury in *Death On The Nile* (Britain)
Best Direction	Ingmar Bergman for *Autumn Sonata* (West Germany)

1979
Ten Best:
In English: (1) *Manhattan* (USA); (2) *Yanks* (Britain); (3) *The Europeans* (Britain); (4) *The China Syndrome* (USA); (5) *Breaking Away* (USA); (6) *Apocalypse Now* (USA); (7) *Being There* (USA); (8) *Time After Time* (USA); (9) *North Dallas Forty* (USA); (10) *Kramer vs. Kramer* (USA).

In Foreign Languages: (1) *La Cage Aux Folles* (France/Italy); (2) *The Tree Of Wooden Clogs* (Italy); (3) *The Marriage Of Maria Braun* (West Germany); (4) *Nosferatu* (West Germany); (5) *Peppermint Soda* (France).

Best Actor	Peter Sellers in *Being There* (USA)
Best Actress	Sally Field in *Norma Rae* (USA)
Best Supporting Actor	Paul Dooley in *Breaking Away* (USA)
Best Supporting Actress	Meryl Streep in *Manhattan* (USA), *The Seduction Of Joe Tynan* (USA) and *Kramer vs. Kramer* (USA)
Best Direction	John Schlesinger for *Yanks* (Britain)

British Academy Awards

The British 'Oscars' have always lived in the shadow of their more glamorous American counterparts, yet the record books show that many of the best picture selections have often been more informed than those of the American Academy.

Only the British Academy, for instance, recognised the genius of Max Ophuls when it named *La Ronde* as the best film of 1951. And only the British Academy voted *Richard III, The Hustler, The Graduate* and *Julia* as best films of their respective years.

The awards were first presented in 1947 when Wyler's *The Best Years Of Our Lives* was selected as the year's best. Acting awards were introduced in 1952 and for sixteen years were split into four categories – Best British Actor, British Actress, Foreign Actor and Foreign Actress. In 1968 the rules were changed and the awards brought into line with those presented at the American Oscar ceremonies – Best Actor, Best Actress, Best Supporting Actor and Best Supporting Actress. Technical awards were also introduced in the sixties.

During the first twenty years (1947-1967) a separate prize was presented for the Best British Film. Lists of nominated pictures sometimes ran as long as eighteen films until they were reduced to a more manageable four pictures per year in 1964.

The awards are presented by the British Academy of Film and Television Arts, formed in 1975 when it replaced The Society of Film and Television Arts (founded in 1967) which, in turn, was an amalgamation of the original British Film Academy and The Guild of Television Producers and Directors.

The Best Film Awards are bronze statuettes created by Henry Moore. The craft and performance awards consist of special plaques. Members of the British Academy of Film and Television Arts vote annually and the awards are presented each March, shortly before the American Oscar presentations.

1947
Best Film, Any Source — *The Best Years Of Our Lives* (USA)
Best British Film — *Odd Man Out*

1948
Best Film, Any Source — *Hamlet* (Britain)
Best British Film — *The Fallen Idol*
Hamlet was named best of the year from seven best picture nominations. Others on the list: *Crossfire* (USA); *The Fallen Idol* (Britain); *Four Steps In The Clouds* (Italy); *Monsieur Vincent* (France); *The Naked City* (USA); *Paisa* (Italy).

The nominated pictures for Best British Film were *The Fallen Idol; Hamlet; Once A Jolly Swagman; The Red Shoes; Scott Of The Antarctic; The Small Voice; Oliver Twist.*

1949
Best Film, Any Source — *Bicycle Thieves* (Italy)
Best British Film — *The Third Man*
Seven pictures were nominated for the Best Film Award: *Berliner Ballade* (Germany); *Bicycle Thieves* (Italy); *The Last Stage* (Poland); *The Set-Up* (USA); *The Third Man* (Britain); *The Treasure Of The Sierra Madre* (USA); *The Window* (USA).

Pictures nominated for Best British Film: *Kind Hearts And Coronets; Passport To Pimlico; The Queen Of Spades; A Run For Your Money; The Small Back Room; The Third Man; Whisky Galore.*

1950
Best Film, Any Source — *All About Eve* (USA)
Best British Film — *The Blue Lamp*
The Best Film nominations: *All About Eve* (USA); *The Asphalt Jungle* (USA); *La Beauté du Diable* (France); *Intruder In The Dust* (USA); *The Men* (USA); *On The Town* (USA); *Orphée* (France).

Six pictures were short-listed for the Best British Film category: *The Blue Lamp; Chance Of A Lifetime; Morning Departure; Seven Days To Noon; State Secret; The Wooden Horse.*

1951
Best Film, Any Source — *La Ronde* (France)
Best British Film — *The Lavender Hill Mob*
Nomination rules were changed in 1951. The Best Film and Best British Film were both selected from a final list of 18 nominated pictures: *An American In Paris* (USA); *The Browning Version* (Britain); *Detective Story* (USA); *Domenica D'Agosto* (Italy); *Edouard et Caroline* (France); *Fourteen Hours* (USA); *The Lavender Hill Mob* (Britain); *The Magic Box* (Britain); *The Magic Garden* (Britain); *The Man In The White Suit*

(Britain); *Miss Julie* (Sweden); *Never Take No For An Answer* (Britain); *No Resting Place* (Britain); *The Red Badge Of Courage* (USA); *La Ronde* (France); *The Sound Of Fury* (USA); *A Walk In The Sun* (USA); *White Corridors* (Britain).

1952

Best Film, Any Source — *The Sound Barrier* (Britain)
Best British Film — *The Sound Barrier*
Best British Actor — Ralph Richardson in *The Sound Barrier* (Britain)
Best British Actress — Vivien Leigh in *A Streetcar Named Desire* (USA)
Best Foreign Actor — Marlon Brando in *Viva Zapata!* (USA)
Best Foreign Actress — Simone Signoret in *Casque d'Or* (France)

Acting Awards were introduced for the first time in 1952. 18 pictures were short-listed for the Best Film and Best British Film Awards, among them: *The African Queen* (Britain); *Angels One Five* (Britain); *Carrie* (USA); *Cry The Beloved Country* (Britain); *Death Of A Salesman* (USA); *Limelight* (USA); *Mandy* (Britain); *An Outcast Of The Islands* (Britain); *The River* (India); *Singin' In The Rain* (USA); *The Sound Barrier* (Britain); *A Streetcar Named Desire* (USA); *Viva Zapata!* (USA).

1953

Best Film, Any Source — *Les Jeux Interdits* (France)
Best British Film — *Genevieve*
Best British Actor — John Gielgud in *Julius Caesar* (USA)
Best British Actress — Audrey Hepburn in *Roman Holiday* (USA)
Best Foreign Actor — Marlon Brando in *Julius Caesar* (USA)
Best Foreign Actress — Leslie Caron in *Lili* (USA)

The short list of contenders for Best Film and Best British Film was increased to 19: *The Bad And The Beautiful* (USA); *Come Back, Little Sheba* (USA); *The Cruel Sea* (Britain); *From Here To Eternity* (USA); *Genevieve* (Britain); *The Heart Of The Matter* (Britain); *Julius Caesar* (USA); *The Kidnappers* (Britain); *Lili* (USA); *The Little World Of Don Camillo* (France/Italy); *The Medium* (Italy); *Mogambo* (USA); *Moulin Rouge* (Britain); *Nous Sommes Tous Des Assassins* (France); *Roman Holiday* (USA); *Shane* (USA); *Les Jeux Interdits* (France); *The Sun Shines Bright* (USA); *Two Pennyworth Of Hope* (Italy).

1954

Best Film, Any Source — *The Wages Of Fear* (France/Italy)
Best British Film — *Hobson's Choice*
Best British Actor — Kenneth More in *Doctor In The House* (Britain)
Best British Actress — Yvonne Mitchell in *The Divided Heart* (Britain)
Best Foreign Actor — Marlon Brando in *On The Waterfront* (USA)
Best Foreign Actress — Cornell Borchers in *The Divided Heart* (Britain)

21 pictures were short-listed for the Best Film and Best British Film Awards: *The Adventures Of Robinson Crusoe* (Mexico); *Bread, Love And Dreams* (Italy); *The Caine Mutiny* (USA); *Carrington, V.C.* (Britain); *The Divided Heart* (Britain); *Doctor In The House* (Britain); *Executive Suite* (USA); *For Better, For Worse* (Britain); *Gate Of Hell* (Japan); *Hobson's Choice* (Britain); *How To Marry A Millionaire* (USA); *The Maggie* (Britain); *The Moon Is Blue* (USA); *On The Waterfront* (USA); *The Purple Plain* (Britain); *Rear Window* (USA); *Riot In Cell Block 11* (USA); *Romeo And Juliet* (Britain/Italy); *Seven Brides For Seven Brothers* (USA); *The Wages Of Fear* (France); *The Young Lovers* (Britain).

1955

Best Film, Any Source	*Richard III* (Britain)
Best British Film	*Richard III*
Best British Actor	Laurence Olivier in *Richard III* (Britain)
Best British Actress	Katie Johnson in *The Ladykillers* (Britain)
Best Foreign Actor	Ernest Borgnine in *Marty* (USA)
Best Foreign Actress	Betsy Blair in *Marty* (USA)

The Best Film and Best British Film were selected from 14 nominated pictures: *Bad Day At Black Rock* (USA); *Carmen Jones* (USA); *The Colditz Story* (Britain); *The Dam Busters* (Britain); *East Of Eden* (USA); *The Ladykillers* (Britain); *Marty* (USA); *The Night My Number Came Up* (Britain); *The Prisoner* (Britain); *Richard III* (Britain); *Seven Samurai* (Japan); *Simba* (Britain); *La Strada* (Italy); *Summertime* (USA).

1956

Best Film, Any Source	*Gervaise* (France)
Best British Film	*Reach For The Sky*
Best British Actor	Peter Finch in *A Town Like Alice* (Britain)
Best British Actress	Virginia McKenna in *A Town Like Alice* (Britain)
Best Foreign Actor	François Périer in *Gervaise* (France)
Best Foreign Actress	Anna Magnani in *The Rose Tattoo* (USA)

The Academy listed 16 pictures from which the Best Film and Best British Film were selected: *Baby Doll* (USA); *The Battle Of The River Plate* (Britain); *Le Defroque* (France); *Gervaise* (France); *The Grasshopper* (USSR); *Guys And Dolls* (USA); *The Killing* (USA); *The Man With The Golden Arm* (USA); *The Man Who Never Was* (Britain); *Picnic* (USA); *Reach For The Sky* (Britain); *Rebel Without A Cause* (USA); *The Shadow* (Poland); *Smiles Of A Summer Night* (Sweden); *A Town Like Alice* (Britain); *Yield To The Night* (Britain).

1957

Best Film, Any Source	*The Bridge On The River Kwai*
Best British Film	*The Bridge On The River Kwai*
Best British Actor	Alec Guinness in *The Bridge On The River Kwai* (Britain)

Best British Actress	Heather Sears in *The Story Of Esther Costello* (Britain)
Best Foreign Actor	Henry Fonda in *Twelve Angry Men* (USA)
Best Foreign Actress	Simone Signoret in *The Witches Of Salem* (France)

The Bridge On The River Kwai was selected from 16 nominated pictures. The other films on the list: *Bachelor Party* (USA); *A Man Escaped* (France); *He Who Must Die* (Italy/France); *Heaven Knows, Mr. Allison* (USA); *A Man Is Ten Feet Tall* (USA); *Paths Of Glory* (USA); *Pather Panchali* (India); *Porte Des Lilas* (France/Italy); *The Prince And The Showgirl* (Britain); *The Shiralee* (Britain); *The Tin Star* (USA); *That Night* (USA); *3.10 To Yuma* (USA); *Twelve Angry Men* (USA); *Windom's Way* (Britain).

1958

Best Film, Any Source	*Room At The Top* (Britain)
Best British Film	*Room At The Top*
Best British Actor	Trevor Howard in *The Key* (Britain)
Best British Actress	Irene Worth in *Orders To Kill* (Britain)
Best Foreign Actor	Sidney Poitier in *The Defiant Ones* (USA)
Best Foreign Actress	Simone Signoret in *Room At The Top* (Britain)

14 pictures were nominated for the Best Film/Best British Film categories: *Cat On A Hot Tin Roof* (USA); *The Cranes Are Flying* (USSR); *The Defiant Ones* (USA); *Ice Cold In Alex* (Britain); *Indiscreet* (Britain); *Nights Of Cabiria* (Italy/France); *No Down Payment* (USA); *Orders To Kill* (Britain); *Room At The Top* (Britain); *Sea Of Sand* (Britain); *The Sheepman* (USA); *Aparajito* (India); *Wild Strawberries* (Sweden); *The Young Lions* (USA).

1959

Best Film, Any Source	*Ben-Hur* (USA)
Best British Film	*Sapphire*
Best British Actor	Peter Sellers in *I'm All Right, Jack* (Britain)
Best British Actress	Audrey Hepburn in *The Nun's Story* (USA)
Best Foreign Actor	Jack Lemmon in *Some Like It Hot* (USA)
Best Foreign Actress	Shirley MacLaine in *Ask Any Girl* (USA)

15 pictures were short-listed for the Best Film and Best British Film categories: *Anatomy Of A Murder* (USA); *Ashes And Diamonds* (Poland); *Ben-Hur* (USA); *The Big Country* (USA); *Compulsion* (USA); *The Face* (Sweden); *Gigi* (USA); *Look Back In Anger* (Britain); *Maigret Sets A Trap* (France); *Northwest Frontier* (Britain); *The Nun's Story* (USA); *Sapphire* (Britain); *Some Like It Hot* (USA); *Tiger Bay* (Britain); *Yesterday's Enemy* (Britain).

1960

Best Film, Any Source	*The Apartment* (USA)
Best British Film	*Saturday Night and Sunday Morning*

Best British Actor — Peter Finch in *The Trials Of Oscar Wilde* (Britain)
Best British Actress — Rachel Roberts in *Saturday Night And Sunday Morning* (Britain)
Best Foreign Actor — Jack Lemmon in *The Apartment* (USA)
Best Foreign Actress — Shirley MacLaine in *The Apartment* (USA)

The Academy listed 17 nominated pictures from which the Best Film/Best British Film were selected: *The Angry Silence* (Britain); *The Apartment* (USA); *L'Avventura* (Italy/France); *La Dolce Vita* (Italy/France); *Elmer Gantry* (USA); *Hiroshima, Mon Amour* (France/Japan); *Inherit The Wind* (USA); *Let's Make Love* (USA); *Never On Sunday* (Greece); *Black Orpheus* (France/Italy); *Les Quatre Cents Coups* (France); *Saturday Night And Sunday Morning* (Britain); *Shadows* (USA); *Spartacus* (USA); *Le Testament d'Orphée* (France); *The Trials Of Oscar Wilde* (Britain); *Tunes Of Glory* (Britain).

1961

Best Film, Any Source — *Ballad Of A Soldier* (USSR) and *The Hustler* (USA)
Best British Film — *A Taste Of Honey*
Best British Actor — Peter Finch in *No Love For Johnnie* (Britain)
Best British Actress — Dora Bryan in *A Taste Of Honey* (Britain)
Best Foreign Actor — Paul Newman in *The Hustler* (USA)
Best Foreign Actress — Sophia Loren in *Two Women* (France/Italy)

11 pictures were short-listed for the Best Film and Best British Film categories: *Ballad Of A Soldier* (USSR); *The Hustler* (USA); *The Innocents* (Britain); *Judgment At Nuremberg* (USA); *The Long And The Short And The Tall* (Britain); *Rocco And His Brothers* (Italy); *The Sundowners* (Britain); *A Taste Of Honey* (Britain); *Le Trou* (France); *Whistle Down The Wind* (Britain); *The World Of Apu* (India).

1962

Best Film, Any Source — *Lawrence Of Arabia* (Britain)
Best British Film — *Lawrence Of Arabia*
Best British Actor — Peter O'Toole in *Lawrence Of Arabia* (Britain)
Best British Actress — Leslie Caron in *The L-Shaped Room* (Britain)
Best Foreign Actor — Burt Lancaster in *Birdman Of Alcatraz* (USA)
Best Foreign Actress — Anne Bancroft in *The Miracle Worker* (USA)

18 pictures were short-listed for the Best Film and Best British Film categories: *Billy Budd* (Britain); *The Island* (Japan); *Jules And Jim* (France); *A Kind Of Loving* (Britain); *The L-Shaped Room* (Britain); *The Lady With The Little Dog* (USSR); *Last Year At Marienbad* (France/Italy); *Une Aussi Longue Absence* (France/Italy); *Lawrence Of Arabia* (Britain); *Lola* (France/Italy); *The Manchurian Candidate* (USA); *The Miracle Worker* (USA); *Only Two Can Play* (Britain); *Phaedra* (Greece); *Thou Shalt Not Kill* (Italy/Yugoslavia/Lichtenstein); *Through A Glass Darkly* (Sweden); *The Vanishing Corporal* (France); *West Side Story* (USA).

1963

Best Film, Any Source	*Tom Jones* (Britain)
Best British Film	*Tom Jones*
Best British Actor	Dirk Bogarde in *The Servant* (Britain)
Best British Actress	Rachel Roberts in *This Sporting Life* (Britain)
Best Foreign Actor	Marcello Mastroianni in *Divorce Italian Style* (Italy)
Best Foreign Actress	Patricia Neal in *Hud* (USA)

The Academy listed 12 nominationed pictures from which the Best Film and Best British Film were selected: *Billy Liar* (Britain); *David And Lisa* (USA); *Days Of Wine And Roses* (USA); *Divorce Italian Style* (Italy); *8½* (Italy); *Four Days Of Naples* (Italy); *Hud* (USA); *Knife In The Water* (Poland); *The Servant* (Britain); *This Sporting Life* (Britain); *To Kill A Mockingbird* (USA); *Tom Jones* (Britain)

1964

Best Film, Any Source	*Dr. Strangelove* (Britain)
Best British Film	*Dr. Strangelove*
Best British Actor	Richard Attenborough in *Guns At Batasi* (Britain) and *Seance On A Wet Afternoon* (Britain)
Best British Actress	Audrey Hepburn in *Charade* (USA)
Best Foreign Actor	Marcello Mastroianni in *Yesterday, Today & Tomorrow* (Italy)
Best Foreign Actress	Anne Bancroft in *The Pumpkin Eater* (Britain)

Nominations for Best Film and Best British Film were reduced in 1964. Just four films were listed in each category.

Pictures nominated for Best Film: *Becket* (Britain); *Dr. Strangelove* (Britain); *The Pumpkin Eater* (Britain); *The Train* (USA).

Pictures nominated for Best British Film: *Becket; Dr. Strangelove; King And Country; The Pumpkin Eater.*

1965

Best Film, Any Source	*My Fair Lady* (USA))
Best British Film	*The Ipcress File*
Best British Actor	Dirk Bogarde in *Darling* (Britain)
Best British Actress	Julie Christie in *Darling* (Britain)
Best Foreign Actor	Lee Marvin in *The Killers* (USA) and *Cat Ballou* (USA)
Best Foreign Actress	Patricia Neal in *In Harm's Way* (USA)

The five Best Picture nominations: *Hamlet* (USSR); *The Hill* (Britain); *The Knack* (Britain); *My Fair Lady* (USA); *Zorba The Greek* (Greece/USA).

Pictures nominated for Best British Film: *Darling; The Hill; The Ipcress File; The Knack.*

1966

Best Film, Any Source	*Who's Afraid Of Virginia Woolf?* (USA)
Best British Film	*The Spy Who Came In From The Cold*
Best British Actor	Richard Burton in *Who's Afraid Of Virginia Woolf?* (USA)
Best British Actress	Elizabeth Taylor in *Who's Afraid Of Virginia Woolf?* (USA)
Best Foreign Actor	Rod Steiger in *The Pawnbroker* (USA)
Best Foreign Actress	Jeanne Moreau in *Viva Maria!* (France/Italy)

Nominations for Best Film: *Dr. Zhivago* (USA); *Morgan – A Suitable Case For Treatment* (Britain); *The Spy Who Came In From The Cold* (Britain); *Who's Afraid Of Virginia Woolf?* (USA).

Pictures nominated for Best British Film: *Alfie; Georgy Girl, Morgan – A Suitable Case For Treatment; The Spy Who Came In From The Cold.*

1967

Best Film, Any Source	*A Man For All Seasons* (Britain)
Best British Film	*A Man For All Seasons*
Best British Actor	Paul Scofield in *A Man For All Seasons* (Britain)
Best British Actress	Edith Evans in *The Whisperers* (Britain)
Best Foreign Actor	Rod Steiger in *In The Heat Of The Night* (USA)
Best Foreign Actress	Anouk Aimée in *A Man And A Woman* (France)

Nominations for Best Film: *Bonnie And Clyde* (USA); *A Man And A Woman* (France); *In The Heat Of The Night* (USA); *A Man For All Seasons* (Britain).

Pictures nominated for Best British Film: *Accident; Blow-Up; The Deadly Affair; A Man For All Seasons.*

1968

Best Film	*The Graduate* (USA)
Best Actor	Spencer Tracy in *Guess Who's Coming To Dinner?* (USA)
Best Actress	Katharine Hepburn in *Guess Who's Coming To Dinner?* (USA) and *The Lion In Winter* (Britain)
Best Supporting Actor	Ian Holm in *The Bofors Gun* (Britain)
Best Supporting Actress	Billie Whitelaw in *Twisted Nerve* (Britain) and *Charlie Bubbles* (Britain)
Best Direction	Mike Nichols for *The Graduate* (USA)

Rules were changed this year and the Best British Film Award discontinued. A Direction Award was introduced and the acting awards brought into line with those of the American Academy, e.g. best actor, actress, supporting actor, supporting actress.

Pictures nominated for best film: *Closely Observed Trains* (Czechoslovakia); *The Graduate* (USA); *Oliver!* (Britain); *2001: A Space Odyssey* (Britain).

1969

Best Film	*Midnight Cowboy* (USA)
Best Actor	Dustin Hoffman in *Midnight Cowboy* (USA) and *John And Mary* (USA)
Best Actress	Maggie Smith in *The Prime Of Miss Jean Brodie* (Britain)
Best Supporting Actor	Laurence Olivier in *Oh! What A Lovely War* (Britain)
Best Supporting Actress	Celia Johnson in *The Prime Of Miss Jean Brodie* (Britain)
Best Direction	John Schlesinger for *Midnight Cowboy* (USA)

Best Picture nominations: *Midnight Cowboy* (USA); *Oh! What A Lovely War* (Britain); *Women In Love* (Britain); *Z* (France/Algeria).

1970

Best Film	*Butch Cassidy And The Sundance Kid* (USA)
Best Actor	Robert Redford in *Butch Cassidy And The Sundance Kid* (USA), *Tell Them Willie Boy Is Here* (USA) and *Downhill Racer* (USA)
Best Actress	Katharine Ross in *Butch Cassidy And The Sundance Kid* (USA) and *Tell Them Willie Boy Is Here* (USA)
Best Supporting Actor	Colin Welland in *Kes* (Britain)
Best Supporting Actress	Susannah York in *They Shoot Horses, Don't They?* (USA)
Best Direction	George Roy Hill for *Butch Cassidy And The Sundance Kid* (USA)

Pictures nominated for best film: *Butch Cassidy And The Sundance Kid* (USA); *Kes* (Britain); *M.A.S.H.* (USA); *Ryan's Daughter* (Britain).

1971

Best Film	*Sunday, Bloody Sunday* (Britain)
Best Actor	Peter Finch in *Sunday, Bloody Sunday* (Britain)
Best Actress	Glenda Jackson in *Sunday, Bloody Sunday* (Britain)
Best Supporting Actor	Edward Fox in *The Go-Between* (Britain)
Best Supporting Actress	Margaret Leighton in *The Go-Between* (Britain)
Best Direction	John Schlesinger for *Sunday, Bloody Sunday* (Britain)

Best Picture nominations: *Death In Venice* (Italy); *The Go-Between* (Britain); *Sunday, Bloody Sunday* (Britain); *Taking Off* (USA).

1972

Best Film — *Cabaret* (USA)
Best Actor — Gene Hackman in *The French Connection* (USA) and *The Poseidon Adventure* (USA)
Best Actress — Liza Minnelli in *Cabaret* (USA)
Best Supporting Actor — Ben Johnson in *The Last Picture Show* (USA)
Best Supporting Actress — Cloris Leachman in *The Last Picture Show* (USA)
Best Direction — Bob Fosse for *Cabaret* (USA)

Best Picture nominations: *Cabaret* (USA); *A Clockwork Orange* (Britain); *The French Connection* (USA); *The Last Picture Show* (USA).

1973

Best Film — *Day For Night* (France/Italy)
Best Actor — Walter Matthau in *Pete 'n' Tillie* (USA) and *Charley Varrick* (USA)
Best Actress — Stephane Audran in *The Discreet Charm Of The Bourgeoisie* (France) and *Just Before Nightfall* (France/Italy)
Best Supporting Actor — Arthur Lowe in *O Lucky Man!* (Britain)
Best Supporting Actress — Valentine Cortese in *Day For Night* (France/Italy)
Best Direction — François Truffaut for *Day For Night* (France/Italy)

Best Picture nominations: *Day For Night* (France/Italy); *The Day Of The Jackal* (Britain/France); *The Discreet Charm Of The Bourgeoisie* (France); *Don't Look Now* (Britain).

1974

Best Film — *Lacombe Lucien* (France/Italy/West Germany)
Best Actor — Jack Nicholson in *Chinatown* (USA) and *The Last Detail* (USA)
Best Actress — Joanne Woodward in *Summer Wishes, Winter Dreams* (USA)
Best Supporting Actor — John Gielgud in *Murder On The Orient Express* (Britain)
Best Supporting Actress — Ingrid Bergman in *Murder On The Orient Express* (Britain)
Best Direction — Roman Polanski for *Chinatown* (USA)

Best Picture nominations: *Chinatown* (USA); *Lacombe Lucien* (France/Italy/West Germany); *The Last Detail* (USA); *Murder On The Orient Express* (Britain).

1975

Best Film — *Alice Doesn't Live Here Anymore* (USA)
Best Actor — Al Pacino in *The Godfather Part II* (USA) and *Dog Day Afternoon* (USA)

Best Actress	Ellen Burstyn in *Alice Doesn't Live Here Anymore* (USA)
Best Supporting Actor	Fred Astaire in *The Towering Inferno* (USA)
Best Supporting Actress	Diane Ladd in *Alice Doesn't Live Here Anymore* (USA)
Best Direction	Stanley Kubrick for *Barry Lyndon* (Britain)

Best Picture nominations: *Alice Doesn't Live Here Anymore* (USA); *Barry Lyndon* (Britain); *Dog Day Afternoon* (USA); *Jaws* (USA).

1976

Best Film	*One Flew Over The Cuckoo's Nest* (USA)
Best Actor	Jack Nicholson in *One Flew Over The Cuckoo's Nest* (USA)
Best Actress	Louise Fletcher in *One Flew Over The Cuckoo's Nest* (USA)
Best Supporting Actor	Brad Dourif in *One Flew Over The Cuckoo's Nest* (USA)
Best Supporting Actress	Jodie Foster in *Bugsy Malone* (Britain) and *Taxi Driver* (USA)
Best Direction	Milos Forman for *One Flew Over The Cuckoo's Nest* (USA)

Best Picture nominations: *All The President's Men* (USA); *Bugsy Malone* (Britain); *One Flew Over The Cuckoo's Nest* (USA); *Taxi Driver* (USA).

1977

Best Film	*Annie Hall* (USA)
Best Actor	Peter Finch in *Network* (USA)
Best Actress	Diane Keaton in *Annie Hall* (USA)
Best Supporting Actor	Edward Fox in *A Bridge Too Far* (Britain)
Best Supporting Actress	Jenny Agutter in *Equus* (USA)
Best Direction	Woody Allen for *Annie Hall* (USA)

Best Picture nominations: *Annie Hall* (USA); *A Bridge Too Far* (Britain); *Network* (USA); *Rocky* (USA).

1978

Best Film	*Julia* (USA)
Best Actor	Richard Dreyfuss in *The Goodbye Girl* (USA)
Best Actress	Jane Fonda in *Julia* (USA)
Best Supporting Actor	John Hurt in *Midnight Express* (Britain)
Best Supporting Actress	Geraldine Page in *Interiors* (USA)
Best Direction	Alan Parker for *Midnight Express* (Britain)

Best Picture nominations: *Close Encounters Of The Third Kind* (USA); *Julia* (USA); *Midnight Express* (Britain); *Star Wars* (USA).

1979

Best Film	*Manhattan* (USA)
Best Actor	Jack Lemmon in *The China Syndrome* (USA)
Best Actress	Jane Fonda in *The China Syndrome* (USA)
Best Supporting Actor	Robert Duvall in *Apocalypse Now* (USA)
Best Supporting Actress	Rachel Roberts in *Yanks* (Britain)
Best Direction	Francis Ford Coppola for *Apocalypse Now* (USA)

Best Picture nominations: *Apocalypse Now* (USA); *The China Syndrome* (USA); *The Deer Hunter* (USA); *Manhattan* (USA).

(Above) Diane Keaton and Woody Allen enjoy the pleasures of early morning New York in *Manhattan* (United Artists)

(Below) Jon Voight and Dustin Hoffman in John Schlesinger's first American film, *Midnight Cowboy* (United Artists)

(Above) Harry Secombe as Mr. Bumble and Mark Lester as the orphan Oliver Twist in Carol Reed's musical *Oliver!* (Columbia), American Academy Award, 1968

(Below) Greer Garson with wounded German pilot Helmut Dantine in MGM's 1942 Oscar-winning *Mrs. Miniver*

Audrey Hepburn in *The Nun's Story* (Warner Bros.), best film, 1959, National Board of Review

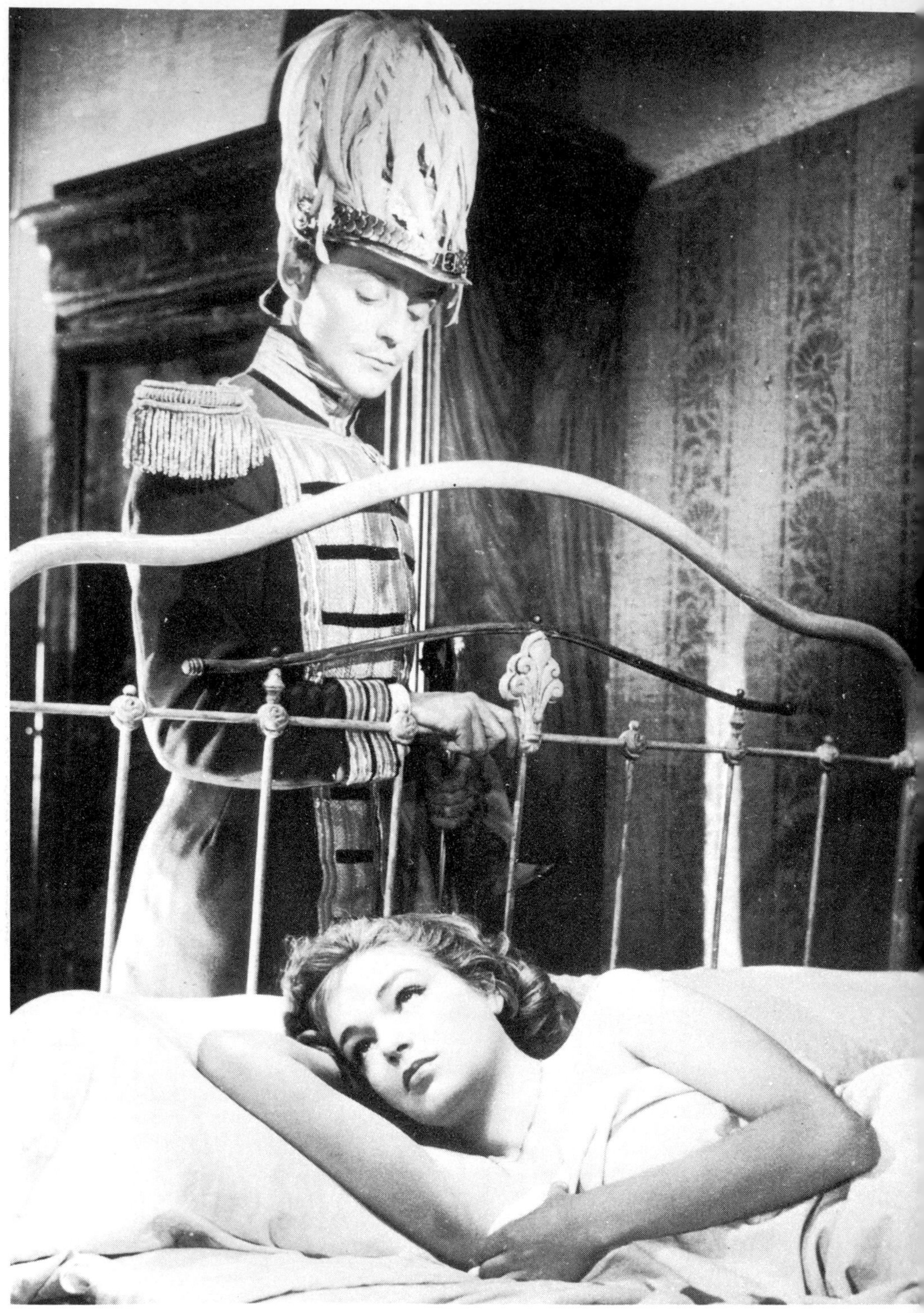

Gerard Philipe and Simone Signoret as part of love's merry-go-round in Max Ophuls' *La Ronde* (Sacha Gordine), voted best film of 1951 by the British Film Academy

Montgomery Clift and Elizabeth Taylor in George Stevens' masterpiece *A Place In The Sun* (Paramount)

Mary Ure and Dean Stockwell in Jack Cardiff's *Sons And Lovers* (20th Century-Fox)

(Above) Thirties con-artists Paul Newman and Robert Redford in the Oscar-winning *The Sting* (Universal)

(Below) Sylvester Stallone battling for the heavyweight championship of the world in *Rocky* (United Artists), directed by John V. Avildsen

(Above) Gloria Swanson's last close-up in Billy Wilder's Hollywood classic *Sunset Boulevard* (Paramount)

(Below) Ann Todd and Ralph Richardson in David Lean's *The Sound Barrier* (British Lion)

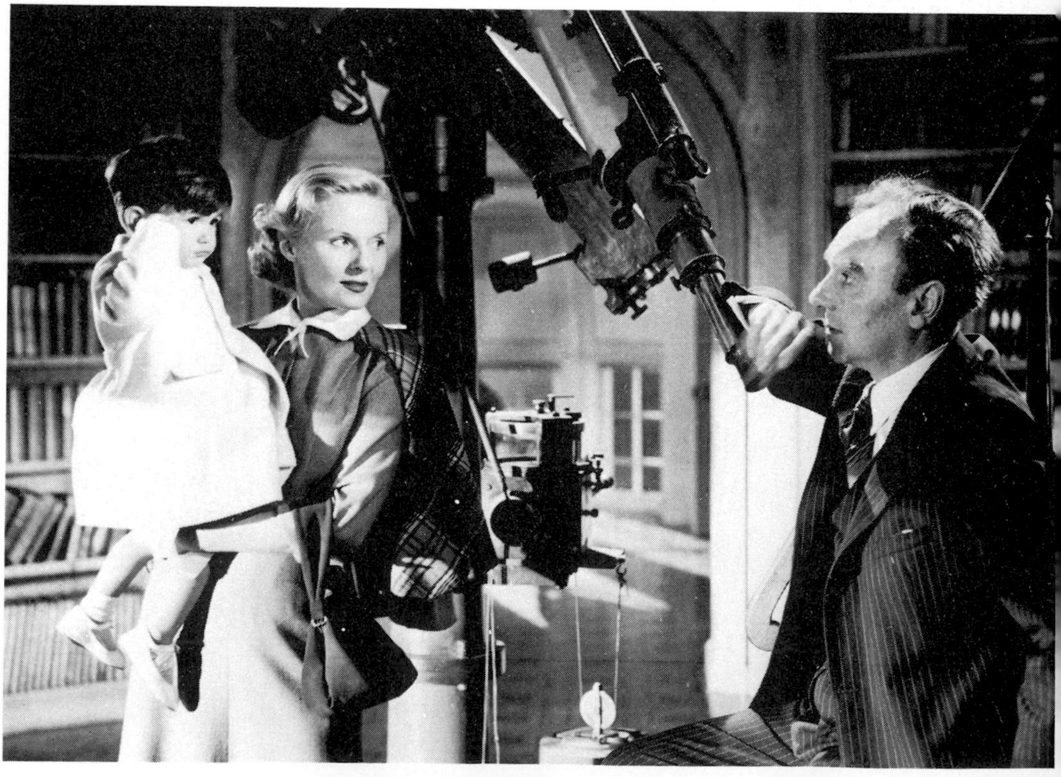

A nervous breakdown in the shower! Susannah York in *They Shoot Horses, Don't They?* (Cinerama), Best Film 1969, National Board of Review

(Above) Ageing ballerina Anne Bancroft in the Herbert Ross soap-opera *The Turning Point* (20th Century-Fox)

(Below) The most famous jury in the movies. E. G. Marshall, Lee J. Cobb and Henry Fonda among the *Twelve Angry Men* (United Artists)

Robert De Niro as Scorsese's violent *Taxi Driver* (Columbia)

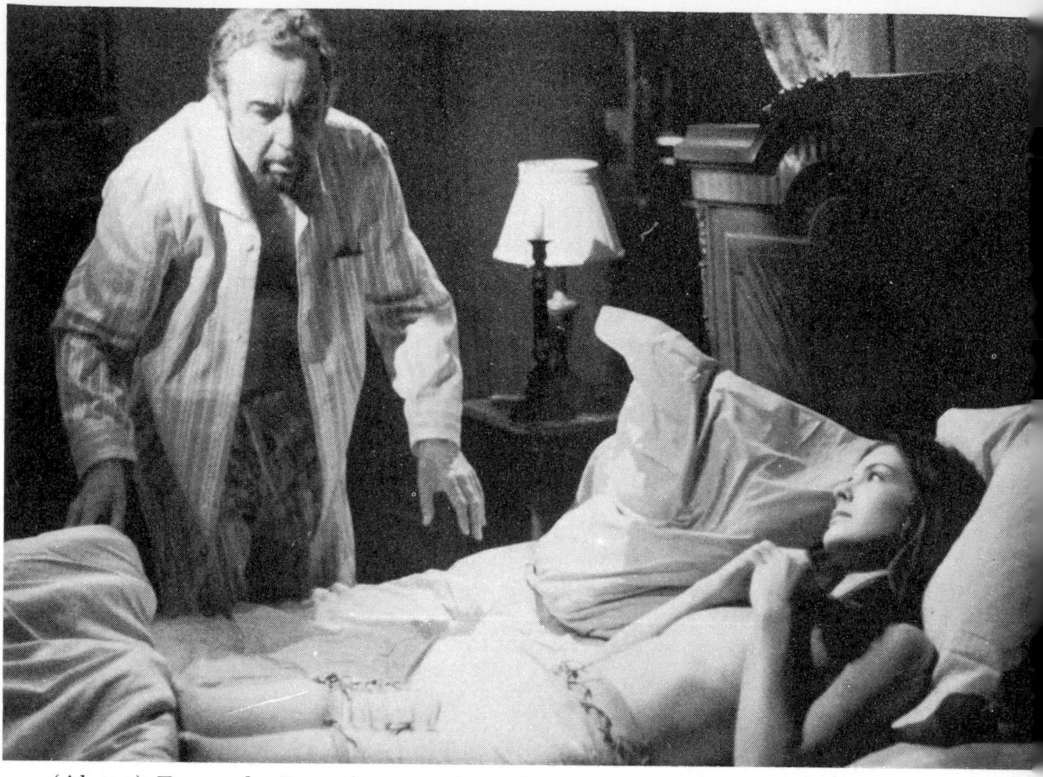

(Above) Fernando Rey, frustrated to the point of distraction in Bunuel's *That Obscure Object Of Desire* (Artificial Eye)

(Below) Tim Holt and Humphrey Bogart defending themselves against Mexican bandits in Huston's *The Treasure Of The Sierra Madre* (Warner Bros.)

Orson Welles as racketeer Harry Lime in Carol Reed's Vienna thriller *The Third Man* (British Lion), Grand Prix, Cannes, 1949

(Above) A blowsy Elizabeth Taylor in *Who's Afraid Of Virginia Woolf?* (Warner Bros.)

(Below) Ingmar Bergman's *Wild Strawberries* (Svensk Filmindustri), Golden Bear, Berlin, 1958

Charles Vanel and Yves Montand suffer their own oil crisis in the Clouzot thriller, *The Wages Of Fear* (Filmsonor/Vera Film/Fono Roma)

(Above) Edward Arnold, James Stewart and Lionel Barrymore in Capra's *You Can't Take It With You* (Columbia)

(Below) Yves Montand in the political thriller *Z* (Reggane Film/ONCIC)

Venice

Venice was the first of the international film festivals and opened in July 1932 as part of the Venice Biennale d'Art.

During the thirties it was the only festival of its kind and 'attempted to raise the status of film to the level of that enjoyed by the more established arts.' Its top prize in the early years was the Mussolini Cup which was awarded to the best foreign film. Acting, directing and other awards were also presented during the period.

In the late thirties the political bias of many of the awards caused bitterness among the competing nations but, after the war when the festival reopened, all animosity was quickly forgotten and the event soon regained its eminence and prestige.

Throughout the post-war years the Golden Lion of St. Mark became the most cherished of all festival prizes and was won by such films as *Rashomon, Les Jeux Interdits, Ordet* and *Aparajito.*

In the sixties the status of the festival was seriously impaired, first by festival director, Luigi Chiarini who introduced an 'art-for-art's-sake' policy at the expense of semi-commercial entries, then by his successor Ernest Laura who 'democratised' the festival by abolishing the awards, claiming that there was no way an international jury could decide which was the best of several types of film in competition.

The abolition of the Golden Lions badly damaged an already ailing festival. With no prizes to aim for, countries opted instead to exhibit their main films at Cannes and Berlin. Venice gradually dwindled to a non-event and finally closed as a festival in 1972.

In its great days Venice was famous for its lavish parties and the splendour of its settings. The festival screenings were held at the Palace of Cinema on the Lido and at the open-air Arena of the Palace of Directors. Retrospectives of the work of directors became a part of its programme in later years.

Biennale cinema director Carlo Lizzani revived the festival with a 'dry run' in 1979 and hopes that the reintroduction of the Golden Lions in 1980 will allow Venice to recapture some of its former glory.

1932
No official prizes were awarded in this first year of the festival but the public were polled about their favourite films in different categories.

The Russian *Road To Life* by Nikolai Ekk was named 'the film most convincingly directed'; René Clair's *A Nous La Liberté* (France) 'the most amusing film'; *Dr. Jekyll And Mr. Hyde* (USA) 'the most original and dramatic film'; and *The Sin Of Madelon Claudet* (USA) 'the film eliciting the greatest emotional response.'

Some voting forms included Mickey Mouse as favourite actor.

Among the other pictures entered in competition: Dovzhenko's *Earth* (USSR); *Mädchen In Uniform* (Germany); *Strange Interlude* (USA); *The Champ* (USA); James Whale's *Frankenstein* (USA) and the Oscar-winning *Grand Hotel* (USA).

1934

Mussolini Cup	*Man Of Aran* (Britain)
Best Actor	Wallace Beery in *Viva Villa!* (USA)
Best Actress	Katharine Hepburn in *Little Women* (USA)

58 films from 17 countries were presented including Feyder's *Le Grand Jeu* (France); Max Ophuls' *La Signora Di Tutti* (Italy); *Queen Christina* (USA); *It Happened One Night* (USA); and Korda's *The Private Life Of Don Juan* (Britain) which received its first ever screening at the festival.

Teresa Confalonieri was voted best Italian film and Gustav Machaty's *Extase* (Czechoslovakia) with a briefly-glimpsed nude Hedy Lamarr — then known as Hedwig Kiesler — was condemned for 'bringing adultery, eroticism and crime against maternity to the screen.'

1935

Mussolini Cup	*Anna Karenina* (USA)
Best Actor	Pierre Blanchar in *Crime And Punishment* (France)
Best Actress	Paula Wessely in *Episode* (Austria)
Best Direction	King Vidor for *The Wedding Night* (USA)

Carmine Gallone's *Casta Diva* received the best Italian film award and Rouben Mamoulian's *Becky Sharp* (USA) was named for its colour.

Sanders Of The River (Britain); *La Dame Aux Camelias* (France) with Yvonne Printemps; *The Eternal Mask* (Austria/Switzerland); *The Informer* (USA); and *David Copperfield* (USA) were among the films also in competition.

1936

Mussolini Cup	*Der Kaiser Von Kalifornien* (Germany)
Best Actor	Paul Muni in *The Story Of Louis Pasteur* (USA)

Best Actress — Annabella in *Veille d'Armes* (France)
Best Direction — Jacques Feyder for *La Kermesse Héroïque* (France)

Other entries included Anatole Litvak's *Mayerling* (France); Capra's *Mr. Deeds Goes To Town* (USA); *The Great Ziegfeld* (USA); *Show Boat* (USA); and René Clair's British Comedy for Korda, *The Ghost Goes West.*

Squadrone Bianco was named best Italian film.

1937

Mussolini Cup — *Un Carnet De Bal* (France)
Best Actor — Emil Jannings in *Der Herrscher* (Germany)
Best Actress — Bette Davis in *Marked Woman* (USA) and *Kid Galahad* (USA)
Best Direction — Mario Camerini for *Il Signor Max* (Italy) and Robert Flaherty and Zoltan Korda for *Elephant Boy* (Britain)

Winterset (USA) which earned a photography prize; *A Star Is Born* (USA); *Victoria The Great* (Britain); Sacha Guitry's *Pearls Of The Crown* (France); *Theodora Goes Wild* (USA); and the Astaire-Rogers musical *Shall We Dance* (USA) were among the films also entered in competition.

Carmine Gallone received his second award in three years when his *Scipione L'Africano* was named best Italian film.

Controversy surrounded the awarding of a special prize to Renoir's pacifist *La Grande Illusion* (France) which many critics felt should have won the premier award. Fascist politics, which had begun to intrude on the festival the previous year, now dominated the prize-giving through a resolution 'empowering the international Chamber of Films to examine film projects that are likely to provoke conflict among peoples and to offend the national honour of countries.'

1938

Mussolini Cup — *Olympia* (Germany)
Best Actor — Leslie Howard in *Pygmalion* (Britain)
Best Actress — Norma Shearer in *Marie Antoinette* (USA)
Best Direction — Karl Ritter for *Urlaub Auf Ehrenwort* (Germany) and Marcel Carné for *Quai Des Brumes* (France)

This was the most controversial Venice Festival since its inauguration, both the British and American delegations angrily accusing the German *Olympia* as being nothing more than blatant Nazi propaganda.

The International Jury, under pressure from political influences, eased itself out of an awkward situation by presenting a vast number of prizes (known as the Minister of Popular Culture Awards) to the following films: *Five Scouts* (Japan); *The Adventures Of Tom Sawyer* (USA);

The Drum (Britain); *Prisons Sans Barreaux* (France); *Giuseppe Verdi* (Italy); *Panen Kutnahorskych* (Czechoslovakia); *Heimat* (Germany); *Pygmalion* (Britain); *Marie Antoinette* (USA); *Mother Carey's Chickens* (USA); *Jezebel* (USA); and *Test Pilot* (USA).

Luciano Serra Pilota was named best Italian film; *Snow White And The Seven Dwarfs* (USA) received an International Art Festival Prize.

1939

Mussolini Cup Not Awarded

This was the last of the pre-war festivals. The United States, who in 1938 had exhibited twelve films, did not compete and no acting prizes were awarded. *Abuna Messias* was named best Italian film; Britain was represented by *The Four Feathers*, Germany by Willy Forst's *Bel Ami* and France by Duvivier's *La Fin Du Jour*, Renoir's *La Bête Humaine* and Carné's *Le Jour Se Leve*.

The 1939 festival closed on August 31 when the German armies were already preparing to invade Poland.

1940-42

The Venice Festival was kept alive during these years but because of the war it ceased to exist as an international event. In 1941 and 1942 its name was changed to the Italian-German Festival.

Competing countries in 1940 included Germany, Italy, Rumania, Sweden, Switzerland and Hungary. Germany's *The Postmaster* and Italy's *The Siege Of The Alcazar* both received prizes.

Award winners in 1941 were Hans Steinhoff's *Ohm Krüger* (Germany) and Alessandro Blasetti's *Helmet Of Iron* (Italy); those in 1942 – *The Great King* (Germany) and *Bengasi* (Italy). Among the countries participating in these years: Argentina, Denmark, Finland, Germany, Italy, Norway, Rumania, Spain, Switzerland, Sweden and Hungary.

After 1942 the festival was cancelled.

1946

International Prize *The Southerner* (USA)

This first festival after the war was more a celebratory occasion than an official event. Talks about the reopening of the festival began in the Spring of 1945, just a month after the liberation of Venice, and the festival was re-staged the following year.

Films shown included many of those made during the war years from as early as 1943 with Fritz Lang's *Hangmen Also Die* (USA) to Rossellini's up-to-the-minute *Open City* (Italy).

Nine films were selected for international prizes with Renoir's *The Southerner* (USA) named as best of the festival. The other eight: Carné's *Les Enfants Du Paradis* (France); Duvivier's *Panique* (France);

Olivier's *Henry V* (Britain); Rossellini's *Paisa* (Italy); Chiaureli's *The Vow* (USSR); Mark Donskoi's *The Unvanquished* (USSR); *Hangmen Also Die* (USA); and *Outcry* (Italy).

1947

International Grand Prix	*Sirena* (Czechoslovakia)
Best Actor	Pierre Fresnay in *Monsieur Vincent* (France)
Best Actress	Anna Magnani in *L'Onorevole Angelina* (Italy)
Best Direction	Henri-Georges Clouzot for *Quai Des Orfèvres* (France)

Prizes for the most original contribution to films were presented to *The Pearl* (Mexico) and *Dreams That Money Can Buy* (USA); the best Italian film was adjudged to be *Ciccia Tragica*.

Among the other pictures in competition: *Glinka* (USSR); *Hets* (Sweden); Autant Lara's *Le Diable Au Corps* (France); Orson Welles' *The Stranger* (USA); and Carol Reed's *Odd Man Out* (Britain).

1948

International Grand Prix	*Hamlet* (Britain)
Best Actor	Ernst Deutsch in *Der Prozess* (Austria)
Best Actress	Jean Simmons in *Hamlet* (Britain)
Best Direction	G. W. Pabst for *Der Prozess* (Austria)

Joint international prizes (runner-up awards) were presented to Robert Flaherty's *Louisiana Story* (USA); John Ford's *The Fugitive* (USA); and *La Terra Trema* (Italy), Luchino Visconti's 160-minute homage to the fishermen of Sicily.

John Bryan received an award for his sets for David Lean's *Oliver Twist* (Britain); Max Steiner a prize for his music for *The Treasure Of The Sierra Madre* (USA); Renato Castellani's *Sotto Il Sole Di Roma* was named best Italian film.

The Red Shoes (Britain); *Gentleman's Agreement* (USA); *The Fallen Idol* (Britain); *The Search* (USA/Switzerland); Ingmar Bergman's *Music In Darkness* (Sweden) and Yves Allegret's *Dédée d'Anvers* (France) were also in competition.

1949

Golden Lion	*Manon* (France)
Best Actor	Joseph Cotten in *Portrait Of Jennie* (USA)
Best Actress	Olivia de Havilland in *The Snake Pit* (USA)
Best Direction	Augusto Genina for *Cielo Sulla Palude* (Italy)

Anatole Litvak's study of mental illness, *The Snake Pit* (USA), *The Quiet One* (USA) and Robert Stemmle's *Berliner Ballade* (Germany) were all awarded international prizes; *Cielo Sulla Palude* was named best Italian film.

William Kellner earned a prize for his designs for *Kind Hearts And Coronets* (Britain); Gabriel Figueroa received an award for his photography of *La Malquerida* (Mexico); and the Jacques Tati comedy *Jour De Fête* (France) won the best screenplay award.

Among the other entries: *Champion* (USA); *Johnny Belinda* (USA); *Scott Of The Antarctic* (Britain); Gustaf Molander's *Eva* (Sweden) and Jean Delannoy's *Aux Yeux Du Souvenir* (France) with Michèle Morgan and Jean Marais.

1950

Golden Lion	*Justice Est Faite* (France)
Best Actor	Sam Jaffe in *The Asphalt Jungle* (USA)
Best Actress	Eleanor Parker in *Caged* (USA)
Best Direction	Jean Cocteau for *Orphée* (France)

International prizes were awarded to Elia Kazan's thriller *Panic In The Streets* (USA); Jean Delannoy's *Dieu A Besoin Des Hommes* (France); and Alessandro Blasetti's *Prima Comunione* (Italy).

Leonide Moguy's *Tomorrow Is Too Late* was voted best Italian film; *La Ronde* (France) won awards for screenplay and design; and *Gone To Earth* (Britain) earned a prize for Brian Easdale's music.

Also in competition: *The Blue Lamp* (Britain); *State Secret* (Britain); *Seven Days To Noon* (Britain); Rossellini's *Stromboli* (Italy); Rossen's Oscar-winning *All The King's Men* (USA); and *Cinderella* (USA) which, together with the short *Beaver Valley* (USA), won a special award for Walt Disney.

1951

Golden Lion	*Rashomon* (Japan)
Best Actor	Jean Gabin in *La Nuit Est Mon Royaume* (France)
Best Actress	Vivien Leigh in *A Streetcar Named Desire* (USA)

The director's prize was discontinued in 1951.

Three unlucky classics each received compensatory international prizes: Bresson's *The Diary Of A Country Priest* (France); Billy Wilder's *Ace In The Hole* (USA); and Renoir's *The River* (India).

Pietro Germi's *La Città Si Difende* was voted best Italian film; Elia Kazan's *A Streetcar Named Desire* (USA) was presented with a special award for 'having reproduced a stage play on the screen, poetically interpreting the lost humanity of the characters, thanks to masterly direction.'

Britain's *The Lavender Hill Mob* (story and screenplay) and America's *Ace In The Hole* (an additional award for music) were other prize-winners. The strong American entry also included *Born Yesterday, Fourteen Hours, Alice In Wonderland* and Fred Zinnemann's *Teresa*.

29 films were in competition.

1952

Golden Lion — *Les Jeux Interdits* (France)
Best Actor — Fredric March in *Death Of A Salesman* (USA)
Best Actress — Not Awarded

Rossellini's *Europe 51* (Italy), John Ford's *The Quiet Man* (USA) and Kenzi Mizoguchi's *The Life Of Oharu* (Japan) all earned international prizes at the festival which included 40 films presented by 14 nations.

Britain was represented by Asquith's version of Oscar Wilde's *The Importance Of Being Earnest, Mandy* and the mining drama *The Brave Don't Cry*; America by Wyler's *Carrie* and *Phone Call From A Stranger* (screenplay award to Nunnally Johnson); and France by *Les Belles De Nuit*.

Les Jeux Interdits, The Quiet Man and *Les Belles De Nuit* were all considered to be possible winners of the Golden Lion. The disappointments of the festival were that Chaplin's *Limelight* was not ready for its world premiere and that Britain did not send David Lean's *The Sound Barrier*.

1953

Golden Lion — Not Awarded
Best Actor — Henri Vilbert in *Le Bon Dieu Sans Confession* (France)
Best Actress — Lilli Palmer in *The Fourposter* (USA)

The International Jury decided that no single film was worthy of the Golden Lion, a decision unique in the history of film festivals. Instead, six Silver Lions were awarded equally to Mizoguchi's *Ugetsu Monogatari* (Japan), Fellini's *I Vitelloni* (Italy), Huston's *Moulin Rouge* (Britain), *The Little Fugitive* (USA), Carné's *Thérèse Raquin* (France) and the Russian production *Sadko*.

The Spanish entry *La Guerra De Dios* and Samuel Fuller's *Pickup On South Street* (USA) were among the films that received Bronze medals.

1954

Golden Lion — *Romeo And Juliet* (Britain/Italy)
Best Actor — Jean Gabin in *Touchez Pas Au Grisbi* (France) and *L'Air De Paris* (France)
Best Actress — Not Awarded

Four remarkable films — Kurosawa's *Seven Samurai* (Japan), Mizoguchi's *Sansho Dayu* (Japan), Kazan's Oscar-winning *On The Waterfront* (USA) and Fellini's *La Strada* (Italy) — shared the Silver Lion runner-up award.

The Special Jury Prize was awarded to the American entry *Executive Suite*; two popular films, Visconti's *Senso* (Italy) and Robert Hamer's *Father Brown* (Britain) with Alec Guinness, failed to share in the final prize-giving.

1955

Golden Lion — *Ordet* (Denmark)

Best Actor — Curt Jürgens in *The Heroes Are Tired* (France) and *The Devil's General* (West Germany)

Kenneth More in *The Deep Blue Sea* (Britain)

Best Actress — Not Awarded

Silver Lions were awarded to Robert Aldrich's Hollywood exposé *The Big Knife* (USA), *The Grasshopper* (USSR), *Ciske De Rat* (Holland) and Antonioni's *Le Amiche* (Italy).

Other films in competition: *The Kentuckian* (USA); *To Catch A Thief* (USA); Fellini's *Il Bidone* (Italy); Franco Rossi's *Friends For Life* (Italy); Andrzej Munk's *Men Of The Blue Cross* (Poland); and Mizoguchi's *Princess Yang Kwei Fei* (Japan).

1956

Golden Lion — Not Awarded

Best Actor — Bourvil in *La Traversée De Paris* (France)

Best Actress — Maria Schell in *Gervaise* (France)

The jury again decided that no film was of a high enough standard to be awarded the Golden Lion. Kon Ichikawa's *The Burmese Harp* (Japan) came closest to winning the prize although Aldrich's anti-war drama *Attack* (USA) received the Italian Critics Award as the best film of the festival.

Among the other entries: Juan Bardem's *Calle Mayor* (Spain); Nicholas Ray's *Bigger Than Life* (USA); *Torero!* (Mexico), a semi-documentary about bullfighting; Luis Berlanga's Spanish comedy *Calabuch*; and Mizoguchi's final film, *Street Of Shame* (Japan).

Note: The entries at Venice in 1956 were screened by a select committee who reduced the films to just 14, regardless of nationality.

1957

Golden Lion — *Aparajito* (India)

Best Actor — Anthony Franciosa in *A Hatful Of Rain* (USA)

Best Actress — Zidra Ritemberg in *Malva* (USSR)

Visconti's *White Nights* (Italy) was awarded the festival's Silver Lion, Fred Zinnemann's *A Hatful Of Rain* (USA) the Italian Critics Prize.

Among the 14 films in competition: Richard Brooks' *Something Of Value* (USA); Nicholas Ray's *Bitter Victory* (France); *Throne Of Blood* (Japan), Kurosawa's version of 'Macbeth'; *The Story Of Esther Costello* (Britain); and André Cayatte's sadistic drama of revenge, *An Eye For An Eye* (France).

The festival closed with an out-of-competition showing of René Clair's *Porte Des Lilas* (France).

1958

Golden Lion — *The Rickshaw Man* (Japan)
Best Actor — Alec Guinness in *The Horse's Mouth* (Britain)
Best Actress — Sophia Loren in *The Black Orchid* (USA)

Two films – Louis Malle's controversial *Les Amants* (France) with Jeanne Moreau, and Francesco Rosi's *La Sfida* (Italy) about racketeering in Naples – earned Silver Lions; the Czech entry *The Wolf Trap* received the International Film Critics Award.

The competition was again restricted to 14 entries (selected by a three-man committee of Italian critics) and included Rolf Thiele's *The Girl Rosemarie* (West Germany) and Anthony Mann's *God's Little Acre* (USA).

1959

Golden Lion — *Il Generale Della Rovere* (Italy/France) and *The Great War* (France/Italy)
Best Actor — James Stewart in *Anatomy Of A Murder* (USA)
Best Actress — Madeleine Robinson in *A Double Tour* (France)

Ingmar Bergman received the Special Jury Prize for *The Face* (Sweden); Claude Chabrol's entry, *A Double Tour* (France) was his first film in colour.

Also competing among the 14 official entries: *Night Train* (Poland); Juan Bardem's *Sonata* (Spain); and *The Boy And The Bridge* (Britain): Billy Wilder's comedy *Some Like It Hot* (USA) was screened out of festival.

1960

Golden Lion — *Le Passage Du Rhin* (France/Italy/West Germany)
Best Actor — John Mills in *Tunes Of Glory* (Britain)
Best Actress — Shirley MacLaine in *The Apartment* (USA)

Luchino Visconti was again passed over for the Golden Lion and received the consolation award – the Special Jury Prize – for his *Rocco And His Brothers* (Italy).

Among the other 14 entries: *Leningrad's Sky* (USSR), an account of the blockade of 1943; *Rat* (Yugoslavia); and Albert Lamorisse's first full-length feature, *Le Voyage En Ballon* (France), a story of an elderly inventor, his little grandson and a balloon!

1961

Golden Lion — *Last Year At Marienbad* (France/Italy)
Best Actor — Toshiro Mifune in *Yojimbo* (Japan)
Best Actress — Suzanne Flon in *Thou Shalt Not Kill* (Yugoslavia)

The Russian comedy *Peace To Who Enters* won the Special Jury Prize.

Others in the 14-strong competition included *Victim* (Britain); Wajda's *Samson* (Poland); Vittorio De Seta's *Bandits Of Orgosolo* (Italy); *Summer And Smoke* (USA); Castellani's peasant saga *The Brigand* (Italy) and Rossellini's *Vanina Vanini* (Italy), an elaborate period melodrama adapted from Stendahl.

1962

Golden Lion — *The Childhood Of Ivan* (USSR) and *Family Chronicle* (Italy)
Best Actor — Burt Lancaster in *Birdman Of Alcatraz* (USA)
Best Actress — Emmanuele Riva in *Thérèse Desqueyroux* (France)

Godard's *Vivre Sa Vie* (France), the story of the fall of a woman into prostitution and a firm favourite for the Golden Lion, received only the Special Jury Prize.

Also in contention: Pasolini's *Mamma Roma* (Italy), Peter Glenville's *Term Of Trial* (Britain) and Kubrick's *Lolita* which was entered as an American film despite being shot in Britain. Two eagerly anticipated entries — Joseph Losey's *Eva* (France/Italy) and Orson Welles' *The Trial* (France/Italy/West Germany) — simply failed to arrive!

1963

Golden Lion — *Hands Over the City* (Italy)
Best Actor — Albert Finney in *Tom Jones* (Britain)
Best Actress — Delphine Seyrig in *Muriel* (France)

Louis Malle's *Le Feu Follet* (France) and Igor Talakin's *Introduction To Life* (USSR) shared the Special Jury Prize.

32 films were entered in competition under the directorship of the new festival head Luigi Chiarini. Included among the entries: Martin Ritt's *Hud* (USA); *Billy Liar* (Britain); *The Servant* (Britain); Weiss' Czech fantasy *The Golden Fearn*; Bardem's *Nunca Pasa Nada* (Spain); and Kurosawa's *High And Low* (Japan), a thriller based on the novel *King's Ransom* by Ed McBain.

1964

Golden Lion — *The Red Desert* (Italy/France)
Best Actor — Tom Courtenay in *King And Country* (Britain)
Best Actress — Harriet Andersson in *To Love* (Sweden)

The Festival's Special Jury Prize was shared between Pasolini's *The Gospel According To St. Matthew* (France/Italy) and Grigori Kozintsev's version of *Hamlet* (USSR).

13 films competed in a drastically pared down festival (still under the

directorship of Chiarini), among them *Girl With Green Eyes* (Britain); Godard's *Une Femme Mariée* (France) and Rolf Thiele's *Tonio Kröger* (West Germany), an adaptation of a novel by Thomas Mann. Robert Rossen's final film, *Lilith* (USA) was withdrawn from competition at the last minute.

1965

Golden Lion	*Vaghe Stelle Dell'Orsa* (Italy)
Best Actor	Toshiro Mifune in *Red Beard* (Japan)
Best Actress	Annie Girardot in *Three Rooms In Manhattan* (France)

Only 11 official entries competed at the festival including Satyajit Ray's *Kapurush* (India), Arthur Penn's *Mickey One* (USA), Godard's *Pierrot-Le-Fou* (France) and Milos Forman's *A Blonde In Love* (Czechoslovakia). The Special Jury Prize was shared between *Simon Of The Desert* (Mexico) and *I Am Twenty* (USSR).

Carl Dreyer's *Gertrud* (Denmark) was shown out of festival.

1966

Golden Lion	*The Battle Of Algiers* (Algeria/Italy)
Best Actor	Jacques Perrin in *The Search* (Spain) and *Almost A Man* (Italy)
Best Actress	Natalie Arinbascarova in *The First Teacher* (USSR)

Robert Bresson received a special homage award for his collective work on film; the Special Jury Prize was shared by the American entry *Chappaqua*, a film about drug addition, and Alexander Kluge's *Yesterday Girl* (West Germany).

Also in competition: Roger Corman's *The Wild Angels* (USA); Truffaut's *Fahrenheit 451* (Britain); Vadim's *La Curée* (France) and Mai Zetterling's sexy and provocative *Night Games* (Sweden) which touched upon 'incest, homosexuality, necrophilia, onanism and all varieties of sado masochism.'

Orson Welles' *Chimes At Midnight* (Spain) contained none of those things and was shown out of festival.

1967

Golden Lion	*Belle De Jour* (France/Italy)
Best Actor	Ljubisa Samardzic in *Dawn* (Yugoslavia)
Best Actress	Shirley Knight in *Dutchman* (Britain)

Special Jury Prizes were awarded to *China Is Near* (Italy) and Godard's *La Chinoise* (France). Other films in competition included Pasolini's *Oedipus Rex* (Italy), Zoltán Fábri's *End Of Season* (Hungary), Jack Clayton's *Our Mother's House* (Britain) and Visconti's *The Stranger* (Italy), an adaptation of the novel by Albert Camus.

1968

Golden Lion	*Artistes At The Top Of The Big Top: Disorientated* (West Germany)
Best Actor	John Marley in *Faces* (USA)
Best Actress	Laura Betti in *Theorem* (Italy)

This was the last Venice festival with an awards ceremony. After 1968, festival director Ernest Laura 'democratised' the competition with the result that prizes for films and acting achievements were discontinued.

Theorem (Italy), directed by Pasolini, was a strong contender for the last Golden Lion; Carmelo Bene's *Our Lady Of The Turks* (Italy) and *Les Socrates* (France) shared the final Silver Lions.

Note: The festival, no longer a major event, continued half-heartedly into the seventies, before coming to a close in 1972.

In 1979, Carlo Lizzani, the new cinema head of the Venice Biennale, revived the festival with a 'dry run.' Golden Lions were not reinstated but two critics associations voted for best films.

The Federation Internationale De La Presse Cinematographique (FIPRESCI) named *La Nouba* (Algeria) and Jean François Stevenin's *Passe Montagne* (France) as best films.

The Italian Film Journalists selected Peter Bogdanovich's *Saint Jack* (USA) as best picture, Evgeni Leonov best actor for *Autumn Marathon* (USSR) and Nobuko Otowa best actress for *The Strangler* (Japan).

Cannes

Although its beginnings were ill-fated — it was scheduled to open on the Cote d'Azur in September, 1939 but had to be cancelled because of World War II — Cannes has become the most illustrious of all European festivals.

Producers, directors, stars, critics and distributors congregate each May to participate in an event that now unspools more than 600 films in a fortnight and boasts as many as seven different sections including the main competition, the critics' week, the directors' fortnight and the busy commercial market place where hectic buying and selling occurs.

The top prize at Cannes was first presented to *The Third Man* in 1949, three years after the festival's official opening. It has been awarded annually ever since except in 1950 when the festival was changed from an Autumn to a May 1951 date and 1968 when political demonstrations led by such respected directors as Truffaut, Godard and Lelouch forced the festival to close in mid-progress.

Between 1949 and 1954 the much coveted main award was known as The Grand Prix; since 1955 it has been known as The Golden Palm.

Acting and technical awards plus jury prizes for runner-up films have been presented since the early days of the festival and awards for supporting performances were introduced in 1979.

When it first began in 1946 Cannes was intended to rival the distinguished festival held each Autumn on the Venice Lido. Although gaudy, commercial and stunt-filled — naked starlets on the Riviera beaches were a regular part of the fifties scene — it has risen above all the glittering razzmatazz and now stands as the premier film showplace in Europe.

1946

Grand Prix	No single Grand Prix was awarded in this first year of the festival. A collective award was shared between 11 films: — *The Red Earth* (Denmark) *The Lost Weekend* (USA) *La Symphonie Pastorale* (France) *Brief Encounter* (Britain) *Neecha Nagar* (India) *Open City* (Italy) *Maria Candelaria* (Mexico) *The Prize* (Sweden) *The Last Chance* (Switzerland) *Men Without Wings* (Czechoslovakia) *The Turning Point* (USSR)
Best Actor	Ray Milland in *The Lost Weekend* (USA)
Best Actress	Michèle Morgan in *La Symphonie Pastorale* (France)
Best Direction	René Clément for *La Bataille Du Rail* (France)

The Special Jury Prize was presented to *La Bataille Du Rail* (France), The Prize for Peace to *The Last Chance* (Switzerland) and an Animation Award to Walt Disney's *Make Mine Music* (USA).

1947

Grand Prix	Again, no single Grand Prix was awarded. 5 films shared prizes under different categories: — Jacques Becker's *Antoine Et Antoinette* (France) was named 'Best Psychological and Love Film'; René Clément's *Les Maudits* (France) was chosen as the 'Best Adventure and Detective Film'; *Crossfire* (USA) was voted the 'Best Social Film'; *Ziegfeld Follies* (USA) the 'Best Musical' and *Dumbo* (USA) the 'Best Animated Film.' No acting awards were presented. Britain's *Mine Own Executioner* received an honourable mention for features.

1948

No Festival.

1949

Grand Prix	*The Third Man* (Britain)
Best Actor	Edward G. Robinson in *House Of Strangers* (USA)
Best Actress	Isa Miranda in *The Walls Of Malapaga* (France/Italy)

Best Direction	René Clément for *The Walls Of Malapaga* (France/Italy)

Among the other films in competition: Fred Zinnemann's *Act Of Violence* (USA); Robert Wise's *The Set-Up* (USA); *Passport To Pimlico* (Britain); *The Queen Of Spades* (Britain); David Lean's *The Passionate Friends* (Britain) and Jacques Becker's *Rendez-vous De Juillet* (France).

Lost Boundaries (USA) was awarded a prize for best screenplay; Autant-Lara's *Occupe-Toi D'Amélie* (France) was named for its decor.

1950

No Festival.

1951

Grand Prix	*Miracle In Milan* (Italy) and *Miss Julie* (Sweden)
Best Actor	Michael Redgrave in *The Browning Version* (Britain)
Best Actress	Bette Davis in *All About Eve* (USA)
Best Direction	Luis Buñuel for *Los Olvidados* (Mexico)

All About Eve (Special Jury Prize) and *The Browning Version* (Best Screenplay) received additional awards and the Powell/Pressburger production *Tales Of Hoffman* (Britain) won a prize for 'Originality of Lyrical Adaptation to Film.' The American entries also included *A Place In The Sun* and *Lights Out*.

1952

Grand Prix	*Two Pennyworth Of Hope* (Italy) and *Othello* (Morocco)
Best Actor	Marlon Brando in *Viva Zapata!* (USA)
Best Actress	Lee Grant in *Detective Story* (USA)
Best Direction	Christian-Jaque for *Fanfan La Tulipe* (France)

André Cayatte's *Nous Sommes Tous Des Assassins* (France) earned the Special Jury Prize; *The Medium* (USA), *Cry The Beloved Country* (Britain), *Police And Thieves* (Italy) and the Somerset Maugham trilogy *Encore* (Britain) were among the other films in competition.

1953

Grand Prix	*The Wages Of Fear* (France/Italy)
Best Actor	Charles Vanel in *The Wages Of Fear* (France/Italy)
Best Actress	Shirley Booth in *Come Back, Little Sheba* (USA)
Best Direction	Not Awarded

Prizes were also awarded for best adventure film — *O Cangaceiro* (Brazil); best entertainment film — *Lili* (USA); best dramatic film —

Come Back, Little Sheba (USA); and best mythical film — *The White Reindeer* (Finland).

Among the other pictures competing: De Sica's *Terminal Station* (Italy) starring Montgomery Clift and Jennifer Jones; Tati's *Monsieur Hulot's Holiday* (France); *The Heart Of The Matter* (Britain); Buñuel's *El* (Mexico); Hitchcock's *I Confess* (USA); Disney's *Peter Pan* (USA); and Juan Bardem's *Welcome Mr. Marshall* (Spain) which received an award for 'good humour.'

1954

Grand Prix	*Gate Of Hell* (Japan)
Best Actor	Not Awarded
Best Actress	Maria Schell in *The Last Bridge* (Austria)
Best Direction	René Clément for *Monsieur Ripois* (Britain/France)

The 1953 Oscar winner *From Here To Eternity* (USA) earned a 'Special Recognition Prize'; the jury also presented 'national recognition awards' to the following 9 films: *The Last Bridge* (Austria); *The Living Desert* (USA); Cayatte's *Avant Le Deluge* (France/Italy); *Two Acres Of Land* (India); *Neapolitan Carousel* (Italy); *Chronaca Di Poveri Amanti* (Italy); *Five Boys From Barska Street* (Poland); *The Great Adventure* (Sweden); and Yutkevich's historical epic, *The Great Warrior, Skanderbeg* (USSR).

Beneath The 12 Mile Reef (USA) and *Knights Of The Round Table* (Britain) afforded Cannes its first view of the CinemaScope process.

1955

Golden Palm	*Marty* (USA)
Best Actor	Spencer Tracy in *Bad Day At Black Rock* (USA) plus a group acting prize to the Soviet actors in *The Big Family* (USSR)
Best Actress	Not Awarded
Best Direction	Serge Vassilev for *The Heroes Of Chipka* (Bulgaria) and Jules Dassin for *Rififi* (France)

Lost Continent (Italy) was awarded the Special Jury Prize.

Also in competition: Kazan's *East Of Eden* (USA) which was named best dramatic film; Carol Reed's *A Kid For Two Farthings* (Britain); *Stella* (Greece); *The End Of The Affair* (Britain); *The Country Girl* (USA); *The Gold Of Naples* (Italy); and the Russian ballet film *Romeo And Juliet* with music by Prokofiev.

1956

Golden Palm	*The Silent World* (France)
Best Actor	Not Awarded
Best Actress	Susan Hayward in *I'll Cry Tomorrow* (USA)

Best Direction — Sergei Yutkevich for *Othello* (USSR)

Other award winners; Clouzot's *The Mystery Of Picasso* (France) which earned the Special Jury Prize; Ingmar Bergman's *Smiles Of A Summer Night* (Sweden) which received an award for 'poetic humour'; and *Pather Panchali* (India) which was honoured as a 'human document.'

Among the festival's other entries: De Sica's *The Roof* (Italy); Cacoyannis' *The Girl In Black* (Greece); Mark Donskoi's remake of the silent classic *Mother* (USSR); *The Harder They Fall* (USA); *The Man In The Gray Flannel Suit* (USA); *The Man Who Knew Too Much* (USA); *Yield To The Night* (Britain); and *The Man Who Never Was* (Britain).

1957

Golden Palm	*Friendly Persuasion* (USA)
Best Actor	John Kitzmiller in *Valley Of Peace* (Yugoslavia)
Best Actress	Giulietta Masina in *The Nights Of Cabiria* (Italy/France)
Best Direction	Robert Bresson for *A Man Escaped* (France)

Andrzej Wajda's *Kanal* (Poland) and Ingmar Bergman's *The Seventh Seal* (Sweden) shared the Special Jury Prize; Grigori Chukrai's *The Forty First* (USSR) received a special award.

Also competing: *The Bachelor Party* (USA); *Funny Face* (USA); *High Tide At Noon* (Britain); *Yangtse Incident* (Britain); *Don Quixote* (USSR); Torre-Nilsson's *The House Of The Angel* (Argentina); and Jules Dassin's *He Who Must Die* (France/Italy).

Mike Todd's *Around The World In 80 Days* (USA) opened the festival out of competition.

1958

Golden Palm	*The Cranes Are Flying* (USSR)
Best Actor	Paul Newman in *The Long Hot Summer* (USA)
Best Actress	Bibi Andersson, Eva Dahlbeck, Barbro Hiort-Af-Ornas and Ingrid Thulin in *Close To Life* (Sweden)
Best Direction	Ingmar Bergman for *Close To Life* (Sweden)

Jacques Tati's second Monsieur Hulot comedy, *Mon Oncle* (France/Italy) received the Special Jury Prize; *Goha* (Tunisia) and *Bronze Faces* (Switzerland) received special awards.

Among the festival's other entries: Arne Sucksdorff's *The Flute And The Arrow* (Sweden), a documentary record of village life in the remote regions of Central India; Anthony Asquith's *Orders To Kill* (Britain); Cacoyannis' *A Matter Of Dignity* (Greece); *Desire Under The Elms* (USA); and *The Brothers Karamazov* (USA).

Shown out of competition were two films (both on the same bill) by two young French directors – the twenty-eight-year-old Claude Chabrol and the young François Truffaut. The films? *Le Beau Serge* and *Les Mistons*.

1959

Golden Palm	*Black Orpheus* (France/Italy)
Best Actor	Dean Stockwell, Bradford Dillman and Orson Welles in *Compulsion* (USA)
Best Actress	Simone Signoret in *Room At The Top* (Britain)
Best Direction	François Truffaut for *Les Quatre Cents Coups* (France)

The Bulgarian/East German production *Sterne*, directed by Konrad Wolf, was awarded the Special Jury Prize; Buñuel's *Nazarin* (Mexico) received the International Prize.

Also in competition: Kinugasa's *The White Heron* (Japan) which received an honourable mention; Castellani's prison drama *Nella Citta L'Inferno* (Italy) starring Anna Magnani; and *Middle Of The Night* (USA).

Alain Resnais' controversial *Hiroshima, Mon Amour* (France/Japan) was shown out of competition as was George Stevens' *The Diary Of Anne Frank* (USA) which closed the festival. Sergei Bondarchuk's *Destiny Of A Man* (USSR), a war film about Nazi brutality, was withdrawn for fear of its causing offence to West Germany.

1960

Golden Palm	*La Dolce Vita* (Italy/France)
Best Actor	Not Awarded
Best Actress	Jeanne Moreau in *Moderato Cantabile* (France) and Melina Mercouri in *Never On Sunday* (Greece)
Best Direction	Not Awarded

Kon Ichikawa's *Kagi* (Japan) was awarded a Special Prize; Ingmar Bergman's *The Virgin Spring* (Sweden) and Luis Buñuel's *The Young One* (Mexico) both received special homage awards.

Michelangelo Antonioni, whose *L'Avventura* (Italy) was booed and hissed at its festival showing, received a prize for 'his contribution towards seeking a new language of cinema.'

Among the other entries: Minnelli's *Home From The Hill* (USA); *Sons And Lovers* (Britain); *Ballad Of A Soldier* (USSR); *The Lady With The Little Dog* (USSR); *Los Golfos* (Spain) and Jacques Becker's last film, the prison escape thriller *Le Trou* (France).

William Wyler's *Ben-Hur* opened the festival out of competition.

1961

Golden Palm	*Viridiana* (Mexico/Spain) and *Une Aussi Longue Absence* (France/Italy)
Best Actor	Anthony Perkins in *Aimez-Vous Brahms* (USA/France)
Best Actress	Sophia Loren in *Two Women* (France/Italy)
Best Direction	Julia Solntzeva for *The Flaming Years* (USSR)

The Polish film, *Mother Joan Of The Angels*, an adaptation of the Devils Of Loudon story by director Jerczy Kawalerowicz, was awarded the Special Jury Prize.

Also competing: Leopoldo Torre-Nilsson's *The Hand In The Trap* (Argentina); *The Mark* (Britain); *A Raisin In The Sun* (USA); and *The Hoodlum Priest* (USA).

1962

Golden Palm	*The Given Word* (Brazil)
Best Acting	Ensemble prizes were awarded to: Katharine Hepburn, Ralph Richardson, Jason Robards, Jr. and Dean Stockwell in *Long Day's Journey Into Night* (USA) and Rita Tushingham and Murray Melvin in *A Taste Of Honey* (Britain)
Best Direction	Not Awarded

Robert Bresson's *The Trial Of Joan Of Arc* (France) and Antonioni's *The Eclipse* (Italy) shared the Special Jury Prize; Cacoyannis' *Electra* (Greece) earned an award for best adaptation and Pietro Germi's *Divorce — Italian Style* (Italy) the prize for best comedy.

Agnes Varda's *Cléo From 5 to 7* (France); *The Innocents* (Britain); Buñuel's *The Exterminating Angel* (Mexico), Satyajit Ray's *The Goddess* (India); *Advise And Consent* (USA); and *All Fall Down* (USA) were among the other films in competition.

The festival was opened by an out of competition showing of *Boccaccio 70* (Italy).

1963

Golden Palm	*The Leopard* (France/Italy)
Best Actor	Richard Harris in *This Sporting Life* (Britain)
Best Actress	Marina Vlady in *Ape Regina* (Italy)
Best Direction	Not Awarded

Masaki Kobayashi's *Harakiri* (Japan) and *Az Prijde Kocour* (Czechoslovakia) shared the Special Jury Prize; Robert Mulligan's *To Kill A Mockingbird* (USA), *Les Abysses* (France), *Lord Of The Flies* (Britain) and Olmi's *The Engagement* (Italy) were among the other competing films.

Hitchcock's *The Birds* (USA) opened the festival out of competition.

1964

Golden Palm — *The Umbrellas Of Cherbourg* (France/West Germany)

Best Actor — Antal Pager in *Pacsirta* (Hungary) and Saro Urzi in *Seduced And Abandoned* (Italy)

Best Actress — Anne Bancroft in *The Pumpkin Eater* (Britain) and Barbara Barrie in *One Potato-Two Potato* (USA)

Best Direction — Not Awarded

Japan's *Woman Of The Dunes*, directed by Hiroshi Teshigahara, was awarded the Jury Prize.

Also entered in competition: Andrzj Munk's *The Passenger* (Poland); George Roy Hill's *The World Of Henry Orient* (USA); and Truffaut's study of adultery *La Peau Douce* (France).

Bergman's *The Silence* (Sweden) and Schaffner's *The Best Man* (USA) were both shown out of festival.

1965

Golden Palm — *The Knack* (Britain)

Best Actor — Terence Stamp in *The Collector* (USA)

Best Actress — Samantha Eggar in *The Collector* (USA)

Best Direction — Liviu Ciulei for *Forest Of The Hanged* (Rumania)

The Japanese *Kwaidan*, based on a collection of ghostly folk tales, received the Special Jury Prize; *317th Section* (France) and Sidney Lumet's *The Hill* (Britain) earned mentions for best screenplay.

Other festival entries included *The Ipcress File* (Britain); Mai Zetterling's *Loving Couples* (Sweden); *Javoronok* (USSR); and Francesco Rosi's film about bullfighting, *The Moment Of Truth* (Italy).

Otto Preminger's *In Harm's Way* (USA) and *Mary Poppins* (USA) opened the festival out of competition.

1966

Golden Palm — *A Man And A Woman* (France) and *The Birds, The Bees And The Italians* (France/Italy)

Best Actor — Per Oscarsson in *Hunger* (Denmark/Norway/Sweden)

Best Actress — Vanessa Redgrave in *Morgan: A Suitable Case For Treatment* (Britain)

Best Direction — Sergei Yutkevich for *Lenin In Poland* (USSR)

Lewis Gilbert's *Alfie* (Britain) was awarded the Special Jury Prize; Orson Welles who starred in and directed *Chimes At Midnight* (Spain) received the Cannes 20th Anniversary Prize for his overall contribution to the cinema.

Also in competition: John Frankenheimer's *Seconds* (USA); Jancso's *The Round-Up* (Hungary), a brutal story of 19th century concentration camps; *Modesty Blaise* (Britain); and the two Polish epics, *Ashes* (about the Napoleonic wars) and *Pharaoh* which opened and closed the festival, respectively.

1967

Golden Palm	*Blow-Up* (Britain/Italy)
Best Actor	Odded Kotler in *Three Days And A Child* (Israel)
Best Actress	Pia Degermark in *Elvira Madigan* (Sweden)
Best Direction	Ferenc Kosa for *Ten Thousand Suns* (Hungary)

Joseph Losey's *Accident* (Britain) and *I Even Met Happy Gypsies* (Yugoslavia) shared the Special Jury Prize.

Other festival entries included Bresson's *Mouchette* (France), Pietro Germi's *The Immoral Man* (Italy) and *Mon Amour, Mon Amour* (France).

1968

Festival Cancelled.

1969

Golden Palm	*If* (Britain)
Best Actor	Jean-Louis Trintignant in *Z* (France/Algeria)
Best Actress	Vanessa Redgrave in *Isadora* (Britain)
Best Direction	Glauber Rocha for *Antonio Das Mortes* (Brazil) and Vojtech Jasny for *Moravian Chronicle* (Czechoslovakia)

Costa-Gavras' political thriller *Z* (France/Algeria) and Bo Widerberg's *Adalen '31* (Sweden), an account of a family of workers on strike in Sweden in the early thirties, shared the Special Jury Prize.

Also in competition: *The Prime Of Miss Jean Brodie* (Britain); Jancso's *The Confrontation* (Hungary); Rohmer's *My Night At Maud's* (France); Malle's *Calcutta* (France); Lumet's *The Appointment* (USA); and Dennis Hopper's *Easy Rider* (USA) which was adjudged the best first work.

The three-hour Russian epic *Andrei Roublev* and the musical *Sweet Charity* (USA) were among the films shown out of festival.

1970

Golden Palm	*M.A.S.H.* (USA)
Best Actor	Marcello Mastroianni in *Drama Of Jealousy* (Italy)
Best Actress	Ottavia Piccolo in *Metello* (Italy)
Best Direction	John Boorman for *Leo The Last* (Britain)

Elio Petri's *Investigation Of A Citizen Above Suspicion* (Italy) was awarded the Special Jury Prize; *The Strawberry Statement* (USA) and *The Falcons* (Hungary) both received special citations.

Buñuel's *Tristana* (Spain), Bergman's *A Passion* (Sweden) and Chabrol's *Le Boucher* (France) were all shown out of competition.

1971

Golden Palm	*The Go-Between* (Britain)
Best Actor	Ricardo Cucciolla in *Sacco And Venzetti* (Italy)
Best Actress	Kitty Winn in *Panic In Needle Park* (USA)
Best Direction	Not Awarded

Visconti's *Death In Venice* (Italy), a hot favourite for the Golden Palm, was awarded the Cannes 25th Anniversary Prize; Dalton Trumbo's *Johnny Got His Gun* (USA) and Milos Forman's first American film, *Taking Off*, shared the Special Jury Prize.

Nicolas Roeg's *Walkabout* (Britain); Bo Widerberg's *Joe Hill* (Sweden); *Loot* (Britain); *Outback* (Australia); and Louis Malle's *Le Souffle Au Cour* (France) were among the other films in competition.

1972

Golden Palm	*The Mattei Affair* (Italy) and *The Working Class Goes To Heaven* (Italy)
Best Actor	Jean Yanne in *Break-Up* (France)
Best Actress	Susannah York in *Images* (Eire)
Best Direction	Miklos Jancso for *Red Psalm* (Hungary)

The Jury Prize was awarded to Andrei Tarkovsky's science-fiction epic, *Solaris* (USSR); a Special Jury Prize was presented to George Roy Hill's *Slaughterhouse-Five* (USA).

Also competing: *The Ruling Class* (Britain); Philippe de Broca's *Chère Louise* (France) and *Jeremiah Johnson* (USA) — the first western ever shown in competition at Cannes.

Fellini's *Roma* (Italy), Huston's boxing drama, *Fat City* (USA) and Polanski's *Macbeth* (Britain) were all shown out of festival.

1973

Golden Palm	*The Hireling* (Britain) and *Scarecrow* (USA)
Best Actor	Gian Carlo Giannini in *Film D'Amore e d'Anarchia* (Italy)

Best Actress — Joanne Woodward in *The Effect Of Gamma Rays On Man-In-The-Moon Marigolds* (USA)
Best Direction — Not Awarded

La Maman Et La Purtain (France) a 220-minute eternal triangle by Jean Eustache, was awarded the Special Jury Prize; *The Invitation* (Switzerland) and *The Sandglass* (Poland) both received special citations.

Among the other films in competition: Lindsay Anderson's *O Lucky Man* (Britain); Marco Ferreri's *La Grande Bouffe* (France); and *Electra Glide In Blue* (USA).

Three potential Golden Palm winners: Truffaut's *Day For Night* (France/Italy), Bergman's *Cries And Whispers* (Sweden) and Chabrol's *Blood Wedding* (France) were all shown out of festival.

1974

Golden Palm — *The Conversation* (USA)
Best Actor — Jack Nicholson in *The Last Detail* (USA)
Best Actress — Marie-Jose Nat in *Les Violons Du Bal* (France)
Best Direction — Not Awarded

Pasolini's venture into Middle East mythology, *A Thousand And One Nights* (Italy) received the Special Jury Prize; Steven Spielberg's *The Sugarland Express* (USA) was named for its screenplay.

Other entries: Robert Altman's *Thieves Like Us* (USA); Alain Resnais' *Stavisky* (France/Italy); *The Nickel Ride* (USA); *The Nine Lives Of Fritz The Cat* (USA); Ken Russell's *Mahler* (Britain); Fassbinder's *Everybody Else Is Called Ali* (West Germany); and Jacques Tati's *Parade* (France).

Fellini's *Amarcord* (Italy/France) opened the festival out of competition.

1975

Golden Palm — *Chronicle Of The Years Of Embers* (Algeria)
Best Actor — Vittorio Gassman in *Scent Of A Woman* (Italy)
Best Actress — Valerie Perrine in *Lenny* (USA)
Best Direction — Michael Brault for *Les Ordres* (Canada) and Costa-Gavras for *Section Spéciale* (France/Italy/West Germany)

Werner Herzog's *The Enigma Of Caspar Hauser* (West Germany) earned the Special Jury Prize; *Man Friday* (Britain); *Alice Doesn't Live Here Anymore* (USA); Miklos Jancso's *Electra* (Hungary); and *A Touch Of Zen* (Hong Kong) were among the other competition entries.

John Schlesinger's *The Day Of The Locust* (USA); Losey's *The Romantic Englishwoman* (Britain) and Antonioni's *The Passenger* (Italy) were all shown out of festival.

1976

Golden Palm	*Taxi Driver* (USA)
Best Actor	José-Luis Gomez in *La Familia De Pascual Duarte* (Spain)
Best Actress	Mari Torocsik in *Deryne, Hol Van* (Hungary) and Dominique Sanda in *The Inheritance* (Italy)
Best Direction	Ettore Scola for *Ugly, Dirty And Mean* (Italy)

Rohmer's *Die Marquise Von O* (West Germany/France) and Saura's *Cria Cuervos* (Spain) shared the Special Jury Prize; Polanski's *The Tenant* (France), Losey's *Mr. Klein* (France), and Alan Parker's all-child musical *Bugsy Malone* (Britain) were among the other competing entries.

Visconti's last film *L'Innocente* (Italy) was shown out of competition and a special day was reserved for the unveiling of Bertolucci's *1900* (Italy) which ran for 5 hours 20 minutes and was shown in two parts — the first at 163 minutes, the second at 157.

1977

Golden Palm	*Padre, Padrone* (Italy)
Best Actor	Fernando Rey in *Elissa, My Love* (Spain)
Best Actress	Shelley Duvall in *3 Women* (USA) and Monique Mercure in *J. A. Martin, Photographer* (Canada)
Best Direction	Not Awarded

Ridley Scott's *The Duellists* (Britain) won The Special Jury Prize.

Also competing: *Car Wash* (USA) which won an award for its music score; Cacoyannis' *Iphigenia* (Greece); Hal Ashby's *Bound For Glory* (USA); the Swiss entry *The Lacemaker* starring French actress Isabelle Huppert; and Ettora Scola's *A Special Day* (Italy/Canada), about the brief liaison between jaded housewife Sophia Loren and homosexual journalist Marcello Mastroianni in pre-war Italy.

1978

Golden Palm	*The Tree Of Wooden Clogs* (Italy)
Best Actor	Jon Voight in *Coming Home* (USA)
Best Actress	Jill Clayburgh in *An Unmarried Woman* (USA) and Isabelle Huppert in *Violette Nozière* (France)
Best Direction	Nagisa Oshima for *Empire Of Passion* (Japan)

Marco Ferreri's *Bye Bye Monkey* (Italy) and Jerzy Skolimovsky's *The Shout* (Britain) shared the Special Jury Prize.

Among the other films in competition: *Who'll Stop The Rain?* (USA); Carlos Saura's *Blindfolded* (Spain); *The Chant Of Jimmy Blacksmith* (Australia); *Passion* (Greece) with Melina Mercouri and Ellen Burstyn; Fassbinder's *Despair* (West Germany); and *Midnight Express* (Britain).

1979

Golden Palm	*Apocalypse Now* (USA) and *The Tin Drum* (West Germany)
Best Actor	Jack Lemmon in *The China Syndrome* (USA)
Best Actress	Sally Field in *Norma Rae* (USA)
Best Supporting Actor	Stefano Madia in *Caro Papa* (Italy)
Best Supporting Actress	Eva Mattes in *Woyzeck* (West Germany)
Best Direction	Terrence Malik for *Days Of Heaven* (USA)

The Russian *Siberiade* was awarded the Special Jury Prize; director Miklos Jancso was presented with a special award for the ensemble of his work.

Also competing among the 20 entries: Wajda's *Rough Treatment* (Poland); *My Brilliant Career* (Australia); *The Bronte Sisters* (France); Bo Widerberg's *Victoria* (Sweden); and James Ivory's *The Europeans* (Britain).

1980

Golden Palm	*All That Jazz* (USA) and *Kagemusha* (Japan)
Best Actor	Michel Piccoli in *Leap Into The Void* (Italy)
Best Actress	Anouk Aimée in *Leap Into The Void* (Italy)
Best Supporting Actor	Jack Thompson in *Breaker Morant* (Australia)
Best Supporting Actress	Carla Gravina in *The Terrace* (Italy) and Milena Dravic in *Special Treatment* (Yugoslavia)
Best Direction	Krzysztof Zanussi for *Constans* (Poland)

Alain Resnais' *Mon Oncle D'Amerique* (France) received the Special Jury Prize and was unanimously voted by the jury as 'being of the same level as that of the two films receiving the Golden Palm.'

Among the other films in competition: *Being There* (USA); *The Big Red One* (USA); *The Long Riders* (USA); *Everyone For Himself* (Switzerland/France); *Loulou* (France); and *Fantastica* (Canada) which opened the festival.

Fellini's *City Of Women* (Italy) was shown out-of-competition.

Berlin

Berlin remains one of the most prestigious of European festivals even though, when first conceived, it was something of a propaganda exercise to help boost West German morale in the gloomy aftermath of World War II.

Established in June, 1951, under the directorship of Dr. Alfred Bauer, it has grown steadily in popularity since the early sixties and with the demise of Venice has taken that distinguished event's place on the festival circuit.

During its early years Berlin awarded its Golden Bear first prize through a unique public ballot system, a policy that was eventually abandoned in the mid fifties when the International Film Producers Association recognised it as a Grade 'A' festival and allowed it the right to adopt an international jury for the prize-giving.

The Berlin Festival has survived two crises, one in 1970 when a political row over the content of one of the entries caused the festival to be abandoned, the other in 1979 when the Eastern bloc (which did not officially compete until 1975) walked out in protest over the out of festival showing of *The Deer Hunter*.

For most of its existence the festival has been held in June, shortly after Cannes. More recently, it has moved to a more advantageous pre-Cannes date of February/March.

Schlesinger, Lumet, Antonioni, Godard, Chabrol and Polanski have all been among the prize-winners at Berlin; *Twelve Angry Men, Wild Strawberries, A Kind Of Loving, Alphaville* and *Distant Thunder* among the films that have won the Golden Bear.

Apart from the main festival, Berlin consists of an International Forum of Younger Cinema (a counterpart to the directors fortnight at Cannes), retrospectives and a Film Fair which is a market place for the trends of various countries.

1951
In this first year of the festival (June 6-18) German judges awarded prizes for films in special categories. *Four In A Jeep* (Switzerland) was adjudged best dramatic feature film: *No Address Given* (France) the best comedy; André Cayatte's *Justice Est Faite* (France) the best criminal and adventure picture; and Disney's *Cinderella* (USA) the best musical.

Cinderella was the only film to be named best of the festival. It was awarded first prize by the public who voted on all the films exhibited in competition. The following nine pictures were placed behind the Disney cartoon in order of merit: (2) *The Browning Version* (Britain); (3) *Justice Est Faite* (France); (4) *Four In A Jeep* (Switzerland); (5) *Lights Out* (USA); (6) *No Address Given* (France); (7) *Dieu A Besoin Des Hommes* (France); (8) *Dr. Holl* (Germany); (9) *Il Christo Proibito* (Italy); (10) *The Mating Season* (USA).

1952
Golden Bear — *One Summer of Happiness* (Sweden)
This was the first year a Golden Bear was awarded for a best film of the festival. The public again voted for the top prize, a policy that continued until the introduction of the jury system in 1956. Votes were indicated on a coupon and the popularity of films gauged by a points system. A Silver Bear was awarded to the second film in the top ten list, a Bronze Bear to the third film.

The nine films placed behind *One Summer Of Happiness* were: (2) *Fanfan La Tulipe* (France); (3) *Cry The Beloved Country* (Britain); (4) *The Voice Of The Other* (Germany); (5) *Miracle In Milan* (Italy); (6) *The Well* (USA); (7) *Death Of A Salesman* (USA); (8) *Three Forbidden Stories* (Italy); (9) *The Deserted Court* (Mexico); (10) *Rashomon* (Japan).

1953
Golden Bear — *The Wages of Fear* (France/Italy)
The voting public placed the following nine films behind *The Wages Of Fear* — (2) *Green Magic* (Italy); (3) *They Found A Homeland* (Switzerland); (4) *The Forbidden Fruit* (France); (5) *Other Times* (Italy); (6) *A Heart Plays False* (Germany); (7) *The Captain's Paradise* (Britain); (8) *The Sun Shines Bright* (USA); (9) *Monsieur Hulot's Holiday* (France); (10) *Man On A Tightrope* (USA).

1954
Golden Bear — *Hobson's Choice* (Britain)
The voting public placed the following nine films behind *Hobson's Choice* — (2) *Bread, Love And Dreams* (Italy); (3) *The Renegade* (France); (4) *The Light Of Love* (Austria); (5) *The Great Hope* (Italy); (6) *Julietta* (France); (7) *Wild Fruit* (France); (8) *Road Without Return*

(Germany); (9) *Neapolitan Carousel* (Italy); (10) *Konig Drosselbart* (Germany).

1955

Golden Bear — *Die Ratten* (West Germany)

The voting public placed the following nine films behind *Die Ratten* — (2) *Marcelino, Bread And Wine* (Spain); (3) *Carmen Jones* (USA); (4) *Bread, Love And Jealousy* (Italy); (5) *Three Men In The Snow* (Austria); (6) *Hiroshima* (Japan); (7) *The Divided Heart* (Britain); (8) *The Young Lovers* (Britain); (9) *Papa, Mama, The Maid And I* (France); (10) *Animal Farm* (Britain).

1956

Golden Bear	*Invitation To The Dance* (USA)
Best Actor	Burt Lancaster in *Trapeze* (USA)
Best Actress	Elsa Martinelli in *Donatella* (Italy)
Best Direction	Robert Aldrich for *Autumn Leaves* (USA)

The 1956 prizes were presented by an international jury which operated for the first time at Berlin. Acting and direction awards were introduced; Olivier's *Richard III* (Britain) was awarded the second prize Silver Bear; and Ealing's *The Long Arm* (Britain) and André Michel's *The Sorceress* (France) both earned honourable mentions.

1956 also marked the last occasion that a public vote was held at Berlin. The top ten — (1) *Vor Sonnenuntergang* (West Germany); (2) *My Uncle, Jacinto* (Spain); (3) *Trapeze* (USA); (4) *Invitation To The Dance* (USA); (5) *The Sorceress* (France); (6) *The Unknown Soldier* (Finland); (7) *Kispus* (Denmark); (8) *The Road To Life* (Mexico); (9) *The Long Arm* (Britain); (10) *Richard III* (Britain).

1957

Golden Bear	*Twelve Angry Men* (USA)
Best Actor	Pedro Infante in *Tizoc* (Mexico)
Best Actress	Yvonne Mitchell in *Woman In A Dressing Gown* (Britain)
Best Direction	Mario Monicelli for *Father And Sons* (Italy)

Among the other entries in 1957: *Teahouse Of The August Moon* (USA); *The Wayward Bus* (USA); *The Spanish Gardener* (Britain); *Manuela* (Britain); and José Urana Forque's Spanish entry *Whom God Forgives* which was awarded the Silver Bear.

1958

Golden Bear	*Wild Strawberries* (Sweden)
Best Actor	Sidney Poitier in *The Defiant Ones* (USA)

Best Actress	Anna Magnani in *Wild Is The Wind* (USA)
Best Direction	Tadashi Imai for *Jun-Ai Monogatari* (Japan)

Other films in competition at the festival included Douglas Sirk's *A Time To Love And A Time To Die* (USA), Britain's *Ice Cold In Alex* and Shantaram's *Two Eyes, Twelve Hands* (India) which won the second prize Silver Bear. Frothy sex was added by Gina Lollobrigida in the Italian *Anna Of Brooklyn.*

1959

Golden Bear	*Les Cousins* (France)
Best Actor	Jean Gabin in *Archimede Le Clochard* (France)
Best Actress	Shirley MacLaine in *Ask Any Girl* (USA)
Best Direction	Akira Kurosawa for *The Hidden Fortress* (Japan)

Among the other festival entries: Helmut Käutner's *The Rest Is Silence* (West Germany), a modern adaptation of the Hamlet story; *That Kind Of Woman* (USA), directed by Sidney Lumet and starring Sophia Loren; Leopoldo Torre-Nilsson's *La Caida* (Argentina) and Britain's *Tiger Bay.* For her performance in the latter film the young Hayley Mills won a special Silver Bear.

1960

Golden Bear	*Lazarillo* (Spain)
Best Actor	Fredric March in *Inherit The Wind* (USA)
Best Actress	Juliette Mayniel in *Kirmes* (West Germany)
Best Direction	Jean-Luc Godard for *A Bout De Souffle* (France)

Other films in competition included Bryan Forbes' acclaimed *The Angry Silence* (Britain); Philippe de Broca's *The Love Game* (France) which won the Silver Bear for comedy; Elia Kazan's *Wild River* (USA); and Cacoyannis' *Our Last Spring* (Greece).

1961

Golden Bear	*La Notte* (Italy/France)
Best Actor	Peter Finch in *No Love For Johnnie* (Britain)
Best Actress	Anna Karina in *Une Femme Est Une Femme* (France)
Best Direction	Bernhard Wicki for *The Miracle Of Father Malachias* (West Germany)

Among the other festival entries: Kurosawa's *The Bad Sleep Well* (Japan); Elio Petri's *L'Assassino* (Italy), a crime drama featuring Marcello Mastroianni; and *Question 7* (USA).

Godard's musical comedy *Une Femme Est Une Femme* (France) was awarded the Special Jury Prize; Jacques Demy's first feature, *Lola* (France), was shown out of competition.

1962

Golden Bear	*A Kind Of Loving* (Britain)
Best Actor	James Stewart in *Mr. Hobbs Takes A Vacation* (USA)
Best Actress	Viveca Lindfors and Rita Gam in *No Exit* (Stateless)
Best Direction	Francesco Rosi for *Salvatore Giuliano* (Italy)

Other films in competition included Jean Renoir's *The Vanishing Corporal* (France), a lightweight 'Grande Illusion' of World War II, and Ozu's *Early Autumn* (Japan). *No Exit*, a version of Sartre's 'Huis Clos', was made in Argentina with American money and was the first feature without a country of origin to be shown at Berlin.

Ingmar Bergman's *Through A Glass Darkly* (Sweden) and Kurosawa's *Sanjuro* (Japan) were both exhibited out of festival.

1963

Golden Bear	*Bushido* (Japan) and *Il Diavolo* (Italy)
Best Actor	Sidney Poitier in *Lilies Of The Field* (USA)
Best Actress	Bibi Andersson in *Alskarinnan* (Sweden)
Best Direction	Nikos Koundouros for *Mikres Afrodites* (Greece)

Other films in competition included Clive Donner's version of Harold Pinter's *The Caretaker* which earned a Special Jury Prize for Britain; Leopoldo Torre-Nilsson's *The Roof Garden* (Argentina); Alain Robbe-Grillet's *L'Immortelle* (France); Huston's *Freud* (USA); and Bardem's *Los Inocentes* (Spain).

1964

Golden Bear	*Waterless Summer* (Turkey)
Best Actor	Rod Steiger in *The Pawnbroker* (USA)
Best Actress	Sachiko Hidari in *She And He* (Japan) and *The Insect Woman* (Japan)
Best Direction	Satyajit Ray for *Mahanagar* (India)

Among the other festival entries: Ruy Guerra's *The Guns* (Brazil) which was awarded the Special Jury Prize; *Of Human Bondage* (Britain); Karel Reisz's remake of *Night Must Fall* (Britain); and Wolfgang Staudte's *Herrenpartie* (West Germany).

1965

Golden Bear	*Alphaville* (France/Italy)
Best Actor	Lee Marvin in *Cat Ballou* (USA)

Best Actress — Madhur Jaffrey in *Shakespeare Wallah* (India)
Best Direction — Satyajit Ray for *Charulata* (India)

Other films in competition included Agnès Varda's *Le Bonheur* (France) and Polanski's *Repulsion* (Britain) — both awarded Silver Bears — and Bo Widerberg's *Love 65* (Sweden).

1966

Golden Bear — *Cul-De-Sac* (Britain)
Best Actor — Jean-Pierre Léaud in *Masculin-Feminin* (France/Sweden)
Best Actress — Lola Albright in *Lord Love A Duck* (USA)
Best Direction — Carlos Saura for *La Caza* (Spain)

Among the other festival entries: Satyajit Ray's *Nayak* (India); Lumet's *The Group* (USA); Chabrol's *La Ligne De Demarcation* (France); and *Georgy Girl* (Britain): Special Jury Prizes were awarded to *Close Season For Foxes* (West Germany) and *Manhunt* (Sweden).

1967

Golden Bear — *Le Départ* (Belgium)
Best Actor — Michel Simon in *The Old Man And The Boy* (France)
Best Actress — Edith Evans in *The Whisperers* (Britain)
Best Direction — Zivojin Pavlovic for *The Rats Awaken* (Yugoslavia)

Other entries included Eric Rohmer's *La Collectioneuse* (France) and *Every Year Again* (West Germany) — both awarded Special Jury Prizes — and Jan Troell's *Here Is Your Life* (Sweden). Irvin Kershner's *The Flim Flam Man* (USA) closed the festival out of competition.

1968

Golden Bear — *Ole Dole Doff* (Sweden)
Best Actor — Jean-Louis Trintignant in *L'Homme Qui Ment* (France)
Best Actress — Stéphane Audran in *Les Biches* (France)
Best Direction — Carlos Saura for *Peppermint Frappe* (Spain)

Among the other festival entries: Makavejev's political allegory *Innocence Unprotected* (Yugoslavia) and *Come L'Amore* (Italy) — both Silver Bear winners; Werner Herzog's *Signs Of Life* (West Germany); Godard's *Weekend* (France); *Charly* (USA); and Orson Welles' first film in colour *The Immortal Story* (France).

1969

Golden Bear — *Early Works* (Yugoslavia)

For the first time since 1955 no acting awards were presented at Berlin.

Silver Bears were awarded to five films — Walter Lima, Jr's. *Brazil Year 2000* (Brazil), about the effects of a nuclear war in South America; *Made In Sweden*, a Swedish anti-capitalist thriller by Johan Bergenstrahle; the West German *I Am An Elephant, Madame*; Brian de Palma's satirical *Greetings* (USA); and Elio Petri's *A Quiet Place In The Country* (Italy) with Franco Nero and Vanessa Redgrave.

Peter Hall's *Three Into Two Won't Go* (Britain) which opened the festival and Schlesinger's *Midnight Cowboy* (USA), considered by many to be the best film in the competition, were both overlooked in the final voting.

1970
Festival cancelled.

1971

Golden Bear	*The Garden Of The Finzi-Continis* (Italy/West Germany)
Best Actor	Jean Gabin in *Le Chat* (France)
Best Actress	Shirley MacLaine in *Desperate Characters* (USA) and Simone Signoret in *Le Chat* (France)
Best Direction	Frank Gilroy for *Desperate Characters* (USA)

Other entries included Pasolini's *The Decameron* (Italy) which received the Silver Bear Special Jury Prize; Stanley Kramer's *Bless The Beasts And The Children* (USA); *Bloomfield* (Israel); *Dulcima* (Britain); and Kon Ichikawa's *To Love Again* (Japan).

Ingmar Bergman's *The Touch* (Sweden), his first film in English, and Tati's *Traffic* (France) were shown out of competition.

1972

Golden Bear	*The Canterbury Tales* (Italy/France)
Best Actor	Alberto Sordi in *Detenuto In Attesa Di Giudizio* (Italy)
Best Actress	Elizabeth Taylor in *Hammersmith Is Out* (USA)
Best Direction	Jean-Pierre Blanc for *The Spinster* (France)

Among the other festival entries: Arthur Hiller's *The Hospital* (USA) which, together with *The Spinster* (France) won a Silver Bear; Werner Fassbinder's *The Bitter Tears Of Peter Vonkant* (West Germany); and Waris Hussein's *The Possession Of Joel Delaney* (USA).

1973

Golden Bear	*Distant Thunder* (India)

No actors, actresses or technicians were cited in the remaining awards.

Prizes were presented to films; directors were mentioned not because each of them won a personal award but more to identify the films themselves.

Silver Bears were awarded to *The 14* (Britain) and David Hemmings 'for sympathetic direction of the juvenile cast'; *The Experts* (West Germany) and Norbert Kueckelmann 'for his involvement in the subject matter of his first film'; *Seven Madmen* (Argentina) and Leopoldo Torre-Nilsson 'for the originality of treatment'; *All Nudity Will Be Punished* (Brazil) and Arnaldo Jabor 'for his realisation of a successful social satire'; and *The Tall Blond Man With One Black Shoe* (France) and Yves Robert 'for his realisation of a diverting and unusual comedy.'

André Cayatte's exposé of political blackmail *No Smoke Without Fire* (France) won the Special Jury Prize.

Chabrol's *Les Noces Rouges* (France); Ulli Lommel's *Tenderness Of Wolves* (West Germany) and *The Blockhouse* (Britain) were all offical entries.

1974

Golden Bear	*The Apprenticeship Of Duddy Kravitz* (Canada)

No acting awards were presented in 1974 although Richard Dreyfuss' performance in *The Apprenticeship Of Duddy Kravitz* (Canada) earned a special mention.

Six films shared Silver Bear awards: *Little Malcolm* (Britain); *Still Life* (Iran); *Rebellion In Patagonia* (Argentina); *Bread And Chocolate* (Italy); *In The Name Of The People* (West Germany); and *The Watchmaker Of St. Paul* (France) which won the Special Jury Prize.

The Soviet Union attended the festival for the first time although its entry *With You And Without You* was shown out of competition — as was Borowczyk's *Immoral Tales* (Poland).

1975

Golden Bear	*Adoption* (Hungary)
Best Actor	Vlastimil Brodsky in *Jacob, The Liar* (East Germany)
Best Actress	Kinuyo Tanaka in *Sandakan, House No. 8* (Japan)
Best Direction	Sergei Solovyov for *A Hundred Days After Childhood* (USSR)

Other entries included Stuart Cooper's *Overlord* (Britain) and Yves Boisset's *Monsieur Dupont* (France), both awarded Special Jury Prizes; Kirk Douglas' western *Posse* (USA); Alan Bridges' *Out Of Season* (Britain); and *Love And Death* (USA) which earned Woody Allen a special comedy award. The Soviet Union entered in competition for the first time.

1976

Golden Bear	*Buffalo Bill And The Indians, Or Sitting Bull's History Lesson* (USA)
Best Actor	Gerhard Olschewski in *Lost Life* (West Germany)
Best Actress	Jadwiga Baranska in *Nights And Days* (Poland)
Best Direction	Mario Monicelli for *Dear Michael* (Italy)

Among the other festival entries: Nicolas Roeg's *The Man Who Fell To Earth* (Britain) and Truffaut's *Pocket Money* (France). *Azonositas* (Hungary) and *Baghe Sanguy* (Iran) both earned Silver Bears; Felipe Cazals' *Canoa* (Mexico) received the Jury Prize.

Alan Pakula's *All The President's Men* (USA) was shown out of competition.

1977

Golden Bear	*The Ascent* (USSR)
Best Actor	Fernando Gomez in *The Recluse* (Spain)
Best Actress	Lily Tomlin in *The Late Show* (USA)
Best Direction	Manuel Aragon for *Black Litter* (Spain)

Other films in competition: Robert Bresson's *The Devil Probably* (France), Paul Sandor's *A Strange Role* (Hungary) and *Los Albaniles* (Mexico), all of which received Silver Bears; Truffaut's *The Man Who Loved Women* (France); Bruce Beresford's *Don's Party* (Australia) and Bernhard Wicki's *The Conquest Of The Citadel* (West Germany).

1978

Golden Bear	Awarded to all the Spanish entries at the festival — *The Trout, What Max Said* and the short *The Lift*.
Best Actor	Craig Russell in *Outrageous* (Canada)
Best Actress	Gena Rowlands in *Opening Night* (USA)
Best Direction	Georgi Djulgerov for *Advantage* (Bulgaria)

Among the other entries: Satyajit Ray's *The Chess Players* (India); *Lemon Popsicle* (Israel); Lina Wertmuller's *A Night Full Of Rain* (Italy/Yugoslavia); and *The Last Wave* (Australia).

The Teacher (Cuba) and *The Death Of The President* (Poland) earned Silver Bears; Brazil's *The Fall* received the Special Jury Prize.

Steven Spielberg's *Close Encounters Of The Third Kind* (USA) ended the festival out of competition.

1979

Golden Bear	*David* (West Germany)
Best Actor	Michele Placido in *Ernesto* (Italy)
Best Actress	Hanna Schygulla in *The Marriage Of Maria Braun* (West Germany)
Best Direction	Astrid Henning Jensen for *Winter-Children* (Denmark)

Other films in competition: Truffaut's *Love On The Run* (France); Peter Brooks' *Meetings With Remarkable Men* (Britain); Werner Herzog's *Nosferatu – The Vampire* (West Germany); *Movie, Movie* (USA); and Youssef Shahine's *Alexandria – Why?* (Egypt) which won the Special Jury Prize.

The East European countries walked out of the festival in protest against the out of competition showing of *The Deer Hunter*.

1980

Golden Bear	*Heartland* (USA) and *Palermo Or Wolfsburg* (West Germany)
Best Actor	Andrzej Seweryn in *The Conductor* (Poland)
Best Actress	Renate Krossner in *Solo Sunny* (East Germany)
Best Direction	Istvan Szabo for *Confidence* (Hungary)

Other entries included *French Leave* (France); *Death Watch* (France) and *Moscow Doesn't Believe In Tears* (USSR).

The Enemy (Turkey), *The Raven's Dance* (Finland) and Jack Hazan's *Rude Boy* (Britain) all received Special Jury Mentions; Athol Fugard earned an anniversary prize for 'his artistic work and engagement', and for his festival film *Marigolds In August* (South Africa).

Nicholas Roeg's *Bad Timing* (Britain) closed the festival out of competition.

Karlovy Vary

The Karlovy Vary Festival in Czechoslovakia was established in 1946, primarily to allow the latest films from Eastern Europe to be seen by visitors from the West and to establish a different kind of festival to those being held in Venice and Cannes.

The aim was to establish a competition for films with a specific social content and which embodied the moral and social humanitarian principles of an idealistic post-war world. These aims were given prominence in such festival mottos as 'For a new man, for a better mankind' and 'For peace, for a new man, for a better world.'

In its initial years Karlovy Vary was the only festival to present productions from Korea, Vietnam, Mongolia and China. In more recent times it has also exhibited many films from the Third World.

The late fifties and the sixties were its most celebrated years; *A Race For Life, The Accused, Capricious Summer* and *Kes* its most notable prize-winning films.

In the late forties the festival was held at Mariánské Lázné but in 1950 it moved permanently to Karlovy Vary, a gracious little spa town that nestles at the bottom of pine-clad mountains. Before it became famous as a centre for a film festival the town was best known for its medicinal hot springs on the Tepl river.

Since 1959, Karlovy Vary has been a bi-annual event, sharing the place on the summer calendar with Moscow. The ideological prizes of the early years — prizes for peace, for labour, etc. — have been replaced by main prizes and jury awards. Presentations are also made for acting, direction and technical merit.

1946
This first festival, held at Mariánské Lázné and Karlovy Vary during August, was non-competitive. It was designed as a shop window for Czech films before an international audience and included pictures of specific and ideologically defined content. Seven countries participated — Czechoslovakia, Russia, France, America, Britain, Sweden and Switzerland — and 13 full-length features (plus shorts) were exhibited.

1947
The second festival was again non-competitive and held solely at Mariánské Lázné. The number of countries exhibiting films increased to 10, the number of features to 14.

1948
Grand Prix *The Last Stage* (Poland)
26 features (from 18 countries) were exhibited at this first competitive festival held at Mariánské Lázné. The festival was held under the slogan, 'For a new man, for a better mankind.'

Madeleine Robinson was named best actress for her performance in *The Bouquinquant Brothers* (France), William Wyler was awarded a direction prize for *The Best Years Of Our Lives* (USA); Mikhail Romm's *The Russian Question* (USSR) won The Peace Prize.

1949
Grand Prix *The Battle Of Stalingrad* (USSR)
Among the other prize-winners: Alexander Borisov who was named best actor for *I. P. Pavlov* (USSR), Luis Daquin, voted best director for *Daybreak* (France), and Gabriel Figuero who earned a prize for his photography of the Mexican *Maclovia*.

Britain's *Scott Of The Antarctic* received a music award, Alexandrov's political drama, *Meeting At The Elbe* (USSR) was awarded The Peace Prize and *An Inch Of Land* (Hungary) the Prize Of Labour.

1950
Grand Prix *The Fall Of Berlin* (USSR)
This was the first festival to be held solely at Karlovy Vary. 25 countries competed with 39 films under the slogan, 'For peace, for a new man, for a better world.'

Vsevolod Pudovkin (maker of the silent classics *Mother* and *Storm Over Asia*) received the direction award for his biography of *Zukovsky* (USSR), the founder of Russian aeronautics, and Gabriel Figuero earned his second consecutive photography prize for *Pueblerina* (Mexico).

Also in competition: René Clair's *La Beauté Du Diable* (France); the Russian musical comedy *Kuban Cossacks* (Prize Of Labour) and Martin Fric's *Steel Town*, about the economic crisis of 1931 and acclaimed as the best Czech film then made.

1951

Grand Prix — *Cavalier Of The Gold Star* (USSR)

In 1951 prizes were awarded for the first time by an international jury.

Jean-Paul Le Chanois was named best director for *Address Unknown* (France); Louis Daquin earned a special mention for *Gods Annointed* (France) as did Czech director Jiri Weiss for *New Warriors Will Arise*, a portrait of life in a Czech village at the end of the 19th century.

Pietro Germi's *The Road To Hope* (Italy), Giuseppe De Santis' *No Peace Among The Olives* (Italy) and Korea's *Young Partisans* were also in competition. Anthony Asquith's *The Browning Version* was the British entry.

1952

Grand Prix — *The Unforgettable Year 1919* (USSR)

Sergei Bondarchuk in *Broken Fetters* (USSR) and Pierre Fresnay in *Mr. Fabre* (France) were awarded best actor prizes; Carlo Lizzani was named for his direction of *Warning Bandits* (Italy), a documentary about the Italian resistance to the Nazi occupation.

Other entries: *Where No Vultures Fly* (Britain), *White Corridors* (Britain) and Poland's *Youth Of Chopin*. Two Czech films, *The Emperor's Baker*, an historical comedy in colour, and *Mikolas Ales*, a biography of the early life of the Czech artist, were both shown out of competition.

Of the major film producing countries, only America was not represented.

1953

No Festival.

1954

Grand Prix	*Close Friends* (USSR) and *Salt Of The Earth* (USA)
Best Actor	Charles Vanel in *The Mauritius Affair* (France)
Best Actress	Rosaura Revueltas in *Salt Of The Earth* (USA)

Other entries included *The Cruel Sea* (Britain); *Genevieve* (Britain); *Heidi* (Switzerland); and André Hunebelle's version of *The Three Musketeers* (France).

Alberto Cavalcanti was voted best director for *Song Of The Sea*, a documentary-styled study of an impoverished peasant family struggling for a new life in Brazil.

1955

No Festival.

1956

Grand Prix	*A Race For Life* (France)
Best Actor	Günther Simon in *Ernest Thalmann, The Leader Of His Class* (East Germany)
Best Actress	Rufina Nifontova in *Children Of Freedom* (USSR)

Among the other films in competition: Tadashi Imai's *Darkness At Noon* (Japan), an indictment of Japanese police methods; Britain's *A Town Like Alice*; the Rumanian comedy *I Take The Responsibility*; and *La Meilleure Part* (France) which starred Gérard Philipe and earned Yves Allégret the direction prize for his imaginative use of CinemaScope.

America, still the only major country not exhibiting, presented *Marty* out of competition. Visconti's *Senso* (Italy) was also shown out of festival.

1957

Grand Prix	*Under The Cloak Of Night* (India)

S. Arnaudov received an acting award for *In The Face Of The World* (Bulgaria); Yves Montand, Simone Signoret and Mylene Demongeot earned a collective acting prize for their performances in *The Witches Of Salem* (France).

Horst Buchholz received a special mention for his role in the West German production of Thomas Mann's *The Confessions Of Felix Krull*.

Other entries: China's *New Year Sacrifice* which won the Special Jury Prize; Zoltán Fábri's *Professor Hannibal* (Hungary); *The Good Soldier, Schweik* (Czechoslovakia) by Karel Steklý whose *Sirena* had received the Grand Prix at Venice in 1947; and two British pot-boilers *Doctor At Large* and *Three Men In A Boat*.

The direction prize was shared by Andrezj Munk for *Man On The Rails* (Poland) and Vladimir Pogacic for *Great And Small* (Yugoslavia).

1958

Grand Prix	*Quiet Flows The Don* (USSR) and *The Stepbrothers* (Japan)
Best Actor	Maxim Shtraukh in *Stories About Lenin* (USSR)
Best Actress	Nargis in *Mother India* (India)

Also entered: *Pillar Of Salt* (Hungary); *The Black Battalion* (Czechoslovakia) about the horrors of the Indo-China campaign; *Barnacle Bill* (Britain); *Operation Teutonic Sword*, an East German documentary of Hans Speidel, a former Nazi turned NATO general; and *The Devil Came At Night* (West Germany), a detective melodrama which earned Robert Siodmak a mention for his direction.

Jacques Tati's *Mon Oncle* (France/Italy) was shown out of competition; America did not compete in the festival.

1959
No Festival. After this year Karlovy Vary became a bi-annual event, alternating with Moscow.

1960

Grand Prix	*Seryozha* (USSR)
Best Actor	Laurence Olivier in *The Entertainer* (Britain) and Erwin Geschonneck in *Men With Wings* (East Germany)
Best Actress	Mari Töröcsik in *Madcap* (Hungary)

Other festival entries included *River Aflame* (Rumania); *Roses For The Attorney General* (East Germany); and *Heroes Of Today* (USSR). The Special Prize of the Jury was awarded to director Roberto Rossellini and actress Giovanna Ralli for their film *That Night In Rome* (Italy), a drama of the last months of the occupation of Rome in World War II.

1962

Grand Prix	*Nine Days Of One Year* (USSR)

No acting prizes were presented in 1962. Tony Richardson's *A Taste Of Honey* (Britain) and Pasolini's *Accattone* (Italy) both won top awards as did Jiri Krejcik's *Midnight Mass*, a Czech film about the Nazi occupation.

France entered Yves Robert's *La Guerre Des Boutons* and the USA, competing for the first time, screened Martin Ritt's *Adventures Of A Young Man*, a compilation of Hemingway's Nick Adams stories.

Karel Zemen's *Baron Munchausen* (Czechoslovakia) opened the festival out of competition.

1964

Grand Prix	*The Accused* (Czechoslovakia)
Best Actor	Wieńczyslaw Gliński in *Echo* (Poland)
Best Actress	Jeanne Moreau in *Diary Of A Chambermaid* (France)

Franklin Schaffner's political drama *The Best Man* (USA) received the Special Jury Prize; István Gaál's *Current* (Hungary), a moving film about the end of adolescence, and Alexander Stolper's *The Living And The Dead* (USSR) a three-and-a-half-hour war epic, were other award winners.

Ingmar Bergman's *The Silence* (Sweden) and Truffaut's *La Peau Douce* (France) were both shown out of competition.

1966

Grand Prix	Not Awarded

Best Actor — Donatas Banionis in *No One Wanted To Die* (USSR) and
Naum Shopov in *The Czar And The General* (Bulgaria)
Best Actress — Not Awarded

For the first time in the history of the festival no Grand Prix was presented, the jury awarding instead main prizes (i.e. runner up awards) to the war films — *Three* (Yugoslavia); *Cold Days* (Hungary) about an atrocity committed by Hungarian troops in World War II; and *Carriage To Vienna* (Czechoslovakia), a pacifist plea concerning a Czech woman and an Austrian soldier in the last days of the war.

Cuba's *Death Of The Bureaucrat* and France's *La Vie De Chateau* shared the Special Jury Prize.

The British entry was *Young Cassidy* and the festival kicked off in some style with the non-competing *The Shop On Main Street*, the first Czech picture to be awarded a foreign language Oscar.

1968

Grand Prix — *Capricious Summer* (Czechoslovakia)
Best Actor — Nikolai Plotnikov in *Your Contemporary* (USSR)
Best Actress — Carol White in *Poor Cow* (Britain)

Richard Brooks' *In Cold Blood* (USA), an account of the murder of a Kansas farming family by two young ex-cons; *When I Am Dead And Gone* (Yugoslavia); *The Long Journey* (Chile); and *Memories Of Underdevelopment* (Cuba) all received jury mentions. The historical epic, *The Sixth Of June* (USSR), a reconstruction of an important day in the history of the Russian Revolution, was awarded a special prize.

1970

Grand Prix — *Kes* (Britain)
Best Actor — Matthieu Carrière in *House Of The Bories* (France)
Best Actress — Natasha Bielokhvostikova in *By The Lake* (USSR)

By The Lake, a 155-minute Russian film about the problems of pollution and conservation, and *Black Angels* (Bulgaria), a story of young resistance workers who sacrificed their lives in the fight against Fascism, both earned Jury Prizes.

Taste Of Black Earth (Poland), Giuliano Monaldo's *God With Us* (Italy), and *On The Way To Lenin* (East Germany), about a young Communist who is en' usted with an important mission to Moscow in 1919, were among the other prize-winners.

1972

Grand Prix	*The Taming Of Fire* (USSR)
Best Actor	Ranjit Ray in *Interview* (India)
Best Actress	Mari Töröcsik in *The Dead Region* (Hungary)

Among the other festival entries: Bulgaria's *The Goat Horn* which was awarded the Special Jury Prize; *Under The Flag Of The Rising Sun* (Japan); *The Flower Girl* (Korea); Ken Loach's *Family Life* (Britain); and the Sidney Poitier directed Western *Buck And The Preacher* (USA).

Cliff Robertson's *J. W. Coop* (USA), a story of an ex-con operating on a small rodeo circuit, was shown out of competition.

1974

Grand Prix	*Romance Of Lovers* (USSR)
Best Actor	Antonio Ferrandiz in *And Your Next Of Kin* (Spain)
Best Actress	Marta Vancurova in *Lovers In The Year One* (Czechoslovakia)

Main prizes at the festival were awarded to Bulgaria's *A Tree Without Roots*; Cuba's *You Can Talk*; De Sica's *Brief Vacation* (Italy) with Florinda Bolkan and Renato Salvatori; and Martin Ritt's *Conrack* (USA), about a white teacher's attempt to educate a backward black school in South Carolina.

Poland's *Dark River* and Argentina's *Quebracho* were also among the prize-winners.

Numerous films were shown in public out of competition e.g. *The Way We Were* (USA), *The Conversation* (USA) and *Lady Sings The Blues* (USA).

1976

Grand Prix	*Cantata Of Chile* (Cuba)
Best Actor	Zygmunt Malanowicz in *Bohdan Poreba* (Poland) and George Dinicu in *Death Game* (Bulgaria)
Best Actress	Karin Schröder in *Man Against Man* (East Germany) and Hildegard Knef in *Even In Death Alone* (East Germany)

Also competing: *Aces High* (Britain); *Stormy Wine* (Czechoslovakia); *May I Have The Floor* (USSR); and the Hungarian *No Man's Daughter* which won Laszlo Ranody the direction award and related the harrowing experiences of a seven-year-old orphan in the thirties.

Satyajit Ray's *Mediator* (India) won the director a special award for 'his contribution to both Indian and world cinematography and his fresh approach to grave issues of contemporary relevance.'

All The President's Men (USA) was shown out of competition.

1978

Grand Prix	*Shadows Of A Hot Summer* (Czechoslovakia) and *White Bim With A Black Ear* (USSR)
Best Actor	Giuliano Gemma in *The Iron Prefect* (Italy) and Peter Faber in *Doctor Vlimmen* (Holland)
Best Actress	Marisol in *A Few Days Of The Past* (Spain) and Marie-José Nat in *A Simple Past* (France)

Mrinal Sen's *A Village Story* (India) and *Autopsy Of Conspiracy* (Algeria) both earned Special Jury Prizes; Jack Gold's *The Sailor's Return* represented Britain, Peter Hyam's *Capricorn One* The United States.

Moscow

Like its Czechoslovakian counterpart at Karlovy Vary, the Moscow Festival is primarily a showcase for new films from the Soviet Union and other East European countries.

The city's first truly international competition was held in 1959 although a solitary pre-war festival to mark the 15th anniversary of Lenin's nationalisation of the Russian film industry had been staged in February, 1935, when Walt Disney and René Clair (for his *Le Dernier Milliardaire*) were among the prize-winners.

The 1959 event was opened with a motorcade through the city and a ceremony, staged before several thousand people, at the Lenin Sports Stadium. 28 features were entered in the main competition in its first year.

Moscow covers a wider field than any other international festival with as many as 100 countries often participating in the main competition. There is no selection committee and countries are free to exhibit one full-length feature (at the Kremlin Palace of Congress) and one short film of their own choice.

Moscow has boasted a number of major prize-winners – *Destiny Of A Man, 8½, Dersu Uzala* and *War And Peace* – in its relatively short history and alternates every other year with Karlovy Vary. It is held in July and numerous prizes are awarded for feature productions, documentaries and shorts.

The festival's recent policy of awarding the Grand Prix to three films is not an unattractive one and, in some ways, a more satisfactory finale to a festival than a solitary first prize award.

1959

Grand Prix — *Destiny Of A Man* (USSR)
Best Actor — Gliski Pavlik and Szewczuk in *The Eagle* (Poland)
Best Actress — Tsuraeviyn Tsevelsuren in *A Messenger Of The People* (Mongolia)

This first international festival in Moscow was opened by Britain's non-competing *Room At The Top*. Among the official entries were Satyajit Ray's *The Music Room* (India), Lewis Gilbert's *A Cry From The Streets* (Britain), and Christian-Jaque's *Babette Goes To War* (France) starring Brigitte Bardot.

Hiroshima, Mon Amour (France/Japan), *Mon Oncle* (France/Italy) and George Stevens' *The Diary Of Anne Frank* (USA) were all shown out of competition. The festival's motto was 'For Humanism in Cinema Art, For Peace and Friendship Among Nations.'

1961

Grand Prix — *Clear Skies* (USSR) and *The Island* (Japan)
Best Actor — Peter Finch in *The Trials Of Oscar Wilde* (Britain) and Bambangu Hermanto in *Fighters For Freedom* (Indonesia)
Best Actress — Yui Lan in *Family Of A Revolutionary* (China)

Other entries at the festival included Luigi Comencini's *Everyone Goes Home* (Italy) which won the Special Jury Prize; *Alba Regia* (Hungary); *Sunrise At Campobello* (USA); and *Tonight A Town Dies* (Poland), a film by Jan Rybkowski about the wartime bombing of Dresden.

Saturday Night And Sunday Morning (Britain) was shown out of competition.

1963

Grand Prix — *8½* (Italy)
Best Actor — Steve McQueen in *The Great Escape* (USA)
Best Actress — Suhihe Sen in *Wedding Circle* (India)

Gold prizes for 'outstanding artistic achievement' were presented to *For We Cannot Forgive* (Czechoslovakia) and *Notorious Girl* (Japan), silver medals to *Black Wings* (Poland) and *A Legend In The Train* (Hungary). Frank Beyer was named best director for the East German *Naked Among The Wolves*. The official British entry was *Sammy Going South*.

West Side Story (USA) and *Some Like It Hot* (USA) were among the films shown out of festival.

1965

Grand Prix	*War And Peace* (USSR) and *Twenty Hours* (Hungary)
Best Actor	S. Zakariadze in *The Soldier's Father* (USSR)
Best Actress	Sophia Loren in *Marriage, Italian Style* (Italy)

Other entries included *Assassination* (Czechoslovakia) and Ciampi's *The Sky Above* (France), both awarded gold medals; *Le Soldatesse* (Italy) which earned the Special Jury Prize; and *The Great Race* (USA) which was named best comedy.

The Adventures Of Werner Holt was the East German entry; John Schlesinger's *Darling* represented Britain. Ion Popescu-Gopo was named best director for *The White Moor* (Rumania).

1967

Grand Prix	*Father* (Hungary) and *The Journalist* (USSR)
Best Actor	Paul Scofield in *A Man For All Seasons* (Britain)
Best Actress	Sandy Dennis in *Up the Down Staircase* (USA) and Grunet Molvig in *The Princess* (Sweden)

Romance For The Bugle (Czechoslovakia), a ballad about a country boy who falls in love with a girl from a fairground, was awarded the Special Jury Prize; Bulgaria's *The Detour* earned a special award; and Dino Ris' *Operation San Gennaro* (Italy) was named best comedy.

Britain's *To Sir With Love* and Stanley Kramer's *Ship Of Fools* (USA) were among the out of competition entries.

1969

Grand Prix	*Lucia* (Cuba) *Serafino* (France/Italy) and *See You Monday* (USSR)
Best Actor	Ron Moody in *Oliver!* (Britain) and Tadeusz Lomnicki in *Colonel Wolodyjowski* (Poland)
Best Actress	Irina Petrescu in *A Woman For A Season* (Rumania) and Anna Maria Picchio in *A Strip Of Sky* (Argentina)

Britain's official entry, *Oliver!* and the 220-minute Soviet adaptation of *The Brothers Karamazov* received Special Jury Prizes; Tati's *Playtime* (France) earned a silver prize; and Kubrick's luckless *2001: A Space Odyssey* which caused some controversy at the festival by being entered as an American film, gained a mention for its technical qualities.

1971

Grand Prix	*White Bird With A Black Mark* (USSR) *Confessions Of A Police Inspector* (Italy) and *Live Today, Die Tomorrow* (Japan)
Best Actor	Richard Harris in *Cromwell* (Britain) and Daniel Olbrychski in *The Birch Wood* (Poland)
Best Actress	Ada Rogovtseva in *Salute, Maria* (USSR) and Idalia Andreus in *The Days Of Water* (Cuba)

Andrzej Wajda received a gold prize for his direction of Poland's *The Birch Wood*; the East German biography of *Goya* earned a special award; and the British ballet film *The Tales Of Beatrix Potter* was named best fairy tale. *Hementhal* (Senegal), *The Key* (Czechoslovakia) and *In The Family* (Brazil) were all silver medal winners.

Out of competition entries included Arthur Penn's *Little Big Man* (USA) and *They Shoot Horses, Don't They*? (USA).

1973

Grand Prix	*Oklahoma Crude* (USA) *That Sweet Word Liberty* (USSR) and *Affection* (Bulgaria)
Best Actor	Sergio Corrieri in *The Man From Maisinicu* (Cuba) and Romaz Chkhikvadze in *The Saplings* (USSR)
Best Actress	Tra Giang in *17th Parallel, Nights And Days* (Vietnam) and Ingrid Vardund in *Lina's Wedding* (Norway)

Also in competition: Britain's *Triple Echo* with Oliver Reed and Glenda Jackson; *Home, Sweet Home* (Belgium) and the Czech *Days Of Betrayal*, an account of the events leading up to Munich. The official Italian entry *The Matteotti Assassination*, earned a Special Jury Prize for its vivid presentation of a political theme.

1975

Grand Prix	*Dersu Uzala* (USSR/Japan) *The Promised Land* (Poland) and *Those Were The Years* (Italy)
Best Actor	Miguel Benavides in *Another Francisco* (Cuba) and Georgy Georgiev-Gez in *A Peasant On A Bicycle* (Bulgaria)
Best Actress	Harriet Andersson in *The White Wall* (Sweden) and Fatima Bouamair in *The Heritage* (Algeria)

The Year Of The Solar Eclipse (Mongolia) was awarded the Special Jury

Prize; *Chorus* (India), *My Brother Has A Cute Brother* (Czechoslovakia) and *Powers Of The Earth* (Peru) all received silver medals. A remake of *Great Expectations* was Britain's official entry; Zoltán Fábri was mentioned for his direction of *Unfinished Sentence* (Hungary).

The Romantic Englishwoman (Britain) and *Murder On The Orient Express* (Britain) were both shown out of competition.

1977

Grand Prix	*The Fifth Seal* (Hungary) *The Long Weekend* (Spain) and *Mimino* (USSR)
Best Actor	Amze Pelya in *The Doom* (Rumania) and Ratko Polic in *The Idealist* (Yugoslavia)
Best Actress	Mary Apick in *The Dead End* (Iran) and Mercedes Karreras in *Crazy Women* (Argentina)

Night Over Chile (USSR) and *Rio Negro* (Cuba) were both awarded Special Jury Prizes; *In The Shadow Of A Castle* (France), *The Swimming Pool* (Bulgaria) and *Omar Gatlato* (Algeria) all received silver medals. Also in competition: *Logan's Run* (USA); *It Shouldn't Happen To A Vet* (Britain); and *The Moving Picture Man* (Venezuela).

1979

Grand Prix	*Christ Stopped At Eboli* (Italy/France) *Seven Days In January* (Spain) and *Camera Buff* (Poland)
Best Actor	Ulrich Thein in *Anton The Magician* (East Germany)
Best Actress	Daisy Granados in *Teresa's Portrait* (Cuba)

Hall Bartlett's *Children Of Sanchez* (USA) and Peter Collinson's *Tomorrow Never Comes* (Britain) were among other festival entries; *Barrier* (Bulgaria), *Take-Off* (USSR) and *The Man With The Axe* (India) were awarded silver medals.

Big events of the festival were out of competition screenings of Coppola's *Apocalypse Now* (USA), *The China Syndrome* (USA) and Fellini's *Orchestra Rehearsal* (Italy). A full print of Eisenstein's *Que Viva Mexico* was also unveiled.

Postscript....

The lists that follow are a kind of potpourri, a statistical summing up of the awards included in this book. They are compiled for fun and also to provide talking points but not to prove that one film, actor or director is better than another.

The net result of all the calculations, however, is that Fellini emerges as the director who has received more best film awards than any other film-maker; that Peter Finch and not Olivier or Brando is the most honoured actor; that Ingrid Bergman rates as the top actress; and that, of the 318 films in the book, just over 20% — 62 — figure among Variety's list of all-time box-office champs. For further confusion read on . . . .

The Top Directors

The following are the leading directors of award-winning movies. The figure after the director's name represents the total number of awards won; the figure after each film denotes the awards won by that particular picture.

FEDERICO FELLINI (14)
- *Amarcord* (3)
- *La Dolce Vita* (2)
- *8½* (4)
- *Juliet Of The Spirits* (2)
- *The Nights Of Cabiria* (1)
- *La Strada* (2)

VITTORIO DE SICA (11)
- *Bicycle Thieves* (4)
- *The Garden Of The Finzi-Continis* (2)
- *Miracle In Milan* (2)
- *Shoe-Shine* (1)
- *Umberto D* (1)
- *Yesterday, Today And Tomorrow* (1)

DAVID LEAN (11)
- *The Bridge On The River Kwai* (4)
- *Hobson's Choice* (1)
- *In Which We Serve* (2)
- *Lawrence Of Arabia* (2)
- *The Sound Barrier* (2)

WILLIAM WYLER (9)
- *Ben-Hur* (3)
- *The Best Years Of Our Lives* (3)
- *Friendly Persuasion* (1)
- *Mrs. Miniver* (1)
- *Wuthering Heights* (1)

FRED ZINNEMANN (9)
- *From Here To Eternity* (2)
- *High Noon* (1)
- *Julia* (1)
- *A Man For All Seasons* (4)
- *The Nun's Story* (1)

INGMAR BERGMAN (8)
Autumn Sonata (1)
Cries And Whispers (2)
Shame (1)
Through A Glass Darkly (1)
The Virgin Spring (1)
Wild Strawberries (2)

RENÉ CLÉMENT (7)
Gervaise (2)
Les Jeux Interdits (4)
The Walls Of Malapaga (1)

JOHN FORD (6)
The Grapes Of Wrath (2)
How Green Was My Valley (1)
The Informer (2)
The Quiet Man (1)

ELIA KAZAN (6)
Gentleman's Agreement (2)
On The Waterfront (3)
A Streetcar Named Desire (1)

AKIRA KUROSAWA (6)
Dersu Uzala (2)
Kagemusha (1)
Rashomon (3)

JOHN SCHLESINGER (6)
Darling (1)
Far From The Madding Crowd (1)
A Kind Of Loving (1)
Midnight Cowboy (2)
Sunday, Bloody Sunday (1)

FRANÇOIS TRUFFAUT (6)
Day For Night (3)
L'Enfant Sauvage (1)
Les Quatre Cents Coups (1)
The Story Of Adèle H (1)

BILLY WILDER (6)
The Apartment (3)
The Lost Weekend (2)
Sunset Boulevard (1)

WOODY ALLEN (5)
Annie Hall (3)
Manhattan (2)

SERGEI BONDARCHUK (5)
Destiny Of A Man (1)
War And Peace (4)

FRANK CAPRA (5)
It Happened One Night (2)
Mr. Deeds Goes To Town (2)
You Can't Take It With You (1)

HENRI-GEORGES CLOUZOT (5)
Les Diaboliques (1)
Manon (1)
The Wages Of Fear (3)

FRANCIS FORD COPPOLA (5)
Apocalypse Now (1)
The Conversation (2)
The Godfather (1)
The Godfather Part II (1)

LAURENCE OLIVIER (5)
Hamlet (3)
Henry V (1)
Richard III (1)

Runners-up: Robert Altman, Luis Buñuel, Joseph L. Mankiewicz, Delbert Mann, Tony Richardson, Roberto Rossellini and Satyajit Ray (4 each).

The Top Actors

The following actors are those who have received the most best acting awards from the organizations included in this book. The figure after each actor's name denotes the number of awards won; the films for which he won his respective prizes are listed beneath his name.

Abbreviations used: BAA (British Academy Award); NYC (New York Critics) and NBR (National Board of Review).

PETER FINCH (9)
A Town Like Alice (BAA, 56)
The Trials Of Oscar Wilde (BAA, 60)
No Love For Johnnie (BAA, 61)
No Love For Johnnie (Berlin, 61)
The Trials Of Oscar Wilde (Moscow, 61)
Far From The Madding Crowd (NBR, 67)
Sunday, Bloody Sunday (BAA, 71)
Network (Oscar, 76)
Network (BAA, 77)

LAURENCE OLIVIER (8)
Henry V (NYC, 46)
Henry V (NBR, 46)
Hamlet (Oscar, 48)
Hamlet (NYC, 48)
Richard III (BAA, 55)
The Entertainer (Karlovy Vary, 60)
Sleuth (NYC, 72)
The Boys From Brazil (NBR, 78)

Note: Olivier was also the winner of a supporting actor award for *Oh! What A Lovely War* (BAA, 69).

MARLON BRANDO (8)
Viva Zapata! (Cannes, 52)
Viva Zapata! (BAA, 52)
Julius Caesar (BAA, 53)
On The Waterfront (Oscar, 54)
On The Waterfront (NYC, 54)
On The Waterfront (BAA, 54)

The Godfather (Oscar, 72)
Last Tango In Paris (NYC, 73)

JACK NICHOLSON (7)
The Last Detail (Cannes, 74)
The Last Detail and *Chinatown* (NYC, 74)
The Last Detail and *Chinatown* (BAA, 74)
One Flew Over The Cuckoo's Nest (Oscar, 75)
One Flew Over The Cuckoo's Nest (NYC, 75)
One Flew Over The Cuckoo's Nest (NBR, 75)
One Flew Over The Cuckoo's Nest (BAA, 76)

Note: Nicholson also won a supporting actor award for *Easy Rider* (NYC, 69).

ALEC GUINNESS (6)
Kind Hearts And Coronets (NBR, 50)
The Bridge On The River Kwai (Oscar, 57)
The Bridge On The River Kwai (NYC, 57)
The Bridge On The River Kwai (NBR, 57)
The Bridge On The River Kwai (BAA, 57)
The Horse's Mouth (Venice, 58)

BURT LANCASTER (6)
From Here To Eternity (NYC, 53)
Trapeze (Berlin, 56)
Elmer Gantry (Oscar, 60)
Elmer Gantry (NYC, 60)
Birdman Of Alcatraz (Venice, 62)
Birdman Of Alcatraz (BAA, 62)

JACK LEMMON (5)
Some Like It Hot (BAA, 59)
The Apartment (BAA, 60)
Save The Tiger (Oscar, 73)
The China Syndrome (Cannes, 79)
The China Syndrome (BAA, 79)

Note: Lemmon also won a supporting actor award for *Mister Roberts* (Oscar, 55).

GENE HACKMAN (5)
The French Connection (Oscar, 71)
The French Connection (NYC, 71)
The French Connection (NBR, 71)
The French Connection and *The Poseidon Adventure* (BAA, 72)
The Conversation (NBR, 74)

PAUL SCOFIELD (5)
A Man For All Seasons (Oscar, 66)

A Man For All Seasons (NYC, 66)
A Man For All Seasons (NBR, 66)
A Man For All Seasons (BAA, 67)
A Man For All Seasons (Moscow, 67)

ROD STEIGER (5)
The Pawnbroker (Berlin, 64)
The Pawnbroker (BAA, 66)
In The Heat Of The Night (Oscar, 67)
In The Heat Of The Night (NYC, 67)
In The Heat Of The Night (BAA, 67)

JAMES STEWART (5)
Mr Smith Goes To Washington (NYC, 39)
The Philadelphia Story (Oscar, 40)
Anatomy Of A Murder (Venice, 59)
Anatomy Of A Murder (NYC, 59)
Mr. Hobbs Takes A Vacation (Berlin, 62)

SPENCER TRACY (5)
Captains Courageous (Oscar, 37)
Boys Town (Oscar, 38)
Bad Day At Black Rock (Cannes, 55)
The Old Man And The Sea and *The Last Hurrah* (NBR, 58)
Guess Who's Coming To Dinner? (BAA, 68)

JON VOIGHT (5)
Midnight Cowboy (NYC, 69)
Coming Home (Cannes, 78)
Coming Home (Oscar, 78)
Coming Home (NYC, 78)
Coming Home (NBR, 78)

Runners-up: Ernest Borgnine, Jean Gabin, Fredric March, Lee Marvin, Ray Milland, Sidney Poitier and Ralph Richardson (4 each).

The Top Actresses

The same rules as before. Again only leading performances are included, although mention is made of supporting roles where necessary.

INGRID BERGMAN (7)

Gaslight (Oscar, 44)
Spellbound and *The Bells Of St. Mary's* (NYC, 45)
Anastasia (Oscar, 56)
Anastasia (NYC, 56)
Inn Of The Sixth Happiness (NBR, 58)
Autumn Sonata (NYC, 78)
Autumn Sonata (NBR, 78)

Note: Bergman also won two supporting actress awards for her part in *Murder On The Orient Express* (Oscar, 74 and BAA, 74).

SIMONE SIGNORET (7)

Casque D'Or (BAA, 52)
The Witches Of Salem (BAA, 57)
Room At The Top (BAA, 58)
Room At The Top (Cannes, 59)
Room At The Top (Oscar, 59)
Room At The Top (NBR, 59)
Le Chat (Berlin, 71)

Note: Signoret also received, along with Yves Montand and Mylene Demengeot, a collective acting award for *The Witches Of Salem* at Karlovy Vary in 1957.

ANNA MAGNANI (7)

Open City (NBR, 46)
L'Onorevole Angelina (Venice, 47)
The Rose Tattoo (Oscar, 55)
The Rose Tattoo (NYC, 55)
The Rose Tattoo (NBR, 55)
The Rose Tattoo (BAA, 56)
Wild Is The Wind (Berlin, 58)

KATHARINE HEPBURN (6)
Morning Glory (Oscar, 33)
Little Women (Venice, 34)
The Philadelphia Story (NYC, 40)
Guess Who's Coming To Dinner? (Oscar, 67)
Guess Who's Coming To Dinner? and *The Lion In Winter* (BAA, 68)
The Lion In Winter (Oscar, 68)

Note: Hepburn also received, along with Ralph Richardson, Jason Robards and Dean Stockwell, a collective acting award for *Long Day's Journey Into Night* at Cannes in 1962.

ANNE BANCROFT (6)
The Miracle Worker (Oscar, 62)
The Miracle Worker (NBR, 62)
The Miracle Worker (BAA, 62)
The Pumpkin Eater (Cannes, 64)
The Pumpkin Eater (BAA, 64)
The Turning Point (NBR, 77)

OLIVIA DE HAVILLAND (6)
To Each His Own (Oscar, 46)
The Snake Pit (NYC, 48)
The Snake Pit (NBR, 48)
The Snake Pit (Venice, 49)
The Heiress (Oscar, 49)
The Heiress (NYC, 49)

JANE FONDA (6)
They Shoot Horses, Don't They? (NYC, 69)
Klute (Oscar, 71)
Klute (NYC, 71)
Coming Home (Oscar, 78)
Julia (BAA, 78)
The China Syndrome (BAA, 79)

AUDREY HEPBURN (6)
Roman Holiday (Oscar, 53)
Roman Holiday (NYC, 53)
Roman Holiday (BAA, 53)
The Nun's Story (NYC, 59)
The Nun's Story (BAA, 59)
Charade (BAA, 64)

VIVIEN LEIGH (6)
Gone With The Wind (Oscar, 39)
Gone With The Wind (NYC, 39)
A Streetcar Named Desire (Oscar, 51)
A Streetcar Named Desire (NYC, 51)
A Streetcar Named Desire (BAA, 52)
A Streetcar Named Desire (Venice, 51)

SOPHIA LOREN (6)
The Black Orchid (Venice, 58)
Two Women (Cannes, 61)
Two Women (Oscar, 61)
Two Women (NYC, 61)
Two Women (BAA, 61)
Marriage, Italian Style (Moscow, 65)

ELIZABETH TAYLOR (6)
Butterfield 8 (Oscar, 60)
Who's Afraid Of Virginia Woolf? (Oscar, 66)
Who's Afraid Of Virginia Woolf? (NYC, 66)
Who's Afraid Of Virginia Woolf? (NBR, 66)
Who's Afraid Of Virginia Woolf? (BAA, 66)
Hammersmith Is Out (Berlin, 72)

LIV ULLMANN (6)
Hour Of The Wolf and *Shame* (NBR, 68)
Cries And Whispers (NYC, 72)
The New Land (NBR, 73)
Scenes From A Marriage (NYC, 74)
Face To Face (NYC, 76)
Face To Face (NBR, 76)

JOANNE WOODWARD (6)
The Three Faces Of Eve (Oscar, 57)
The Three Faces Of Eve and *No Down Payment* (NBR, 57)
Rachel, Rachel (NYC, 68)
The Effect Of Gamma Rays On Man-In-The-Moon Marigolds (Cannes, 73)
Summer Wishes, Winter Dreams (NYC, 73)
Summer Wishes, Winter Dreams (BAA, 74)

BETTE DAVIS (5)
Dangerous (Oscar, 35)
Marked Woman and *Kid Galahad* (Venice, 37)
Jezebel (Oscar, 38)
All About Eve (NYC, 50)
All About Eve (Cannes, 51)

GLENDA JACKSON (5)
Women In Love (Oscar, 70)
Women In Love (NYC, 70)
Women In Love (NBR, 70)
Sunday, Bloody Sunday (BAA, 71)
A Touch Of Class (Oscar, 73)

SHIRLEY MACLAINE (5)
Ask Any Girl (Berlin, 59)
Ask Any Girl (BAA, 59)
The Apartment (Venice, 60)

The Apartment (BAA, 60)
Desperate Characters (Berlin, 71)

PATRICIA NEAL (5)
Hud (Oscar, 63)
Hud (NYC, 63)
Hud (NBR, 63)
Hud (BAA, 63)
In Harm's Way (BAA, 65)

Runners-up: Shirley Booth, Julie Christie and Edith Evans (4 each).

50 That Nearly Made It!

For those of you who have looked belatedly for a film you are sure has won a best picture award this list might provide some consolation. The 50 films were all runners-up at festivals or nominated at Academy Award time. The list is wide-ranging but the selection is a personal one. The losing picture is on the left, the winning picture on the right.

Accident	Cannes, 67	*Blow-Up*
Ace In The Hole	Venice, 51	*Rashomon*
Adalen '31	Cannes, 69	*If*
Alfie	Cannes, 66	*A Man And A Woman* and *The Birds, The Bees And The Italians*
Les Amants	Venice, 58	*The Rickshaw Man*
Anatomy Of A Murder	Oscar Nomination, 59	*Ben-Hur*
Le Bonheur	Berlin, 65	*Alphaville*
Bonnie And Clyde	Oscar Nomination, 67	*In The Heat Of The Night*
Chinatown	Oscar Nomination, 74	*The Godfather Part II*
Crossfire	Oscar Nomination, 47	*Gentleman's Agreement*
Death In Venice	Cannes, 71	*The Go-Between*
Deliverance	Oscar Nomination, 72	*The Godfather*
Doctor Zhivago	Oscar Nomination, 65	*The Sound Of Music*
Double Indemnity	Oscar Nomination, 44	*Going My Way*
The Eclipse	Cannes, 62	*The Given Word*
The Exorcist	Oscar Nomination, 73	*The Sting*
Une Femme Est Une Femme	Berlin, 61	*La Notte*
Le Feu Follet	Venice, 63	*Hands Over The City*
Foreign Correspondent	Oscar Nomination, 40	*Rebecca*
Giant	Oscar Nomination, 56	*Around The World In 80 Days*
The Gospel According To St. Matthew	Venice, 64	*The Red Desert*
The Great Dictator	Oscar Nomination, 40	*Rebecca*
Great Expectations	Oscar Nomination, 47	*Gentleman's Agreement*
Guess Who's Coming To Dinner?	Oscar Nomination, 67	*In The Heat Of The Night*

Hamlet (USSR)	Venice, 64	*The Red Desert*
It's A Wonderful Life	Oscar Nomination, 46	*The Best Years Of Our Lives*
Jaws	Oscar Nomination, 75	*One Flew Over The Cuckoo's Nest*
Kanal	Cannes, 57	*Friendly Persuasion*
Kwaidan	Cannes, 65	*The Knack*
The Little Foxes	Oscar Nomination, 41	*How Green Was My Valley*
The Magnificent Ambersons	Oscar Nomination, 42	*Mrs. Miniver*
The Maltese Falcon	Oscar Nomination, 41	*How Green Was My Valley*
Mr. Smith Goes To Washington	Oscar Nomination, 39	*Gone With The Wind*
Network	Oscar Nomination, 76	*Rocky*
The Red Shoes	Oscar Nomination, 48	*Hamlet*
Repulsion	Berlin, 65	*Alphaville*
The River	Venice, 51	*Rashomon*
Rocco And His Brothers	Venice, 60	*Le Passage Du Rhin*
Seven Brides For Seven Brothers	Oscar Nomination, 54	*On The Waterfront*
Seven Samurai	Venice, 54	*Romeo And Juliet*
The Seventh Seal	Cannes, 57	*Friendly Persuasion*
Shane	Oscar Nomination, 53	*From Here To Eternity*
Solaris	Cannes, 72	*The Mattei Affair* and *The Working Class Goes To Heaven*
Stagecoach	Oscar Nomination, 39	*Gone With The Wind*
Star Wars	Oscar Nomination, 77	*Annie Hall*
La Terra Trema	Venice, 48	*Hamlet*
To Kill A Mockingbird	Oscar Nomination, 62	*Lawrence Of Arabia*
The Trial Of Joan Of Arc	Cannes, 62	*The Given Word*
Twelve O'Clock High	Oscar Nomination, 49	*All The King's Men*
Vivre Sa Vie	Venice, 62	*The Childhood of Ivan* and *Family Chronicle*

The Box Office Hits!

The 62 pictures listed below have all grossed more than four million dollars at the box-office. They do *not* represent the top 62 commercial hits of all time, just the most popular listed in this book. Figures quoted are from *Variety's* list of all-time box-office champs and refer to receipts in the United States and Canada.

The most popular *award movies* of all time are as follows:

1.	*The Godfather*	$86,275,000
2.	*The Sound Of Music*	79,000,000
3.	*The Sting*	78,889,000
4.	*Gone With The Wind*	76,700,000
5.	*One Flew Over The Cuckoo's Nest*	59,000,000
6.	*Rocky*	54,000,000
7.	*The Graduate*	49,078,000
8.	*Butch Cassidy And The Sundance Kid*	46,039,000
9.	*M.A.S.H.*	36,720,000
10.	*Ben-Hur*	36,650,000
11.	*The Godfather Part II*	30,673,000
12.	*All The President's Men*	30,000,000
13.	*Patton*	28,100,000
14.	*The Deer Hunter*	26,927,000
15.	*The French Connection*	26,315,000
16.	*Around The World In 80 Days*	23,120,000
17.	*Apocalypse Now*	22,855,657
18.	*Midnight Cowboy*	20,325,000
19.	*Cabaret*	20,250,000
20.	*West Side Story*	19,450,000
21.	*Annie Hall*	18,093,000
22.	*The Longest Day*	17,600,000
23.	*The Bridge On The River Kwai*	17,195,000
24.	*Tom Jones*	16,950,000
25.	*Manhattan*	16,908,439
26.	*The Turning Point*	16,845,000
27.	*Oliver!*	16,800,000
28.	*Lawrence Of Arabia*	16,700,000
29.	*A Clockwork Orange*	15,800,000
30.	*Who's Afraid Of Virginia Woolf?*	14,500,000
31.	*The Greatest Show On Earth*	14,000,000

32.	*Julia*	12,953,000
33.	*A Man For All Seasons*	12,750,000
34.	*Cinderella*	12,450,000
35.	*From Here To Eternity*	12,200,000
36.	*My Fair Lady*	12,000,000
37.	*Taxi Driver*	11,600,000
38.	*The Best Years Of Our Lives*	11,300,000
39.	*In The Heat Of The Night*	10,910,000
40.	*Barry Lyndon*	9,200,000
41.	*The Lion In Winter*	9,053,000
42.	*Five Easy Pieces*	8,900,000
43.	*Nashville*	8,744,000
44.	*La Dolce Vita*	8,000,000
45.	*Alice Doesn't Live Here Anymore*	7,800,000
46.	*Gigi*	7,300,000
47.	*Z*	7,100,000
48.	*The Apartment*	6,650,000
49.	*Going My Way*	6,500,000
50.	*Blow-Up*	6,350,000
51.	*A Man And A Woman*	6,300,000
52.	*They Shoot Horses, Don't They?*	5,980,000
53.	*The Nun's Story*	5,750,000
54.	*Mrs. Miniver*	5,500,000
55.	*Friendly Persuasion*	5,050,000
56.	*Dr. Strangelove*	5,000,000
57.	*Becket*	5,000,000
58.	*A Streetcar Named Desire*	4,800,000
59.	*The Lost Weekend*	4,300,000
60.	*On The Waterfront*	4,200,000
61.	*Scarecrow*	4,200,000
62.	*Yesterday, Today And Tomorrow*	4,100,000

Note: List complete until January 1, 1980.

Index:

Winning Films

A guide to all the award-winning movies included in this book.

All Films

This second index includes every film mentioned in the book and allows for a quick check on where your favourite films lost out at awards time. The index consists primarily of the runners-up and nominated best pictures although winning films are again included as they also feature in the latter sections of the book.